# RE-READING LEAVIS

*Also by Gary Day*

THE BRITISH CRITICAL TRADITION (*editor*)
BRITISH POETRY 1900–50: Aspects of Tradition
(*co-editor with Brian Docherty*)
BRITISH POETRY 1950s—1990s: Identity, Politics and Art (*editor*)
PERSPECTIVES IN PORNOGRAPHY (*editor*)
READINGS IN POPULAR CULTURE (*editor*)

# Re-Reading Leavis

## Culture and Literary Criticism

Gary Day

*Senior Lecturer in Critical and Cultural Theory*
*De Montfort University, Bedford*

First published in Great Britain 1996 by
**MACMILLAN PRESS LTD**
Houndmills, Basingstoke, Hampshire RG21 6XS
and London
Companies and representatives
throughout the world

A catalogue record for this book is available
from the British Library.

ISBN 0–333–62900–0

First published in the United States of America 1996 by
**ST. MARTIN'S PRESS, INC.,**
Scholarly and Reference Division,
175 Fifth Avenue,
New York, N.Y. 10010

ISBN 0–312–16419–X

Library of Congress Cataloging-in-Publication Data
Day, Gary, 1956–
Re-reading Leavis : culture and literary criticism / Gary Day.
p.   cm.
Includes bibliographical references (p.     ) and index.
ISBN 0–312–16419–X
1. Leavis, F. R. (Frank Raymond). 1895–1978.   2. English
literature—History and criticism—Theory, etc.   3. Literature and
society—England—History—20th century.   4. Criticism—England–
–History—20th century.   5. Structuralism.   6. Consumption
(Economics)—England—History—20th century.   7. Capitalism and
literature—England—History—20th century.   8. Industrial
management —England—History—20th century.   9. Books and reading–
–England—History—20th century.   I. Title.
PR55.L43D39   1996
801'.95'092—dc20                                                96–24143
                                                                  CIP

10   9   8   7   6   5   4   3   2   1
05   04   03   02   01   00   99   98   97   96
Printed in Great Britain by
The Ipswich Book Company Ltd
Ipswich, Suffolk

# Contents

|  |  | Page |
|---|---|---|
| *List of Abbreviations* | | vii |
| *Introduction* | | ix |
| *Acknowledgements* | | xvi |

1 'MASS CIVILISATION AND MINORITY CULTURE' — 1
- Definitions and Standards — 2
- 'Signals', Standards and Standardisation — 5
- Metaphor: the Gold Standard, 'Race' Consciousness — 7
- The Economics of Excess — 13
- Culture, Metaphor and Metonymy — 21
- Advertising and Book Clubs — 24
- The Work of Repetition in 'Mass Civilisation and Minority Culture' — 28
- Leavis Reading and the Use of 'America' — 32
- The Obvious, Desire and Footnotes — 37
- Reading Culture Twice — 42

2 CULTURE AND ENVIRONMENT — 47
- Leisure and Consumerism — 47
- Work and Leisure — 50
- Literature, Literary Criticism and the Wheelwright's Craft — 55
- Consciousness, Modernity and Tradition — 59
- Leavis Reading Sturt — 64
- Culture, Leisure and Substitution — 73
- Leavis, Lacan and Value — 75
- Culture, Consciousness, Civilisation and the Body — 82
- Literature, Advertising, Science and Speech — 87
- Connection, Example, Quotation — 96
- Gender and Bliss — 100

3 LITERATURE AND SOCIETY — 107
- Leavis and Marxism — 108
- Scientific Management and the Organic Community — 112
- Leavis, Lefebvre and Marxism — 115

Criticism, Scientific Management and Professionalism        117
The Problem of Cultural Autonomy                            120
The Body of the 1930s                                       123
Modernity: Disembodiment and Desire                        128
Lacanian Psychoanalysis, Leavisian Criticism and
the Contract                                               130
Literature and Society                                     134
Leavis and Bateson                                         143
Restraint, Excess, Metaphor and 'Life'                     149
Negation and the Body                                      152
The Body in Pieces                                         155
Leavisian Criticism and Consumersim                        157
Public and Private                                         159
Freud, Leavis and Judgement                                162
Reading and the Nature of Criticism                        163

4   THE 'THIRD REALM'                                       169
The 'Double' Existence of the Poem                         169
The 'Third Realm' and *Différance*                         171
Negative Dialects and the 'Third Realm'                    176
Adorno and Leavis                                          179
Leavis and Wittgenstein                                    183
Boundaries and the Space of Reading                        186
Surveying the Body                                         190
Tradition and Advertising                                  197
Terms and Transcendence                                    201
Reading by the Body                                        204
Leavis, Derrida and 'Force'                                206
The Problem of Intention and the 'Third Realm'             209
Leavis, Lacan and 'Recognition'                            211
Meaning and Significance                                   218
Leavis and Adorno                                          221

Conclusion                                                 229

Notes                                                      235
Bibliography                                               285
Index                                                      302

# List of Abbreviations

| | | |
|---|---|---|
| *AB* | – | Adam Bede |
| *AK* | – | Anna Karenina: Thought and Significance in a Great Creative Work |
| *BTME* | – | Bunyan Through Modern Eyes |
| *C & P* | – | Literary Criticism and Philosophy |
| *CE* | – | Culture and Environment: The Training of Critical Awareness |
| *E U & C* | – | English, 'Unrest' and Continuity |
| *EWL & L* | – | Mr. Eliot, Mr. Wyndham Lewis and Lawrence |
| *HJ & TFOC* | – | Henry James and the Function of Criticism |
| *HTTR* | – | How To Teach Reading: A Primer For Ezra Pound |
| *J & A* | – | Judgement and Analysis |
| *J & TRW* | – | Joyce and the 'Revolution of the Word' |
| *JA* | – | Johnson and Augustanism |
| *JAP* | – | Johnson as Poet |
| *JOVB* | – | Justifying One's Valuation of Blake |
| *KS & CV* | – | Keynes, Spender and Currency Values |
| *L & S* | – | Literature and Society |
| *LD* | – | The literary discipline and liberal education. |
| *LS* | – | Literary Studies: a reply |
| *M B & C* | – | Mill on Bentham and Coleridge |
| *MCC* | – | Marxism and Cultural Continuity |
| *MC & MC* | – | Mass Civilisation and Minority Culture. |
| *MN* | – | Mutually Necessary |
| *MOW* | – | Memories of Wittgenstein |
| *NB* | – | New Bearings in English Poetry |
| *P C & SH* | – | Pluralism, Compassion and Social Hope |
| *PP* | – | The Pilgrim's Progress |
| *R* | – | Revaluation: Tradition and Development in English Poetry |
| *RFC* | – | Restatement for Critics |
| *RC* | – | The Responsible Critic: or the function of criticism at any time |
| *ROP* | – | Reading Out Poetry |
| *S & L* | – | Sociology and Literature |
| *SC* | – | Standards of Criticism |

*T L & O*     –   Thought, Language and Objectivity
*TC*          –   Two Cultures? The Significance of Lord Snow
*TIOC*        –   Luddites? or There is Only One Culture
*T L & O*     –   The Living Principle: English as a Discipline of Thought
*T & M*       –   Tragedy and the Medium
*TMA*         –   The Marxian Analysis: A Review of The Mind in Chains
*T M & S*     –   Thought, Meaning and Sensibility: the problem of value judgement
*TP & TP*     –   The Present and the Past: Eliot's Demonstration
*T.S.E. & EL* –   T.S. Eliot and English Literature
*TSOC*        –   Towards Standards of Criticism
*T W & C*     –   Thought, Words and Creativity: Art and Thought in Lawrence
*UWKB*        –   Under Which King Bezonian
*VC*          –   Valuation in Criticism
*WWWC*        –   What's Wrong With Criticism

# Introduction

In 1992 F.R. Leavis was the second most popular critic on English literature courses in polytechnics and colleges. The first was Roland Barthes and the third was Terry Eagleton.[1] In 1995, Ian MacKillop's biography of Leavis[2] appeared attracting widespread if not exactly sympathetic reviews. Taken together these two incidents suggest that Leavis continues to exert an appeal or to arouse hostility.

But who is this Leavis who can have such an effect? Although there are many critics who have argued against his particular judgements and although some have challenged one or other of his general assumptions or procedures there is no one, according to Francis Mulhern, who has 'produced anything even resembling an integrated account and assessment of his aesthetic and critical position'.[3] This is a more sober version of Garry Watson's view that Leavis's work has been systematically distorted and ridiculed with critics ignoring what he does say in favour of what they believe he says – or even want him to say.[4] It is this absence of a comprehensive account of his criticism that has given rise to a myth of Leavis[5] which is the source of the strong reactions that his name can still provoke, nearly 20 years after his death.[6]

And yet there is no shortage of criticism of Leavis's work, even though there may not exist that overarching study that Mulhern believes is necessary. There are books which combine biography with exposition such as Ronald Hayman's *Leavis*[7] and William Walsh's *F.R. Leavis*.[8] Then there are books which focus on the criticism alone such as R.P. Bilan's *The Literary Criticism of F.R. Leavis*[9] and Robert Boyer's *F.R. Leavis: Judgement and the Discipline of Thought*.[10] Philosophical approaches include John Casey's *The Language of Criticism*[11] and Michael Tanner's essays on the relationship between literature and philosophy.[12] There are books such as Fred Inglis's *Radical Earnestness: English Social Theory 1880–1980*[13] and Lesley Johnson's *The Cultural Critics: From Matthew Arnold to Raymond Williams*[14] which place Leavis in the tradition of English social commentary. Elizabeth and Tom Burns assay a sociological analysis in *The Sociology of Literature and Drama*[15] while accounts of Leavis's role in the development of English can be found in Chris Baldick's *The Social Mission of English Criticism*

*1848–1932*[16] and Bernard Bergonzi's *Exploding English: Criticism,Theory, Culture.*[17]

In fact there is a wealth of books, chapters in books and articles in journals covering this or that aspect of Leavis's criticism.[18] The amount of material, however, is not matched by its diversity. There is a broad acceptance that Leavis viewed literature in moral rather than formal terms and critics either applaud or deplore this approach depending on their point of view. Rightly or wrongly, Leavis seems to be the sort of writer who either inspires discipleship or excites enmity, neither of which is particularly conducive to insightful comment.

Two studies which I have found particularly impressive are Francis Mulhern's *The Moment of 'Scrutiny'* and Michael Bell's *F.R. Leavis.*[19] The former offers a detailed account of the development of Leavis's thought as it appeared in *Scrutiny*, the magazine he edited with his wife, Q.D. Leavis, for nearly 20 years, and anyone who writes on Leavis is greatly indebted to this fine work. The same is true of Bell's book. This has a narrower focus, comparing Leavis's understanding of language's relation to 'life' with Heidegger's understanding of language's relation to 'Being', but it is a salutary reminder that Leavis is a more complex thinker than is sometimes supposed.

Perhaps the most salient fact about criticism of Leavis is that there has been no sustained post-structuralist account of his work. I am using the term post-structuralism to refer first to Saussure's claim that, in the words of Catherine Belsey, 'language is not … a way of naming things which already exist, but a system of differences with no positive terms'.[20] Language, the argument goes, 'precedes the existence of independent entities, making the world intelligible by differentiating between concepts'.[21] In short, language creates the meanings which order our perceptions and organise our ideas about the world. The second sense in which I use the term post-structuralism is to refer to the writings of Derrida, Foucault and Lacan. These thinkers have radically changed the study of literature in this country and it is surprising that post-structuralism, which established itself in opposition to Leavisian criticism,[22] should have done so without a thorough deconstruction of his work. True, there have been local engagements such as Catherine Belsey's critique of Leavis's reading of George Eliot's *Daniel Deronda*[23] and Christopher Norris's engagement with Leavis's essay on *Othello*[24] but, to my knowledge, there has been no comprehensive post-structuralist engagement with Leavis.

There are two possible reasons for this. The first is that one of the effects of post-structuralism has been to dislodge literature from its special place in the academy. Literary language is no longer regarded as a unique or privileged form of writing but as something which has been invested with those qualities so as to better reproduce the existing power relations of society. Once literature is seen in terms of its ideological effects it loses its aura and can be analysed in the same way as other discourses. In Antony Easthope's view, there is nothing to distinguish 'literary' texts from those of popular culture. They are both forms of textuality which must be discussed in terms of '[i]nstitution, sign system, gender, identification, ... subject position [and] the other'.[25] The dissolution of the category of literature eliminated the problem of valuation which was Leavis's special concern and so there was no need to engage with him. Arguably, however, it was this very indifference to valuation that has led to its re-emergence as an issue today.

The second reason why there has been no post-structuralist reading of Leavis is a subliminal awareness that there are similarities as well as differences between the two positions, and to confront these would undermine post-structuralism's claim to be a radical departure from the kind of thought associated with Leavisian literary criticism. To put it simply, Leavis shares with post-structuralism the ideas that works are not explicable in terms of their author's intentions; that the meaning of works is not fixed but changes over time and, perhaps most importantly, that reality is an effect of language.[26]

Catherine Belsey in characterising Leavis as an 'expressive realist', that is, someone who believes art is a reflection of life and an expression of the author's experience, glosses over the complexity of Leavis's position and how it mirrors, in part at least, her own.[27] It is necessary to be careful here. The claim is not that Leavis is a post-structuralist or that post-structuralists are Leavisites in disguise. The similarities I have mentioned conceal significant differences of understanding and emphasis. For example, although Leavis believes that reality is an effect of language his conception of both these terms is not at all the same as what a post-structuralist's might be.[28]

Nevertheless there are affinities between Leavisian and post-structuralist criticism and this makes it inappropriate to see them purely in terms of opposition. Post-structuralism's failure to acknowledge these similarities has not only driven the ideas of value and evaluation 'into the critical unconscious where they continue to exercise force but without being available for analytic scrutiny'[29], it also represents a lost opportunity to build on what might be useful in Leavis for its own project.

Accordingly, one of my aims is to draw attention to the parallels between aspects of Leavis's work and of post-structuralism as represented in the writings of Derrida and Lacan but particularly the latter. In doing so I hope to show that Leavis's texts are more plural than has hitherto been recognised and that they are therefore available for more progressive readings than they have been given in the past. At the same time, I try to use Leavis as a corrective to what I consider to be the limitations of post-structuralism, for example its anti-humanism, and, to this end, I draw on Adorno, whose ideas about the relation of art and society can be shown to resemble Leavis's own. Further, just as there are post-structuralist elements in Leavis's thought, so there are in Adorno's[30], and both writers are also moved by a concern for human significance. Adorno, however, is by far the more subtle thinker and this, together with his greater sociological awareness, means that he can be used to focus and develop some of the insights that Leavis struggles to express.

In addition to reading Leavis through post-structuralism and post-structuralism through Leavis and Adorno, I also aim to outline some of the connections between Leavisian criticism, scientific management and mass consumerism, all of which began to take shape in 1930s Britain.[31] These connections occur at the levels of structure, logic, rhetoric and vocabulary. The image of the body is also common to all three and it is suffused with an anxiety for what can only loosely be described as 'something more', a phrase whose multiple meanings will become clearer as the argument develops. At its simplest it refers, in scientific management, to increased productivity; in consumerism it denotes the 'something more' of advertising – 'bread is not just bread'[32] and, in Leavisian criticism, it refers to a whole cluster of problems ranging from the need to supplement definitions to the nature of literary value. These different aspects of 'something more' are negotiated in each discourse through an image of the body. An image, moreover, which was by no means stable for the body was being reimagined in 1930s Britain as society moved from one which understood itself as based on production to one which understood itself as based on consumption.

In Leavis, the problem of 'something more' is initially understood in terms of an increased amount of reading material and its 'heterogeneity'.[33] This perception of 'more', of a sense of accumulation and profusion cannot be divorced from mass consumerism's celebration of the fact 'that there is too much'.[34] For both Leavisian criticism and consumer society the problem is how to organise this abundance. Leavis develops a 'technique' (*HTTR*, p. 40) of reading that limits it whereas consumer society emphasises it through the 'stack' and the 'display'.[35]

The kind of language that Leavis uses to describe his technique of reading is consistent with that of scientific management. He speaks of the need to 'improve[] one's apparatus, one's equipment, one's efficiency as a reader'.[36] Similarly his belief in the efficacy of a *method* of reading set out, for example, in *How To Teach Reading: A Primer for Ezra Pound* reflects the importance attached to 'method' and technique by scientific management as opposed to 'rule of thumb'.[37]

The aim of scientific management was to increase profits and productivity by eliminating waste and inefficiency.[38] Similarly Leavis aimed to develop a technique that would cut down on the amount the student had to read – so much '*profitless* memorizing' (*HTTR*, p. 26, italics added) – in order that he or she would be better 'equipped to *profit*' (p. 42, italics added) from literature. Leavis proposed a 'scheme of work' (p. 38), essentially a concentrated reading of representative works from 'the tradition', that would develop and refine students' critical faculties (pp. 25–49).

It is worth noting, in passing, that Leavis's phrase, 'scheme of work' is now part of the language of the National Curriculum which, with its 'aims and objectives', 'attainment targets' and 'criteria of assessment' represents an approach to literature that he would have found deplorable. And yet he can be regarded as in some sense responsible for initiating a train of thought that has culminated in the bureaucratisation and codification of learning. Leavis may have associated literature with 'life', with what cannot be measured or precisely defined but his logic belongs to that of scientific management which disregards human significance in the interests of what can be quantified.

The aim of reading, then, is to 'save the student from ... laborious dissipation' and to enable him or her 'to organise, extend and consolidate [their reading]' (*HTTR*, pp. 7-8). But, according to Leavis, reading should also aim at 'something more' (p. 4). The technique of reading should thus aim to generate a double surplus, one of which, expressed through the metaphor of 'profit', throws his whole concept of valuation into crisis while the other, 'something more' is vague because of its multiple meanings. And this semantic plurality is itself an instance of that 'tropical profusion of topics and vocabularies' (*WWWC*, p. 88), that 'concourse of signals so bewildering in their variety and number'[39] which called Leavisian criticism into being in the first place. Conceived as an exercise in limitation, Leavisian criticism enacts the overproduction it seeks to restrict, and this constitutes one of its main tensions.

Leavis also develops his technique of reading in response to 'the thought-frustrating spell of "Form", "pure sound value"'[40] which is most evident in poetry that is incantatory. This poetry of 'enchantment'[41] of 'insidious ... spell[s]' (*NB*, p. 45) so lulls the reader through its soft sounds and soothing rhythms that his or her 'resistance' is 'weaken[ed]'[42] to the point that he or she 'surrender[s] at last' (*R*, p. 43). The language of seduction is unmistakable here. A certain type of poetry works on the body rather than the mind, thereby coinciding with the discourses of consumer culture which proclaim the body as 'a vehicle of pleasure'[43] and which are 'centred around the hedonistic lifestyle'.[44] This orientation of consumer culture is at the expense of consciousness understood as a self-reflective process, as something which transcends the body. In consumer society the body not the mind, the outer not the inner, is seen as the true location of identity.[45]

The poetry of 'enchantment' and the character of consumer culture bring about a separation between consciousness and the body. In Leavis, this is felt as a loss of control; the senses are delighted by a poetry which bewitches the mind, thus overturning the traditional hierarchy in which the body is secondary. This experience mirrors the loss of 'distinction and dividing lines' (*MC & MC*, p. 31) which Leavis views as the essential factor of modernity.

But, in trying to restore the supremacy of consciousness by forging a technique of reading that ensures 'the closest and fullest working attention, the most acutely perceptive, the most delicately discriminating responsiveness'[46] Leavis is in danger of exiling the notion of pleasure from his literary criticism. And this point is given greater emphasis when it is realised that the sort of heightened consciousness which is required for reading – close and full attention and acute perceptiveness – approximates to that state of watchfulness which is characteristic of the super ego from whom 'nothing can be hidden'.[47]

Although Leavis endeavours to promote consciousness over the body and to develop a technique of reading that will guard it against the siren calls of the poetry of 'enchantment' he does not quite succeed in his task. Time and again in his criticism the body returns to disrupt the operations of consciousness and, in fact, it is the relation between consciousness and the body which forms the second main tension of his criticism, the first being that between limitation and 'something more'.

These form the main focus of my argument and they are examined in detail in the following chapters. What I hope to achieve is a change in the way Leavis is perceived. To this end I have concentrated on texts which have either not been discussed for some time or else which have appeared in the two posthumous collections edited by G. Singh, *The Critic As Anti-Philosopher* and *Valuation in Criticism and Other Essays*.[48] Second, I have approached Leavis from a broadly post-structuralist perspective which is, in any case, inevitable since, in one form or another, this constitutes the dominant paradigm of literary studies at present. And third, I have tried to situate Leavis more firmly in his social and historical context than I believe has hitherto been attempted.

The first section offers a detailed reading of 'Mass Civilisation and Minority Culture' focusing particularly on the logic and metaphors of the text. The second section concentrates on *Culture and Environment: The Training of Critical Awareness'*.[49] This offers a reappraisal of the organic community and analyses what Leavis means by reading. The third section examines Leavis's relation to Marxism and considers his understanding of the relationship between literature and society as represented, for example, in his dispute with F.W. Bateson.[50] The final section investigates Leavis's concept of the 'third realm' from a number of points of view and also draws together some of the ways that Leavisian criticism is implicated in production and consumption.

Approaching my chosen texts in the way I have indicated will, I hope, not only challenge traditional accounts of them but will also show that Leavis still has a contribution to make to literary and cultural studies.

# Acknowledgements

I would like to thank the following for their time, ideas, inspiration and encouragement: Catherine Belsey, Clive Bloom, Elena Bonelli, Martin Coyle, Terence Hawkes, Ian MacKillop, Christopher Norris and Richard Storer. I owe special thanks to Charmian Hearne for her patience and commitment to this project and I am enormously indebted to Jane Page who nurtured and wordprocessed the manuscript from its scribbled beginnings to its fevered revisions. Without her this book would not have been completed so speedily or do efficiently. I am also indebted to my colleagues Russell Barnes, Jane Dowson, Peter Doyle, Michael Faherty, David James, Maureen Little, Michael Spindler, Geraldine Stoneham, Alistair Walker, Clare Walsh and Carole Wood for their support, generosity and stimulating scepticism. And without the invaluable aid of Margaret Griffiths I would never have been able to track particularly obscure references.

My greatest debt, however, is to my beloved wife Deborah, whose constant support made this book possible. It is therefore dedicated to her and our darling daughter Charlotte, who was born during the writing of it.

# 1

# 'Mass Civilisation and Minority Culture'

## INTRODUCTION

Francis Mulhern suggests that the importance of 'Mass Civilisation and Minority Culture'[1] is that it contained, in embryonic form, *Scrutiny*'s governing theme: '"industrialism" and its destructive effects on society and culture'.[2] While it cannot be denied that Leavis's essay, which originally appeared in pamphlet form in 1930, has some relation to the concerns of *Scrutiny*, such an observation hardly does justice to either its rhetoric or the complexity of its arguments. Accordingly, my purpose is to address these in some detail in order to show that there is far more to 'Mass Civilisation and Minority Culture' than is evident in Mulhern's account of it.

If the essay is read transparently its argument is clear: the relation between culture and civilisation[3] is being severed by industrialisation, which is leading to the increasing standardisation of language and therefore experience since, in Leavis's thought, the two cannot be dissociated. Culture, in the form of creative literature, is being confined more and more to a minority by the emergence of new discourses of mass culture, such as those associated with the Book Society and the Book Guild, which have manufactured the word 'High-Brow' – 'an ominous addition to the English Language' (*MC & MC*, p. 38) in order to exclude further the already marginalised cultured minority.

Even this brief summary should be sufficient to raise at least two questions regarding the Leavis myth.[4] First, Leavis's elitism appears to be as much the construct of mass culture as it is of his own pronouncements on art and literature. His argument is that culture is prevented from contributing to the life of society, not that it is the exclusive property of an elite. Second, re-reading Leavis on 'mass civilisation' it is hard not to wonder whether he has a point. His comments on the work of John B. Watson (*MC & MC*, p. 40)[5] who advocated, among other things, the development of techniques for the control of emotions, show an alertness to the ways in which the modern subject was being mapped, defined and organised that resembles Foucault. Of course, the latter's analysis of the disciplines of modernity, particularly the prison, the army and the school[6] is a great deal more sophisticated than anything offered by Leavis. Nevertheless, both thinkers are aware, to different degrees, of the various mechanisms by which the subject is dominated and his or her experiences 'normalised'.

Foucault claims that there is always resistance to this process but the emphasis in his works falls on how the modern subject has come to be dominated, not on how it resists domination.[7] Leavis's work on the other hand, while lacking the historically detailed analysis which characterises Foucault's studies,[8] is resolutely oppositional and inter-ventionist. This is evident in the way his writings refuse the reductions and conformities of mass culture, promoting instead the virtues of multiplicity, complexity and difference.


## DEFINITIONS AND STANDARDS

To read 'Mass Civilisation and Minority Culture' in a transparent manner, as Mulhern and others have done, is to take the process of reading for granted, which is profoundly ironic given that it is an essay which raises the whole question of what it means to read. The problem appears in the very first paragraph where Leavis, commenting on certain phrases from Matthew Arnold's *Culture and Anarchy*, writes, 'Today one must face problems of definition and formulation where Arnold could pass lightly on' (*MC & MC*, p. 13). Hence Leavis cannot simply refer an enquirer about the meaning of culture to *Culture and Anarchy* for 'I know that something more is required' (p. 13). This points to a lack in the very cultural heritage that is supposed to be a corrective of modern life. What 'is needed [now] as never before' is 'a strong current of criticism' (p. 31). This would consist of identifying major writers and their successors and, by so doing, allow people to 'profit ... by the finest human experience of the past' (p. 15). This strategy is unrealistic, however, because the conditions of modern culture severely curtail the relevance of these past experiences.

For Leavis, one of the functions of criticism in the present time is to protect language from being wholly appropriated by mass culture, which sees it as merely 'a "method of symbolising human thought"'.[9] And yet there is a problem here for while Leavis wants to assert that language always exceeds the purposes for which it is used and hence can never really be 'scientifically improved' (*MC & MC*, p.42), it is also the case that he adheres very closely to the qualities of exactitude and precision which he identifies with Richard Paget's proposed reforms for English.[10] This is implicit in the key words and phrases of his essay, for example, 'discerning appreciation' (p. 13), 'subtle' (p.15), 'finer living' (p. 15), 'delicate [...] adjustments' (p. 17), 'fastidious' (p. 23) and 'discriminating' (p. 30). All these suggest a desire for a clearly articulated and refined response to 'life'.

But such fine gradations of response as Leavis calls for are not consistent with his view of language as always being more than 'a method of symbolising humane thought'. On the contrary, what these words and phrases indicate is a desire to 'symbolise' or present thought as accurately as possible. 'Symbolising' thought is precisely Leavis's ambition – despite his assertion that the essence of language resides in 'something more'.

This striving for clarity seems to be at odds with his recognition, expressed at the outset of the essay, that definitions and formulations constitute a problem, so much of one in fact that he regards his own definition of culture, one of the key terms of his argument, not as 'tight' but 'as adequate by anyone who is likely to read the pamphlet' (*MC & MC*, p. 15). The assumption here is that his reader will share his values and therefore assent to his definition of culture. There is, in Leavis's formulation, an appeal to 'implicit standards' (p. 15) which he and his readers have in common. Since these standards are implicit, they remain unspoken and, in so far as they remain unspoken, they can be said to constitute that 'more' which Leavis seeks to preserve. On the other hand, the very fact that those standards are implicit means that they do not achieve that clarity for which Leavis is striving. There is, in other words, a tension between the aim of a clearly defined response to life and/or art and an appeal to implicit standards where the response is by definition more muted.

This tension is aggravated by the relation that Leavis assumes between implicit standards and, for want of a better phrase, explicit responses. It is the former which 'order the fine living of an age [determining] the sense that this is worth more than that, this rather than that is the direction in which to go, that the centre is here rather than there' (*MC & MC*, p. 15). These implicit standards constitute 'the heritage' (p. 44). The survival of this heritage depends upon 'the use of words' (p. 44) but, as has been seen, the use of words is associated with clarity, explicitness, accuracy and precision, with being 'as aware as possible' (p. 46). The relationship between the implicit and the explicit in this essay is therefore problematic. Implicit standards depend on explicit responses or judgements, while these latter draw their authority from the tacit criteria which inform them.

Leavis's implicit standards must not be seen solely in relation to explicit responses or judgements. Their implicit nature, which confers on language its ability to transcend purely instrumental purposes, links them with a feature of modern culture deplored by Leavis, namely that it is a 'concourse of signals so bewildering in their variety and number' (*MC & MC*, p. 31) that it is hardly possible to discriminate between them. Although 'signals' are different from 'standards', both participate in an economy of excess. The excess in implicit standards inheres in their implicitness while the excess of signals is to be understood as the loss of clearly defined boundaries since 'the distinctions and dividing lines have blurred away' (p. 31). In the latter case, excess is a negative phenomenon while in the former it is positive.

But although this is true at one level it is not at another. Earlier Leavis has argued that one of the purposes of implicit standards is to prevent the 'spirit' from being 'thwarted and incoherent' (*MC & MC*, p. 15). But Leavis does not define 'spirit' and it is therefore a potentially ambiguous term. As such, it has an affinity with those 'implicit' standards which, in not being articulated, also have an air of equivocation about them. And, since this is the case, they cannot be appealed to in order to make the spirit less thwarted or more coherent. Consequently, the ambiguity in implicit standards connects them with the disorientation Leavis identifies with the signals of mass culture. The problem of implicit standards is not confined to their participation in an economy of excess for, as previously noted, Leavis has a commitment to clarity and precision which means that these implicit standards, sooner or later, must be expressed. This, in fact, constitutes a contradiction at the heart of Leavis's writings. On the one hand, there is an appeal to implicit standards, on the other a demand for a fully conscious, articulated response or judgement.

## 'SIGNALS', STANDARDS AND STANDARDISATION

In the process of being made explicit a sense of depth is lost – what was implicit has been inscribed on the surface. This loss of depth is perhaps consistent with Leavis's use of the word 'signals' which he opposes to culture, language and standards. 'Signals' connotates something superficial, instant and momentary. Adorno also uses the term 'signals' to describe 'mass culture'.[11] As in Leavis, the term signifies a loss of depth. '[M]ass culture', writes Adorno, 'is a system of signals that signals itself'[12] that is, it 'exhibits itself ... show[ing] how its products are made and how everything in it functions'.[13] In signalling itself, mass culture reveals a repetitive character 'whose perpetual sameness', according to Adorno, 'always expresses an identical meaning'.[14] This has the effect of making 'history come[ ] to a standstill'.[15] There is no direct parallel for this in Leavis but he is concerned that he writes in an age where there is 'no living tradition of poetry' (*MC & MC*, p. 30) and where proposed reforms of the English language will eliminate 'the living subtlety of the finest idiom' with the result that the heritage will 'die[ ]' (p. 44). In short, Leavis, like Adorno, fears that modern civilisation blunts the historical sense.

For Adorno, this results in an 'abstract present'[16] which is contrasted to the 'sensuous individuation'[17] of art. Leavis also relies on art – or rather tradition – as a corrective to those abstractions of civilisation which manifest themselves in attempts to 'scientifically improve [ ]' (*MC & MC*, p. 42) English. Both see the space of art being progressively squeezed. Adorno sees art disappearing, as 'the borderline between culture and empirical reality becomes more and more indistinct' and, though Leavis too notes the 'blur[ring] away' (p. 31) of distinctions and dividing lines, he explains culture's shrinking sphere in terms of the creation of a discourse intended, as he sees it, to marginalise critics and artists. The addition of 'high brow' to the English language is a sign that '[t]he minority is being cut off as never before from the powers that rule the world' (pp. 38–9).

Another way in which art is under attack relates directly to mass culture as a system of signals. Adorno equates these signals with mass culture disseminating information about itself. Such information points to how mass culture functions and 'refers constantly to what has been preformed, to what others already know'.[18] 'Furthermore,' writes Adorno, 'this information is [w]renched from all context'[19] and this 'promote[s] the decay of the aesthetic image'.[20] A similar view is found in Leavis. The 'concourse of signals' represents the dissolution of tradition which provides the context for change and development. Without this context 'it becomes increasingly difficult for anyone to know whether he knows what he is talking about or not'.[21]

Two consequences follow from this. The first is that as tradition decays it becomes impossible to tell the difference between 'high' and popular culture, and the gradual erosion of this distinction helps to create that depthlessness characteristic of modern civilisation. The second consequence is that, as tradition dissolves and is replaced by technique, so the 'sensuous movement of art transforms itself under the eyes of mass culture into the measurement, comparison and assessment of physical phenomena'.[22]

In both Leavis and Adorno the term 'signals' indicates a loss of depth. Adorno also claims that, 'as a system of signals' mass culture 'culminates in the demand that no-one can be any different from itself'.[23] A similar relation between signals and conformity can be discerned in Leavis. Signals belong to the surface and so are different from standards which belong to depth. But, as has been argued, standards in being articulated lose their implicit character and in becoming visible are associated with signals. This complex relation is apparent in the meanings of the term 'standard' in the text. As a noun, it signifies quality and difference but, as a verb, 'standardisation' (*MC & MC*, p. 18 and *passim*) it denotes quantity and sameness, a drive to conformity. This is also evident in the use of 'standard' as a noun since standards are to do with 'order' and 'adjustment' (pp. 15, 17) and thus they function in manner similar to standardisation which seeks to order and adjust according to a norm.

The play between implicit standards and standardisation is facilitated by the absence of 'an informed and cultivated public' (*MC & MC*, p. 29). The purpose of this public is to endorse the 'first hand judgement[s]' of 'the "few" who are capable' of making such appraisals (p. 14). Without this public the confirmation of these judgements and the authority of the implicit standards on which they are based, is in jeopardy. Leavis's reasoning here would suggest that since there is no 'informed and cultivated public' so too there are no implicit standards, only standardisation.

Lacking a public to whom he can appeal for the safeguard of implicit standards Leavis then resorts to trying to redefine the phrase 'the standard of living', his aim being 'to wrest [it] from the economist' (*MC & MC*, p. 17). This strategy seems tacitly to acknowledge two things: first that the relations between implicit standards and explicit judgements involve a number of contradictions and, second, that there may very well be no implicit standards, given the absence of an 'informed and cultivated public'. If there is indeed no such public, problems of evaluation cannot be resolved by an appeal to implicit standards. The same would also apply to meaning, given that Leavis wants to alter the meaning that economists have given to the phrase 'the standard of living'. That is, meanings are not intrinsic but have to be contested. Leavis's work thus has a potentially radical dimension: it admits meaning is created in accordance with certain interests, a view that recalls Pierre Macherey's remark about literary discourse, that it is 'a contestation of language rather than a representation of reality'.[24]

The contestation over the meaning of 'the standard of living' is related to what Leavis considers to be an important 'use of words' (*MC & MC*, p. 44), namely the maintenance of tradition. But since keeping tradition alive entails making explicit what is implicit, tradition is deprived of that very quality for which it is desired; its ability to transcend, in a resonant way, the surface of life. The use of words, in short, has an effect beyond what Leavis intends. But this excess is hardly the 'something more' which he apprehends in language and which will prevent it from being reduced to purely instrumental purposes. This surplus of meaning problematises the notion of the contestation of meaning, which implies a struggle over distinct meanings. What 'Mass Civilisation and Minority Culture' shows is that meaning is far from distinct and this is particularly evident in the behaviour of metaphor in the text.

## METAPHOR: THE GOLD STANDARD, 'RACE' CONSCIOUSNESS

Metaphor is important in Leavis's argument. It must first of all be understood in relation to the problem of definition and formulations which it supplements. The first appearance of metaphor is almost immediately after the claim 'that something more is required' (*MC & MC*, p. 13). Hence metaphor has partly to be understood in terms of that 'something more'. And it is as 'something more' that metaphor prevents language from being only 'a method that symbolises human thought'. As such, it is related to those implicit standards which perform the same function.

Leavis deploys a number of different metaphors in his text. The first concerns the notion of valuations which 'are a kind of paper currency based upon a very small proportion of gold. To the state of such a currency the possibilities of fine living at any time bear a close relation' (*MC & MC*, p. 14). This metaphor verges on being literally true for fine living does indeed depend on currency. Moreover, it has a certain topical significance given that Britain's return to the gold standard in the 1920s helped to prepare for the financial crisis of 1931 and the return of a National government.[25] Leavis, writing in 1930, resorts to a metaphor whose economic basis is quite at odds with his criticism of civilisation. His metaphor suggests quantity whereas he is concerned with quality. The metaphor of orthodox financial policy serving as a guarantee of sound critical practice thus ties criticism into society despite the oppositional role that Leavis wants to give it. Moreover, it is precisely at the point where Leavis asserts that 'fine living' depends on the state of the currency that his metaphor starts to appear as if it is literally true, thus, perhaps, calling into question the very nature of metaphor itself.

This wavering between a literal and a metaphoric meaning does not seem to trouble Leavis himself. 'There is no need,' he writes 'to elaborate the metaphor' (*MC & MC*, p. 14).[26] Yet, immediately after he states that 'the nature of the relation [between valuation and fine living] is suggested well enough by this passage from Mr. I.A. Richards, which should by now be a *locus classicus*' (p. 14). The reference to Richards cannot but be regarded as a form of elaboration. But the nature of this elaboration needs to be carefully considered. Richards is appealed to as authority, as 'proof' that '[t]here is no need to elaborate the metaphor'. The quotation from Richards is designed to prevent the metaphor from being disruptive, to prevent it, indeed, precisely from operating as a metaphor. Richards is invoked as a guarantee of the self-evident nature of the metaphor, its 'obviousness', but to stress this aspect of it is almost to suppress its very nature as metaphor, assimilating it instead to the so-called transparency of plain speech.

This suppression of metaphor is ironic in a text where the metaphoric aspect of language has to be insisted upon if Leavis is to succeed in convincing his readers that language is more than 'a method of symbolising human thought'. However, it is consistent with the desire for clarity and explication which also runs through the essay. But the commitment to clarity involves a denial of metaphor which reintroduces the very lack it was intended to supplement. Even this is not the end of the matter for, by citing Richards to support the claim that '[t]here is no need to elaborate the metaphor', Leavis provides precisely the elaboration which he says the metaphor does not require. Quotation acts as elaboration.

Quotation explains metaphor just as metaphor is meant to explain, to fill out the deficiencies of definition. In short, metaphor itself seems to evince a lack and therefore it cannot act as a supplement. Metaphor, a sign of excess, is itself exceeded by quotation. And what is the purpose of Richards's quotation? To endorse Arnold's view that poetry is a criticism of life.

> For the arts are inevitably and quite apart from any intentions of the artist an appraisal of existence. Matthew Arnold, when he said that poetry is a criticism of life, was saying something so obvious that it is constantly overlooked.[27]

What is significant here is that Arnold's position is taken for granted in contrast to Leavis's problematising it in the opening paragraph of the essay. But in quoting Richards, who in turn refers to Arnold, Leavis reinstates the authority of Arnold that he began by calling into question.

Drawing attention to the inadequacy of Arnold's formulations and proposing to remedy them by 'something more' generates the kind of problems mentioned above. The only escape from these internal pressures is to refer to another text, hence the use of quotation which, though presented to illustrate a point, functions to solve a problem. The project of Leavis's essay is to provide 'something more' which supplements Arnold and which guards language against instrumental appropriation. But in the process the text reveals that it too requires 'something more' – hence the use of quotation.

The notion of 'something more' is a complicated one: is it an inherent or an added quality? The logic of Leavis's argument would seem to suggest that it is both. It is inherent to the extent that Leavis assumes that language is more than a 'method of symbolising human thought' and it is an added quality to the extent that it supplements the definition of culture. The problem deepens when Leavis uses language as a metaphor for culture (*MC & MC*, p. 14) since this suggests less an addition to culture than a substitution for it. Further, once language occupies the place of culture it, that is culture, no longer needs supplementing since, as language, it already contains within itself that 'something more' it previously lacked.

Another feature of Richards's quotation which is worth emphasising is the remark that Arnold 'was saying something so obvious that it

is constantly overlooked'. This echoes Leavis's claim that there is no
need to elaborate his metaphor. Both Richards and Leavis trust in the
obvious, yet the problem of how to read the obvious lies at the heart
of 'Mass Civilisation and Minority Culture'. The obvious is always
underwritten. Leavis states that there is no need to elaborate his
metaphor, yet immediately does so by referring his readers to
Richards, who refers to Arnold, noting that what he says is 'so obvious
that it is constantly overlooked' and hence must be glossed. The
meaning of the obvious is never fully present in the obvious and so
it is always less than itself.

Not only does Richards's quotation gloss Leavis's metaphor, it
also provides him with another one. 'This last sentence gives the hint
for another metaphor' (*MC & MC*, p. 14). The sentence in question
refers to the poet who 'is the point at which the growth of the mind
shows itself'.[28] Leavis uses this remark as a cue for his second
metaphor, that the minority 'constitute the consciousness of the race'
(p. 15). Thus the use of Richards to play down metaphor – Leavis
quoting Richards as proof that '[t]here is no need to elaborate the
metaphor of currency' (p. 14) merely gives rise to the creation of
another metaphor. The attempt to suppress metaphor only leads to
more metaphor.

The term 'race' evokes the social Darwinism of the early part of the
century which saw competition between nations in racial terms.[29] This
prompted anxiety about the health of the British working class, which
led to measures to make it a more efficient workforce. Race was thus
tied up with class and cannot be considered apart from the values of
industrial capitalism.[30] These connotations of race affect Leavis's use
of the term, as does the context in which it appears – the concern with
the continued and healthy growth of consciousness. This reflects, in
displaced form, a cultural anxiety about mental health in the period.[31]
It was feared that 'the feeble minded'[32] would, along with the
'improvident', the 'unproductive' and the 'incompetent'[33] reproduce
'at the expense of the [nation's] better stocks'.[34] Leavis's concern for
the state of consciousness is, then, part of a wider worry about Britain's
ability to compete in international trade. His fear that tradition will
disappear under a concourse of signals reflects the panic of a middle
class who fears it will be swamped by the rising birth rate of the 'lower
orders'. Thus, despite Leavis wanting to assert the independence of
'culture' from 'civilisation' two of his key metaphors, the gold standard
and health are drawn from and reflect the concerns of the latter.

One way of understanding the metaphor of the mind's growth, of the minority as the consciousness of the race is by looking at its affinities with social and economic concerns. Another is to highlight the element of recognition. Recognition is not just something which can be conferred, it is also something which is desired. Leavis requires that the minority have their judgements endorsed by a slightly larger group who are capable of 'genuine personal response' (MC & MC, p. 14). Without this endorsement the minority's judgements would seem to be rather precarious; though it is hard to see why, given that they are authenticated by 'first hand judgement' (p. 14). What Leavis's logic seems to demonstrate is that the personal, the genuine, the authentic – terms by which he sets such great store – are, because they require recognition, in some sense deficient, hence they too partake of the lack which characterises civilisation and so cannot be used to remedy it.

This aspect of Leavis's argument can be focused by a comparison with Adorno. Adorno criticises the idea that 'genuineness'[35] provides a standard against which other ideas can be judged. In this respect, he claims, it behaves like gold in the economy,[36] thus highlighting the implicit connection in Leavis's argument between the gold standard and a genuine personal response. However, where Leavis treats gold and genuineness as if they were foundations, Adorno observes that they 'precisely express only the fungibility, the comparability of things … they are not in themselves, but for others'.[37]

Adorno's remarks clarify what is the source of the problem of valuation in the early Leavis, namely that he conceives of value as a foundation while the weight he gives to recognition – whether of the literary lineage or the judgements of the minority – suggests that it is indeed relational. The tension between the assumption of foundation, for example, in implicit standards, and the practice of criticism, persuading others to recognise the rightness of a judgement, may account for why the problem of 'something more' cannot be resolved. This problem arose because of the absence of foundations but while Leavis acknowledges this absence he fails to 'recognise' that he is trying to make recognition do the work of foundations, that is to found and stabilise the notion of value.

Another aspect of this metaphor of the minority as 'the consciousness of the race' is that it brings together consciousness and metaphor to the point where they begin to merge; consciousness appears as metaphor and metaphor appears as consciousness. This suggests that consciousness is dependent on language and, if this is so, then it cannot transcend language in order to use it in the ways prescribed by Leavis. The identification of consciousness and metaphor highlights the linguistic nature of the former, making it difficult to conceive of the transcendent status which Leavis would like to give it. Throughout his work, Leavis insists on the inseparability of language and consciousness,[38] but his position is always that consciousness is in control of language, whereas his metaphor of the minority as consciousness of the race in 'Mass Civilisation and Minority Culture' would seem to indicate that it is the other way around.

This has a bearing on the problem of 'something more' which consciousness looks to metaphor to provide. But, as metaphor and consciousness appear to be one and the same then consciousness itself becomes that 'something more' and is thereby rendered opaque; it cannot know itself in the way that Leavis requires that it should. Consciousness, like metaphor, is thus implicated in an economy of excess, which is embraced as a means of preventing language from being reduced to a 'method of symbolising human thought' but which is also repudiated because it contradicts the insistence on clarity, precision and discrimination.

This tension complicates the roles assigned to consciousness, for example in recognising the literary lineage. If consciousness is bound up with the text's complicated play of metaphor then any recognition it can offer can only be partial. Perhaps this helps to explain why Leavis feels the need of an 'informed and cultivated public' (*MC & MC*, p. 29) to endorse the 'first hand judgement[s]' (p. 14) of the 'very small minority' (p. 13) for this public can then guarantee the perceptions of a consciousness that is not as authoritative as Leavis would wish it to be. This desire for recognition, together with the compromised ability of consciousness to recognise authority, lineage and true worth further complicates the act of reading, which Leavis conceives in precisely these terms.

The complex nature of metaphor in 'Mass Civilisation and Minority Culture' stems from the fact that it is both a tool of argument, the means of clarifying a point and, at the same time, that 'something more' which the text desires. It is thus both the object of a text and a trope of argument. In the latter capacity it generates a multiplicity of meanings and this gives it an affinity with the 'concourse of signals so bewildering in their variety and number' (*MC & MC*, p. 31) which Leavis identifies as the chief characteristic of civilisation. This multiplicity seems to answer the text's need for 'something more', something, that is, which cannot be reduced to 'a tight definition' (p. 15) and which is more than a 'method of symbolising human thought'. But 'something more' is also implicated in the blurring of boundary lines, therefore making 'it increasingly difficult for anyone to know whether he knows what he is talking about or not'.[39] What the text desires, 'something more', turns out to be part of what it deplores, that 'concourse of signals, so bewildering in their variety and number' (*MC & MC*, p. 31).

## THE ECONOMICS OF EXCESS

The notion of 'something more' deserves closer scrutiny. It is inscribed in the text in at least three ways. The first has to do with the overwhelming number of signals which characterise modern civilisation, the second refers to the currency metaphor and the third concerns reading, to which I shall return. The first lends a negative value to 'something more' despite the text's investment in the logic of excess. The second is altogether more complicated.

Initially, the valuation of literature is seen in economic terms, '[t]he accepted valuations are a kind of paper currency based upon a very small proportion of gold' (*MC & MC*, p. 14).[40] This metaphor makes literary judgements quantifiable, a notion which Leavis vigorously repudiates elsewhere in his work.[41] Moreover, in presenting criticism in economic terms Leavis unwittingly allies himself with the Marxists whom he took to task for assuming that cultural problems will disappear when economic ones are solved, since his metaphor collapses the difference between the two spheres.[42] The economic metaphor also suggests the potential to articulate a value, thereby calling into question the notion of 'something more' which, according to the logic of the argument, should be beyond 'symbolisation'. Indeed, it is possible to go one step further and say that the economic metaphor does perform the work of 'symbolising human thought' in that it presents Leavis's notion of value. But this leaves metaphor, supposed to symbolise 'something more' than thought, symbolising only thought. The literary trope which is deemed to resist the instrumentalisation of language itself becomes the prime instance of it.

Although the economic metaphor lends itself to this reading, it also generates a kind of excess. This is apparent when Leavis quotes, with approval, Norman Angell on the declining quality of newspapers. Angell also uses the image of money to make his point.

Just as in commerce debased coin, if there be enough of it, must drive out the sterling, so in the contest of motives, action which corresponds to the most primitive feelings and impulses, to first thoughts and established prejudices, can be stimulated by the modern newspaper far more easily than that prompted by rationalised second thought.[43]

Here, excess is seen to be inflationary and devaluing so that the 'more' of the economic metaphor becomes something to be avoided. As Leavis puts it, 'The currency [of standards] has been debased' (*MC & MC*, p. 21). By seeing criticism in terms of an economic metaphor Leavis is able to give that sense of 'something more' which is essential to his argument but, ironically, that same metaphor reveals 'something more' to be undesirable.

The quotation from Angell suggests a relationship between economics and psychology: the former is used to illuminate the latter. The psychology presented is of a simplistic nature, 'primitive feelings and impulses' as opposed to 'rationalised second thought'. This schema is reminiscent of the Freudian divide between the conscious and the unconscious, and the phrase 'rationalised second thought' recalls especially the notion of secondary revision.[44] Furthermore, Angell's distinction finds an echo in Leavis's text since the latter talks about the desirability of a 'critically adult public' (*MC & MC*, p. 32), thereby implying the existence of an uncritical, childish one.

This division between adult and childish publics is conceived in terms of their critical capacities. The former, being 'a very small minority' (*MC & MC*, p. 32) are equated with 'consciousness' (p. 15) whereas the latter are identified with emotion in its 'cheapest' form (p. 21). The divide between the adult and childish public is seen therefore in terms of greater or lesser consciousness and, as such, it lends itself to an understanding along the lines of the Freudian model, though it cannot be reduced to it. One of the key concepts of psychoanalysis is the Oedipus complex and this offers a way of understanding the relations between the 'adult' and the 'childish' public. For example, Leavis observes that 'parents are helpless to deal with their children' (p. 17) and this is consonant with the problems surrounding the recognition of the *paternal* lineage that constitutes the tradition.

Such observations are justified by the association of the economic and the psychological in the quotation from Norman Angell and by Leavis's conception of an 'adult' and 'childish' public which lends itself to a psychoanalytic interpretation. They are, furthermore, examples of how the economic metaphor cannot be confined to questions regarding standards of criticism. Another manifestation of excess in the economic metaphor is, therefore, the number of different meanings which accrue to it. These ensure that the metaphor is repeated throughout 'Mass Civilisation and Minority Culture'. The appeal of newspapers is, for example, 'cheap' and so too is the response to them (*MC & MC*, pp. 21–2). This widespread use of economic terms represents a steady accumulation, a textually generated excess since it cannot be made to yield any one single meaning.

On the one hand, the economic idiom suggests the possibility of articulating a value precisely, and this is something of which Leavis approves, but, on the other, it is a metaphor for that inflation, for that 'bewildering variety' of signals (*MC & MC*, p. 31) which make such precise articulation impossible. And yet as excess, as 'something more', the economic metaphor provides Leavis with a defence against those who see language as nothing more than a 'method of symbolising human thought'. The situation is rendered even more complex by the fact that the economic metaphor at once serves as an illustration of a point and simultaneously produces or enacts it. Thus, while it helps to give a concrete sense of the inflationary devaluation of standards it also, by virtue of its recurrence throughout the text, produces that inflation of which it is supposed to be an instance. It is little wonder then that Leavis, right at the beginning of his essay, should seek to suppress metaphor – '[t]here is no need to elaborate the metaphor' (p. 14) – since it proves so uncontrollable.

The economic metaphor can be a source of inflation because it conditions a view of language as 'currency', thus inflation refers not just to money, but also to meaning. One example of this inflation is additions to the currency. Hence Leavis remarks that 'the age ... has given currency to the term "highbrow"' (*MC & MC*, p. 39). He sees this word, along with 'worthwhile', as examples of the Americanisation of English, and this is something to be deplored (p. 36) on the grounds that such additions to the language do not come from the native tradition and their intrusion helps to undermine it. They belong specifically to the vocabulary of advertising, whose sole purpose is to foster and exploit 'the cheap response' (p. 22). In this way advertising devalues the subtlety and complexity of the living language, hence 'making things more difficult for the fastidious' (p. 23).

Additions to the language are inflationary because they devalue its discriminatory capacity, on which judgements of worth depend. Leavis is adamant that American additions to English should be resisted. This opposition to America certainly fits Leavis's argument at one level since he is concerned with the 'consciousness of the race' (*MC & MC*, p. 15) and the shaping of 'the national temperament',[45] both of which are threatened by 'the American enterprise' (p. 18) which means 'that we are being Americanised' (p. 17). At the same time, however, Leavis relies heavily on America to read the crisis of culture. America, as it is used throughout his argument, provides Leavis with the means of conceptualising England and he therefore refers to it repeatedly. Therefore, far from repudiating it, he transports it to the heart of English culture.

Another consequence of additions to the language is that they effect a breach between civilisation and culture, making them 'antithetical terms' (*MC & MC*, p. 39). Leavis does not clearly define either culture or civilisation but the difference between them can perhaps be explained as the difference between technique and tradition. Leavis claims that 'technique ... is to replace the ... traditional ways' (p. 40). Technique is associated, in the quotations Leavis presents, with control of emotion and belief, and this suggests that Leavis recognises and tries to find ways of opposing the demands of disciplinary society so carefully analysed by Foucault.[46] Tradition, by contrast, is a matter of 'delicate adjustments [according to] mature, inherited codes of valuation' (p. 17).

'Addition' then, although it seems to answer to the desire for 'something more' represents an 'alien' intrusion and creates a faultline between culture and civilisation. But these negative effects perhaps only make manifest what is intrinsic to the term itself. 'Addition' suggests something which can be clearly computated and this is not what Leavis has in mind when he talks about 'something more'. He defines that 'something more' only negatively, meaning that language is more than a 'method of symbolising human thought'. The 'something more' is therefore unquantifiable and is not well served by the term 'addition'.

Another way in which 'addition' is negative is that it is ultimately repetitive. Writing about the Book Society and the Book Guild, Leavis notes that both 'make great play with the American adjective "worthwhile"' (*MC & MC*, p. 36). For Leavis, this American 'addition' to the English language flattens out all distinctions between different texts, making them part of an 'atmosphere of uplift and hearty mass sentiment' (pp. 36–7). In this respect 'addition' parallels that 'concourse of signals so bewildering in their variety and number' which have 'blurred away distinctions and dividing lines' (p. 31). And, as if to underline the connection, Leavis notes that a further feature of this 'concourse of signals' is that 'the same words are used with different meanings' (p. 31). Thus 'additions' to the language are achieved at the cost of other words which may help to sharpen powers of discrimination. 'Addition', in Leavis's logic, seems to be the replacement of many terms by one. Since 'addition' suggests that the same words are used with different meanings, it can be seen as a form of repetition and, as such, it functions as a conservative force. Thus, Leavis's objection to it can perhaps be interpreted in a progressive light. His oppositional stance would seem to indicate not that he is against change but that he is for it – as long as it goes along considered and principled lines.

But this openness to change has to be set alongside the fact that his own writings can be seen in terms of repetition. Anne Samson has noted Leavis's 'willingness to republish',[47] the fact that his major books 'were made up from articles published in *Scrutiny*[48] and how '[s]triking is the continuity of [the] later criticism with the earlier'.[49] Such repetitions may be seen either as an adherence to principle or a failure to develop thought and, if the latter, then Leavis's writing can be seen to parallel the conservative work of 'addition' when it functions like repetition.

Repetition comes out of 'addition' and 'addition' itself is related to the metaphor of the gold standard which, in one form or another, recurs throughout 'Mass Civilisation and Minority Culture'. The metaphor of the gold standard is historically resonant. 'Mass Civilisation and Minority Culture' appeared in 1930, one year after the Wall Street Crash and one year before the British financial crisis. The gold standard is therefore a dubious image of stability. Moreover, its very nature as metaphor militates against it fixing values. The meanings of this economic metaphor extend far beyond those which Leavis ascribes to it and this plurality makes it similar to the 'concourse of signals'. It is because of the protean quality of this metaphor that it can expand and contract to accommodate many different readings and this demonstrates its intrinsically economic nature; it validates, as it were, the very notion of economy to the extent that it promotes the exchange, circulation and currency of meaning. Whether Leavis likes it or not economics is quite literally the prop of culture.

The idea of language as a currency, as a circulation of terms, suggests that value is a relative, not an absolute phenomenon. As the example of 'highbrow' shows, new words can always be added to the language and given currency. The effect of this particular addition is to unify different cultural groups, by appealing to their shared democratic pleasures against the elitism of 'highbrows'. This necessarily entails a revaluation of the relations between 'high' and 'popular' culture. Again there is a parallel with Adorno, who argues that the function of the 'culture industry' is to eliminate difference by 'impress[ing] the same stamp upon everything'.[50] One aspect of this involves 'forc[ing] together the spheres of high and low art',[51] with the result that both are weakened. 'High' art is forced to justify itself in the market place while 'low' art has to suppress its more vulgar and exuberant elements in the interests of the dominant morality.[52]

The welding together of 'high' and 'low' art, argues Adorno, means that the distinction between image and reality is eliminated.[53] This is most clearly seen in film. 'Real life,' claims Adorno, 'is becoming indistinguishable from the movies'.[54] The purpose of cinema, continues Adorno, is to teach people 'how to move and speak according to the scheme it has fabricated'.[55] Leavis also sees film as a threat to art, specifically literature, because it closes the gap between cultural and empirical reality. Films, he writes, 'provide ... a compellingly vivid illusion of actual life' (*MC & MC*, pp. 20–1) and this characteristic rivals 'the concrete livingness, the immediacy of sensuous and life charged presentation'[56] that can be found in literature. Since films only present the illusion of life they cannot be seen as interrogating it, they lack that 'exploratory creation'[57] which Leavis associates with literature, hence film is a more conservative medium. 'Low' culture imitates 'high' culture in a movement that fuses them together, depriving each of them of their respective strengths. This process is supplemented by the creation of a discourse that marginalises the representatives of culture. Consequently, though they appear united, culture and civilisation 'are coming to be antithetical terms' (p. 39) or, as Adorno expresses it, they 'are torn halves of an integral freedom, to which, however, they do not add up'.[58]

Leavis's argument shows that a commercial enterprise, in this case the Book Society, can generate a discourse that includes terms like 'highbrow' which re-align the values of culture. This suggests that how language is used is more important than the meaning of individual words. The problem is that this seems to conflict with his view about standards. Leavis seems to imply that they enable the critic to discover the essential worth of cultural artifacts. This is due to the standards themselves being 'implicit' (MC & MC, p. 15), a quality which ensures that what they designate as having true worth cannot be questioned on rational grounds.

Thus there appears to be an ambiguity in Leavis's position. On the one hand he wants to be able to point to the absolute value of an artifact while the logic of his argument, particularly economic metaphors, which gives rise to terms like currency, suggests that value can only be relative.[59] Indeed, the economic metaphor, with its associations of circulation and exchange, does not sit easily with Leavis's overt claims about culture having a definite and recognisable centre (MC & MC, p. 15). This ultimately suggests something static which is in stark contrast to the movement that characterises an economy. Its essential dynamism and inevitable fluctuations prevent the achievement of the subtlety, delicate adjustment and discernment at which Leavis aims, for these depend on a fixed and stable order.

But although Leavis seems to posit the existence or at least the desirability of such an order it is also the case that he exploits what he seems to lament – the shifting and relative nature of value. Hence Leavis can talk about 'wrest[ing] the phrase [the standard of living] from the economist' (MC & MC, p. 17). This indicates that Leavis does not regard value as intrinsic but dependent on context and motivation. Hence, value and, by extension, meaning seem to be the result of contestation. Both appear to be the outcome of struggle rather than a matter of being able to recognise an object's true and essential worth.

By drawing attention to the contingent nature of value, the economic metaphor enables Leavis to resist and oppose what he regards as the pernicious effects of 'civilisation'. He may imply that culture has an inherent worth but his metaphor suggests that it is a site of struggle. And indeed, the accent of his work falls precisely on this struggle. The economic metaphor, so unsatisfactory in many ways, nevertheless enables Leavis to take up the cudgels on behalf of a beleaguered culture.

Furthermore, by revealing, albeit unintentionally, the arbitrary nature of value and then arguing with great earnestness and conviction for his own particular conception of culture, Leavis challenges the reader to consider his or her own views on the subject. His challenge is no less effective because there is a gap between his tacit view that culture has essential worth and his metaphor which suggests the opposite. On the contrary, this tension underlines the difficulty involved in thinking about culture, which is in itself salutary since it prevents the reader from being too glib about the topic.[60]

The gap between Leavis's assumption about value and the way his metaphor projects it may be viewed positively in one light but not in another. For the fact is that Leavis is blind to the persistence of the metaphor in his text and to its multiple effects. This blindness contrasts with his avowed aim that criticism is a matter of full conscious recognition of its object. Can this be achieved when the discourse of criticism cannot fully recognise itself? What seems most apparent here is that criticism's perception of its object is, at least in part, a function of its own lack of self-awareness. This can lead to projecting onto other critics qualities that inhere in one's own critical discourse. Hence Leavis is scornful of Arnold Bennett, whose critical vocabulary is deemed 'gross' because it contains phrases like 'value for money' (*MC & MC*, p. 28). Yet the economic metaphor in 'Mass Civilisation and Minority Culture' implies something similar since it suggests judgements are quantifiable. Bennett's terminology evokes bargains, Leavis's the proper price, but both belong to the idiom of the market. Since Leavis fails to recognise that he and Bennett share the same idiom it is doubly ironic that he should further accuse Bennett of wilful self-ignorance, claiming that Bennett's 'would be confession' about his lack of knowledge of prosody is really 'self betrayal' (p. 29). Leavis may not 'betray' himself but he certainly shares with Bennett an inability to control the meaning of what he has written and this gives a peculiar aptness to his plea that there should be a critically informed public who can endorse the judgement of the minority. The danger is that this public may recognise the text in a way in which it cannot recognise itself.

Though the play of the economic metaphor reveals certain blindspots in Leavis's view of his text, it does resolve two of the conflicting demands of Leavis's argument – that language should be something more than a 'method of symbolising human thought' and simultaneously a precise expression of thought. The metaphor of the gold standard combines both of these by being at once precise and polyvalent. Precise because it conveys Leavis's belief that literary value exists and must be defended, and polyvalent because it connotates a whole range of meanings not relevant and even contrary to his purpose. However, it remains true that the success of metaphor in fusing these contradictory demands is achieved at the expense of a certain loss of textual self-reflexivity so that metaphor, at least in its capacity of being 'something more', actually entails something less:

a diminution of consciousness understood as Leavis's being unaware of how his metaphor means 'more' than he intends. And yet, at another level, Leavis does seem aware of the irrepressibly generative nature of his metaphor since he attempts to repress its metaphoric status by claiming its meaning is obvious. Later, Leavis's retrenchment will be mirrored by the National Government's package of cuts to deal with the sterling crisis of 1931. In literature and in the economy the endeavour to conserve value is carried on by the same means. There is a symmetry here if not a connection.

## CULTURE, METAPHOR AND METONYMY

The economic metaphor and the metaphor of the minority as the consciousness of the race involve, then, a number of problems both in themselves and about the nature of metaphor generally. Leavis's third metaphor, as previously mentioned, is that of language, which is a metaphor for culture. But this metaphor is more complicated than the previous two because it 'is a metonymy also and will bear a good deal of pondering' (MC & MC, p. 15). What is not clear is how metaphor can be equated with metonymy, and the problem is accentuated by Leavis being less than explicit in regard to what he means by metonymy. Metonymy is usually defined as a 'figure of speech in which the name or attribute of a thing is substituted for the thing itself'.[61] Thus language, as a part of culture, comes to stand, in Leavis's formulation, for the whole of culture itself. But then it is difficult to imagine any part of culture that is *not* language or surrounded by language. Painting is not a language of words but it is a language of line, brushstroke, colour and so forth. Furthermore, it is made to mean through, among other things, the discourse of art history and exhibition catalogues. Therefore it is possible to argue that language is culture and not simply a part of it.[62]

But perhaps Leavis's error, if it can be called that, springs less from his failure to think through metonymy than from an ambiguity within the term itself. This resides in the notion of substitution which has also been used to define the operation of metaphor in language. Roman Jakobson, for example, equates metaphor with the paradigmatic axis of language, which is the vertical line where words can be substituted one for another. By contrast, he equates metonymy with the syntagmatic axis, which is the horizontal line where words are placed next to one another in a relationship.[63] In this formulation,

metaphor seems like the standard definition of metonymy. It may be
objected that metaphor is a trope whereby one thing is described in
terms of another whereas metonymy is simply a part of a thing
standing in for the thing itself. But this does not dispose of the problem
since, in both cases, a substitution is involved. Both metaphor and
metonymy emphasise one quality of a thing at the expense of another
and so both elevate the part at the expense of the whole. In addition,
metaphor, like metonymy, implies some form of movement. In the
original Greek, *metaphora* means 'carrying from one place to another',
and the movement of metonymy is evident in the way words are
linked together to produce meaning. If, therefore, metaphor and
metonymy are not so readily distinguishable[64] it is hardly surprising
that Leavis's reference to them should be less than explicit.

The blurring of the distinction between metaphor and metonymy
may have consequences for Leavis's argument in that it shows the
precariousness of setting up oppositions. Leavis implies that metaphor
and metonymy are two separate tropes yet the fact that he does not
articulate what he considers to be the difference between them has
the effect of bringing them closer together. This makes those
distinctions in his argument such as 'culture' and 'civilisation' (*MC
& MC*, p. 39) or 'active' and 'passive' (p. 21) much less tenable. The
former particularly since, although Leavis defines culture as the 'use
of' language (p. 15) he also discusses civilisation in exactly the same
terms. For example, he looks at how advertising uses language
(pp. 22–3) and at some of the ideas for 'scientifically improv[ing]
English' (p. 42).

Both culture and civilisation have to do with the use of language,
rather than with the relation of language to the world. They both seem
to share the assumption that reality is generated by using language
in particular ways and it is this, not language's correspondence with
the world which matters. The question then is how and for what
purposes language will be used. Leavis is explicit on this point: it is
to 'keep alive the subtlest and most perishable parts of the tradition'
(*MC & MC*, p. 15); it is 'to discriminate' (p. 31) and to know 'that the
centre is here rather than there' (p. 31). But Leavis does not seem
cognisant of the full implications of his emphasis on the use of
language, which anticipates the neo-pragmatism of, for example,
Richard Rorty. One aspect of the latter's thinking, which is certainly
present in a latent form in Leavis's argument, is that there are no
ultimate grounds which sanction our ethics or our epistemology.[65]
Because these lack firm foundations they are always going to be

provisional and subject to change.[66] Leavis's advocacy of the use of language suggests an anti-foundationalist stance in his argument, thus calling into question his notion of implicit standards which, precisely because they are implicit, ground his particular form of criticism. But he does not seem to register this inconsistency in his argument, thereby demonstrating how his commitment to consciousness seems to be accompanied by unconsciousness.

Culture and civilisation, then, are similar in that both are to do with the use of language though each conceives of this use in different ways. Leavis, however, only asserts that *culture* is the use of language. Perhaps it is here that Leavis's view about language being 'a metaphor that is metonymy also' becomes a little clearer. If language is a metaphor for culture, it does not seem unreasonable to suppose that the *use* of the language is metonymy. If this is the case then metaphor, which Leavis used to supplement Arnold's definitions and which functioned as the 'something more' that resisted the instrumentalisation of language, itself appears as a lack needing to be supplemented by metonymy.

The effect of metonymy supplementing metaphor is to destabilise Leavis's argument. It will be remembered that metaphor, in so far as it stands for 'something more' which cannot be precisely articulated, is linked to Leavis's implicit standards. These implicit standards function transhistorically to the extent that they are implicit. Their non-articulation protects them from historical erosion. By not being defined, they cannot be challenged. Metaphor and implicit standards therefore provide a fixed reference point, a sense of plenitude which enables the act of discrimination to take place. Since, however, metaphor has to be supplemented by metonymy, its transhistorical character begins to waver. Metonymy is the introduction of history into metaphor and yet the whole purpose of metaphor in Leavis's argument is to oppose history, understood here as 'civilisation'. Without knowing it, Leavis was right, his 'metaphor that is metonymy also [does indeed] bear a good deal of pondering' (*MC & MC*, p. 15).

What Leavis seems to mean by metonymy is the use of language. 'Use' is a key word in the Benthamite tradition which Leavis so vigorously repudiates,[67] but by repeating so insistently his view that what matters is the use of language Leavis is in danger of delivering language over to those agencies who want to completely instrumentalise it. Leavis's emphasis on use seems less to combat the administrative mentality than to reinforce it. Both he and the bureaucrat are interested in 'use', though Leavis would claim that what distinguishes him from the bureaucrat would be that his 'use' is connected to a purpose – the survival of tradition. But this defence is not good enough. For Leavis, the chief use of language is discrimination and, it can be argued, this is similar to how language functions in its administrative and bureaucratic capacities. There, it catalogues and classifies according to a norm and the same can be said of Leavis's criticism, his nuanced responses all taking their cue from those implicit standards which should orientate psychology and behaviour. Adorno is sensitive to this aspect of culture, noting that it 'betrays from the outset an administrative view, the task of which, looking down from on high, is to assemble, distribute, evaluate and organise'.[68] An emphasis on 'use' therefore is only partly progressive. It lends itself too easily to the way language is made to work by the institutions of society itself.

To counteract this it is necessary to stress how 'Mass Civilisation and Minority Culture' shows that language is 'something more' than use. In other words it is necessary to distinguish between the use of language and how language works. Leavis may want to *use* language for the purpose of discrimination but the logic of his text shows that this goal is not so easily achieved. Hence it seems to say something 'other' than what Leavis would like it to say. This suggests that language cannot be reduced solely to how it is used and thus it can never be wholly appropriated by those branches of civilisation which want to standardise it. A desire to subordinate language to given ends seems to entail an excess that transcends those ends. The problem is how to turn that excess into an effective critique, if one is necessary, of those ends.

## ADVERTISING AND BOOK CLUBS

As already mentioned, the use of language for Leavis is discrimination and what Leavis wants to discriminate between in this text is culture and civilisation. He concentrates on two examples of civilisation, advertising and book clubs, and attacks them both from the standpoint of culture. The problem is that these examples of civilisation exhibit features that belong to culture. Leavis's insistence on difference reveals similarities. One of the first comments Leavis makes about advertising is that the word 'may be taken to cover a great deal more than comes formally under that head' (*MC & MC*, p. 22). Yet this also applies to culture which, as language, is 'a metaphor that is metonymy also and will bear a good deal of pondering' (p. 15). Advertising and culture thus contain qualities that are not included in the commonly accepted definition of each term. Civilisation is associated with techniques which 'symbolise ... thought' (p. 42), whereas culture, as language, is always 'something more': yet so too is advertising, one of the manifestations of civilisation in the text. In his desire to distinguish between culture and civilisation Leavis may condemn advertising for 'becoming increasingly exact every day' (p. 22) but, as has been argued, his own text promotes the principle of exactitude in response to the dissolution of traditional boundary lines manifest in that 'concourse of signals' so 'bewildering' in their variety. Again, culture and civilisation seem more to mirror than to differ from one another.

This demonstrates Leavis's failure to recognise the actual state of the relations between culture and civilisation and this is highly ironic considering his impatience at those who cannot see what he can even though it is so 'obvious' (*MC & MC*, pp. 15, 16, 17, 20 and *passim*). What Leavis fails to note is how culture and civilisation complement one another and this makes him a good example of Adorno's remark that 'culture is blind to its entanglement with the social totality'.[69] And yet Leavis ought to be able to perceive this given that he, like Adorno, is aware that culture has been 'removed from any possible relation to praxis'.[70] This, indeed, is the theme of 'Mass Civilisation and Minority Culture', but the conclusion which Leavis fails to draw from this is that, by being severed from the concrete realities of everyday life, culture is more easily integrated into the social whole and thus lacks that oppositional force with which he would like to invest it. The text shows this even though Leavis does not say it. 'Mass Civilisation and Minority Culture' is 'something more' than the expression of his thought. Its structure negates his intended meaning, calling into question reading as a process of becoming fully conscious of the object of criticism whether it be a work of literature or an aspect of society.

Culture's resistance to civilisation is further weakened by the continuity between 'minor' literature and commercial discourses. '[A]dvertising', writes Leavis, 'is carrying on the work begun by Mr. Rudyard Kipling' (*MC & MC*, p. 23). These are also allied with the discourse of popular culture, creating the impression of a seamless totality wholly exclusive of literature, that is, Leavis's tradition, which it defines as 'other', specifically, 'highbrow'. Initially, this analysis may seem to restore a sense of opposition to literature, showing that culture need not necessarily underwrite the imperatives of civilisation. It also suggests that the yoking together of various aspects of 'high' and 'low' culture may not have been as effective as Adorno fears.

Closer examination, however, reveals that though literature may exist in opposition to civilisation there is no sense of how this opposition can function. It is a structural rather than a practical opposition. Indeed, it is an opposition created *by* civilisation, and literature can therefore be seen as fulfilling a pre-ordained role. The sort of literature which is *effective*, which *works*, is that which reinforces and reproduces the values of the social whole. Leavis's literature – tradition – is abstract compared to the concrete functioning of minor literature and this is ironic given the stress Leavis places on the concrete throughout his career. By the terms of Leavis's own argument, literature is deprived of all efficacy and can only serve as an object of aesthetic contemplation.

But this need not be interpreted in a negative light for the very 'uselessness' of such literature acts as a reproach to the use-dominated consciousness of society. Similarly, the claim that culture repeats civilisation need not preclude the possibility of opposition. For it is in its 'doubling' of civilisation that culture allows the latter's absence of meaning to emerge and reveal itself precisely in all its negativity. To be able to appreciate the oppositional force of 'Mass Civilisation and Minority Culture' it is necessary to heed Leavis's advice about being fully conscious of a work, but it is also necessary to take warning from his example that the pursuit of a fully conscious reading – here of the relation between culture and civilisation – involves 'something more' that escapes conscious attention – an unconsciousness which means that there can always be other readings – even of Leavis.

If advertising shares certain qualities which Leavis elsewhere assigns to culture alone this may be because advertising comes to be an expression of the effect which Leavis would like literature to have. It is not simply that advertising shares certain characteristics with literature, but that it seems to exaggerate them and, by doing so, articulates Leavis's desire that literature have more of an impact on society. For, in the end, advertising accomplishes what Leavis would like to do, namely persuade people to take up certain products rather than others and it does so by seeking to perfect ways of determining and controlling response. Leavis's critical project operates along similar lines, it simply lacks the resources and techniques of advertising. Advertising, therefore, can be seen as an expression of desire, of Leavis's desire that certain privileged works elicit the sort of response appropriate for members of the minority, whose cultural product is then endorsed by a sufficiently educated mature and adult public. Unwittingly, Leavis articulates his cultural criticism in the grammar of mass civilisation and this suggests that, if it is to be a force of resistance, culture's relation to society needs to be thought out in terms other than its opposition to civilisation.

That opposition, at least as Leavis conceives it, is untenable. The relation between culture and civilisation is rather one of desire and, since Leavis desires the influence and rhetorical powers of advertising, this relation comes closer to illustrating Lacan's notion that 'man's desire finds its meaning in the desire of the other'.[71] This might explain why, in Leavis's essay, the 'desire' of culture, though it appears to be the same as that of civilisation, is nevertheless expressed in opposition to it. In any case, the idea that criticism should articulate a fully conscious response to an object is, once more, called into question. A focused and sustained reading may be the declared aim of criticism but this takes no account of desire as part of its constitution. This relationship between an unconscious desire and a conscious goal strengthens the idea, noted earlier, that 'Mass Civilisation and Minority Culture' is structured in a manner analogous to the Freudian schema of the conscious and the unconscious, whereby what is consciously rejected is unconsciously desired.

This pattern of desiring what is repressed is also apparent in Leavis's comments on the Book Society and the Book Guild. His first objection to these organisations is that they usurp the critic's role by 'guid[ing]' and 'help[ing]' the 'very small critically adult public' (*MC & MC*, p. 32). The book clubs attempt to determine what is and is not worth reading and the criteria they use are that a book should have both literary merit and popular appeal.[72] Although Leavis is hostile to this enterprise, whereby book clubs 'tak[e] into their keeping the future of English taste', he does acknowledge that people will get through 'a greater amount of respectable reading than before' (pp. 34–5). His chief objection is expressed through the analogy of a manufacturer who wanted to reduce the number of patterns he had for the same article, which he achieved by concentrating on a small number of them, advertising those in colour and the rest in black and white. Leavis's comment on this process is that it merely reveals how '[s]tandardisation advances to fresh triumphs' (p. 36).

It is fair to say that the book clubs have the power and authority which Leavis feels should belong to culture (*MC & MC*, p. 39). The book clubs minister to a public in need of guidance and, furthermore, their criteria of what constitutes a good book resemble Leavis's own view, that is, literature should be 'at once popular' and 'appreciated only by an educated minority' (p. 38).[73] In addition, the book clubs are in the business of moulding *English* taste (p. 34) which, as has been seen, is Leavis's specific concern, evident in his asides on race and national temperament. Thus the book clubs, like advertising, reveal Leavis's desire. He reviles them not because they are different from culture but because they have the influence which he would like to reserve for his minority. Leavis's critique of civilisation thus betrays a will to power that conflicts with the more democratic notion of recognition mentioned earlier.

Leavis's description of the strategy of the manufacturer is also a description of himself. In reducing his patterns the manufacturer does nothing more than Leavis would like to do. Leavis has complained about the adverse effects of the 'concourse of signals', how they have blurred distinctions and problematised knowledge, and how one concrete manifestation of this is 'the smother of new books' (*MC & MC*, p. 30). His remedy for this is 'a limited set of signals' or, in literary terms, 'severe thought and long continued intercourse with the best models' (pp. 30–1). These constitute the 'tradition' which may be regarded as similar to those few patterns on which the manufacturer concentrates; the best models are variations on the implicit standards of tradition, just as the restricted number of patterns are variations of 'the same article'.[74] Thus, although Leavis uses this analogy to point up the sheer commercialism of the book clubs and the consequent commodification of literature, it also parallels Leavis's own project by organising the plethora of texts around a few basic models. Civilisation may cause the problems of culture but it also provides a solution for them. In doing so it effects a *rapprochement* between these two terms which Leavis finds so antithetical. Civilisation, it might be said, accomplishes what culture desires.

## THE WORK OF REPETITION IN 'MASS CIVILISATION AND MINORITY CULTURE'

Civilisation, then, in the form of advertising and the book club, seems to mirror culture and in the process exaggerate it. In this respect it appears to be 'more' than culture and thus to provide that excess which Leavis requires if language is not going to lapse into nothing more than a 'method of symbolising human thought'. Far from being, as Leavis argues, a lack, civilisation is in fact the plenitude which culture lacks. It achieves this condition by repeating or mirroring, on a large scale, some of the qualities of culture as culture repeats or mirrors some of the qualities of civilisation for, ultimately, it is impossible to tell which is the 'original' and which the repetition in this relationship. One effect of repetition is to bridge the gap between culture and civilisation, since repetition is as much about continuity as discontinuity, unity as much as about division. The repetition of civilisation by culture and culture by civilisation is not a conscious strategy but a structural feature of Leavis's argument and, as it functions as the site of productive possibilities it offsets Leavis's declared pessimism.

Repetition is not, however, without problems. For example, it can be considered inimical to notions of narrative and progress. This is because repetition replaces the cause and effect relationship which Leavis sets up to explain the relation between culture and civilisation. The former's decline is blamed firmly on the machine, specifically the 'automobile', which has 'radically affected religion, broken up the family and revolutionised social custom' and so has destroyed 'delicate traditional adjustments [and] mature, inherited codes of habit and valuation' (*MC & MC*, p. 17). The result of this is that 'concourse of signals' where there are no boundaries or dividing lines. There is a sense of claustrophobia, of a conflation of the centre with the periphery: 'What is taking place is not something that ... stops short ... at the periphery' (pp. 23–4). In the absence of clearly defined relations, repetition becomes an ordering principle. The question then arises as to whether this principle merely reproduces the same, since repetition, as repetition, seems to preclude the notion of development. And yet this need not necessarily be the case for, as civilisation repeats aspects of culture and vice versa, so it modifies them through exaggeration and this difference may prove fruitful.

Repetition can also be understood as a way of making manifest what was hidden. This is best understood by considering how civilisation comes to express certain desires of culture, which are not immediately apparent, for example, a desire for control or domination. Indeed civilisation, at times, seems like a wish fulfilment of culture. Civilisation seems to be like a mirror, angled to reflect culture in certain ways. It is also like a screen onto which culture projects certain characteristics of its own. In this latter capacity, civilisation appears as culture's 'other'. For example, civilisation has to do with quantitative valuation but that process is also implicit in culture. By projecting it onto civilisation however, culture purifies itself. This projection is not a conscious matter, it is simply a consequence of the textual logic of 'Mass Civilisation and Minority Culture'. It is therefore possible to argue that culture does not recognise itself, and this observation should then be placed against the text's desire for recognition expressed in the idea that the minority need their judgements endorsed by a critically adult public. However, this desire is one which asks for confirmation of what already is the case; it is, as it were, a plea for confirmation of the mirror image. What the reader is faced with instead is a mirror-like play between culture and civilisation, which shows that neither is exactly as Leavis claims them to be. It is this that the reader recognises, not the image which Leavis would like confirmed.

Another way of approaching repetition is to consider it in relation to metonymy. Metonymy refers to the way words, sentences and ideas are connected, to the way, in fact, in which words are used. It also implies some form of progressive accumulation and this is different from repetition, which is more to do with the play of the same. Further, since it is to do with the use of words, with their combination in sentences whose meaning unfolds in time, metonymy has a temporal dimension. By contrast, repetition's insistence on the same seems to preclude the possibility of change. The temporal dimension of metonymy opens it to history and change, and it is therefore closely tied to civilisation. Thus, what matters to Leavis, the use of words, that is, culture, is ultimately connected to the very process against which the use of words is directed, that is, civilisation. Repetition on the other hand, because it resists the temporal dimension, is best seen in relation to culture and its implicit standards, which Leavis wants to preserve from historical erosion. But this, at least on a superficial reading, is hardly to be regarded as a recommendation for culture, which now appears as that which cannot adapt but only repeat itself. However, as has been argued, culture can be rescued from this plight by emphasising repetition as a play between culture and civilisation.

What follows from this is that repetition complicates the relation between metaphor and metonymy. Leavis seems to regard them as synonymous when he notes that culture, as the discriminatory use of language, is 'a metaphor that is a metonymy also' (*MC & MC*, p. 15). Discrimination is thus rooted in an initial conflation of tropes. However, as was argued earlier, it is difficult to distinguish clearly between metaphor and metonymy, though this does not help Leavis's case since it destabilises the oppositions on which it is built. It is only through the work of repetition that a sense of discontinuity between metaphor and metonymy becomes apparent.

As a force of conservation, repetition is associated with culture which is conceived metaphorically in terms of the minority as 'the consciousness of the race' and a gold standard. By implication, therefore, repetition is linked with metaphor and in as much as repetition is contrasted with metonymy so too, by extension, is metaphor. Further, metaphor answers the problem of 'something more' in 'Mass Civilisation and Minority Culture', and repetition can be seen as a form of 'something more' in that, by its very nature, it is a type of excess. As a type of excess, however, its status as a force of conservation becomes problematic. A similar ambiguity affects metaphor in that, in providing 'something more', it threatens to deliver too much and thus Leavis tries to curb the fertility of metaphor by refusing to elaborate or expand upon it.

This strategy leaves only one option, that of repetition, which is inscribed in Leavis's text in two ways. The first consists of 'restat[ing] the obvious' (*MC & MC*, p. 15) and the second, the play between civilisation and culture, has already been discussed. In respect of the former, repetition constitutes an excess but, at the same time, it is redundant since it adds nothing to what is not already 'obvious'. Hence 'something more' acquired by the logic of the text appears, through the work of repetition, as mere superfluousness. Repetition is more productive when seen as part of the complex interrelation between culture and civilisation since it offers a different way of conceiving the two terms from that presented by Leavis. Another positive approach to repetition is to see it in contrast to Leavis's claim regarding the 'breach in continuity' (p. 17) which he regards as the crisis of culture. The double layer of repetition in his text seems to present, in formal terms at least, a unity that refutes the notion of any such 'breach'.

Like metaphor and metonymy, repetition is an important aspect of 'Mass Civilisation and Minority Culture'. Unlike metaphor and metonymy it receives no mention from Leavis. Repetition can thus be seen as the 'unconscious' of Leavis's text. Moreover, as is clear from the above, it seems to have a number of different meanings and effects but, even taken together, these do not appear to be able to account for it. It has a force beyond any of its particular manifestations and this gives it a somewhat demonic character. Freud relates the demonic character of repetition to the death instinct, noting that while repetition binds energies together this ultimately allows it only to propel the organism towards dissolution.[75] The contradictory character of repetition in 'Mass Civilisation and Minority Culture' lies in seeking, by 'restat[ing] the obvious', to bind together those 'few who are capable of unprompted first hand judgement' with the minority 'who are capable of endorsing such first hand judgement by genuine personal response' (*MC & MC*, p. 14), while, at the same time dissolving distinctions, such as those between culture and civilisation, thus helping to promote the blurring of boundaries which Leavis deplores.

Repetition, along with metaphor, metonymy and the relation between implicit standards and explicit responses, make it very difficult to read 'Mass Civilisation and Minority Culture' in a transparent manner. Leavis encourages a transparent reading by his frequent appeals to the 'obvious' but the operations of his text show that there can be no such thing. Nor, indeed, can there be the sort of alert and fully tuned conscious reading that he assumes exists. In the first place, it is hard to reconcile such a conception of reading with an appeal to the obvious whose (apparent) self-evidence simply does not require the kind of detailed attention that characterises Leavis's view of reading. In the second place, Leavis's obliviousness to the role and perhaps even the presence of repetition in his text shows that there is indeed nothing 'obvious' about a text and so it does therefore require the reader to be more than usually conscious in his or her approach to it. Leavis, it can be said, vindicates his method of reading precisely by failing to apply it.

## LEAVIS READING AND THE USE OF 'AMERICA'

What Leavis reads in 'Mass Civilisation and Minority Culture' is not a text but culture. His reading is both diagnostic and curative. He attempts to reveal the state of culture and then offers to remedy it.

Although his reading is diagnostic it also claims to be saying nothing more than what is already known. Hence he can write '[i]t is a commonplace today that culture is at a crisis' (*MC & MC*, p. 15). But what is at issue is whether this commonplace is 'understood' for 'realisation of what the crisis portends does not seem to be common' (p. 16). This suggests that the crisis of culture lies more in the future than in the present but that it can be read if the signs of what is happening now are correctly understood. Reading, on this interpretation, is prognosis and, as such, its validity is open to question until such a time as it can be empirically verified. More importantly, these questions reveal the central ambiguity of Leavis's conception of reading: that it is intended to highlight what should really be obvious. Hence Leavis, since he believes that 'realisation of what the crisis portends [is] not … common' feels that it is 'not unnecessary to restate the obvious' (p. 16).

However, restatement of the obvious constitutes a repetition in the text and, in so doing, offers to break with the 'obviousness' of the 'obvious'. This threatened rupture is a source of anxiety for immediately afterwards Leavis writes that, in order to support his view that the present state of culture is unprecedented, 'it is enough to point to the machine' (*MC & MC*, p. 16). The argument thus seems somewhat circular. The present condition of culture is 'obvious' but not so 'obvious' that it cannot be restated; yet, in order to restate it, 'it is enough' to point to one aspect of it which, by that very phrase, returns the reader to the obvious from which Leavis started. This, of course, can be dismissed as a common device in polemical and horatory writing but to do so would be to give preference to the general rule above the particular case and, moreover, it safeguards Leavis from a rigorous reading, leaving the generally reductive estimate of his work intact.

Leavis's anxiety about the rupture with which repetition threatens the obvious should be seen in relation to the 'breach in continuity' (*MC & MC*, p. 17) that Leavis claims is part of the crisis of the culture. The purpose of reading in this context, therefore, is to heal the breach in continuity. But reading is by no means a straightforward process and, conceived as the making plain of what should already be obvious, functions to institute a breach rather than to heal one. Together, these points suggest that the operation of clarifying the 'obvious' renders it more obscure than transparent. The 'obvious', in short, is problematised.

This links it with metaphor, which is also a highly problematic term in 'Mass Civilisation and Minority Culture'. More precisely, Leavis tries to assimilate metaphor to the obvious by denying the metaphoric status of the gold standard, claiming that there is 'no need to elaborate the metaphor' (*MC & MC*, p. 141). But if this brings metaphor and the 'obvious' closer together, it also provides a means of distinguishing between them, for while Leavis may deny the nature of metaphor as metaphor, he insists on the 'obviousness' of the 'obvious'. There is, however, a further twist, for the emphasis on the 'obvious' is itself paralleled by the repeated recourse to metaphor, making it, in the end, almost impossible to disentangle metaphor from the 'obvious' or the 'obvious' from metaphor.

The problem of the obvious in 'Mass Civilisation and Minority Culture' is further illustrated by Leavis's references to America. His claim that, in order to grasp the crisis of culture 'it is enough to point to the machine', is supported by reference to R.S. and H.M. Lynd's study of a community in the American middle west, *Middletown*.[76] Thus America is used to read the crisis of English culture. America is witness to the devastating effects of the machine, how it has 'radically affected religion, broken up the family and revolutionised social custom' (*MC & MC*, pp. 16–17). '[T]he same processes,' Leavis writes, 'are at work in England' (p. 17). What is obvious in England, therefore, can best be understood through seeing it in America. America is both an illustration of what is happening to England and a form of repetition that makes clear what should already be 'obvious'. The relation between England and America in the text partakes of the logic surrounding the 'obvious'. By itself the 'obvious' ought to be self-sufficient but it is not, and so it needs to be highlighted and this is precisely how the text places America in relation to England.

It is also the case that the England–America relation in the text is conditioned by another logic, that pertaining to the relation between implicit and explicit standards. The function of Leavis's minority is to make explicit what is implicit and this is what America seems to do for England since it reveals, in their finished form, possibilities, tendencies and potentialities in English culture. As Leavis writes, 'It is true that in America change has been more rapid, and its effects ... intensified ... [b]ut the same processes are at work in England' (*MC & MC*, p. 17). America, therefore, is necessary to Leavis's argument; without it, it would be difficult to understand what is happening to and going to happen to English culture. At the same time Leavis would like to repress what America represents. This is seen in his deploring the introduction of book clubs into England modelled on the American Book of the Month Club (p. 32). Leavis, in wanting to repress what America stands for, links it to metaphor, which he also wants to repress but which is a source of illumination, as indeed is America. The association of America with metaphor means that it starts to function as that 'something more' which the text requires.[77] Thus, it cannot simply be seen as an *example* of tendencies in English culture. Through its relation with metaphor America constitutes an excess that makes it more than an illustration of a point in an argument.

If the text's use of America parallels its use of metaphor it is also fair to claim that America has a metonymic dimension too. Here, it is important to remember that Leavis's conception of America is taken from *Middletown*, which is the study of only one particular area. Leavis extrapolates the whole of America from one part of it and, to this extent, his idea of it corresponds to that aspect of metonymy which concerns the substitution of the part for the whole.

Metonymy is also a principle of combination, that is, it connects and organises different elements, building them into a whole. It is thus on the side of hierarchy, distinction and division and, if this is the case, then America as metonymy functions less as excess that disrupts boundary lines than as the possibility of their very existence. Moreover, with its metonymic capacity of connecting things America offers a way of healing the breach which Leavis sees as constituting the crisis of culture. Thus America appears less as an example of cultural degeneration than as a means of renewal.

Since America partakes of both metaphor and metonymy in the text, it parallels Leavis's characterisation of culture, that is the use of language as a 'metaphor that is a metonymy also' (*MC & MC*, p. 15). Language is used to discriminate and to make explicit what is implicit. It is possible to question whether these uses are, in fact, compatible. In broad terms, discrimination is sensitivity to difference whereas making explicit what is implicit is a form of repetition. However, as has been argued, repetition, for example in the case of the 'obvious', can have the effect of introducing difference. Certainly it is the case that America cannot be seen just as an example of the crisis of English culture, though that is how it is deployed in the text.

A key point here is that America is seen as what will happen to England. It makes manifest what is only latent in English culture. Thus America is read as a sign not of itself, but of England. The fact that America is a sign of England draws attention to how, in Leavis's argument, it functions more as a linguistic unit than as a real place and its primarily linguistic status is further underlined by the manner in which it parallels the movement of metaphor and metonymy. These complicate a straightforward understanding of America, which makes the reader suspicious of the ease with which Leavis 'reads' it. The point about America is that it problematises reading at the very moment it is used to 'read' England.

From the way Leavis uses America it would seem that he conceives of reading as identifying a tendency and then finding examples of it. In its capacity as an illustration, an example is usually thought of as

something secondary but, in 'Mass Civilisation and Minority Culture',
it appears to be primary for, without America, the crisis of English
culture, though 'obvious', cannot be understood. But this notion of
having to repeat the 'obvious' before its 'obviousness' is apparent is
suspect since Leavis does not deem it necessary to question the
'obviousness' of *Middletown*. He regards its conclusions as if they were
transparent and self-evident, and applies them without modification
to English culture. Yet his whole point is that the 'obvious' cannot be
taken for granted, that it needs to be seen from elsewhere before it
leaps into focus. That claim, however, collapses as Leavis accepts the
'obviousness' of America without question. This is all the more
problematic in that America appears in the text as a prediction of
England's future and so the two are not even temporally coincident.

Leavis uses America to read English culture, specifically to make
explicit what is only implicit. But what is presented explicitly is never
quite the same as what existed implicitly. The process of reading, in
other words, opens a gap which is the very opposite to what Leavis
intends. Reading should heal 'breach[es] in continuity' (*MC & MC*,
p. 17), not institute them. Thus America, in being used to read England,
cannot be equated with it. Indeed, in trying to equate England with
America Leavis's analysis betrays symptoms of the very standardisation – the suppression of difference – that he sets out to criticise.
Or, to put it in the idiom of the economic metaphor, Leavis's conflation
of England and America parallels the work of the exchange relation
which ignores the unique identity of goods, reducing them to
measurement in terms of money. The goods themselves do not matter,
only their price.

But the principle of equivalence which characterises the relation
between England and America in 'Mass Civilisation and Minority
Culture' is disrupted by a conception of reading that is not stated by
Leavis so much as enacted by his text. Leavis's view is that reading
is a recognition of what should, in any case, be 'obvious'. It is being
'as aware as possible' (*MC & MC*, p. 46) of what is already and self
evidently there. In short, reading is fidelity to whatever is being read
– almost, the implication is, to the point of repeating it. The rhetorical
operations of the text, however, show that repetition creates an
element of difference and so reading cannot be conceived in terms of
fidelity to its object. Moreover, not only is reading not coincident with
its object but the object is not even coincident with itself, since what
Leavis says about reading is not borne out by his text which shows
that textual considerations curtail any notion of a transparent reading.

Leavis himself draws attention to the rhetorical procedures of 'Mass Civilisation and Minority Culture' by his comments on, for example, metaphor but, at the same time, he tries to repress them.

Ironically, it is what he tries to repress, textuality, that seems to offer the best prospects for culture. This is because, as 'Mass Civilisation and Minority Culture' shows, textuality is inseparable from ideas of otherness and difference, suggesting that 'mass production' and 'standardisation' cannot eradicate these qualities or make unique works equivalent. Whenever the discourses of civilisation try to assimilate the discourses of culture a sense of difference will always assert itself as the expression of 'something more', of a residue which cannot be absorbed by the processes of mass production or the discourses of bureaucracy and administration. To analyse 'Mass Civilisation and Minority Culture' in this way is not to ignore Leavis's opinion that readers should be 'as aware as possible' (p. 46), rather it is to try and be *more* aware of Leavis's text than he himself was so as to counter more effectively the processes of sameness and standardisation.

## THE OBVIOUS, DESIRE AND FOOTNOTES

Leavis, then, uses America to make 'obvious' what should already be 'obvious'. His concern regarding the 'obvious' is evident in the many comments he makes about it: 'It is enough' (*MC & MC*, p. 19), '[a]ll this, again, is a commonplace, again, on which it seems necessary to insist' (p. 20), '[a]ll this seems so obvious' (p. 21) and 'the standardising influence of broadcasting hardly admits of doubt' (p. 21). The tone is by turns confident and diffident. There seems to be no way of demonstrating what is 'obvious' and the only remaining resource is to insist on it. Such insistence, however, is not sufficient to convey the meaning of the 'obvious'. Paradoxically, the more Leavis insists on the 'obvious', the further it recedes. Its very ubiquity renders it invisible. Consequently, the 'obvious' cannot be 'read'. Instead, it is reproduced.

This is evident in Leavis's next move which is 'to bring ... home, [with] a little concrete evidence' his repeated claim that 'the currency has been debased and inflated' (*MC & MC*, p. 24). Leavis moves from insisting on the obvious to providing evidence for it. But the evidence turns out to be no evidence at all, it is merely an attack on the literary judgements of Arnold Bennett which, Leavis claims, can only be made in a period where 'there [are] no standards, no living tradition of poetry spread abroad, and no discriminating public' (p. 30). The absence of the latter perhaps can be seen as contributing to the problem of 'the obvious' since the text solicits the recognition of this group in order that readings of the minority can be validated. But the text admits that this public is nowhere to be found yet it appeals to it constantly and so it is caught up in a process of soliciting recognition while being aware that none is forthcoming. It thus constitutes itself as desire.

The term desire evokes notions of the unconscious and so it is appropriate to remember that the Freudian understanding of consciousness structures, in part, Leavis's approach to the crisis of culture, for example, his view of the relations between the adult minority and the childish or infantile majority. Furthermore, it will be remembered that the recognition of the literary lineage lends itself, again only in part, to an Oedipal reading. Desire in the text is for the sort of influence on the course of literature that is wielded by Bennett. His favourable opinion of a book increases its sales dramatically (*MC & MC*, p. 26). But to desire this is to desire the commodification of literature. It is to desire the translation of literary value into cash terms. Of course Leavis does not desire this in any conscious sense but it is already implicit in his economic metaphor, which conceives of literary value in terms of the gold standard. Furthermore, there can be little doubt that Leavis *would* like to exercise the sort of power and authority commanded by Bennett, since it is these very qualities which Leavis believes are being wrenched from the minority (p. 39). What Leavis desires and, to a certain extent may later be said to have achieved, is the position of 'the most powerful maker of literary reputations in England' (p. 26). Again, none of this is stated directly but the implications are clear and, moreover, they are consistent with the way the rhetoric and logic of 'Mass Civilisation and Minority Culture' produce meanings that are different from those which Leavis intends.

This is not to suggest that there is a strict division between conscious and unconscious meanings in the text, for there is a certain defensiveness in Leavis's introduction to his discussion about Bennett – he hopes 'to avert the charge of extravagant pessimism' (*MC & MC*, p. 24) – which indicates he is half aware that latent meanings may lurk behind his manifest ones. This would certainly be a plausible explanation for his efforts to suppress metaphor. The question of where exactly the border can be drawn between conscious and unconscious crops up again in the relation between the footnotes and the main body of the text.

Leavis advocates being 'as aware as possible', yet earlier he quotes, in a footnote, a passage from *Middletown* which suggests that it is better to let certain ideas stay just below the level of consciousness for then their effect is greater:

> One gains a distinct impression that the religious basis of all education was more taken for granted if less talked about thirty five years ago, when high school 'chapel' was a religious inspirational service with a 'choir' instead of the 'pep session' which it tends to become to-day.[78]

Since Leavis quotes this passage uncritically it is reasonable to assume he agrees with the idea it expresses. Yet this goes against his project of combating that 'vast and increasing inattention' (*MC & MC*, p. 16) which is part of what he considers to be the malaise of culture. The footnote, directly below the main body of the text, appears in the guise of its unconsciousness, and this is particularly apt since it promotes the virtue of not examining things but taking them for granted. And, in this respect, the footnote is allied with those implicit standards by which Leavis sets so much store.

The notion of the footnote is therefore implicated in the play between implicit standards and 'something more' and also, in the example of this particular footnote, the relation between implicit standards and consciousness. By its very nature the footnote appears as 'something more', an addition or supplement to the main body of the text.[79] Here, however, the footnote is less a complement to the main argument than a contradiction of it. This is, therefore, not the kind of 'something more' that the text desires. Yet, because the footnote contradicts the central claim about consciousness it is for that very reason consistent with those rhetorical operations of 'Mass Civilisation and Minority Culture' which offer opposing readings of the problem of culture to those which Leavis gives. From this perspective, the footnote is part of, not separate from the main body of the text. Nevertheless, its position on the page argues that, while it may stand out from the argument, it still contributes something to it.

And yet there is a problem here. Leavis's argument requires 'something more' on two counts. The first is to supplement definitions which can no longer be taken for granted and the second, more vague, is an insistence that, because of an intrinsic 'something more', language cannot be reduced to a 'method of symbolising human thought'. The footnote seems to answer the first sense of 'something more', but in this capacity it does not seem to add anything and therefore appears as redundant. This is best illustrated by Leavis's use of Matthew Arnold, not least because Arnold is Leavis's starting point in 'Mass Civilisation and Minority Culture'. Leavis argues for the necessity of a minority who can 'sense that this is worth more than that, this rather than that is the direction in which to go, that the centre is here rather than there' (*MC & MC*, p. 15). He then supports this view with a quotation, to the same effect, from Arnold in a footnote. Thus Leavis, who begins his argument by noting that, although he can refer his readers to *Culture and Anarchy*, he 'know[s] that something more is required' (p. 13). Yet, in place of that 'something more', is a quotation from *Culture and Anarchy*. The footnote returns the reader to Arnold instead of supplementing him. In this particular instance, the footnote, whose very nature is supplementary, does not advance the text by supplying it with 'something more' but returns it to the very absence with which the text commences and which it aims to fill.

The complex exchange between footnotes and the main body of the text vividly dramatises that blurring of boundaries which Leavis identifies as the modern condition. The various permutations of the relation between the footnotes and the main body of the text show that there is no clear demarcation between consciousness and unconsciousness or between the centre and the periphery of a work. There are no dividing lines, only constantly shifting relations and this helps to explain Leavis's problem with the 'obvious', for the 'obvious' can only be 'obvious' where there is a measure of stability and where there are definite boundaries which mark it off from other things which are not obvious. 'Mass Civilisation and Minority Culture' is itself an instance of that confusion of borders which it deplores. This is not, however, to denigrate it. On the contrary this observation can be used to support its claims.

Further, viewing culture in terms of borders and boundaries is not merely some idiosyncrasy on Leavis's part, for Adorno also discussed culture in these very same terms.[80] Once again there is a direct connection between the two thinkers, right down to the use of the same words and the same imagery. This similarity to a major European thinker at least makes Leavis a less provincial figure than he has sometimes been portrayed and, moreover, if two thinkers can, independently of each other, coincide so closely in their analysis, then their opinions are worth serious consideration.

The dissolution of boundaries which precipitates the mingling of different phenomena raises the question of how they might be connected or related. This is a task which falls to reading since reading, in the discriminatory sense proposed by Leavis, assumes its importance against the background of the 'breach in continuity' (*MC & MC*, p. 17). Reading is an attempt to heal that breach, to reconnect what has been broken. Only the minority can achieve this, their reading must repair and maintain the continuity of tradition shattered by modernity, it must bridge gaps and heal divisions. Reading, in short, is a process of unification. As such, however, it is in danger of smearing out the differences between what is read so that it is as difficult to make valid distinctions and to know what one 'is talking about' in this area as it is in civilisation where there has been a blurring of boundaries and dividing lines. Reading, in other words, is in danger of reproducing what it is meant to resolve.

It is in any case questionable whether reading should aim at closing gaps and eliminating divisions since without them Leavis would have nothing to support his notions of hierarchy and tradition. Leavis may deplore modernity as a break with the past but he too needs to be able to think in terms of breaks if he is to be able to articulate differences of worth. Reading may therefore be more about instituting divisions than about unifying them.[81] Without these divisions, which spatially organise the field of literature, Leavis would not be able to assert that 'the centre is here rather than there' (*MC & MC*, p. 15).

A further twist to this argument can actually make Leavis's position less incompatible with civilisation than he would willingly acknowledge. For example, his repeated assertion that modern civilisation has brought about a breach in continuity suggests that civilisation, far from having dissolved boundaries, has in fact erected them by distancing itself from the past. Civilisation thus lays the foundation for the sort of discrimination that is the goal of reading. And, if civilisation is characterised by definite borders between one phase and another, then it cannot have blurred away divisions and dividing lines. On the contrary, this situation seems to be the result of reading which suppresses difference in the interest of continuity. However, the logic of Leavis's argument also requires that reading should be a process of apprehending difference so that value judgements can be made.

The overlap between the attributes and processes of civilisation and reading show, once more, that 'Mass Civilisation and Minority Culture' cannot sustain the oppositions on which it is based. This presents a problem for how is it possible to discriminate without some notion of opposition? Does not the collapse of oppositions usher in that unbounded flux which Leavis identifies with civilisation? But these questions can only be asked from within a paradigm that structures perception in terms of opposition when what is required is the ability to think beyond it. The challenge of 'Mass Civilisation and Minority Culture' is to make the reader think the necessity of discrimination without recourse to opposition. This involves a respect for what Leavis is trying to say and an awareness of what the logic of his text allows him to say. Without the former, according to Derrida, 'critical production would risk developing in any direction at all and authorise itself to say almost anything'[82] but without the latter commentary would only double the text. '[R]eading', observes Derrida, 'must always aim at a certain relationship unperceived by the writer, between what [s]he commands and what [s]he does not command of the patterns of language that [s]he uses'.[83]

In 'Mass Civilisation and Minority Culture', this relationship is the tension between Leavis's statement of opposition between culture and civilisation and the system of logic which undermines that opposition. By insisting on the opposition of culture and civilisation 'as static blocks which discreetly oppose one another',[84] Leavis shows that he is 'under the spell of ... reification'.[85] But, as Adorno observes, '[n]o matter how reified both categories are in reality, neither is totally reified'[86] and this is apparent in the text's deconstruction of the opposition which allows the reader to conceive of a more mutual and less hostile relationship between civilisation and culture. This does not mean that the two terms are equated, rather the result of such an endeavour would be to maintain a notion of difference in a society where 'repetitions ... self sameness, and the ubiquity of modern mass culture tend to make for automatized reactions and to weaken the focus of individual resistance'.[87] The problem is not to let a commitment to difference decay into an indiscriminate toleration of whatever proclaims itself as such. To read 'Mass Civilisation and Minority Culture' in the Derridean sense is to face up to that responsibility.

## READING CULTURE TWICE

As noted above, the logic of 'Mass Civilisation and Minority Culture' gives two meanings to reading and it is therefore appropriate that this is a text which reads culture twice. This is somewhat ironic since Leavis had earlier refused to elaborate even something so small as his currency metaphor, regarding its meaning as perfectly plain. In this context it is worth recalling a remark Leavis made many years later. '[T]he offered parallel of a language and a monetary currency is', he wrote, 'profoundly revealing; it exposes the desperate plight of our civilization'.[88] Such an observation underscores how little Leavis understood the significance of his key metaphor in his analysis of civilisation.

It seems as if a refusal or, in the light of the above, an inability to read a part of the text is compensated for by the whole text being a reading of culture, twice. The first time Leavis makes his point by insisting on the 'obvious', which is a form of repetition, and the second time he resorts to a form of empiricism, 'concrete evidence' (*MC & MC*, p. 24) which turns out to be no more than a criticism of the criteria which Arnold Bennett uses for evaluating literature.

What does this second reading of culture reveal? In some ways little more than the first. Both are introduced by the same economic metaphor (*MC & MC*, pp. 14, 24) and both deplore the absence of 'standards' and a 'discriminating public' (pp. 13–15, 21, 30). Thus the second reading can be seen as 'repeating' the first and, by doing so, perhaps even inflating it, therefore contributing to that debased and inflated state of the currency of which Leavis complains. Nevertheless, the second reading does represent a development of the first.

It begins with Leavis deploring the absence of 'standards', a 'living tradition of poetry' and a 'discriminating public' (*MC & MC*, p. 30). The 'new' element here is the 'living tradition of poetry'. But it is the lack of all three which constitutes 'the plight of culture'. This plight is footnoted, and at the bottom of the page is a quote from I.A. Richards declaring that there is 'no ... gulf between poetry and life ... There is no gap between our everyday emotional life and the material of poetry.'[89] This remark seems to contradict Leavis's statement that there is no 'living tradition of poetry', a remark which has already been rendered dubious by his earlier claim that the minority keeps this tradition alive (p. 13). Footnote and main text clash and there seems no way of resolving their conflict. Further, by footnoting the sentence '[i]t is the plight of culture generally that is exemplified here', Leavis seems to suggest that *the* plight of culture has to do *only* with the relation between poetry and life and not with the other points mentioned in the previous sentence. Yet the plight of culture exemplified in the footnote turns out to be the very thing which Leavis desires for culture, a continuity between life and poetry.

Having just stated what the plight of culture is, Leavis then goes on to lament the 'bewildering variety' of signals which blur distinctions and dividing lines. Then, in almost exactly the same words he has just used he declares that '[h]ere we have the plight of culture generally' (*MC & MC*, p. 31). Very nearly the same words are used in regard to a different point and this ironically parallels that trait of civilisation whereby 'the same words are used with different meanings'. *The* plight of culture is therefore at least two different things. Indeed, it is possible to argue that the plight of culture is plurality.

As plurality, culture comes to stand for that 'more' which the text desires but at the same time refuses whenever it is actually manifested. To be acceptable, 'more' must remain latent. Leavis wants to reduce this plurality so reading becomes, as it were, a cutting exercise. But at the same time as it cuts, reading also produces. Culture is read twice in 'Mass Civilisation and Minority Culture'. The second reading repeats the first but, in doing so, adds to it and thus introduces difference where the same is, apparently, being asserted.

Reading is therefore highly problematic. Reading is, as has been mentioned, diagnostic and curative, but both these modes seem equally chimerical for they depend on a transcendent position which the text simply does not sustain. Reading is always doubled just as the 'obvious' is. The fact that reading is always doubled, either by Leavis or the reader means that it can never capture its object. Leavis wants to articulate the significance of the 'obvious' but he can only repeat it and repetition, it will be remembered, breaks with what is repeated, which means that with each repetition, the 'obvious' becomes something different. The double treatment of reading is intended as clarification but, after reading culture twice, Leavis concludes that it is '[s]o difficult ... to understand what it is that is being discussed' (*MC & MC*, p. 44). Reading thus seems to draw a veil over what is read rather than remove one and perhaps this links with that element of defensiveness noted earlier. But in hiding something the text at least finds a way of establishing that 'more' which it so desires.

'Mass Civilisation and Minority Culture' begins by declaring the necessity of adding to or supplementing Arnold and yet where Arnold is quoted in footnotes (*MC & MC*, pp. 13, 15, 35, 45) it is to illustrate or clinch Leavis's argument. Arnold, in other words, functions as an authority, not as a thinker whose definitions require 'something more'. Thus Leavis endorses Arnold in the same way that he requires the critical public to endorse the readings of his minority. In this way, the text seems to come full circle – except that in repeating Arnold, Leavis breaks with him as, according to the text's logic, all second readings are fated to do.

Since 'Mass Civilisation and Minority Culture' problematises reading, it warns the reader not to take Leavis himself at face value. To concentrate on how 'Mass Civilisation and Minority Culture' works, as much as on what it says, makes it a richer and potentially more productive piece of writing than has hitherto been recognised. 'Mass Civilisation and Minority Culture' is a reminder of how difficult it is to think about culture since it shows how key concepts deployed for the study of culture seem to disintegrate under the work they are required to do. This argues for an openness to the problems of culture which in turn means, among other things, a willingness to consider the question of value, which theory has only recently begun to acknowledge.[90] Leavis's writing, though flawed and inconsistent, at least considers this issue.

The next section will consider the question of reading and the relations between culture and civilisation as Leavis develops them in *Culture and Environment*, the book he co-authored with Denys Thompson. An attempt will be made to integrate the primarily textual approach of this chapter with a historical and sociological one in the next. In this way it is hoped to contextualise the issues with which Leavis deals.

# 2

# Culture and Environment

## INTRODUCTION

*Culture and Environment* develops the analysis of society begun in 'Mass Civilisation and Minority Culture'. It also proposes a solution to the problems it diagnoses and that solution is a particular type of reading. A consideration of Leavis's exploration of the relation between 'culture and environment' and his conception of reading will form the main part of this chapter. First, however, it is necessary to question the standard approach to *Culture and Environment* by situating its concerns within the general anxieties of the 1920s and 1930s.

It was Raymond Williams who was responsible for the notion that *Culture and Environment* presented a mythic view of history.[2] His section on the organic community in *Culture and Society* remains, in the words of Michael Bell, 'the classic critique'.[3] But it is important to remember that Williams was not wholly critical of Leavis's approach. On the contrary, he agreed with him that the mass media deliberately exploited 'the cheapest emotional responses' (*CE*, p. 3).[4] Williams also had high praise for *Culture and Environment* as 'an educational manual'.[5] But in order to understand what is at issue in *Culture and Environment* it is necessary to do more than draw attention to the range of Williams' comments upon it. What needs to be stressed is that *Culture and Environment* was one of many texts concerned with the problems of the relation between work and leisure.

## LEISURE AND CONSUMERISM

It was generally agreed, from the 1920s onwards, that mechanisation limited the number of hours that people needed to work. This created more leisure or free time which meant that the conventional definition of it as a period of recuperation from or compensation for labour time had to be re-thought.[6] One idea was that leisure was an opportunity for fulfilment that was denied by the monotony of work. Another was that it was this very monotony that prevented people from making the most of their newly found leisure. Hence L.P. Jacks insisted in 1927 that free time could never be free if it was not coupled with interesting work, an observation which Constance Harris set out to prove in her study of the working class in Bethnal Green.[7] That Leavis shared this view is evident from his remark that the nature of modern work disables people from 'making the *positive* effort without which there can be no true recreation' (*CE*, p. 100).

The anxiety over increased leisure was partly due to the traditional identification of it with 'improvident spending and an erosion of the work ethic'.[8] Regarding the former, Thorstein Veblen argued that leisure time devoted to wasteful displays of social status undermined the discipline needed for efficient production.[9] Rexford Tugwell agreed, noting that 'for the old morality of service, of workmanship and of pride in skill, there is substituted the morality of display'.[10]

Tugwell's remark suggested that work and leisure had become separate spheres. Leavis also notes that, whereas they were integrated in the past, they now exist in opposition: work is 'meaningless' so people 'live only for their leisure' (*CE*, p. 68). This view is challenged by Adorno, who argues that there can be no rigid distinction between work and leisure since there are leisure industries such as camping and tourism which are 'organised for the sake of profit'.[11] Similarly sport, one of the biggest leisure industries, cannot just be seen as an end in itself since the discipline and fitness it imposes are also useful for the work place.[12]

Despite the mutual reinforcement of work and leisure it is true that they are nevertheless perceived as separate spheres and Adorno explains this is terms of the division of labour characteristic of bourgeois society. His claim is that, just as work must have nothing to do with leisure, so leisure must in no way reflect work and this, Adorno adds, accounts for 'the inanity of many leisure activities'. The absoluteness of the division between work and leisure also serves to disguise the kinship between them. Hence leisure can always hold out the promise of fulfilment that work denies and this forestalls any radical criticism of the capitalist system as a whole. Adorno concludes his analysis of leisure by claiming that it is not just the monotony of work that renders people incapable of enjoying their leisure but 'the social totality' itself. It atrophies and deforms their imagination:

[T]he reason why people can actually do so little with their free time is that the truncation of their imagination deprives them of the faculty which made the state of freedom pleasurable in the first place.[13]

In his excellent book, *Time and Money: The Making of Consumer Culture*, Gary Cross argues that there was a struggle over how to define the newly increased free time. Business wanted to define it in terms of consumerism, whereas a whole array of others, intellectuals and local and national organisations, 'sought to define it in terms of '[a] politics of democratic leisure'.[14] The latter referred to personal or communal activities that led to self fulfilment or social realisation. Henry Overstreet believed that the dullness of work could be relieved by 'adventuring with thought'[15] while E.B. Castles argued that hobbies were the best antidote to the 'deadening compulsion'[16] of work. The emphasis on community was evident in the BBC's encouragement of the formation of 'wireless groups' to discuss educational radio programmes and also in local education authorities promoting classes in, among other things, folk dancing.[17]

These and other initiatives were not, however, strong enough to counter the influence of consumerism. It provided goods to a working class which before had been out of their reach. Moreover, an increasingly sophisticated system of advertising stimulated a longing for more goods, making this, rather than the fear of poverty, a motivation for work. In addition, consumerism seemed to offer a freedom of choice which the politics of democratic leisure, couched in a discourse of moral coercion – what people ought to do – seemed to deny. As Cross notes:

The quest was not for the intellectual's dream of social interaction in highminded discussion groups or didactic holiday tours; rather people strove for a society of consumer symbols where individuality was projected onto goods.[18]

But though consumerism seemed to promise freedom from poverty and to promote individual choice it was also the case that freedom and choice were severely constrained. There was, for example, the deliberate manipulation of advertising which 'attempted to turn the consumer's critical functions away from the product and toward him [her] self'.[19] Then there was the fact that the concept of freedom was debased by being identified with consumer choice. Finally, the allure

of consumerism won people over to a system that thwarted them in
other ways, such as health, housing, education and work. As Orwell
noted, 'Whole sections of the working class who have been plundered
of all they really need are being compensated, in part, by cheap
luxuries which mitigate the surface of life.'[20]

If consumerism was not as liberating as it appeared, neither was
democratic leisure solely a patronising attempt by intellectuals to direct
the people's free time while disregarding what they really enjoyed.
While it may be true, as Cross observes, that both left and right saw
commercial leisure as a threat to genuine working-class culture and
therefore sought to '"uplift" the masses'[21] it was also the case that

> the democratic leisure movement in the 1930s partly transcends the
> conservative social agenda of its late nineteenth century founders:
> the overriding concern with disorder partially gave way to a broader
> service and participatory ethic.[22]

As such, the movement both challenged commercialised leisure and
provided models for social interaction outside the state and the
workplace.[23]

This, then, is the context in which *Culture and Environment* should
be understood. It too is concerned with the relation between work and
leisure. Leavis notes their separation and how the tediousness of
work prevents people from using their new found leisure creatively.
He also demonstrates repeatedly, though unawares, Adorno's point
that the distinction between work and leisure or between culture
and environment, is by no means clear cut. In this respect, language
betrays Leavis into truth. Furthermore, in common with other thinkers,
he tends to see freedom from work in terms of a release of libido that
threatens high culture[24] since he associates leisure with 'satisfaction
at the lowest level and ... immediate pleasures' (*CE*, p. 3). Having
established that *Culture and Environment* reflects in a general way the
anxiety about leisure, the next step is to consider, in more detail,
Leavis's analysis of this problem, and the solution he proposes for it.


## WORK AND LEISURE

The organic community provides the standard by which Leavis
judges the character of work in modern society. In the organic
community, work involves the whole person: 'their heads, their

brains, imagination, conscience, sense of beauty and fitness – their personalities were engaged and satisfied' (*CE*, p. 75). Satisfaction provides the motive for work, not money. This is in contrast to the modern world where people are 'merely concerned for their wages' (p. 75). Thus, the inhabitants of the organic community lived 'for the most part' in their work while the labourer, factory worker or clerk 'live only for their leisure' (p. 68). Further, there was not that divorce between work and leisure in the organic community which Leavis finds in modern life. The 'art of speech' (p. 71), for example, was part of the 'rich traditions of recreation and the use of leisure' (p. 68) but it was not practised only in leisure time since people 'talked at work and at rest' (p. 72).

What the organic community offers, in short, is an image of wholeness as opposed to the fragmentation of modern life. This is a somewhat idyllic view but it cannot be dismissed altogether. George Ewart Evans, for example, notes that the term organic community involves 'no value judgement' but simply describes 'a community where co-operation and inter-relatedness was a stark economic necessity'.[25] E.P. Thompson in his introduction to *The Wheelwright's Shop* notes that Sturt's 'testimony', upon which Leavis drew for his views of the organic community, though not by any means complete, deserves to be 'weigh[ed] in the scales of judgement'.[26]

In any case, there is more at stake in Leavis's view of the organic community than a lament for the stultifying impact of modern work. This will be examined in detail when Leavis's reading of Sturt is discussed. For now it is sufficient to note that part of the appeal of the organic community for Leavis lies in the discipline it imposes on its inhabitants. The demands work makes on the body ensure that the body is not able to enjoy sensuous pleasure unless it is related to production. What Leavis most fears about the new leisure industries is that they offer 'pleasures' without 'effort' (*CE*, p. 3). Since 'effort' is equated with 'consciousness' (p. 5) and 'pleasures' with the body (p. 3) it can be seen that Leavis views the separation between work and leisure as a division between mind and body.

The key point, however, is that by placing a high value on work, Leavis's conception of the organic community cannot be read as wholly oppositional to mass civilisation. The centrality of work in the organic community can be read in a number of ways. First, work in the organic community is more satisfying than work in a factory. Second, this work is seen as productive and so it connects with concern about falling production rates in steel, shipbuilding and coal.[27] Third, as a dream of production the organic community could be read as a critique of mass unemployment in the early 1930s. In this connection it is worth noting that unemployment began to fall in 1933,[28] the year *Culture and Environment* was published.

Another way of reading the relation between work in the organic community and unemployment in Britain is in terms of a concern with social order. Leavis's fears about the disruptive effects of leisure reflect fears about social unrest brought on by the enforced 'leisure' of unemployment. Work disciplines both the private and the social body, ensuring their pleasures are neither subversive nor *in* subversion.

The structure of the organic community finds a parallel in the corporatist development of the British economy after the General Strike of 1926.[29] The word corporate comes from the Latin *corporare*, meaning to form into a body and, as Evans has observed, the phrase 'organic community' is itself 'a figure of speech on the analogy of a body comprising members working separately yet in co-operation with the whole'.[30] This also describes the working of the corporate economy where different groups subordinate their own interests to 'a wider system of order'.[31] Society was being redefined in terms of the body just as the individual body was being redefined in terms of consumption instead of production. The main point, however, is that the organic community becomes a concentrated image of corporate society.

According to Harold Perkin, the 'corporation [is] the institutional framework of professional society', whose driving force is 'the professional social ideal', that is the service professions perform for society.[32] *Culture and Environment* may be regarded in this light since it defends the study of literature in terms of the contribution it makes to cultural 'health[]' (*CE*, p. 5) and provides a programme of training to ensure this. Brian Doyle has written an excellent history of the 'professionalisation' of literature[33] and Francis Mulhern has traced *Scrutiny*'s involvement in this development. His argument is that *Scrutiny* generated a new discourse for literary criticism suited to the maintenance of a talent-governed career structure which eventually came to dominate the profession as a whole.[34]

*Culture and Environment* then, may lament the modern nature of work by a comparison with the organic community but that comparison reveals other meanings in the term 'work' which diminishes the effectiveness of the organic community as a critique of modern civilisation. The organic community is further problematised when its structural similarities with corporatism become apparent. Both ignore the divisions of class which were all too clear in the early 1930s and both promote an image of society based on the body, where all the constituent parts co-operate for a common purpose. Finally, for all its aloofness from modern civilisation, *Culture and Environment* is an example of the ethic of professionalism which provides corporatism with its *raison d'être*.

The richness of leisure in the organic community stems from its relation with work. 'Talk' was an important ingredient of this leisure, in contrast to modern day activities such as 'reading newspapers, or going to the cinema or turning on the loudspeaker or the gramophone' (*CE*, p. 72). These are all passive activities, 'form[s] of daydreaming or "fantasying"' (p. 100). By contrast talk, rooted in work and tradition, is active.

> In farmyard, in taproom, at market, the details [of 'folk knowledge'] were discussed over and over again, [the men] gathered together for remembrance in village workshop; carters, smiths, farmers, wheelmakers in thousands landed on each his own little bit of understanding, passing it to his own son or the wheelwright of the day, linking up the centuries.[35]

Talk is an act of 'remembrance'. It is the medium through which skills are passed on to the next generation, 'linking up the centuries'.

According to Leavis 'the art of social intercourse hardly exist[s]' (*CE*, p. 65) in the modern world. The advent of the machine caused the disappearance of craft-based communities and the resulting loss of tradition has created 'a gap in the continuity of consciousness'.[36] No longer bound up with tradition, '[t]he decisive use of words today' is 'in association with advertising, journalism, best sellers, motor cars and the cinema' (p. 82). Talk that endlessly renewed the folk wisdom (p. 80) of the organic community has been superseded by a variety of commercial discourses. In Leavis's words, there has been 'a debasement of emotional life, and of the quality of living' (p. 48).

Adorno too speaks of the 'debasement' of language.[37] He argues that the demands of, for example, advertising and administration, mean that words are emptied of their history and connotations with the result that the word ... becomes so fixed to the thing that it is just a petrified formula. This affects language and object alike. Instead of making the object experiential, the purified word treats it as an abstract instance, and everything else (now excluded by the demand for ruthless clarity in expression ...) fades away in reality.[38]

Having their history suppressed means that words function only in the present, a view which chimes with Debord's claim that 'bureaucratic society lives in a perpetual present'.[39]

To live in this present is not the same as to experience it. Debord argues that '[a]ll that was once directly lived has become mere representation'.[40] He describes this state of affairs as the society of the spectacle. This is a difficult concept but basically it refers to the dominance of the commodity[41] which, in the form of images of advertised goods, mediates the social relationship between people.[42] The commodity offers an image of 'the spectator's' needs and desires with which he or she then identifies.[43] Thus to buy goods is to buy the self. In this way, Debord argues, there has been a degeneration from *'being* into *having'*.[44]

Although Leavis emphasises the difference between modern leisure and leisure in the organic community this difference is not absolute since both produce conformity. Newspapers 'give[] the public what it wants' (*CE*, p. 36), making sure, Leavis implies, that they first tell the public what it wants. Having established what 'the public' wants it then becomes very difficult 'for an unfamiliar opinion to gain headway against accepted opinion'.[45] And this public is, of course, a creation of the newspapers, whose ploy of giving 'the public' what it wants is simply a technique for homogenising conflicting and shifting groups into a single body that speaks with one voice. Popular fiction too promotes conformity by affecting a literary style which gives a cultural gloss to these character traits such as 'vision' and 'purposeful[ness]'[46] which best typify the personality of the capitalist entrepreneur. This fusion of culture and commerce smothers the former's critical impulse towards the status quo. As such, culture is recruited to the service of conformity. In the words of Adorno, 'Culture ... proclaims: you shall conform'.[47]

The leisure of the organic community also produces conformity. This leisure, it will be remembered, is defined in terms of talk, which is continuous with but not wholly identifiable with work. Talk centres on the body of folk knowledge whose 'details were discussed over and over again'.[48] The repetition suggests that this knowledge is renewed but never added to or challenged. Moreover, that which is renewed is, in material terms, the hierarchal structure of the organic community itself. This hierarchy is expressed in terms of the relation between employer and employee, which shows that Leavis's valuation of the organic community is bound up with an essentially conservative view of labour relations. Work, like leisure, is associated with renewing the body of folk knowledge. In 'watching Cook put a wheel together,' Sturt writes that he 'was watching practically the skill of England, the experience of ages'.[49] Cook's assembling of the wheel, putting each part in its place, is analogous to the way talk, in work and leisure, helps to reproduce society as socially differentiated.

Leavis contrasts the leisure of the organic community with modern leisure to the detriment of the latter. Leisure may have been scanty in the organic community but it was more satisfying and fulfilling than its modern counterpart. But this claim is open to question on the grounds that leisure, defined as talk, is to do with 'remembrance'. This suggests a nostalgia on the part of the members of the organic community which itself points to a lack at the heart of it. If this is the case then the leisure of the organic community threatens to be as hollow as modern leisure. Its nostalgic quality means that it turns away from reality, which is precisely Leavis's criticism of modern leisure as a species of 'daydreaming' (*CE*, p. 100). The leisure of the organic community thus appears to be as escapist as, Leavis claims, the cinema or popular fiction. Moreover, the connection between work and leisure in the organic community means that the satisfaction of work is also thrown into doubt. The repetitive nature of talk makes the wheelwright's shop seem as drearily monotonous as the routine of any factory.

It should be clear that although Leavis uses the organic community to critique work and leisure in the modern world this is not a wholly successful strategy for, in some ways, the organic community is continuous with and even underpins the ideology of that world. Having described what he considers to be the escapist quality of modern leisure Leavis then proposes a way of resisting its effects.

## LITERATURE, LITERARY CRITICISM AND THE WHEELWRIGHT'S CRAFT

The barren nature of work and leisure are, Leavis claims, the result of the dominance of the machine. It is the machine, he goes on to say, that is responsible for the loss of the organic community (*CE*, pp. 3, 87–8). This has created 'a gap in the continuity of consciousness'.[50] In Leavis's words, 'there has been virtually a loss of memory, the memory that preserves the "picked experience of ages"' (p. 97). The loss of tradition is mirrored in the dehumanised nature of work and leisure, and also in the debased quality of language in journalism and popular fiction. '[T]his debasement', writes Leavis, 'is not merely a matter of words; it is a debasement of emotional life, and of the quality of living' (p. 48). Leavis does not propose to remedy this situation by a return to the organic community. '[W]e must beware', he warns, 'of simple solutions. We must, for instance, realize that there can be no mere going back' (p. 96). What he proposes instead is to promote literature as a means of resisting the debasement of the language and as a focus of 'our spiritual tradition ... the "picked experience of ages"' (p. 82).

Literature is a substitute for talk. Talk was concerned with remembrance and, as noted above, that task has now fallen to literature. What was remembered was tradition and tradition was defined in terms of work and so, by implication, are literature and literary criticism. Leavis makes this explicit when he adds to a remark from Sturt – 'in watching Cook putting a wheel together I was watching practically the skill of England, the experience of ages'[51] – the following: 'just so a good critic or cultivated person of sure judgement is exhibiting more than merely individual taste' (*CE*, p. 82).

The parallel between literary criticism and the wheelwright's craft highlights the notion of work common to both. In literary criticism, Leavis rediscovers the meaning of sensuous labour that has been lost in modern work. Cook's knowledge of his craft is 'not by theory but [by] his eyes and fingers'.[52] It is in this sensuous apprehension of work that a basis may be found for Leavis's anti-theoretical stance. The standards of criticism 'are assumed' he writes 'nothing more ... need[s] to be said'.[53] But the nature of work in *The Wheelwright's Shop* is not wholly sensuous. Sturt's descriptions of his men are based on his non-involvement with their work. He watches them: 'I ... watched the work'.[54] This watching is of a 'supervis[ory]'[55] nature, particularly in respect of the 'pace'[56] of work. In this way, Sturt anticipates the time and motion studies pioneered by Frederick Winslow Taylor, who was keen to eliminate what he called 'soldiering' or 'slow working' so that competitiveness could be improved.[57] Sturt, in other words, is not only concerned with the expressive qualities of labour but also with whether it makes his business 'pay'.[58]

This aspect of Sturt's text helps to define certain parallels between *Culture and Environment* and the principles of scientific management. The aim of the latter is 'to secure the maximum prosperity for the employer, coupled with the maximum prosperity for each employee'.[59] This, Taylor argues, will be achieved by making workers produce more than they are at present. Leavis too aims to produce 'something more'. One of the tasks of literary criticism is to reveal the presence of tradition in language thereby showing that it is not reducible to the commercial imperatives of advertising, journalism and popular fiction. But readers have to be trained to do this – the subtitle of *Culture and Environment* is *The Training of Critical Awareness* – in the same way that workers have to be trained to substitute 'scientific for rule of thumb methods'.[60] This points to a contradiction in Leavis between technique and tradition. It was seen in the last chapter how Leavis deplored the replacement of tradition by technique, but here he seems to embrace the idea of technique as a means of restoring a sense of tradition.

Leavis regards tradition, above all, as a form of order (*CE*, pp. 80–2). The different works compose a tradition in the same way that spokes and felloes make a wheel. Moreover, the hierarchy of the literary tradition can be regarded as a compensation for the lost hierarchy of the organic community. The organisation of tradition stands in contrast to the fragmentation of modern society brought about by the dissolution of boundary lines. The sense of 'something more' is bound up with the idea of tradition as an ordered whole. However, the analogy of literature with talk presents problems for this view. Specifically, the details of this talk 'were but dimly understood' so that 'the whole body of knowledge was a mystery'.[61] In other words, the idea of tradition exceeds any expression of it. The various parts cannot be fitted to the whole and it is this which generates the sense of 'something more' not the idea of tradition as an apprehended unity. Thus tradition appears to be as formless as modern society itself. Nevertheless, it is this very formlessness that provides Leavis with that elusive 'something more'.

Literature's relation with tradition lies in its preservation of 'the subtlest and finest use [of language]' (*CE*, p. 82). This will help combat what Leavis considers to be the debasing use of language by the mass media. Literature is characterised by the vitality of its language in contrast to the inert, formulaic language of, for example, journalism and popular fiction. This 'otherness' of literature prevents it from succumbing to the commercial and conformist pressures which affect other discourses. As such, it offers a perspective from which civilisation can be critiqued.

Literature, then, nourishes and maintains tradition. But it is also the case that tradition supports literature. Indeed, the 'vigour and potency' of words depends on their 'being used in association with such traditions as the wheelwright's' (*CE*, p. 81). But since this tradition is dead then words cannot have the power that Leavis claims for them. They have lost their connection with 'life' and this reduces the distance between literature and commercialised discourses. Of course, it could be argued that literature's strength comes from drawing its own traditions but this leads to self-referentiality and merely reinforces the sense of separation between words and experience – precisely what Leavis criticises in James Joyce.[62]

The sense of literature's isolation from experience is reinforced by a consideration of that phrase the 'picked experience of ages' (*CE*, p. 82). These experiences were valued because they were rooted in a way of life. If literature preserves them now that way of life has been superseded it is in danger of fetishising them. Thus literature appears not to be able to close the gap between past and present, only to repeat the former which suggests an inability to come to terms with the latter. Moreover, the value attached to these experiences suggests a desire to relive them which runs counter to Leavis's claim that 'there can be no ... going back' (p. 96).

Literature's problematic relation with tradition weakens it as a means of resistance against what Leavis calls 'civilisation'. Perhaps it is his subliminal awareness of this that leads him to declare that 'the training of literary taste must be supplemented by something more' (*CE*, p. 4). Irony is piled upon irony here. In 'Mass Civilisation and Minority Culture' Leavis looked to literature to provide that 'something more' which would protect language from being appropriated for purely commercial ends. In *Culture and Environment* Leavis adopts the same strategy but seems to suggest that the study of literature is not enough. In addition, people need to be trained to be aware 'of the immediate environment, physical and intellectual – the ways in which it tends to affect taste, habit, preconception, attitude to life and quality of living' (pp. 4–5). The problem is that the model for the training of critical awareness is the literary, the very thing that training in discrimination is intended to supplement. For example, Leavis attacks 'the stylistic tricks ... of the "best seller" [and] pretentious authors' (p. 49), noting 'the cheapness and vulgarity of the kind of writing that aspires to "style" by the affectation of literary mannerisms and pseudo-archaisms' (p. 51). The 'immediate environment' is criticised according to literary standards which were earlier deemed insufficient to cope with the complexity of modernity. Thus *Culture and Environment* shows that literary taste turns out to be its own supplement.

The circularity of this argument recalls the return to those 'picked experience[s]' (*CE*, p. 82) mentioned earlier. These returns of Leavis upon himself have a certain symmetry when it is recalled that the task of the literary critic is analogous to the wheelwright's craft. The circularity of the argument is aptly symbolised in the shape of a wheel. This raises the difficult problem of the relation between metaphor and logic in *Culture and Environment*. The return of Leavis upon himself in the matters of 'picked experience' and 'literary taste' shows that his argument seems unable to advance and this may be due to the constraints of the metaphor of the wheel. This suggests that it has a negative meaning but it also has a positive one because the craft of the wheelwright – and by extension the work of the critic – shows how tradition is maintained and renewed. The tension between textual logic and metaphor means that *Culture and Environment* cannot be read in quite the straightforward manner that it has been. The standard criticism of it as an idealisation of the organic community represents a failure to engage both with its complexity and respond to its challenge.

## CONSCIOUSNESS, MODERNITY AND TRADITION

The training of critical awareness involves a 'commitment to more consciousness' (*CE*, p. 5), and consciousness is viewed as a defence against 'the competing exploitation[s] of the cheapest emotional responses, [of] satisfaction at the lowest level' (p. 3). Implicit in this remark is an awareness of how modernity makes numerous demands on a person's attention. Georg Simmel discusses this aspect of modernity in his essay 'The Metropolis and Mental Life'.[63] He argues that the essential nature of the metropolitan experience is 'the swift and continuous shift of external and internal stimuli'.[64] Their 'rapid fluctuations and discontinuities'[65] threaten profound psychological disruption unless people protect themselves 'through the intensification of consciousness'.[66] Both Leavis and Simmel, then, conceive of consciousness as a defence against stimuli.

The result of this, according to Simmel, is a split between reason and 'feelings and emotional relationships'.[67] The latter, he claims, 'are rooted in the unconscious levels of the mind and develop most readily in the steady equilibrium of unbroken customs'.[68] Simmel argues that the emphasis on consciousness to the exclusion of emotions and feelings undermines the capacity for experience. Walter Benjamin makes a similar point when he writes that 'the more ... consciousness has to be alert as a screen against stimuli ... the less do these impressions enter experience'.[69] Part of what Benjamin means by experience is remembrance, which is to be distinguished from memory in that the former lies beyond the reach of consciousness. Memory, the product of consciousness, lacks the aura of remembrance which, if chanced on as in the famous case of Proust's madeleine, can transport a person back to the past with a vivid immediacy and sense of relatedness that illuminates the experience in question.[70] In being identified with consciousness, memory can be connected with Simmel's 'reason' while remembrance can be connected with those 'feelings and emotional relationships' which belong to 'the unconscious levels of the mind'.[71]

If consciousness is seen as a means of preventing experience and as a dulling of the sense of the past then Leavis's commitment to it seems misplaced.[72] Indeed, it is odd that he should value consciousness so highly when the kind of experience he desiderates is based on its absence. Sturt describes his men as living 'unawares ... as integral parts in the rural community'[73] and Leavis adds that it is precisely this unawareness that 'constitute[s] an organic community' (*CE*, p. 86). If consciousness is a problem in *Culture and Environment* so too is tradition. Here, the distinction between remembrance and memory is important. The talk of the organic community is to do with 'remembrance'[74] while tradition is associated with 'memory' (p. 97). The former, on Benjamin's reasoning, is removed from consciousness and is therefore consistent with the general state of unawareness in the organic community while the latter belongs to consciousness which cannot accommodate that qualitative sense of the past which, for Leavis, should be embodied in tradition. The task Leavis assigns to consciousness cannot be performed by it and this creates difficulties in understanding the role of consciousness in *Culture and Environment*. Those difficulties diminish, but do not disappear, if consciousness is examined in the light of the writings of Simmel and Benjamin.

Briefly, Leavis sees consciousness as a solution to modernity when it may be better understood as its symptom. Simmel and Benjamin have described how the metropolis stimulates consciousness more than the other faculties and one source of stimuli must be the emerging consumerism where products compete for attention. The importance Leavis attaches to consciousness, in other words, may in part be explained by the nature of modernity rather than by any intrinsic merit in consciousness itself. One thing is certain. If consciousness, by definition, cannot capture 'feelings and emotional relationships' then the sense of 'something more' is not something outside consciousness but rather is constitutive of it. Ironically, therefore, the more Leavis invests in consciousness as a means of recovering qualitative experience, the more such experience recedes since it is premised, if Sturt is to be believed, on 'unawareness' (*CE*, p. 86).

Although consciousness is bound up with the notion of tradition in *Culture and Environment* it may be possible to view the latter in a way that frees it from some of the problems associated with the former. 'Tradition' writes Lyotard, 'needs to be rethought'.[75] He believes that a study of the traditional narratives of the Cashinahua would be a valuable contribution to this rethink. These narratives are characterised by the fact that the recipients 'are part of [the] narrative while still being so and so in the Cashinahua system'[76] and they are also 'in the position of listener[s]'.[77] The narrator of the stories, Lyotard adds, is someone who presents himself not by giving his own name, but as someone who has 'first been the addressee of a story of which he is now the teller'.[78] Lyotard finds in this anonymity and variety of different relationships both within and outside the narratives a refreshing contrast to the West's 'fascination with autonomy'.[79]

Leavis's conception of tradition suggests that what Lyotard finds in the exotic other of Europe can, in some measure, be discerned in the West. For example, the impersonality which is characteristic of Cashinahua narratives is very much a feature of Leavis's tradition, which 'constitutes a surer taste than any individual can pretend to' (*CE*, p. 82). The notion of 'picked experience[s]' (p. 82) can be understood as narrating those who relay them and those who listen to them for they are, in some sense, assumed to be definitive. More particularly, Leavis endorses the idea that the artist 'does not belong to him [her] self'.[80] Further, Leavis's conception of the relations between the artist, the critic and the educated public in respect of tradition implies ideas of community and participation that are not wholly dissimilar to the relations obtaining between the Cashinahua storyteller and his audience.

One of the misconceptions about tradition is, according to Lyotard, that it is a form of 'identity without difference'.[81] But, as he points out, though narratives may be repeated, they are never identical. Lyotard's point is that repetition involves both a 'nonforgetting' and a 'forgetting'; a 'nonforgetting' because the narrative is recalled and a 'forgetting' because certain details are changed or slightly altered, thereby affecting the narrative as a whole. What is of particular interest to Lyotard is the way in which the 'forgetting' of certain details 'make[s] for a nonforgetting of time'.[82] The slight alteration in details or a shift of emphasis is a mark of change which is a reminder of time. Lyotard continues:

> Tradition is that which concerns time ... Whereas what the West wants from autonomy, invention, novelty, self-determination, is the opposite – to forget time and to preserve, acquire and accumulate contents. To turn them into what we call history, and to think that it progresses because it accumulates.[83]

History is a denial of time because it 'accumulate[s] contents'. Nothing is allowed to disappear and therefore there is no sense of change and hence none of time. Adorno describes how consumerism entails that no one should 'concentrate upon anything other than what is presented to him [her] in the given moment'.[84] And, as has been mentioned, Debord notes that 'bureaucratic society lives in a perpetual present'.[85] There is a measure of agreement therefore on the question of time in late capitalist society. Lyotard looks to tradition to redeem time, which it does through the dialectic of 'forgetting' and 'nonforgetting' in the Cashinahua narratives.

Leavis also looks to tradition to enliven a sense of time:

> if you eliminate the past from the present ... you destroy the essential human achievement, that which makes civilization a spiritual reality. To say as I've done that only in the present can the past live is not to deny that the past *is* past ... past, present, time and change are necessary words ... but they cover irreducible complexities of experience, shifting indefinables and uneliminable equivocations ... there is something – I will call it 'cultural continuity' – that has its life in time, and, transcending 'present' and 'past', gives time its meaning and humanity its grasp of a real ...[86]

'Cultural continuity' can be regarded as synonymous with tradition. The claim is not that Leavis's idea of tradition corresponds to Lyotard's understanding of the term but that both share a common concern and, for this reason, Lyotard may be used to develop a new and more productive analysis of Leavis's notion of tradition than Eagleton's dismissal of it as 'a kind of petty-bourgeois version of the upper-class chauvinism which had helped to bring English to birth in the first place'.[87]

Specifically, the concern for time in Leavis's tradition can be read as a critique of the denial of time in consumer society. If Lyotard's analysis is correct, then Leavis's tradition would involve both a 'forgetting' and 'nonforgetting' of time. This would not just be a matter of how 'picked experience[s]' (*CE*, p. 82) were recreated in a different form each time they were repeated, it would also have a bearing on what Leavis *excludes* from, for example, his 'great tradition'. He has, of course, been rightly criticised for what he has omitted in his account of what is important in the development of the novel.[88]

But simply to include what has been left out is to miss the radical potential inherent in Leavis's tradition – that it is a reminder of time, and therefore of the possibility of change in a society whose consumerist ethos denies both. To include works in an existing tradition or to create a new one does not address this issue. Nor does it even acknowledge that all traditions or groupings of texts are governed by a principle of exclusion as much as by one of inclusion. While the recovery of neglected works is important, it is necessary that it does not turn into a process of accumulation for that, if Lyotard is to be believed, is to conspire with those forces which repress time; in part by calling it history.

Lyotard may also be used to read the relationship in Leavis between consciousness and tradition. It will be remembered that consciousness, by its very nature, cannot grasp the experiences that constitute tradition since they are based, by Sturt's own admission, echoed by Leavis, on 'unawareness' (*CE*, p. 86). However, if tradition involves a forgetting then its link with consciousness is weakened. Moreover, what is forgotten, what has slipped beneath consciousness, has the potential to become an element of remembrance in the way that Proust's madeleine was. The slight shift toward remembrance from memory creates the possibility, in tradition, for an accidental or spontaneous return of what has been forgotten in the manner of an epiphany. This does not mean the return of a particular experience, rather the present being suffused by the form or nature of a 'picked experience' (p. 82) to which consciousness is simply not attuned. It must be conceded that all this remains highly abstract, nevertheless, Lyotard's analysis of tradition does seem a promising way of reviving Leavis's understanding of the term.

## LEAVIS READING STURT

The training of critical awareness and of literary taste, training, in other words, in how to read, reflects Leavis's 'commitme[nt] to more consciousness' (*CE*, p. 5). '[T]he analysis of prose and verse' (p. 6) will, Leavis believes, be a useful technique in helping the student or worker 'resist' (p. 5) the blandishments of 'popular' culture. The commitment to consciousness involves a repression of the body in so far as the body is associated with the 'immediate pleasures' of civilisation rather than those which are got through 'effort', that is, work (p. 3). But if reading begins with a repression of the body it is also the case that its goal is the recovery of the body.

What is prized in the organic community is the sensuousness of the body in relation to its environment. Sturt observes of Turner, one of the inhabitants of the village, that '[h]is day's work is his day's pleasure' and this pleasure is related to his 'senses'.[89] Leavis focuses on the senses of the craftsmen, noting how they 'were trained to discriminate extreme delicacies of difference' (*CE*, p. 105). It is this relation to the environment that helps to constitute the organic community (p. 86).

Not only is the body the central feature of the organic community, the very term itself evokes the notion of the body.[90] Thus, in valuing the organic community, Leavis is valuing the body and, as literature is a 'substitute' (*CE*, p. 1) for the organic community it cannot be separated from considerations of the body. Hence key terms in Leavis's criticism such as 'sensuous concreteness'.[91]

Reading, then, aims to recover the working body integrated with its environment. Of course it cannot do this literally; it cannot experience this body, only apprehend it in the form of the literary work, 'the essential whole' (*JOVB*, p. 16). But this working body, this 'structure of a fine and complex organism'[92] cannot be regarded as a whole if the model for the literary text is the body both *in* and *of* the organic community, for what that body lacks is consciousness. To repeat Sturt's comment of his men, 'unawares they lived, as integral members of the organic community'.[93] *Culture and Environment* thus seems to begin with a repression of the body by consciousness and end with the repression of consciousness by the body. It appears trapped in a binary opposition of mind and body whose roots ultimately lie in the division of labour.

Consciousness involves being critical of the press, advertising and popular fiction. To read is to be critical. But reading should not be understood simply as an analysis leading to a value judgement. Leavis's criticism of advertisements reflects, above all, a need to maintain the hierarchy that sustains social order. Here, for example, are the exercises which Leavis recommends for pupils who have studied adverts similar to the ones he has collected:

i) Describe the type of person represented.

ii) How are you expected to feel towards him?

iii) What do you think his attitude would be towards us? How would he behave in situations where mob passions run high? (*CE*, p. 17)

It is evident that these encourage the reader to distance him/herself from the person depicted in the advert. It assumes that this person is male and that 'he' is likely to have an antagonistic attitude towards 'us'. This is heightened in the last question which refers to 'mob passions run[ning] high'.

It is this concern for social order which prevents Leavis from reading Sturt critically. One striking example of this is Leavis's description of 'the art of speech as *essential* to the old popular culture' (*CE*, p. 2, italics added) while Sturt, who is Leavis's main source for that culture, describes its inhabitants as 'taciturn'.[94] What Leavis finds in Sturt is an expression and confirmation of his own anxieties about social disintegration and this blinds him to specific details of Sturt's text which do not conform to his overall impression of it.

Sturt discusses '[u]nrest' in terms of 'the class war'.[95] The mention of class comes as something of a surprise for, hitherto, Sturt's idyllic descriptions have given no hint of a *class* structure in the village. The reason for this is that he takes its class structure for granted. It is part of the natural order blending with it to such an extent that it is invisible. Class only becomes visible when Sturt shifts his focus away from the village. He acknowledges 'the immensity of changes which have overtaken labour throughout the civilised world'[96] and then goes on to ask the following question: 'What is to become of us all if the dockers will not sweat for us or the miners risk their lives?'[97] For civilisation to 'flourish' he continues, 'a less-civilised working class must work'.[98] He traces the problems of 'working class unrest' to 'machinery' which has made work 'less and less pleasant to do'.[99]

Leavis quotes uncritically the sentence, '[t]hat civilisation may flourish a less civilised working class must work' (*CE*, p. 91) adding, by way of parenthesis, that it is not just the working class who suffer from the loss of organic community but that '[w]e all [do]'. It is noteworthy that 'the working class' is presented here as suffering when earlier the implication is that they are the cause of suffering. Perhaps the hesitation between these two conceptions of 'the working class' – which has its source in Sturt – is a factor in Leavis's ambiguous relation to Marxism.

Both Sturt's and Leavis's concern with the problem of order gives a new meaning to the organic community; it is desirable not so much because it sustains and expresses the 'whole' person but because it is a model of social stability. For Sturt, work is a spectacle. Describing Turner he writes that '[t]o see him putting young cabbage plants in rows is to realise what a fine thing it is to know the best way of going to work'.[100] The idea of spectacle is a constant motif in the analysis of consumer society. Adorno refers to mass culture as 'one great exhibition'[101] and Guy Debord refers to modern society as the society of the spectacle. The trend reaches its apotheosis in Baudrillard where the spectacle, which preserved some sense of the distinction between true and false has been superseded by the simulacrum which not only makes it impossible to tell the difference between true and false but makes the very question itself irrelevant.[102] Sturt's analysis of work in terms of the spectacle thus anticipates later approaches to the study of culture and this suggests a continuity between the 'organic community' and consumer society. Hence the two cannot simply be opposed to one another or the former be used as a standard by which to judge the other. Work, as a spectacle, is what others do and this gap between those who watch and those who work constitutes a potentially destructive division in this otherwise 'coherent and self explanatory village life' (*CE*, p. 74). Village life is only self-explanatory from Sturt's, not Turner's point of view; and Sturt was an employer.

What Leavis picks out from Sturt's description of the wheelwright's business, which he inherited from his father, is the relation between employer and employees. The latter 'taught their master the business' (*CE*, p. 75) declares Leavis. They were never merely 'hands' but always 'the men' and they were so because their work 'engaged their hands, their brains, imagination, conscience, sense of beauty [and] fitness, [hence] their personalities were ... satisfied' (p. 75). Yet, as Sturt makes clear, the hours were 'long', the work was 'laborious' yet the men 'welcomed overtime ... because ... with their 24s. for an ordinary week they were underpaid and were glad to get the money'.[103] Leavis's uncritical reading of Sturt is painfully evident here. The claim that 'the men' were 'satisfied' in their work is at odds with the remarks about its 'laborious' character, the 'long' hours and the poor pay.

Leavis, like Sturt, stresses the fulfilment the men found in their work so that 'they could, without a sense of oppression, bear with long hours and low pay' (*CE*, p. 77). Sturt similarly comments that though '"the men" were [o]verworked and underpaid they nonetheless enjoyed life, I am sure'.[104] The problem with this argument is that Sturt has stressed how 'unaware' 'the men' are. He writes that, '"unawares they lived as integral parts of the rural community ..."'[105] and Leavis immediately adds '[m]en in such a relation to the environment and one another constitute an organic community' (p. 86). Fulfilment or satisfaction in their work, then, depends on 'the men' living 'unaware' of how they are being exploited. In this way, *Culture and Environment* endorses a form of unconsciousness as being necessary for good labour relations. The 'unrest' on which both Sturt and Leavis comment can, in this context, be seen as the growth of consciousness. Of course, *Culture and Environment* is 'committed to more consciousness' (p. 5) but, in the matter of labour relations, 'unconsciousness' seems to be preferred.

'The men' are represented to the reader from the standpoint of their employer, Sturt. They are not 'hands' he comments, but 'the men',[106] a description which encourages the reader to see them as whole persons rather than as mere functionaries. Ultimately, however, the phrase 'the men' no more individualises them than does 'the hands'. There is no difference between them. The 'hands', a Victorian term for factory workers, conceived of people solely in relation to work and the phrase 'the men' is no different since both Sturt and Leavis describe them in terms of their craft. In Leavis's words, 'it was in their work for the most part that the folk lived' (*CE*, p. 68). Further, even if the men are 'individualised' as in the case of Turner and Cook, they merely serve as representative figures of a way of life. In watching Cook, for example, Sturt declares that he was watching 'practically the skill of England, the experience of ages'.[107]

It seems, then, that 'the men's' lack of awareness means that they can be content in their exploitation. But if they are unaware of the contradiction in their condition so too, since neither register it, are Sturt and Leavis. This points to an unconsciousness on their part which is particularly evident in the case of Sturt. Writing about his workshop he observes that '[n]either my partner nor myself realised at all that a new world ... had begun to form all around us'.[108] He then remarks that 'in my old-fashioned shop the new machinery had forced its way in,' adding, finally, that '[un]intentionally, I had made them [the men] servants'.[109] Sturt's apparent powerlessness here may stem from his role as observer. It will be recalled that his relation to the organic community, in so far as it is defined through work, is that of the onlooker, someone to whom work is a spectacle. This lack of involvement compromises his ability to 'read' what is happening to the organic community and this failure to 'read' is repeated by Leavis who merely quotes Sturt without commenting upon him. In a sense, to quote is not to read.

Sturt's failure to read the organic community from his position of observer undermines the notion of a transcendent reading. Such a reading carries connotations of disinterest and objectivity which are not borne out by a careful examination of Sturt's description of labour relations. However, this is not a cynical exercise on Sturt's part. He is not deliberately disguising from his readers the true import of his text. Rather, his position as a transcendent reader conceals *from himself* his own interest and involvement in what he describes. The opposite of a transcendent reading is an immanent one and Leavis seems to propose something like the latter when he writes that 'poetry invite[s] us, not to "think about" and judge but to "feel into" or "become" – to realise a complex experience that is given in words'.[110] The view of reading expressed here is in contrast to the sort of reading deemed appropriate for the mass media. What counts there is the adoption of a transcendent position vis-à-vis the subject matter to be discussed. Culture seems to invite an immanent reading, civilisation a transcendent one. The problem is to try and reconcile the two for both, as Adorno has argued, are necessary if cultural criticism is to generate insights worthy of notice.[111]

It has been argued that Sturt does not read the 'organic community'. But what justification is there for using the term 'read' in this context? Sturt himself describes the various features of the countryside as a text, 'these details [landscapes, cornfields, meadows, woods, and so on] are themselves like an interesting book'.[112] Thus the countryside and, by implication, the organic community lend themselves to being read. Reading is the metaphor by which they are to be understood.

As the phrase 'these details are like an interesting book' implies, they can be read in and for themselves. They are legible and comprehensible on their own terms and do not have to be referred to the whole – the organic community – of which they are a part. This self-evident character is consistent with the description of village life as 'coherent and self-explanatory' (*CE*, p. 74). The term 'read' therefore seems to be justified.

Leavis too assumes that reading is a self-evident process. Hence he assumes that his reader will find the quotations he takes from Sturt as transparent as he himself does. This proves impossible, however, because Leavis often isolates a line or two from a lengthy quotation (see, for example, *CE*, pp. 86, 88) which has the effect of making the rest of the quotation appear as an excess. Even the highlighting of the remark can be seen as a form of excess since it repeats what has just been quoted. Excess thus complicates the ideal of transparency which lies behind Leavis's use of quotation and adds a further dimension to the problem of 'something more'.

Sturt's isolated details and Leavis's single quotations seem to offer their meaning spontaneously, they do not need to be 'placed' in a system. But this is because they already are so placed. Sturt's details only make sense within the organic community while Leavis's quotations derive their particular force from the educational project of *Culture and Environment*. This needs to be examined in a little more detail.

To begin with, there is a contradiction. Sturt asserts that details are, in their singularity, 'legible'.[113] But this clarity or legibility soon disappears for, in talking about the details of 'folk-knowledge' which are the very same details referred to earlier, Sturt writes that they 'were but dimly understood'.[114] It is difficult to account for this discrepancy. The legibility of detail is related to 'country craftsmanship'[115] but so is the fact that it is but 'dimly understood' since in the latter context detail refers to making a wheel. Thus details are both readable and not readable. Their non-readability comes from their hazy relation to the whole body of folk knowledge which is 'a mystery'.[116] Thus, both part and whole are inaccessible because the relation between them is not clear. And yet Sturt emphasises the importance of things being fitted together. A wheelwright's brain has to 'fit itself' to the local wisdom, 'just as his back had to fit into the suppleness needed in the saw pit'.[117]

Reading too is understood as a process of fitting things together. For example, Leavis encourages the reader to make connections between *Culture and Environment* and the reader's 'own observation and experience' (*CE*, p. 23). Moreover, just as the wheelwright's craft depends on a knowledge of tradition, so also does the literary critic's. Words, being 'the chief link with the past' constitute the 'hope of keeping in touch ... with the picked experience of ages'.[118] In being associated with the wheelwright's craft, however, reading is also implicated in a state of unawareness. This is partly because the details of the wheelwright's craft are 'but dimly understood'[119] and partly because labour relations themselves are mystified, '[s]o unawares, they lived as integral parts in the rural community'.[120] As a result of this, reading can be seen as both progressive and conservative. Progressive because, by not being integrated into the whole, the part is free to be interpreted in a number of different ways and conservative because the emphasis on 'fit' suggests that the part can only find its meaning in relation to the whole. It is this conservative aspect of reading which Leavis seems most to endorse since he clearly admires 'the almost incredible complexity and subtlety of adaptation and correlation that every part of a waggon exhibits' (p. 78).

But this can be read the other way round. Fitting or connecting things in a different way opens up new possibilities while isolated or 'dimly understood' details can be viewed conservatively since they belong to that state of unawareness which Leavis identifies as essential to the organic community and which characterises labour relations, 'the men' not seeing how they are exploited. Reading, as not connecting or fitting things together, reinforces a divided social order whose members are blind to its divisions. The difference between the organic community and modern society is that the members of the latter are aware of its divided nature and it is precisely this awareness which is a potential threat to stability. Consciousness and awareness are consciousness and awareness of division.

But reading, as the expression of consciousness and awareness, is not directed at a text's divisions but at its integrity. The text is perceived as a unified whole, a quality manifested by its transparency. This transparency, moreover, seems to eliminate the need for criticism and this is evident in those places in *Culture and Environment* where quotation far exceeds commentary (see, for example, pp. 84–5, 87–9, 94–5). It is assumed that these quotations 'speak' for themselves. But, if this is the case, then criticism is redundant and the project of *Culture and Environment* superfluous. Reading turns out to be not critical discernment but an absolute fidelity to the integrity of the text. Indeed, there is a sense in which critical intervention is an assault on this integrity.

What is at stake, in other words, is not the meaning of a text but its inviolateness. This regard for the unity and wholeness of a text amounts to a non-reading of it, to, in fact, an unawareness or unconsciousness of it. Unconsciousness is precisely what *Culture and Environment* addresses itself to in the hope of turning it into consciousness but, if the above analysis is correct, what seems to happen is that the text only manages to circle back to unconsciousness. This return of the text upon itself makes it fitting that the chief image of the organic community should be the wheelwright's wheel. Such an image suggests, contrary to Leavis's claim, that there is indeed a 'going back', though whether it is a 'mere' one is another matter (*CE*, p. 96).

This non-reading, in a text designed to teach reading, is manifested in Leavis failing to read what Sturt has written. For example, prior to a lengthy quotation Leavis writes: 'Sturt describes a new process, the devising and executing of which exhibits the skill and resource of "the men"' (*CE*, p. 79). Yet in the very first sentence of the extract, Sturt described how he was 'disturbed by a feeling of something wrong about it, something clumsy'. And he goes on to say that

> these men were but uninstructed amateurs at this particular job, I do not wonder that the details of it strike me as clumsy now I remember them. They were a crude replacement of an older method, when wheels were not tyred but shod.[121]

Leavis reads not what is there but what he wants to be there, namely the ability of the men to use their skills so as to adapt to a new situation. This misreading of Sturt shows that desire is an operative force in reading. The desire is to find, in this extract from Sturt, evidence for the survival of tradition, for this would make it easier to believe that it can continue in the form of literature. This desire is not conscious since, consciously, Leavis is quite emphatic that the organic community 'has gone' (*CE*, p. 87).

Reading as the endeavour to be fully conscious of the integrity of the text also involves an unconscious desire that violates that integrity. It does so by refusing to acknowledge what is there in an effort to establish what it would like to be there. In this context, reading becomes a species of 'day-dreaming or "fantasying"' (*CE*, p. 100) which Leavis says characterises leisure or, as he terms it, 'substitute

living' (p. 99). Reading, by contrast, is associated with what is real
(p. 101). It penetrates through to the reality behind appearances.
Reading brought to bear on, for example, advertising is meant to
expose the 'optimism' which makes it 'an offence against society to
recognise that anything [is] wrong' (p. 58). Reading, however, cannot
penetrate through to the reality of desire. The fact that desire, or
fantasy, is a component of reading makes it difficult to sustain that
opposition between reading and daydreaming which is so crucial to
Leavis's critique of modern civilisation. This opposition is rooted in
a conception of reading that does not read itself, whose lack of self-
reflexivity prevents it from seeing or making the connections between
its own processes and the dream-like evasions of 'substitute living'
(p. 99).

The Leavis's failure to make connections matches Sturt's inability to
connect or build details into a whole. Writing of change Sturt
comments that

> nobody saw what was happening. What we saw was some
> apparently trivial thing, such as the incoming of tin pails instead
> of wooden buckets ... Seen in detail the changes seemed so much
> trumpery and, in most cases, real improvements. That they were
> upsetting old forms of skill ... occurred to nobody.[122]

Sturt's failure to make sense of details in relation to a whole recalls
the craftsman's inability to do the same; for them, too, 'the details were
but dimly understood; the whole body of knowledge was
a mystery'.[123]

The ability to build details into a whole is one of the meanings of
reading in *Culture and Environment*. It is the aim of reading to show
how a work is highly organised, everything in it being significant in
relation to the whole. This mirrors the structure of the organic
community where everyone has 'a dignified notion of their place in
the community' (*CE*, p. 105). The manner in which everything has its
place in order to create a working whole recalls the image of the
wheel which can now be seen as a symbol of a literary work as well
as of the organic community. But as a circular object, the wheel exists
in some tension with notions of order and hierarchy. They suggest a
fixed, vertical structure whereas the wheel, circular and mobile,
suggests the return of the same. As such, the wheel is a fitting model
of criticism which aims to be so faithful to the work as to almost

reproduce it: the critic 'is pre-occupied with *referring* as sensitively, faithfully and closely to the work as [s]he is able'.[124]

Furthermore, this same image also counteracts Leavis's claim that the organic community has vanished and that there can be 'no going back' (*CE*, p. 96) for the circularity of the wheel suggests that there will indeed be returns. The wheel, in other words, offers a cyclical view of history in contrast to the linear one which otherwise governs *Culture and Environment*. However it is necessary to be cautious for, as was argued in the previous chapter, returns and repetitions always introduce differences into what is returned or repeated. This is well illustrated in psychoanalysis with the concept of the return of the repressed, where the same returns in a different guise. If this is applied to Leavis's model of reading it would seem that, far from presenting the self-evidence of the text, reading, in fact, returns what is hidden from it. Nor is this a perverse interpretation of Leavis's view of reading since the idea of reading as an enhancement of consciousness already implies that the text is in some way secret to itself.

## CULTURE, LEISURE AND SUBSTITUTION

The 'secret' of *Culture and Environment* is the similarity between the culture and civilisation. This similarity is disguised by Leavis's characteristic method of juxtapositioning which is intended to make the difference between them self-evident.

The similarity between culture and civilisation is apparent in the fact that literature and leisure are understood in terms of substitution. Both literary education and leisure activities are seen as substitutes for the organic community (*CE*, pp. 1, 99). More particularly, writing is substituted for speech. The organic community is characterised in terms of speech, the modern world in terms of writing, that is literature and the press. As Leavis expresses it, '[i]nstead of *reading* newspapers ... people *talked*' (p. 72, italics added). The speech of the organic community, as noted earlier, is connected with work and memory.

Literature, as a substitute for the organic community, approximates to speech (*CE*, p. 52) and is also associated with work and memory. The link with work is evident in the vocabulary Leavis uses to describe the reading of literature. It is necessary to make an 'effort' (p. 3), indeed, the aspiring reader must be 'train[ed]' (p. 3) so that 'the critical habit is systematically inculcated' (p. 5) into him or her. Such diction, as has already been mentioned, does not belong to the tactile character of work in the organic community but to the discourse of scientific management which had begun to affect British industrial relations as early as the 1890s.[125] Thus the very terms Leavis deploys against 'mass production' are borrowed from a discourse designed to increase it by making it more efficient. Literature *itself* may be said to preserve the character of work in the organic community by its emphasis on the concrete, on the sensuous detail. Literature is viewed as a form of memory because it is where the 'subtlest and finest use of [the language] is preserved ... keeping [readers] in touch with ... the "picked experience of ages"' (p. 82).

Since leisure is the opposite of work it is more difficult to see it as a substitute for the organic community. Nevertheless, Leavis uses the term '[s]ubstitute [l]iving' (*CE*, p. 99) to describe leisure. In contrast to the speech of the organic community, leisure appears as writing. 'The decisive use of words to-day', writes Leavis, 'is ... in association with advertising, journalism, best-sellers, motor-cars and the cinema' (p. 82). Such writing does not 'link[ ] up the centuries'[126] rather it 'debas[es]' the 'important words' (p. 53) of the tradition so that there is no continuity between past and present. This 'debasing' helps to account for that 'gap in the continuity of consciousness'[127] which Leavis so deplores. But the gap between work and leisure, as Adorno has argued, is not so marked as Leavis believes for 'advertising, journalism, best-sellers, motor-cars and the cinema' are as much a part of the world of commerce and manufacture as they are of leisure. Leavis's failure to connect leisure with work reflects his failure to make connections between Sturt's observations. The latter is perhaps understandable given Leavis's view of reading as fidelity to the text but the former is less so because earlier in *Culture and Environment* Leavis had drawn attention to 'the relation between mass production ... and advertising' (p. 30).

If leisure is linked with work then it is easier to see it as a substitute for the organic community. Another way in which leisure can be seen as a substitute for the organic community is that both are associated with a state of either 'unawareness' or 'fantasying' (*CE*, p. 100). In this respect, neither leisure nor the organic community are adapted to 'see[ing] things as they are' (p. 58). Moreover, it is hard to claim that both leisure and literature are substitutes for the speech of the organic community when Sturt notes that the men of such a community were 'often taciturn'.[128]

## LEAVIS, LACAN AND VALUE

Substitution is very much the act of metaphor. As Lacan puts it, '*One word for another*: that is the formula for metaphor'.[129] Central to Lacan's conception of metaphor is the idea of repression. At first glance, repression seems to have little relevance to Leavis's notion of substitution, which is a purely conscious matter. Leavis knows what has been lost and what must substitute for it, literature, and what has been substituted for it, leisure. And yet the matter is not quite so straightforward. For example, Leavis claims 'there has been virtually a loss of memory' (*CE*, p. 97), implying that substitution, understood here as metaphor, entails at least a forgetting. According to Lacan, 'every successful symbolic integration involves a sort of normal forgetting'[130] thus literature, as a 'symbolic integration' in the form of tradition, forgets even as it remembers the organic community.

But Lacan has a more radical notion of metaphor, which is that it precipitates 'the formations of the unconscious'.[131] The relevant point, in a highly complex argument, is that the unconscious comes into existence with the acquisition of language. What is most important in this process is that the subject is not even aware of what has been repressed in the formation of the unconscious. This is because of the dialectic between need, demand and desire.[132] Simplifying drastically, the physiological nature of need cannot be reproduced in language – here understood as demand – hence any attempt to articulate it means that it can only return to the speaker in an alienated form. It is this split between need and demand, this difference between physiological basis and linguistic expression that gives rise not just to desire but to its 'eternalization'.[133] Desire is eternal because 'it is not articulable'[134] and therefore has no possibility of being satisfied; constituted by language it continually escapes it.

This whole process is dramatised by the Oedipus complex, where the acquisition of language is bound up with the recognition of paternal authority. The 'formations of the unconscious' observes Lacan, can be explained by the '*formula of the metaphor or of signifying substitutions*'.[135] He goes on to write that 'the metaphor of the Name-of-the-Father ... substitutes this Name in the place first symbolized by the operation of the absence of the mother'.[136] The myriad physiological promptings that characterised the relation with the mother are transformed, according to Lacan, into an identification with the father. This transformation denies these multiple stirrings any expression and so the subject is never conscious of them. They are created as desire precisely because they are not expressed and it is as desire that they constantly unsettle the subject's attempts to use language to create a unified and settled identity.

Any parallels between Lacan's account of metaphor and Leavis's notion of substitution can only be suggestive. Nevertheless, both writers discuss the passage from one state to another in terms of language. It is interesting that both writers focus on language when discussing major changes in the psyche and society respectively. The question arises as to why they do. The answer lies in the fact that the 1930s was a time when European intellectuals, for the first time in history, had to come to terms with mass consumerism and what that implied for culture.[137] More specifically, one of the effects of the new consumerism was the creation of a number of discourses pertaining to leisure activities such as motoring, the cinema and the phonograph. These discourses complemented those pertaining to work, for example scientific management, which themselves grew out of discourses of social regulation appearing in the early part of the century, marking the transition from *laissez-faire* to monopoly capitalism.[138] Given the growth of these new discourses it is not unreasonable to suppose that one consequence of them was the highlighting of questions of language.

Clearly, Lacan looks at language in a different way from Leavis, although it is worth noting that both view it in terms of the body.[139] Lacan, however, is interested more in language's structure, Leavis in its quality. Lacan is concerned with the acquisition of language whereas Leavis merely charts its degeneration from the speech of the organic community to the writing of civilisation. He does not posit a time prior to language nor does he discuss what is involved in its emergence. Having said that, however, it remains the case that both writers use a model of language to illustrate profound changes of condition and this makes for certain similarities between them.

In particular, both Lacan and Leavis regard substitution as crucial in their respective accounts of language. For Lacan it is substitution through metaphor that gives rise to language while for Leavis substitution refers to both the ideal substitution of literature for the speech of the organic community and the actual substitution of leisure for the work of the organic community. Another similarity is that, just as Lacan sees the entry into language as a loss, since 'the play of displacement and condensation' which defines language means that a person is 'doomed' to be 'a subject to the signifier' and therefore can never 'aim at being whole',[140] so too does Leavis regard the passage to 'civilisation' as a fall. Leisure replaces work but it cannot make people 'feel self-fulfilled [or] make life significant, dignified and satisfying' (*CE*, p. 69). In addition, both Leavis and Lacan emphasise the impossibility of recovering what has been lost and their work is accordingly motivated towards the future. This does not mean that the past is abandoned but rather that it is brought into relation to some projected goal. Leavis notes that '[i]f we forget the old order we shall not know what kind of thing to strive towards' (p. 97) while Lacan remarks that the aim of analysis is 'true speech and the realization by the subject of his history in relation to a future'.[141] Leavis does not aim at 'true speech' but he does advocate the reading of literature, which is the only thing that approximates to speech in all the writing of civilisation.

For both Leavis and Lacan, then, a certain type of language or language in general institutes a split in the subject which can never be healed. This similarity allows the reader to focus more clearly on the problem of desire in Leavis. It is present in the plea for recognition which characterised 'Mass Civilisation and Minority Culture' and in the misreading of Sturt.

Desire is related to leisure, since leisure is characterised by 'day-dreaming or "fantasying"' (*CE*, p. 100). However, these are conscious desires compared to the desire which animates *Culture and Environment*, and this is ironic because *Culture and Environment*, a text 'committed to more consciousness' (p. 5), particularly in respect of reading, appears to be unconscious of its motives in reading other texts, notably Sturt. The presence of desire at the heart of *Culture and Environment* negates Leavis's claim that by avoiding the allurements of hypnotic leisure activities like the cinema, he is able 'to see things as they are' (p. 58) for, as Lacan points out, 'in ... relation to desire, reality appears only as marginal'.[142]

But if the centrality of desire causes problems at one level of *Culture and Environment*, at another it resolves them, for desire can be interpreted as that 'something more' which Leavis requires to defy the reductions of civilisation. In brief, desire is that 'something more' to the extent that it eludes and exceeds all expression.

Bearing in mind the similarities between Leavis's and Lacan's conception of language it can be argued that desire in Leavis is a consequence of the move from the organic community to civilisation. At the risk of being schematic, experience in the organic community is rather like need in Lacan. One may be sensuous and the other physiological but neither is articulated. Experience in the organic community, it will be remembered, is characterised by 'unawareness' and 'taciturnity'. Furthermore, just as demand cannot reproduce need except in a distorted form neither can the experience of the organic community be reproduced by literature.

The split between sensuous experience and the expression of that experience roughly corresponds to Lacan's account of the relation between need and demand. It is the difference between them that gives rise to desire. Similarly, it might be argued that the difference between experience and its expression is what gives rise to desire in Leavis. However, the parallel with Lacan means that while desire provides the necessary 'something more' in Leavis it also gives it a negative instead of a positive quality.

Desire for Lacan is unknown and so too is the organic community for Leavis, as can be seen in his (mis)reading of Sturt. As something unknown and something which can never be satisfied, desire 'eternally stretch[es] forth'[143] into nothingness. Desire therefore hollows out the 'being and enacting'[144] of literature. It sabotages its efforts to present presence, showing that the 'something more' of language is not the sensuous particularity with which Leavis would like to counter the abstractions of civilisation, but a 'going beyond' that undermines language itself. Desire means that language can never be closed and hence texts can never be self-contained and, since this is the case, criticism can never reproduce them. On the contrary, the parallel with Lacan encourages the reader to see the relation of criticism to the literary work in much the same terms as the relation of literature to the organic community, that is, the impossibility of equivalence creating the dynamic of desire.

It will be recalled that Lacan links the entry into language with the recognition of and identification with paternal authority. Something similar occurs in Leavis where entry to literature and the literary tradition – in short culture – depends on the recognition of a succession of *male* authors (*MC & MC*, p. 15). The specifically paternal aspect of this is highlighted by a comparison with Sturt who frequently refers to his employees as 'children',[145] thus emphasising the paternalistic character of labour relations in the organic community.

In Lacan the identification with the 'Name-of-the-Father' is a metaphor, a substitute for the connection with the mother.[146] In Leavis, literature is a substitute for the speech of the organic community though this is problematised by the community also being characterised by taciturnity. Central to the recognition of paternal authority in Lacan is an awareness of who occupies which place in the field of family relations. Recognition of the male heritage in Leavis entails an awareness of who belongs where in the tradition. Moreover, just as the paternal metaphor inscribes the beginning of language and thus of *consciousness* in Lacan so too is recognition of the literary lineage in Leavis a mark of consciousness, belonging to the 'critically adult public' (*MC & MC*, p. 32) as opposed to the imputed 'unconsciousness' and 'infantalism' of the non-critically adult public.

In general terms it is somehow fitting and not fitting that Leavis should insist on the authority of a paternal line, on the authority, that is, of a father figure. Fitting, for this will be the decade of the dictators: Benito Mussolini, General Franco and Adolf Hitler. Not fitting because there were no dictators in Britain, only the aspiring Oswald Mosley. Yet, as Valentine Cunningham has pointed out, one of the main features of 1930s' popular culture was admiration for the strong man.[147]

The effect of comparing Leavis with Lacan is to highlight the role and nature of substitution as metaphor in *Culture and Environment*. The relation between literature and the organic community approximates to the process of language acquisition described by Lacan. The organic community is silent and sensuous, a state that is then substituted by literature in much the same way as demand is substituted for need. However, there are important differences, notably the fact that the organic community is highly structured and therefore cannot be compared to that state of chaotic flux which exists prior to entry into language. Moreover, the organic community is riddled by contradiction since it is simultaneously portrayed as both silent and clamorous with speech. However, comparisons need not correspond point to point in order to yield fruit.

There are two types of metaphor in *Culture and Environment*. The first is literature, which is a metaphor, in the sense of a substitution for the organic community. The second is language itself since language, according to Lacan, begins with a metaphoric substitution or, as Lacan calls it in his earlier work, a 'symbolisation'.[148] This process is evident in Leavis in the substitution of literature for the organic community, that is, of silence for 'speech'. Furthermore, this substitution is perceived as an enhancement of consciousness which makes it consonant with – though by no means equivalent to – Lacan's claim that symbolisation marks the beginning of consciousness. 'To think,' writes Lacan 'is to substitute the word … for [the thing]'.[149]

The fact that language is a substitute and therefore a metaphor for 'experience' has a number of consequences for Leavis's criticism. First, his assumption that literature is a 'being' and an 'enactment' is untenable. The gap between the 'experience' and its expression prevents any such fusion. Second, the fundamental fissure in language means that the literary work cannot be conceived as a unified whole. And, since language cannot capture its object – an object which, according to Lacan, it consistently misrecognises as its true desire, so criticism cannot coincide with or reproduce the work. Third, to view language as a substitute for a 'reality' makes it difficult to view it in terms of a correspondence with that reality. This has immediate consequences for Leavis's reading of Sturt. Leavis reads the latter in a transparent manner but the assumption that Sturt's texts refer directly to the villagers and their way of life is severely compromised by the fact that *Culture and Environment* shows language to be a metaphoric substitution while practising a form of reading that suggests it is referential.[150]

The above points are all valid but they reflect a limited interpretation of Lacan's account of metaphor as it applies to Leavis's work. Specifically, the notion that language is a metaphoric *substitution* encourages the reader to think of a prior 'reality' which is infinitely richer than any words used to describe it. What needs emphasising is that language creates and reflects upon 'reality' or 'experience' which are only ever encountered in language. This is the view expressed in *Culture and Environment* and, although the text hesitates between a perception of language as constitutive of experience (*CE*, pp. 22, 53, 54, 81) and as a judgement brought to bear on it (pp. 53, 82) it never wavers from the belief that language, 'reality' and 'experience' are deeply entwined with one another. The use of language therefore involves questions of responsibility. Leavis recognises the power of advertising and journalism to evoke 'realities' and construct 'experiences' but he considers this to be an irresponsible use given that the 'realities' and 'experiences' which are so constructed could be much richer according to the resources of the language. The use of language calls for the exercise of responsibility which is based on a value choice. This is the challenge of Leavis's work.

However, it is hard to accept this challenge because the vocabulary of value has fallen into disuse. This, Leavis asserts, is due to advertising, popular journalism and fiction which promote a limited vocabulary that reinforces conventional values and encourages an absolutist mode of thought – something is either good or bad – rather than an acknowledgement and exploration of complex issues. Furthermore, as was seen in the last chapter, the word 'highbrow' is used to marginalise those who might extend the parameter of the debate. It is a term against which 'we' can unite, confirming 'us' in our 'democratic normalacy' and establishing a consensus of value from which any deviations can be seen as elitist. This creates a climate in which it is difficult to discuss value either as an aesthetic or as an ethical phenomenon and may be one reason for what Barbara Herrnstein Smith calls the 'exile of evaluation' from the literary academy.[151]

Steven Connor also notes that there has been 'a decisive swing away from a concern with judgement and toward a concern with meaning and interpretation'.[152] However, as Connor goes on to argue, 'value and evaluation have not been so much exiled as driven into the critical unconscious, where they continue to exercise force but without being available for analytic scrutiny'.[153] Undoubtedly, the study of literary texts has benefited from the change that Connor describes. For example, there can be few who would now dispute that aesthetic value masks and perpetuates certain definite relations of power. However, this is not to claim that aesthetic value is no more than a mystification of the will to power or the naturalisation of the bourgeois worldview.

Leavis's writing has a bearing on these and other problems. First, he provides a vocabulary that may help to retrieve from 'the critical unconscious' questions of 'value and evaluation'. And the fact that Leavis's own discourse has an unconscious dimension makes his work especially relevant in this context. Second, Leavis began to write at a time when education was being divided along academic or vocational lines. The Haddow Report of 1926, for example, proposed two types of secondary school, the grammar school and the 'modern' school.[154] Implicit in Leavis's writing is the recognition that this division would lead to the long-term decline of literature or culture generally. Nor was he far wrong. There has been an assault on the humanities in high education, an assault which amounts to

> a rejection of the concept of an evaluative discipline in favour of a positivist and instrumentalist model of education as training, a model which was itself derived from a narrowly idealized version of scientific and technical education in which fact, knowledge and interpretation have an ascendancy over values and the process of value judgement.[155]

Leavis upheld the notion of value against such a view of education. Post-structuralist theory, by contrast, has retreated from the notion of value and could therefore be claimed to have facilitated the developments described above.[156] Leavis's resistance may be simplistic but it is a resistance. His call for responsibility in the use of language is a recognition that subjects are not just driven by desires or are the effects of discursive formations but that they are also purposive agents. This stance is bound up with a view of literature as a resource in the construction of reality and experience that forces the reader of Leavis to consider how ethics and aesthetics are related in his writing.[157]

This is not to oppose Leavis to post-structuralist theory. On the contrary, it is impossible, since the paradigm shift of the 1970s, to read Leavis except through the work of, for example, Foucault, Lacan and Derrida. The aim is rather to find a way of allowing Leavisian criticism and critical theory to 'read' and be 'read' by each other so as to discover the parallels, differences and productive tensions between them. Juxtaposing Leavis and Lacan allows certain common themes to emerge; the importance of language as a model of understanding consciousness and social change; the organising power of patriarchal authority and the fact that language cannot be considered apart from questions of surplus. These are merely the basis for a ground clearing exercise but it is worth mentioning that the notion of surplus – desire in Lacan and the problematic 'something more' in Leavis – could be aligned and used to counter the tendency to deprecate value judgements.

This would not be easy and a number of difficult questions have to be asked. For example, how is it possible to bring a psychoanalytic understanding of desire to bear on questions of literary value and literary tradition? But the difficulty of the task should not be regarded as a reason for failing to undertake it. To desist from the enterprise would be to endorse what some see as an intellectually and morally bankrupt climate.[158] The challenge is therefore to think differently and one way of doing that is to look at how a particular aspect of the English tradition can illuminate and be illuminated by the French thought that has dominated and to a large extent still continues to dominate thinking in the humanities.

## CULTURE, CONSCIOUSNESS, CIVILISATION AND THE BODY

The divisions precipitated by metaphor threaten to give language a fundamentally binary character which would inhibit reading in its quest for nuance, subtlety and finely articulated relations. These divisions are mirrored in the separation of culture and civilisation which necessitates two types of reading. The first is an analysis of advertisements, popular fiction and so on. The second is a recognition of the value of literary works. The former requires the reader to adopt a transcendent position and, though this also seems to be a requirement of the latter, it is much less pronounced, the accent falling on the need for an 'inward acquaintance with the work[ ] of literature'.[159] In both cases reading is identified with consciousness. As analysis, it endeavours to transcend the 'body' of civilisation which attempts to work its seductions on the body of the reader. As recognition, it seeks to merge with, to 'recreat[e]' (*VC*, p. 278) the play, novel or poem. The division of reading reflects the division between culture and civilisation rather than challenges it. Indeed, it accepts as given the distinction between the 'language' of civilisation and the 'literature' of culture. Reading thus operates within a predetermined framework which it re-finds and legitimates at all times.

Leavis makes it clear, at the beginning of *Culture and Environment*, that there is an intimate relation between reading and consciousness. The 'commit[ment] to more consciousness' (*CE*, p. 4) is to be achieved by refining reading skills and extending them beyond 'prose and verse ... to the analysis of advertisements ... followed up by comparison with representative passages of journalese and popular fiction' (p. 6). The commitment to consciousness can be seen as a reaction to behaviourist psychology, notably the work of J.B. Watson, with whom Leavis took issue in 'Mass Civilisation and Minority Culture'. 'The time [has] come,' Watson proclaimed, 'when psychology must discard all reference to consciousness'.[160] Instead, interest should focus on the 'correlat[ion] of stimulus with response and response with stimulus'.[161] Adorno argued that psychology joined forces with 'films, and soap operas ... delv[ing] into the deepest recesses [with the result that] people's last possibility of experiencing themselves has been cut off by organised culture'.[162]

Leavis would seem to want to preserve consciousness as an interior experience by his emphasis on the inwardness of the literary critical act. And yet the commitment to consciousness does not include consciousness reflecting on itself. Consciousness is always directed to objects outside consciousness. It seems to flee the interior as if that area had been colonised in the manner described by Adorno.

In relation to literary criticism, consciousness seems to escape into the work. It attempts to merge with the work, not to keep a distance from it. Such a distance would imply that the work was something different which required commentary. Criticism seeks to show that it is within the work, accenting, pronouncing and articulating it. Criticism disappears so that the work can appear. If consciousness disappears in literary criticism, its presence is strongly felt in its relation to advertising or popular fiction. There, consciousness is sharply defined by its opposition to such examples of the mass media. It is against such phenomena that consciousness defines itself. It can never aim at being one with them as it can with literature, but it is precisely this difference which enables consciousness to enjoy the sort of prominence Leavis would like to give it.

Critical consciousness, then, seems to be either immanent or transcendent. Both these represent ways of reading. Literature is read immanently, popular culture transcendently. This reflects a division in reading which itself reflects the division between culture and civilisation and this division can be read in terms of Lacan's theory of metaphoric substitution, that initial split that brings language into being.

It is also necessary to understand these two kinds of reading according to the internal logic of *Culture and Environment*. As has been mentioned, one of the dominant images of both the organic community and civilisation is the body. The body is not as visible in the organic community as it is in civilisation, where different bodies constantly pass one another in the shops and streets of the big towns and cities. As Pasi Falk notes,

> in hierarchal ... society both the body and the signs surrounding it were bound directly to status. But in a society of 'free' subjects and moving positions, where bodies are in principal equal, the body and its signs become something to acquire and to achieve.[163]

Hence there is a need to project individual identity, which is achieved by a pattern of consumption that emphasises the status value and symbolic meaning of the commodities purchased.

This attempt to differentiate one body from another also heightens the visibility of bodies, drawing attention to their physicality. By the logic of Leavis's argument these are dangerous bodies because they are defined not through production, as in the organic community, but consumption. They are bodies of pleasure rather than bodies of work and they therefore offend and pose a threat to reading which, as was noted earlier, is described in terms of a discourse of work. In the early

1930s the literal unemployed body was considered dangerous. As John Stevenson has pointed out, concerns about the effect of unemployment led to fears 'that the unemployed would turn to crime, riot in the streets or join extreme political groupings'.[164] Leavis's diction and his logic thus reflect wider social and political anxieties even though they are addressed to the problem of criticism. In doing so, they show that culture and civilisation are not as separate as Leavis claims.

The body that reading suppresses is a compound body. It is the unemployed body that presents a threat to order and the body of consumption whose pleasures are disruptive of reading. The attempted suppression of the former body shows that Leavis's values are ironically consistent with the social formation that *Culture and Environment* critiques. The suppression of the body leaves consciousness disembodied as is apparent in its relationship with the mass media which it transcends. In the organic community, consciousness was embodied in work: 'It was in their work for the most part that the folk lived' (*CE*, p. 68).

The consciousness that was embodied in the organic community is not, however, the sort of consciousness which Leavis promotes in *Culture and Environment*. This is a critical consciousness, one of whose characteristics, manifested in reading, is the ability to connect details to a whole, something which was not managed in the organic community. It is this consciousness which needs to be embodied, and it seeks embodiment by being incorporated into the literary text. This is apparent in the vocabulary of Leavis's literary criticism. What pleases Leavis in Keats is the latter's 'tactual effects', his 'sureness of touch and grasp' and his 'sensuous firmness' which ultimately reveals 'a fine and complex organism' (R, p. 202). Keats's poetry is discussed in bodily terms.

However, the problem, as argued earlier, is that the literary text is also understood as consciousness and hence it cannot simply serve as a means of embodiment for literary criticism. Even at the level of literature, there is a divorce between mind and body. This should not, on reflection, appear surprising for it will be recalled that the organic community is similarly split and literature, as its substitute, is bound to have certain of its characteristics.

Reading, then, is split. One type stands outside the text, another endeavours to be 'inward' with it. Since reading bifurcates in this way it cannot achieve the central task Leavis assigns it; to heal the rift between culture and civilisation which is also expressed as 'a gap in the continuity of consciousness'.[165] These divisions ultimately refer

back to the initial fracture consequent upon language acquisition. The
earlier discussion of that process showed that language was driven
by desire of which it could never be conscious. This desire means that
language can never really fulfil the demands Leavis makes on it.
'[W]ords', writes Lacan, 'introduce a hollow, a hole ... in the real'.[166]
As such, language cannot be seen as a form of enactment for this
presupposes a coincidence between event and expression which is
prevented by its very structure. Leavis's text reveals what Leavis
cannot know: that it is not simply forces acting upon language, such
as the press, which undermine its capacity for sensuous particularity
and concrete realisation, but also the very nature of language itself.
The press cannot de-base a language that has no base; no foundation
on which it ultimately rests. As a substitute for 'reality,' language
cannot be rooted in it and so cannot body it forth.

Reading is a process of connection, but Leavis never explains what
it is that needs connecting. The inference is that it is culture and
civilisation but these categories are too general to serve any useful
purpose. The irony is that Leavis, who is so passionate in his advocacy
of the particular, of the sharply realised, should himself promote and
rely on such vague abstractions. Culture and civilisation can be broken
down into mind and body and Leavis certainly deploys these terms
throughout Culture and Environment. However, they are charged with
certain meanings or are undergoing certain mutations in society at
large which are not always helpful to his argument. Mind, or
consciousness, is being redefined by psychoanalysis and behaviourist
psychology so that it cannot have that transcendent quality Leavis
would like it to have. Similarly, the body is being redefined by
unemployment, consumerism and the new discourses of health and
fitness. These amount to its fetishisation, whereas Leavis wants the
body to stand for concrete relations in respect of work, others and the
community.

The task which Leavis assigns to reading is, in any case, impossible.
Reading cannot heal divisions that are the result of complex economic,
social, cultural and political processes. It cannot connect parts into a
whole and, in this respect, reading begins to imitate the mentality of
the inhabitants of the organic community who understood 'details
... but dimly'[167] and so they could not grasp either their interrelation
nor their relation to a whole. Consequently 'the whole body of
knowledge [remains] a mystery'.[168] The only way reading can
envisage a whole is if it transcends what is read. This is the case in
its relationship with advertising, popular fiction and the press. It is

also the case in Sturt's relationship with the organic community. This can serve as a model of integration – and therefore reproach to the modern world – only because Sturt stands outside it as an observer. The price of wholeness is the non-experience of it and this immediately transforms the organic community into an abstraction in much the same way that Leavis does the mass media.

An 'inward' or an immanent reading is also problematic. Again, using the organic community as an analogy, it can be seen that an 'inward' reading, such as is practised by its inhabitants, entails an inability to grasp the whole of which they are a part. Individual details may be 'legible'[169] but they cannot be composed into a whole by those, like Turner, who read them. This has implications for Leavis's literary criticism, which seeks to be 'inward' with a work. Such 'inwardness' is meant as an act of fidelity to the work, a respect for its wholeness but, as can be seen from a comparison with the inhabitants of the organic community, inwardness precludes a perception of the whole. The literary work, viewed in terms of the organic relation between part and whole, is undone by a form of reading intended to make manifest precisely that relation.

## LITERATURE, ADVERTISING, SCIENCE AND SPEECH

Training people to read means training them 'to discriminate and to resist' (*CE*, p. 5). Leavis's own reading, as exemplified by *Culture and Environment*, shows little evidence of discrimination and this is because he operates within the framework of a division between culture and civilisation, or as he here refers to the latter, 'environment'. His aim is to demonstrate the difference between the two, a difference which is 'obvious'. Since this difference is 'obvious' the need for discrimination is lessened. *Culture and Environment* may assert the necessity of discrimination but its logic calls that necessity into question. Leavis believes that the 'obvious' difference between culture and environment should be immediately apparent by the simple technique of comparison and juxtaposition, neither of which it should be noted, correspond to the two main types of reading, transcendent and immanent, necessitated by his argument. 'Juxtapositions' of various adverts for Stratford-upon-Avon which rest their appeal on references to Shakespeare are 'so obviously irrelevant to – incompatible with – an interest in Shakespeare' that they make it 'easy to explain convincingly in what ways such writing is insincere, sentimental and vulgar' (p. 51). Similarly, 'comparisons [of advertisements] with passages from essays and novels [will] expose the cheapness and vulgarity of the kind of writing that aspires to "style" by the affectation of literary mannerisms and pseudo-archaisms' (p. 51).

Although Leavis includes numerous examples of what he considers to be pretentious writing he does not include, for the purpose of comparison, any examples of what he would call literature. Thus he cannot really be said to be either juxtaposing or comparing one type of writing with another. This undermines the appeal to the 'obvious' since that presupposes a difference between two types of writing while here there is only one. Furthermore, the exclusion of literature from the comparison means that Leavis cannot demonstrate his central point that culture and civilisation are two completely separate entities.

Leavis's failure to demonstrate his claim is ironic in view of his heavy reliance on scientific vocabulary in *Culture and Environment*. Traditionally, the truth or falsity of a hypothesis is demonstrated by scientific experiment, but there is neither demonstration nor experiment in Leavis's text. What his reliance on scientific vocabulary does demonstrate, however, is that culture and civilisation are not so distinct as Leavis imagines. For example, the use of a scientific idiom was, in the 1930s, inseparable from ideas about training which were most apparent in 'scientific management'.

*Culture and Environment* itself exemplifies a commitment to training since its principal aim is to '*train* critical awareness' (*CE*, p. 5). This emphasis on training is hardly to be differentiated from those '"technique[s] for learning how to behave emotionally or unemotionally"' (*MC & MC*, p. 42) which Leavis criticises in 'Mass Civilisation and Minority Culture'. What he objects to is the intrusion of scientific thinking into language which, he argues, is not reducible to scientific principles. Yet in *Culture and Environment* Leavis draws on scientific vocabulary to defend language from the depredations of advertising. Terms like 'experiment (*CE*, p. 8), 'method', 'analysis', 'classification' (p. 13). 'specimen' (p. 16) and 'field work' (p. 18) all suggest that advertising is best approached from the scientific rather than the literary standpoint, and this goes against Leavis's earlier claim that '[p]ractical [c]riticism' (p. 6) should be the chief means of inculcating the critical habit. His attack on one aspect of civilisation, advertising, proceeds not from culture, but from another aspect of civilisation, science.

Leavis's scientific vocabulary not only shows the extent to which it has penetrated into those areas from which he would like to exclude it, but also reveals a different view of language from the one presented by *Culture and Environment*. The scientific use of language is one of correspondence. Leavis notes the claims of advertisers and then refers them to science. On this scheme, language's claims about the world are either true or false. It is therefore strictly referential. This view contrasts with the one which states that popular fiction, journalism and advertising are responsible for the 'debasement' of language, which 'is not merely a matter of words, it is a debasement of the emotional life, and of the quality of living' (*CE*, p. 48). Here, language is seen to be more constitutive of experience and, as already noted, the text never really either acknowledges or resolves these two ideas about language.

The question arises as to why, given Leavis's hostility to science, does he use its terms in order to expose the claims of advertisements, especially when he has argued that this can be achieved by practical criticism (*CE*, p. 6)? The answer seems to be that the language of advertising and the language of literature resemble one another too closely for Leavis to condemn advertising by any strategy that belongs to either literature or literary criticism alone. The resort to the vocabulary of science is as much to disguise the kinship between advertising and the literary as it is a criticism of advertising. The frequent use of the word 'obvious' fulfils a similar function in that it appeals to the reader's recognition of the differences between the discourses of literature and advertising so that they do not then have to be analysed.

Advertising resembles literature in a number of ways. Take the following example:

### THE TOBACCO OF TYPICAL TWIST

"Yes, it's the best I've ever smoked. But it's deuced expensive." "What's the tuppence extra? And anyway you get it back – *an'* more. Burns clean and slow – that's the typical twist – gives it the odd look. Cute scientific dodge. You see they experimented ..." "Oh! cut the cackle, and give us another fill, You talk like an advertisement." Thereafter peace and a pipe of Two Quakers. (*CE*, p. 16)

Without doubt, this advert which Leavis includes to show its obvious difference from literature, exhibits certain 'literary' characteristics. There is alliteration. There is 'naturalistic' dialogue evident in the foreshortening of 'an'' and in the absence of a subject for 'Burns'. This 'naturalisation' co-exists with a modernist – or perhaps even post-modernist – self-consciousness about the medium: '"[y]ou talk like an advertisement"'. There is also an element of parody of other advertisements evident in this self-consciousness, adding yet another 'literary' element to the advert. Finally, there is a mischievous pun on 'Two Quakers' since 'to quack' can mean 'to talk loudly and foolishly' with the further sense of 'puff or advertise extravagantly' and this underlines the scientific 'quackery' which, Leavis has asserted, characterises the claims of many adverts.

One of the ways in which Leavis has characterised literature is as a substitute for the organic community (*CE*, p. 1). But if literature is a substitute, so too are advertised goods. They come, according to Adorno, close to standing in for a person. '[P]ersonality', he notes, 'scarcely signifies anything more than shining white teeth and freedom from body odour and emotions'.[170] Leavis, quoting Sinclair Lewis, makes the point more strongly:

> Those standard advertised wares – toothpastes, socks, tyres ... were his symbols and proofs of excellence; at first the signs, then the substitutes, for joy and passion and wisdom.[171]

Advertising is implicated in a process whereby originary experiences are substituted for synthetic ones and this parallels the way literature is substituted for the organic community. But what is also interesting about this is the mention of the notion of sign which stands midway between the experience and the substitution. This positioning would seem to suggest that the sign bears some relation to 'reality' whereas substitution does not. That is to say, the sign acknowledges the existence of a 'reality' to which it refers and thus ensures the possibility of distinguishing between it and that reality. This disappears with substitution since that replaces a 'reality' rather than signifies one.

Substitution in advertising occurs when the representation of the product becomes independent of it. This corresponds, in some measure, to the independence of literature from the organic community. The 'decline of referentials'[172] in advertising is accompanied by a move away from an 'emphatically rational mode of argumentation supported by essentially falsifiable "evidence" of product utility towards representations of the satisfaction that comes from using the product'.[173] As this trend was apparent at least as early as 1911,[174] Leavis's scientific approach to the claims of advertisers seems to offer another instance of how he can misread what is in front of him. This is further underlined by Leavis's literary approach to advertisements which ignores their other components such as the increasingly important visual one.[175]

At the heart of this change in advertising 'from a product-centred argumentation and representation to a thematization of the product–user relationship'[176] is the idea that the product is 'something more' than itself. As an American advertising man expressed it in the 1930s, 'Bread is not just bread.'[177] The idea that the product offers 'something more' than itself suggests a further link between the discourse of advertising and Leavis's literary criticism. One way of understanding this link is in terms of desire. Leavis's early writings evince a desire for 'something more' but that 'something more' is never identified. This can be accounted for by Lacanian psychoanalysis which argues that desire is born of the difference between need and demand.

The details of this argument were discussed earlier. The relevant point is that desire comes into being with language but can never be expressed by it. A similar process is at work in the relationship between the organic community and literature. Lacan's ideas also have some bearing on advertising since advertising makes the product 'promise[] to fill in the "empty space"' that consumers feel is there *'even though they do not know how to name it'*.[178] Advertising operates like language in that the presentation of the product makes the consumers aware of a lack which they desire to remedy. However, they cannot name this remedy because, although it is associated with the product, it also transcends it. As with language itself, advertising seems to be implicated in the creation of a desire which escapes being named but which structures the relation with the commodity.

Both literature and advertising are caught up in an economics of 'something more'. Leavis looks to literature for this elusive quality, the consumer to commodities. Although this 'something more' remains elusive it is associated with wholeness. In advertising, 'the fundamentally nameless "it" becomes thematized in the domain of satisfaction and wholeness'.[179] Literary criticism, meanwhile, seeks to find in literature the memory of a unified social order in contrast to the fragmented present. What both advertising and literary criticism have in common is a desire to find a sense of completeness from an object – product or book – rather than through a relation with others. Writing of the commodity, Marx noted that 'the definite social relation between men ... assumes here, for them, the fantastic form of a relation between things'.[180] Leavis endorses Sturt's description of the organic community as 'men' living in an integral relation 'to the

environment and one another' (*CE*, p. 86). As a substitute for the
organic community, literature offers, instead of a relation between
men, a fetishised relation between a reader and a text.

The reader's relation to the text is similar to the consumer's to the
product. In both cases there is, as was noted above, a relation with
an object instead of with an other. There also seems to be little
difference between the categories of reader and consumer. Both are
ideal constructs. Leavis's belief that '[t]here *is* ... a point of view
above classes' and that 'there *can* be intellectual, aesthetic and moral
activity that is not merely an expression of class origin and economic
circumstances'[181] implies that anyone can become a discerning and
discriminating reader. All he or she has to do is suppress the
contingencies of their existence such as class, gender and ethnicity.
Terry Eagleton has criticised this view of the reader, pointing out that
it betrays its ideology at the very moment it tries to rise above it.[182]
The ideology of the Leavisite reader is apparent in the way his or her
reading of a text is expected to endorse a conception of order
inseparable from that of the organic community. The type of reader
Leavis promotes is therefore bound up with concerns about the
stability of the social formation.

The ideal reader is matched by, in Baudrillard's phrase, the
'[u]niversal [b]eing'.[183] The entire discourse on consumption, writes
Baudrillard, 'aims to transform the consumer into the Universal
Being, the general, ideal and final incarnation of the human species'.[184]
This construction of the consumer aims to suppress his or her
historicity, as does the construction of the ideal reader. Both the
discourses of consumerism and culture appeal to the abstract category
of the individual while differentiating between real individuals on
the basis of taste. Some consumers are held to be more cultivated than
others as are some readers. This, however, simply reinscribes the
values of class as matters of individual preference. The suppression
of class also has the effect of making consumers and readers solitary
and cellular in contrast to producers since, 'as a consequence of the
division of labour, each labourer presupposes all others'.[185] Because
of the structural similarity between Leavis's reader and the category
of the consumer, the former cannot merely be opposed to the latter.
Indeed, consumerism appropriates the idiom of culture, for example
'taste', thus neutralising it as a critical force.

The similarities between the reader and the consumer offers the
possibility of a *rapprochement* between the two types of reading,
immanent and transcendent. Briefly, the commodity is presented as

something which the consumer lacks. It is therefore outside of him or her. He or she sees it on a television screen, a poster or an advertisement in a magazine. This positioning of the consumer and the commodity is similar, in formal terms, to the relationship between the reader and the various texts of popular culture. The difference is that Leavis's reader does not desire and would therefore repudiate these texts whereas the consumer does desire the commodity. However, this difference may be more apparent than real when it is remembered that Leavis's criticism of, for example, advertising and book clubs betrays a desire for the very things he criticises.

At the same time as the commodity is outside the consumer it is also the case that his or her relationship with it is a profoundly inward one. This is because the lack which consumers experience is not for the commodity itself but for the sense of wholeness which it connotates. This lack of wholeness is experienced internally as, ultimately, is the commodity for, as Falk observes, advertising, which is the production and play of signs of commodities, creates 'inner being'.[186] That is to say, the meaning of the commodity is realised as the experience of the self.

The consumer's relation with the commodity offers, then, a synthesis of immanence and transcendence. But this synthesis is a travesty of the kind Adorno has in mind. This would

> relate the knowledge of society as a totality and of the mind's involvement in it to the claim inherent in the specific content of the object that it be apprehended as such.[187]

What the consumer's relation with the commodity shows is how, once again, civilisation appropriates the operations of culture with the result, noted by Adorno, that it is becoming increasingly difficult to tell them apart.

Adorno distinguishes between culture and administration rather than between culture and civilisation. He defines culture as 'the perennial claim of the particular over the general' whereas administration 'represents ... the general against [the] particular'.[188] He argues that mass culture tries to abolish this difference by creating an identity between them. Administration takes on the characteristics of culture, making it seem as if culture still flourishes. The difference is that the particular, instead of opposing the general, now serves it. The advantage of Adorno's analysis is that it helps to focus what is implicit in Leavis's writing on culture and civilisation, namely that they are not as distinct as he maintains.

Literature, it should now be clear, cannot be distinguished from advertising in terms of its proximity to reality. Both are forms of writing and ironically, given Leavis's desire to differentiate between them, each is described in terms of use. Advertising is 'a use of words' intended to evoke a response rather than point to any facts (*CE*, p. 20) and literature is the 'finest use' (p. 82) of words. Thus, both culture and civilisation converge when Leavis's whole intention is to distinguish them. Advertising, literature and literary criticism are all rhetorical, designed to bring out a desired response. Leavis may conduct his argument against advertising by an appeal to science but this amounts to an admission that he cannot criticise advertising by using literary techniques since these bear too close an affinity to the gaucheries of publicity. To approach advertising scientifically undermines the explicit claim of *Culture and Environment* that it is only by cultivating a literary sensibility that the pernicious effects of advertising can be resisted. Furthermore, it calls into question Leavis's own hostility to science, which he believes involves a reduction of 'the human'. He makes this point by quoting G.H.L.F. Pitt-Rivers who notes that '[s]cience ..... has produced vast machinery. But what sort of man has the machine produced? What sort of man is best adapted to turn a lever from left to right all day long in a factory?'[189] And yet, to defend 'the human' against the depredations of advertising, Leavis turns to the 'non-human' science. This inconsistency does, however, have the advantage of disguising the kinship between literature and advertising.

The application of scientific criteria to advertisements implies that science is distinct from publicity, but this is not the case. Just as advertising is closely related to literature so it is to science: '[t]he advertising expert, guided by years of carefully recorded and tabulated experiments ... sets "scientifically" to work to get a given reaction out of the public' (*CE*, p. 12). The identity of advertising thus wavers between that of a science and an art, problematising both. It questions their traditional boundaries as epistemological and affective discourses respectively. This situation is not without precedent. In describing the wheelwright's task, Sturt claims that the work 'was more of an art ... than a science'.[190] He does not say that it was *not* a science, rather it is a question of proportion; 'in this art, as I say, the brain had its share'.[191] Art is distinguishable from the brain which belongs to 'science'. There is, then, a mixture of 'art' and 'science' in the organic community and the fact that advertising oscillates similarly between the two indicates a continuity between the organic community and civilisation whereas Leavis wants to emphasise a radical disjunction between them.

Leavis eventually turns to speech in his persistent attempt to distinguish literary discourse from that of advertising. Advertising is felt to be false in so far as it departs from speech. Leavis presents an advert asking the reader to '[m]ark the expressions in it that you would not use in speaking' (*CE*, p. 52). The implication is that speech is the touchstone of genuine writing, but this is dubious because Leavis has indicated that the 'art' of 'speech' only survives 'where the relics of the old culture linger' (p. 72) and the 'motor coach, wireless [and] cinema are rapidly destroying them' (p. 2). Thus it is hard to see how he can appeal to speech when it is geographically marginalised and on the point of extinction. Furthermore, Leavis seems to be working with the notion that there is a single, unified phenomenon called speech but this is contrary to his observation (p. 2) that it is different in different parts of the country. Hence he cannot really claim that there is a common speech which can be used to determine the authenticity or otherwise of writing.

Leavis's claim that the artifice of advertising and journalism is opposed to the naturalness of speech is further troubled by the following extract where the aim is to teach the prospective writer to write *as if speaking*:

> It is quite likely that you may know it all and feel enormously sorry for the Great B[ritish] P[ublic] for not having enjoyed all your advantages. But the Great B.P. is not always impressed. Very frequently it is bored stiff. Silly and presumptuous of it, but there it is. Amuse it and clear it up. Chat to it. Bully it a little. Tickle its funny bone. Giggle with it. Confide in it. Give it, now and again, a good old cry. It loves that. But don't, for your success's sake, come the superior highbrow over it.[192]

This shows that a certain kind of writing, popular journalism, can behave like the modes of 'ordinary' speech but, in so doing, it challenges the ordinariness and naturalness of that speech. Here, speech is a product of writing, rather than an entity which writing imitates. In other words, writing generates a conception of speech upon which speech, in order to be authentic, must model itself. Since speech appears as a function of writing it cannot have that immediacy which

Leavis attributes to it. Writing approximates to literature the closer
it approximates to speech but if speech is an effect of writing then
literature cannot be seen as being based on speech.


## CONNECTION, EXAMPLE, QUOTATION

The fact that Leavis tries so many ways of distinguishing between
'high' and popular culture shows that the difference which he regards
as obvious is anything but. Each new manoeuvre betrays an awareness
of the failure of the previous one. But this awareness is never
articulated in a conscious manner, showing, once more, how a text
'committed to more consciousness' (*CE*, p. 5) nevertheless remains
'unconscious' of itself. The remedy for this lies in making the kind of
connections between 'high' and popular culture that have been made
in this chapter for, paradoxically, it is only by noting similarities that
differences begin to emerge.

In part, reading is about making connections. Leavis certainly
encourages the reader to make connections between, for example, his
or her 'own observation and experience' (*CE*, p. 23) and the analysis
he offers of advertisements. But the *text* demands the reader make
other connections, ones of which Leavis seems unaware. *Culture and
Environment* is a text of bits and pieces. That is to say, there are pages
of continuous prose, pages of prose and 'adverts', the latter in italics
or small type; there are pages of only adverts or extracts, pages of
quotation only, chapters are of unequal length and there is no
symmetry between commentary and quotation. The text is
simultaneously analysis, example, question, extract, quotation,
prescription and also, ironically, an advertisement for books which
support its case. What this format does is call into question the generic
concept of 'book'. The fragmentary form of *Culture and Environment*
undermines the idea of the integrated work of art symbolised by the
organic community. In promoting a particular idea of a book – the
ordered whole of a literary work – *Culture and Environment* presents
the reader with a text in pieces.

*Culture and Environment* is a polyphony of registers, meaning that
it cannot be regarded as a text which teaches the reader how to read.
What it does is put into play a variety of different reading positions.
This means that there is no single vantage point from which to view
the text, an impression strengthened by an uncertainty as to whom
it is addressed. At times it is directed to teachers, though whether in

schools or colleges or institutes of higher edcuation is uncertain, and at other times to students though, again, the sort of institution is not specified. And, moreover, different audiences are addressed on the same page (*CE*, p. 39) thus fracturing further an already fissured text.

As Leavis notes, 'The manner of presentation differs to some extent from part to part of the book' (*CE*, p. 9). This, together with the different registers and the address to different audiences all make it difficult to read the text in a straightforward manner from beginning to end. The numerous breaks and interruptions also inhibit a linear reading. In addition, Leavis himself signals that the text cannot be understood purely in terms of chronology. For example, on page 27 he refers us to page 57. On page 30 he notes that '[r]elevant considerations will be found later on' and on page 46 he writes that '[t]his question was suggested on page 39'. The text thus moves back and forth aware that meaning is rarely where it appears to be but has to be produced by making connections across a temporal divide. This lends it a diachronic character which is at odds with Leavis's favoured way of reading, juxtaposition and comparison. These, together with quotation, suggest that meaning is seen to be self-contained and self-evident. However, it is hard to sustain this view when faced with the text's continual revelations that meaning is always elsewhere and with the fact that parts of it are repetitions of 'Mass Civilisation and Minority Culture'. These repetitions echo meaning, each articulation inflecting it in a slightly different way so that meaning is seen to constantly differ from itself, thus undermining any notion of it being 'obvious' or manifestly 'there'.

The problem of connecting different parts of the same text together – never mind the problem of connecting different texts together – is raised in acute form by Leavis's use of 'examples'. They are to be regarded as expositions, 'i.e. suggested exercises bringing home the point at issue' (*CE*, p. 9). They appear in the early part of the book but '[a]s the book proceeds they are offered much less frequently – at any rate in explicit form' (p. 9). They do, however, appear at the end of the book, their order 'corresponding to the phases of the argument' (p. 9). They are intended to enforce it and they also 'contain much that could not be included in the body of the text without blurring the outline' (p. 9). Nevertheless, the outline is blurred, making this text a graphic enactment of Leavis's description of the borderless condition of modernity.

Although the word 'example' includes the idea of exercise, '[f]act or thing illustrating general rule ... problem or exercise designed to do this',[193] the word exercise does not include the idea of example. The nearest definition of exercise for Leavis's purpose is a '[t]ask set for ... training'.[194] There is, then, a certain tension between example and exercise; they cannot be mapped exactly on to one another. This perhaps explains why Leavis puts 'examples' in quotation marks, as if to indicate some instability in the term as he employs it. The example is an 'exposition' *and* an 'exercise' designed to 'bring ... home the point at issue' (*CE*, p. 9). Generally, the example constructs the reader as both passive and active; passive in that the reader simply has to witness the illustration of a point and active in that the example, as exercise, requires the reader to demonstrate the point for him or herself. The example as example functions to make the reader the recipient of the text – he or she is not involved in it – whereas the example as exercise seeks to involve the reader in the text as someone actively helping to construct its meaning. However, the distinction between active and passive is by no means clear cut since the 'active' exercise is 'passive' in as much as it requires the reader to confirm or reproduce the point that has already been made.

This raises the important question of whether an example is subordinate to an argument in the sense of merely illustrating it or whether in fact it exceeds it by having its own structure and logic. This latter is hinted at by the fact that 'further exercises ... could not be included in the body of the text without blurring the outline' (*CE*, p. 9). But, as has been argued, there is no outline to blur. *Culture and Environment* is a patchwork of texts rather than a single one bounded by a clear idea. And Leavis admits as much when he claims, contrary to what he stated at the beginning of the book, that education should mean more than reading (p. 104). This excess is mirrored in the examples which do indeed produce 'something more'.

This is anticipated in Leavis's use of quotation. Quotation works like an example because both are forms of exposition. The quotations from Sturt contain more information than Leavis either needs or uses to make his point. The same is true for at least some of his examples. When they take the form of questions in response to extracts, they do not take account of all the extracts or the information in them. After three extracts on 'the connection between Fiction and Advertising' Leavis writes:

> The relation between advertisements and the rest of the magazine may be important without being as obvious as this. In what ways

would you have to alter the account to make it apply to English magazines as you know them? (*CE*, pp. 47–8).

This remark applies only to the extract immediately above it, not to the two, one quite lengthy, which precede it. Since Leavis's remark does not focus attention on them they seem somewhat superfluous, an impression strengthened by his saying that the first two 'have some bearing on the answer' to the 'question … suggested on p. 39' (*CE*, p. 46) indicating that they more properly belong there than here.

They are out of sequence and this disjointedness creates an excess which is compounded by a repetition. The same question that is asked on page 39, '[f]rom the advice given above regarding Journalism for Profit what conclusions would you draw concerning Fiction-Writing for Profit?' is asked again on page 46. There is sufficient material on page 39 to answer the question. Indeed, it is possible to argue that only one of the extracts given there is necessary to produce the desired response. When the question is repeated, more material, in the shape of two further extracts, is offered, creating a surplus like the one described above.

The relevance of this to the general argument is that it shows the excess of 'something more' of literary language is also a consequence of the disjunction between a question and the material to answer it. This disjunction produces that same sense of being overwhelmed as is characteristic of the dissolution of borders. The irony, of course, is that Leavis intends *Culture and Environment* to re-establish and shore up those borders, not to contribute to their effacement.

The problem of sequence can also be seen at the end of the book where Leavis provides a long section (*CE*, pp. 110–45) entitled 'Further Examples'. He claims that these correspond to the phases of the argument. This is not strictly true. The second example in this supplementary section concerns the question of whether advertising is a form of literature, an issue not directly addressed in the main text until about half way through. Moreover, examples which develop the idea of organic community by referring to the culture of the inhabitants of Tepoztlan (p. 134) come *before* an example of advertising (p. 139) which reverses the order of the main text where the organic community is considered *after* the role of advertising. By not corresponding to or even reversing the stages of Leavis's argument the examples in the last section of *Culture and Environment* threaten to create an order among themselves. This, together with their varying length, their use of quotation, polemic, straightforward description or eyewitness testimony problematises their status as mere examples, illustrative of a point in an argument.

In effect, the examples in the last section of the book further contribute to that sense of dissolution which Leavis tries to check by his conception of reading. Central to this is the balanced and mutually sustaining relationship between the part and the whole. But this relationship seems increasingly improbable given that one form of it, the example and the argument, has been shown to be asymmetrical. The project of reading is thus rendered still more difficult.

The disorganisation of the relation between part and whole recalls Walter Benjamin's observation that, in the modern age, 'things press too closely on human society'.[195] This, argues Benjamin, makes criticism impossible since '[c]riticism is a matter of correct distancing. It was at home in a world where perspectives and prospects counted and where it was still possible to take a standpoint'.[196] Leavis seems to illustrate Benjamin's point. He attempts to distance culture from civilisation only to show how they are conjoined. Leavis echoes Benjamin in another respect. His criticism begins with the perception that dividing lines are blurred and borders dissolved so that 'things [do] press too closely'. Where he differs from Benjamin is in his conclusion. Benjamin accepts 'the decay of criticism',[197] Leavis wants to renew it.

But if criticism depends on distance, *Culture and Environment* shows the impossibility of attaining that distance; what Leavis wants to separate remains locked together. The loss of distance in this area has repercussions for the reader. That is, by eroding distances, *Culture and Environment* disables the reader from adopting a transcendent position in relation to the text. In a sense, it constructs the reader as one of Sturt's labourers, as someone who cannot read if reading is to be understood as standing outside what is read.

## GENDER AND BLISS

It will be recalled that Sturt's labourers are required to fit the part to the whole. The labourer's task is to put a wheel together. Like criticism, this involves 'correct distancing'. As Sturt notes, '[a] good wheelwright knows the proportion to keep between spoke and felloes'.[198] Making a wheel is analogous to reading, each entails a 'subtlety of adaptation' (*CE*, p. 78). The wheelwright makes the spokes and hub into a wheel, the critic assembles a tradition from different works. However, at the same time that the wheelwright's skill depends on a knowledge of fitting part to whole it is also true that this is the very knowledge he lacks: 'details were but dimly understood; the whole body of knowledge was a mystery'.[199] The reader too finds him or herself in this double bind. The textual logic of *Culture and Environment* has collapsed the distance between the reader and the work which allowed him or her to perceive it as a whole.

It is worth emphasising the analogy between Sturt's workmen and the reader. The latter is presented as a labourer or craftsman. But, unlike the craftsman, the reader is also someone who needs to be trained. However, as Sturt implies, training is the very opposite of craftsmanship.[200] Training, as already noted, is one of the key terms of scientific management, whose aim was to promote efficiency and maximise output from the factory. Leavis's reader, in other words, is a combination of the old-fashioned labourer and the modern industrial worker. Above all, he is male.

The 'maleness' of Sturt's men is conveyed through the nature of their labour, their success in which 'prov[es] their manhood'.[201] Leavis's reader achieves the same effect partly through the 'effort' (*CE*, p. 3) or labour of reading and partly by not succumbing to the pleasures of mass culture, which are associated with the feminine. Women do not 'care ... about facts'.[202] Popular fiction should 'have a strong feminine appeal and a happy ending is essential'[203] and it is women 'especially [who] seek in the vicarious realm of fiction ... to satisfy their natural craving'.[204] Women are associated with the body, their 'natural craving' giving them an affinity with those 'immediate pleasures' (p. 3) which must be suppressed in the interests of critical reading.

If reading is premised on the repression of mass culture and mass culture is identified with the feminine then reading can be seen as a repression of the feminine. Maleness is thus dependent on making the feminine invisible. Reading as discrimination is indeed just that, a discrimination against women, and if this is so then reading is again about instituting divisions and not making connections. But this is true only on a superficial level for, as has been argued, culture and civilisation are neither distinct nor discontinuous. Hence, the feminine cannot be identified exclusively with civilisation. Indeed, Leavis acknowledges this, albeit in an offhand manner when he criticises the English Tripos examination at Cambridge University. He uses the male pronoun to describe the typical candidate but admits, in parenthesis, that 'it's often a woman'.[205] So, despite the fact that the reader is constructed as male, the excluded feminine returns through the working of the text. And, if Leavis's comment is to be believed, the feminine is already a strong component of reading.

The confluence of male and female in the position of the reader raises, once more, the problem of the body. The 'natural craving' of women gives them an animal-like quality which diminishes their humanity. In this way, *Culture and Environment* repeats the dehumanising process it criticises (*CE*, p. 69). The text aims to restore that humanity by a process of reading which evokes the sensuous engagement of labour in the organic community. The problem is that the humanity of the organic community is illusory, not merely because of its exploitative labour relations but also because it resolves itself into animality. Sturt describes 'the men' as animals. They are adapted to their environment '[a]s a wild animal species to its habitat'.[206] To be associated with animals connects 'the men' to women who are also depicted in animal-like terms. Animality suggests an absence of conscious reflection and indeed this is the case with both women and 'the men'. Women enjoy escapist fiction while 'the men' live 'unawares'. As a consequence, *Culture and Environment* constructs a reader very different from the one Leavis has in mind. His is conscious and discriminating rather than instinctual and unreflective.

The position of the reader, then, is a combination of male and female understood in quite specific ways. Since each is unaware and animal-like, the body becomes prominent. This 'reading' body is precisely the body of 'immediate pleasure' that reading must overcome, committed as it is to 'more consciousness'. In fact the text does not transcend this body but produces it as the body of the reader. It is a body that combines male and female qualities, thus representing another lost boundary, this time between the sexes. The feminine component gives rise to anxieties about the nature of reading evident in Leavis's habit of describing it in forthright, masculine terms such as 'athletic', 'tough' and 'discipline[d]' (*MB & C*, pp. 2, 30, 37). This emphasis on masculinity can be understood as an antidote to 'the traditional female associations of literature' that went with a literary culture of 'social poise and hedonistic impressionism'.[207] However, Leavis also deploys terms like 'delicate' (*NB*, p. 39) and 'exquisite' (*NB*, p. 46) in his critical vocabulary which have feminine rather than masculine connotations and so the feminine remains an important part of his conception of reading. The fact that Leavis did not come to terms with it invites a feminist investigation of this neglected aspect of his work.

The animality of the body of the reader is expressed through the phrase 'natural craving'. Craving suggests the sort of impossibility of satisfaction that is characteristic of desire. Further, just as desire escapes language so too does craving because it is associated with the formulae of civilisation rather than the discourses of culture. Because both desire and craving escape language, they are in excess of it thus constituting that 'something more' which Leavis feels to be lacking. The irony is that the source of that 'something more', specifically the body, is the very thing *Culture and Environment* sets out to repress. That it should have this negative attitude to the body is strange given that the body functions as one of the chief metaphors of the text. The book itself is seen as a 'body' (*CE*, p. 10) while the renewal of culture is located not so much in reading as in 'instinct', (p. 4) which surpasses, in physiological terms, the word 'craving' and is the very essence of the body. As in 'Mass Civilisation and Minority Culture' a single metaphor – there the gold standard, here the body – comes to represent within itself contradictory meanings and thus, though used to distinguish between culture and civilisation or culture and environment, in fact shows their unity.

Since craving and desire are an energy in excess of language they threaten its ability to discriminate and set in order. Similarly, as both inhere in the position of the reader they jeopardise what Leavis considers to be an important part of the reader's text, the relating of part to whole. This general disruptiveness corresponds to Barthes's notion of bliss. He distinguishes between pleasure and bliss, 'pleasure can be expressed in words, bliss cannot'.[208] Pleasure is associated, among other things, with 'culture' and the 'art of living'.[209] Bliss, on the other hand,

discomforts [and] unsettles the reader's historical, cultural, psychological assumptions, the consistency of his [her] tastes, values, memories, brings to a crisis his [her] relation with language.[210]

These distinctions have some bearing on the problems of *Culture and Environment*. The organic community is an 'art of life' (*CE*, p. 1) and so can be associated with pleasure, as indeed can culture. The analogy between culture, specifically criticism, and the craft of the wheelwright confers on culture a sensuous character which highlights the element of pleasure involved. Barthes even uses the word '[d]elicacy'[211] to describe the pleasure of the text, a term which, as

noted, features quite strongly in Leavis's critical vocabulary. The fact
that Barthes also defines the pleasure of the text in terms of *'praxis'*[212]
also serves to bring out the analogy between criticism and
craftsmanship. It is evident from this that pleasure has an object, the
text or the wheel. Bliss, however, 'is absolutely intrasitive'.[213] It has
no object, and in this respect it can be associated with desire which
lacks an object to the extent that it cannot be satisfied by one. In
addition, the unsettling power of bliss is matched by that of desire.
Moreover, just as bliss 'brings to a crisis [the reader's] relation to
language' so too does desire. It reveals a hollow in language which
prevents it from enacting what it speaks.

*Culture and Environment* seems, then, to be a text of pleasure and
bliss. The fact that the two can co-exist simultaneously shows that they
are not radically distinct. Pleasure, like bliss, is an 'excess' that exists
'outside any imaginable finality'[214] and hence it dislocates the text
leaving it 'in pieces',[215] an effect also produced by the 'cut[ting]'[216]
action of bliss. Both are to do with the body. Pleasure, for example,
is 'when [the] body pursues its own ideas … [b]ut we also have',[217]
writes Barthes, 'a body of bliss'.[218] The continuity between pleasure
and bliss is another way of articulating the continuity between male
and female. The association of pleasure with '[m]astery'[219] links it to
the maleness of criticism and craftsmanship while the intensity of bliss
evokes the feminine 'craving' discussed earlier. But, just as 'there is
only a difference of degree'[220] between pleasure and bliss so it is
difficult to differentiate completely between male and female in the
position of the reader.

Pleasure and bliss help to focus what is implicit in *Culture and
Environment*: that the reader, the act of reading and the text itself can
be understood in terms of the body and its desires. This body
challenges gender divisions and belongs neither to the 'immediate
pleasures' of civilisation nor to the sensuous apprehensions of the
organic community. As such it is an excess, something produced *by*
the text but not represented *in* it. Consequently, the notion of the body
becomes problematic, making it difficult to rely on bodily terms to
describe poetic achievements such as Keats's or to refer casually to
'the body of the book' (*CE*, p. 10).

Escaping totalisation, the body exists in pieces, thus matching the
very format of *Culture and Environment* with its advertisements,
commentaries, questions and different typographical features. The
layout of the book means that it does not teach reading so much as
stage the problem of how to read. In this, *Culture and Environment*

behaves very much like a modernist text which requires the reader to organise the separate parts into a whole.[221] And, in behaving in this way, *Culture and Environment* problematises the dividing line between criticism and literature, demonstrating, once more, how it dissolves boundaries in the very act of trying to establish them.

All this has consequences for that elusive 'something more' which Leavis requires. 'Something more' is a going beyond the reductions of civilisation and the definitions of culture. It is the task of reading to establish this 'something more' but the strategy of reading is one of limitation. Reading connects, discriminates and draws boundary lines which, of its very nature, 'something more' must transgress. The body is important in this process since desire, 'natural craving', pleasure and bliss all belong to the logic of 'something more'. Reading should therefore value the body but instead, it repudiates it, again showing how the method of reading seems to contradict the goal of reading.

The problem of the body recurs in Leavis and the next chapter will examine, among other things, how it figures in Leavis's understanding of the relation between literature and other elements of the social formation.

# 3

## Literature and Society

In the early 1930s Leavis wrote two articles attacking what he saw as the limitations of Marxism. The first, 'Under Which King, Bezonian?' appeared in *Scrutiny* on 3 December 1932, the second, 'Marxism and Cultural Continuity' formed the prefatory statement to Leavis's first collection of essays, *For Continuity*, published in 1933. A third article, 'Restatement for Critics', which appeared in *Scrutiny* on 4 March 1933, also addressed the challenge of Marxism though this was not its major concern.[1]

The year 1932 was a troubled one in Britain. In February there were riots in Bristol and in October there were four days of rioting when hunger marchers joined supporters in Hyde Park protesting against the means test and unemployment. By the standards of 1932, 1933 was quiet but there were one or two ominous developments. In January, unemployment reached almost 3 million while on the continent Hitler became Chancellor of Germany. The domestic peace was shortlived, however, for in the following year, the National Unemployed Workers' Movement (NUWM) organised a mass lobby of parliament and there were also disturbances at the Olympia meeting of the British Union of Fascists (BUF).

Demonstrations continued in various parts of the country until the outbreak of war. In 1935 there were protests against the new Unemployment Assistance Board regulations. Then 1936 saw the famous Battle of Cable Street when anti-fascist demonstrators attempted to prevent the BUF from marching through the Jewish districts of East London and in 1938 and 1939 there were demonstrations in London by the NUWM as part of a campaign for winter relief for the unemployed. Hunger marches were also a regular feature of the 1930s, the most famous being the Jarrow March of the unemployed to London in 1936.

The Marxist analysis of these events was that the poverty and unemployment consequent on the financial crashes of 1929 and 1931 were a sign of the coming collapse of capitalism. In such a time of crisis, the forces of reaction would unite to protect their interests and it was therefore incumbent on progressive intellectuals to inspire the proletariat to seize the initiative and usher in the revolution. Leavis's analysis of these same events was that 'only a dedicated concern for "culture" could guarantee a fruitful approach to the problems of the contemporary world'.[2]

## LEAVIS AND MARXISM

That is one way of putting the matter but it is unfair to Leavis, whose relation to Marxism, Francis Mulhern believes, 'require[s] a lengthy study in its own right'.[3] It would be wrong to see Leavis's position as diametrically opposed to that of the Marxists. A.L. Morton, a Marxist contemporary, did not think it was. On the contrary, he greeted 'Bezonian' as a 'challenge ... welcome to Marxists'[4] and further claimed that the social and cultural values of *Scrutiny* were also the objectives of the socialist revolution. Leavis himself noted that 'there seems to be no reason why supporters of *Scrutiny* should not favour some kind of communism as the solution to the economic problem' (*UWKB*, p. 38). Nor did he deny the Marxist insight that society has to be understood in its totality. Indeed he felt it not unreasonable that 'scrutineers' should 'warn [themselves] now and then against making the perception of the complexity of problems an excuse for complacent inattention [for] special duties are not ultimately served by neglect of the more general' (*UWKB*, p. 38). Leavis even described himself as a 'Marxist' (*RFC*, p. 50) to the extent that he recognised 'there [was] a sense in which economic problems [were] prior' (*MCC*, p. 33) and therefore believed that some form of 'economic communism [was] inevitable and desirable' (*RFC*, p. 50).

The qualifying phrase is important. Leavis agreed that the economic base was important but not that it determined every aspect of society (*MCC*, p. 33). In particular, Leavis wanted to argue for the autonomy of the cultural sphere which, he believed, Marxists wanted to reduce to a mere reflex of 'the "methods of production"' (*UWKB*, p. 40).

Iain Wright has criticised Leavis on the grounds that in his dispute with Marxism

[h]e consistently chose as his targets the most naïve and reductive examples of Marxist cultural thought and literary criticism ... and therefore never engaged with those aspects of historical materialism which might have helped him to clarify his own analysis.[5]

Wright's criticism, however, does not bear 'scrutiny'. In the first place, it is a matter of dates. The kind of 'Marxist cultural thought and literary criticism' to which Wright refers is found, according to Wright, in the pages of *Left Review* which appeared from October 1934 to May 1938. The first issue, in other words, is published *after* Leavis's comments on Marxism and he cannot therefore be criticised for not engaging with the ideas debated in the journal. Of course Wright would claim that Leavis should have modified his views in the light of these debates but, as David Margolies points out, the 'most general premise' of *Left Review* was 'that all art is class art',[6] which was precisely Leavis's perception of '[t]he Marxist ... [who] admits no reality but the Class War' (*MCC*, p. 35). It is true that Wright also refers to the historian, Herbert Butterfield, as someone from whom Leavis could learn that 'to be a Marxist was not to be a "crude economic determinist"'[7] but what he omits to mention is that Butterfield argues this very case in the pages of *Scrutiny* itself.[8]

Furthermore, Wright overlooks the fact that Butterfield is a *historian* and Leavis a *literary critic*. It is Leavis's project to establish literary criticism as a separate discipline and, to that end, he is committed to affirming its identity as distinct from that of history (see, for example, *CE*, pp. 6–7). He is also commited to safeguarding the new and rather vulnerable profession of criticism from being absorbed into, as Leavis would see it, generalised theories of history and society such as Marxism. It is ironic that Wright, who accuses Leavis of being 'closed off ... from the ... complex historical shifts of the decade'[9] should fail to note that the very opposite was the case: Leavis was the spearhead of one of those 'complex historical shifts', namely the movement to professionalise literary criticism and this *necessitated* his opposition to another historical shift, Marxism.

Another factor in Leavis's opposition to Marxism may, in an uncanny fashion, be class itself. As Perry Anderson has noted, 'Marxism became fashionable'[10] in the 1930s, attracting a number of writers and artists from the more privileged classes in society. Leavis himself noted, in a somewhat dismissive manner, that much of the 'enthusiasm' for Marxism came from 'the Middle and Public School classes'.[11] The tone of the remark may be attributed to Leavis's petit bourgeois origins. This class was traditionally opposed to the flamboyant displays and modish opinions of those above it. Furthermore, it was precisely from this group that Leavis was wresting control of literary studies so there may have been a professional as well as personal element in his 'jibe' (*TMA*, p. 203) at public school Marxists. Class, which Leavis rejects as a mode of explanation, may nevertheless be applied to an understanding of his position, showing that, in this respect at any rate, the Marxists may have had more of a case than Leavis allowed.[12]

But, it must be stressed, Leavis was not resolutely anti-Marxist. As already mentioned, he agreed with the Marxists that economic problems were prior and needed to be urgently addressed if 'civilization' was to 'be saved from disaster' (*RFC*, p. 50). His quarrel with Marxism was one of degree and concerned the autonomy of culture. In this, he anticipated the work of Louis Althusser, who reformulated the canonical base–superstructure relation. Society, Althusser insisted, is a structurally complex totality, a dynamic ensemble of relatively autonomous practices each with their own specific effectivity. Hence, in the words of Francis Mulhern:

> It was unnecessary, and probably mistaken, to analyse literature as the complicated appearance of the essentially simple reality of classes and their struggles. Rather it must be grasped as a distinct practice, carried on by specific means and with specific ideological effects within an always complex social history.[13]

Leavis's claim that 'there is a sense in which economic conditions are prior' (*MCC*, p. 33), but that literature cannot be explained simply in terms of those conditions opens his work to an Althusserian reading.[14] So does the fact that he conceived of the study of literature in terms of a 'distinct practice carried on by specific means'. This is clearly illustrated by the programme of *Culture and Environment* and by Leavis's declaration that one of the functions of *Scrutiny* was to

> provide [and] foster in schools and in education generally an anti-acquisitive and anti-competitive moral bent, on the ground (there are others) that the inherited code is disastrously and obviously inappropriate to modern conditions (*RFC*, p. 51).[15]

It would seem, then, that Leavis's relation to Marxism could be more fruitfully discussed in relation to Althusser than to the Marxism of the 1930s. However, it should be stressed that whereas Leavis seems to claim an absolute independence for culture, '[t]here *is* a point of view above classes' (*MCC*, p. 35), Althusser would argue that culture, specifically art, has a special relationship with ideology which 'does in the last analysis, arise from the relations of production'.[16] Furthermore Leavis was a humanist – 'there *is* a "human culture" to be aimed at that must be achieved by cultivating a certain autonomy of the human spirit' (*MCC*, p. 35) – whereas Althusser's work, in trying to develop Marxism as a science, has been described by both himself and others as anti-humanist.[17]

But even if Leavis cannot be discussed in terms of Althusserian Marxism, it could be argued that he was more 'revolutionary' than the Marxists since he saw in their preoccupation with 'economic problems' the 'consummation of capitalism' (*MCC*, p. 33; see also *UWKB*, p. 44). What he meant by this was that Marxism, like capitalism, addressed itself only to economic matters not cultural ones and hence there was a profound continuity between the two systems. Leavis, by contrast, wanted to undermine capitalism by promoting a cultural sensibility whose values were opposed to it.

In perceiving a continuity between Marxism and capitalism Leavis again anticipates a more recent thinker, this time Baudrillard, who maintains that since Marxism

fail[s] to conceive of a mode of social wealth other than that founded on labour and production, [it] no longer furnishes in the long run a real alternative to capitalism.[18]

Baudrillard, in other words believes that Marxism, in deploying the categories of labour and production, fails to break with capitalism whose entire structure Baudrillard maintains, rests on these very notions.

Although there are differences between the terms of their comparisons it is nevertheless noteworthy that both Leavis and Baudrillard detect a complicity between Marxism and capitalism. Baudrillard's terms, however, highlight how Leavis's literary criticism, despite being cast in an oppositional role to political economy, nevertheless only seems to 'redouble'[19] it. Specifically, Leavis's idea of literary criticism and the literary text are, as argued in the previous chapter, based on a certain conception of labour. Literary criticism is viewed in terms of training while the structure of the literary text is analogous to the structure of the organic community which is itself

defined through work. In short, the idea of productive labour lies at
the heart of Leavis's criticism and it is this which makes it consonant
with scientific management whose main concern is also productive
labour.

## SCIENTIFIC MANAGEMENT AND
## THE ORGANIC COMMUNITY

However, it is necessary to distinguish carefully between Leavis's view
of criticism and his view of literature. The former is couched in the
vocabulary of scientific management, the latter in the vocabulary of
the organic community. The vocabulary of scientific management has
a number of elements which are reflected in Leavis's criticism.[20]
Some of these have already been mentioned such as the concern with
increasing output, which parallels Leavis's pursuit of 'something
more'.[21] Another concerns the way Taylor believes that the application
of the principles of scientific management will morally improve
workers so that they 'live ... better, begin to save money, become more
sober, and work more steadily'.[22] One of the aims of *Scrutiny* was the
creation of 'a morally responsible public'[23] showing how Leavis too
envisaged some kind of moral change in those who engaged in the
critical study of literature. Literature itself is closest to the organic
community when it has such 'life and body that we hardly seem to
be reading arrangements of words'.[24] Literature's characteristic
'immediacy of presentment' (*J & A*, p. 95) also evokes 'the coherent
and self explanatory nature of village life'.[25]

But the distinction between criticism and literature in terms of
training and serious and fulfilling labour is difficult to maintain
because there are aspects of the organic community which are
assimilable to the concerns of scientific management. First, both Sturt
and Taylor focused their attention on manual labourers and both saw
them, ultimately, in terms of animals; Sturt saw sawyers as 'wild
animals'[26] while Taylor notes that

> one of the very first requirements for a man who is fit to handle
> pig iron as a regular occupation is that he shall be so stupid and so
> phlegmatic that he more nearly resembles in his mental make up
> the ox than any other type.[27]

The quotation points to another feature common to both the organic community and scientific management: the strict division of labour. This is evident in the employer–employee relations of the organic community and, more particularly in the demarcations between the sawyers and the wheelwrights.[28] Taylor is quite explicit about the necessity for a division of labour: 'one type of man is needed to plan ahead and an entirely different type to execute the work'.[29] This, he continues, will 'ensure the work can be done better and more economically'.[30]

A third point of comparison between the organic community and scientific management is a concern for order. Sturt, it was argued earlier, is anxious about unrest because it unsettles class divisions while Taylor's hope is that the application of the principles of scientific management will 'render[] labour troubles of any kind or a strike impossible'.[31] The time and motion study is a means to this end. It is a process of observing the worker either with a view to improving his or her performance or as a way of ensuring that optimum performance is maintained.[32] There are, of course, no time and motion studies in the organic community but, nevertheless, Sturt's relationship to his workers is primarily through observation. His gaze is the gaze of the employer observing his employees.

Despite an apparent commitment to individuality in both Sturt and Taylor the effect of such observation is to turn workers into objects. Taylor declares 'the importance of individualizing each workman'[33] but what this means is fitting each worker to a 'job … for which [s]he is … mentally or physically … suited',[34] the aim being to improve productivity and increase savings. The 'individualizing' of the worker, in short, has as its goal not the worker's all round development but the company's improved efficiency. In Sturt, individuals may be named but they function as *types* of the organic community. They are representative figures, not distinct characters. In any case, these named individuals, Cook and Turner, are eventually absorbed into that term 'the men' which may, unlike the Victorian term 'the hands', be intended to denote their humanity but only succeeds in suppressing their individuality.[35]

The parallels between the organic community and the principles of scientific management render ambiguous a key term in Leavis's criticism: 'organization'. The 'business of criticism,' writes Leavis – oblivious to the irony of that '*business*' – is to 'help to form – and organize [the contemporary sensibility]'.[36] It should 'deal with the … organization of the total response to the [work]' (*TSOC*, p. 229).

Judgement of any work, observes Leavis, is a 'problem of organization' requiring 'discipline and training' (*RFC*, p. 47). In general terms, what Leavis means by organisation is the meaningful order of tradition which orientates a response to a work. This is in contrast to the shapeless flux of the modern world brought about by the dissolution of boundaries and dividing lines. The organisation of tradition preserves a sense of 'the human' which, according to Leavis, is lost in the modern world where everything is a matter of technique.

But this sense of 'the human' that Leavis tries to maintain by the term organisation is precisely what is being filtered out of it in society at large. This is evident in Taylor's declaration that: 'In the past, man has been first; in the future the system must be first.'[37] Following on from this, Harold Perkin notes that 'industrial administration became a technical study in which the "human factor" was [subordinated] to "a pure theory of organization" applicable equally to "government, churches or armies" as well as production'.[38] The term 'organization' thus had a contradictory relationship to 'the human', both highlighting and eclipsing it.

This simultaneity of mutually exclusive meanings imposes a limit on how far the term organisation can be deployed either by Leavis or the practitioners of scientific management. Its instability ensures that it can never be wholly appropriated by either. The difference between Leavis and the practitioners of scientific management is that whereas they want to restrict a word to one meaning, Leavis, in another context, regards such a move as a 'reductive absurdity' noting that a word cannot mean '*this* or *that*' but can have '*both* meanings at once' (*J & A*, p. 102; italics in original). The problem is that he does not recognise the implications of this view for his own criticism, itself riven by a commitment to clarity and an insistence that analysis 'yield ... instances of the co-presence [in a passage] of the disparate, the conflicting or the contrasting' (p. 108).

Leavis's criticism, then, depends on a conception of labour which has affinities with scientific management. Thus it helps to reproduce an ideology of work that does more to sustain than undermine capitalism. Even if this were not the case, the organic community still could not be regarded as an effective critique of the unfulfilling nature of work in capitalism. This is because there is a divorce between thought and feeling in the work of the organic community, just as there is in the work of capitalism. 'The men', it will be remembered, are 'unaware'. Only in literature is it possible for Leavis to find a fusion between thought and feeling, 'sensibility and intelligence' (*J & A*, p. 77).

The substitute, the inferior version, turns out to have the very qualities that were attributed to what is replaced. The separation of the faculties in the organic community again make it just as continuous as discontinuous with capitalism.

This continuity means that what Leavis says of Marxism also applies to him: that in criticising the system he too unwittingly reproduces it. Leavis's criticism of the Marxists may also blind him to how his own position is more Marxist than he imagines. As already noted, he agrees with the Marxists on the *ultimately* determining character of the forces of production but differs from them on the question of class and the relative autonomy of the cultural sphere.

## LEAVIS, LEFEBVRE AND MARXISM

There is, however, another element in Leavis's criticism that may be described as Marxist and that is his concern with the alienating character of both labour and leisure. In the modern world 'for very few indeed can the breadwinning job give anything like a sense of fulfilment or be realized in itself a significant part of a significant process' (*UWKB*, p. 41). Leavis argues that civilisation only considers important what can be 'measured, aggregated and averaged',[39] a remark echoed almost exactly by Adorno, who writes '[a]nything that is not reified, cannot be counted and measured, ceases to exist'.[40] Leavis continues:

> With this Philistinism goes the elimination of the day-by-day creativity of human response that manifests itself in the significances and values without which there is no reality – nothing but emptiness that has to be filled with drink, sex, eating, background music and what the papers and the telly supply. (*T.S.E. & EL*, p. 142)

Some may find it easy to dismiss such pronouncements as elitist but this represents a failure to engage with them. One way of engaging with them is to note how Leavis's comments evoke in spirit, if not in analytical rigour, Marx's concept of alienation.

Henri Lefebvre criticises those Marxists who want to restrict the term purely to the exploitative nature of the relations of production since Marx himself 'analyses alienation under several headings'.[41] Lefebvre uses this to justify applying the concept to an analysis of everyday life. He argues that the immediacy of everyday life, examples of which include the café, the funfair, shopping and television,[42] contains and conceals 'economic reality', 'social practice', 'ideological forces', 'political superstructures' and 'political consciousness'.[43] It is only by analysing 'the simplest event – a woman buying a pound of sugar for example' that 'the sum total of capitalist society' can be 'grasped'.[44] The part, in other words, represents the whole, and this kind of thinking characterises much of Leavis's literary criticism where parts are 'organic constituent[s] of the whole' (*J & A*, p. 106). Lefebvre's claim is that only by apprehending the totality contained in the apparently discreet and fragmentary nature of everyday life 'will [we] be able to extract what is living, now, positive – the worthwhile needs and fulfilments – from the negative elements: the alienations'.[45]

Lefebvre's observations make manifest a potential Marxism in Leavis. Leavis, like Lefebvre is concerned with the quality of everyday life and his approach to literature, seeing the part in the whole and vice versa, is similar to Lefebvre's Marxist approach to the analysis of society. Lefebvre's *Critique of Everyday Life* is an attack on those Marxists who wanted to 'define socialism solely by the development of productive forces'.[46] In Lefebvre's view, socialism 'can only be defined *concretely* on the level of everyday life, as a system of changes in what can be called lived experience'.[47] It is precisely this attention to the concrete, to lived experience which characterises Leavis's criticism: '[t]o be concerned ... for literary criticism is to be vigilant and scrupulous about the relation between words and the concrete' (*UWKB*, p. 43). This attention to the particular is in contrast to what Leavis saw as the 'abstractions', 'dogma[s]' and 'pat' answers of the Marxists (pp. 43–4).

There is, then, a possible Marxist aspect to Leavis's thought if it is compared to Lefebvre's rather than to the British Marxism of the 1930s. Leavis himself, unlike his 'Marxist' contemporaries, acknowledged the existence of more than one Marxism. Indeed, it was this which made 'it difficult to determine what precisely orthodoxy is' (*UWKB*, p. 39). The fact that this perception has escaped the notice of those like Wright who concentrate on Leavis's 'anti-Marxist' stance suggests that there is a cultural imperative not to read him progressively.

A consequence of this is the loss of a vocabulary concerned with, among other things, the concrete, creativity, the quality of life, value and vitality. These are difficult and challenging terms and, as such, offer a contrast to at least one branch of cultural studies which collapses complex problems into a simple relationship of domination and resistance.[48] Another prominent term in cultural studies is pleasure.[49] No one would want to deny that this is an important element in a response to cultural artifacts but an undue emphasis on the term – which is in any case highly subjective – can obscure not only real differences between works themselves but also problems of class, unemployment, poverty and education, all of which condition access to and ability to analyse, appreciate or otherwise appropriate these works. At a very basic level Leavis's commitment to the unique particular is an attempt to bring a work 'to a fulfilment determined by the essential and fundamental tendencies of [its] nature',[50] to preserve it from being 'measured by norms not inherent to it and which have nothing to do with the quality of the object but rather with some type of abstract standards imposed from without'.[51]

## CRITICISM, SCIENTIFIC MANAGEMENT AND PROFESSIONALISM

But this characteristic of Leavis's criticism is compromised by its entanglement with the discourse of scientific management. One way of understanding this entanglement is through Raymond Williams's scheme of 'dominant', 'residual' and 'emergent'.[52] These refer to the internal dynamics of a given social formation. The dominant expresses the chief norms, ideas, values and practices of a society. The residual designates experiences and meanings formed in the past but which may still be active in the present. The emergent describes 'new meanings and values, new practices, new relationships and kinds of relationships'[53] which 'depend[] crucially on finding new forms or adaptations of form'.[54] The emergent appears not to be as relevant to Leavis's criticism as the dominant and the residual. The dominant strain would be scientific management, the residual would be the organic community. Williams argues that the residual can be either oppositional to the dominant culture or else incorporated into it. And, perhaps with Leavis in mind, he illustrates this point with the 'rural community' which

is in some limited respects alternative or oppositional to urban industrial capitalism, though for the most part it is incorporated,

as idealization or fantasy, or as an exotic leisure function of the
dominant order itself.[55]

Williams might here have referred to the nostalgia for the
'traditional' England in the inter-war years. This crossed class and
political lines, attracting the socialist George Lansbury as much as the
conservative Stanley Baldwin. No wonder, then, that Lancashire
textile workers dreamed of vacationing in the country lanes of Devon
– though all they could afford was 'a few days at a tacky commercial
resort'.[56] This pervasive nostalgia helps to place the organic
community as part of a widespread cultural phenomenon though it
is to Leavis's credit that he did not subscribe to this nostalgia since
he was quite adamant that there could be no return to the past.
Nevertheless, the fact that the organic community can be identified
as part of the ideology of 'traditional' England further weakens its
oppositional force, already undermined by its relationship to scientific
management. The former is a clear instance of how the organic
community is incorporated by the dominant ideology, the latter
points to an altogether more complicated process whereby an ideology
of work in the present is underpinned by an ideology of work from
the past, despite an apparent discontinuity between them expressible
in terms of technique and tradition. A lively perception of this
difference may entail a blindness to how, at a deeper level, the past
can support and strengthen the present – and this is precisely the case
with Leavis's conception of the organic community.

The consequences for Leavisian criticism are twofold. In the first
place it will be remembered that there is a theoretical difference
between Leavis's conception of criticism and literature. The vocabulary
of the former parallels that of scientific management while the latter
resonates with metaphors relating to the organic community. This
difference means that criticism cannot be faithful to a text nor respect
its integrity; instead, criticism can only translate the organic 'nature'
of literature into the idiom of scientific management. This process is
facilitated by the way in which both coalesce around a conception of
labour, making the difference between criticism and literature more
apparent than real.

In the second place, Leavisian criticism *can* be faithful to a text *and*
respect its integrity precisely because it shares with literature a
vocabulary and attitude that pertains to the ethos of scientific
management. This is certainly *not* what Leavis means by criticism's
'more than ordinary faithfulness' (*VIC*, p. 278) to a work since he

opposes its concern with the concrete to the abstractions represented by discourses such as scientific management. The 'real' fidelity of criticism therefore escapes him showing that critical faithfulness is not, as Leavis claims, a matter of 'more consciousness' (*CE*, p. 15) but of less.

Leavis's relation to Marxism is, then, more complex than commentators such as Wright allow. Even though Leavis was faced with a crude version of Marxism he still acknowledged that it had a certain application. His disagreement with Marxism over the autonomy of culture was something that could be found within Marxism itself, though *not* in England. The case of Lefebvre's dispute with the Stalinist Marxists in France comes to mind here. But to concentrate on Leavis's relation to Marxism obscures what is perhaps the more important relation to scientific management. The parallels between his criticism and the principles of scientific management are not surprising when it is remembered that Leavis was trying to professionalise criticism as the latter was an attempt to professionalise management.

To focus on Leavis's relation to Marxism is to accept, and to some extent reproduce, his reading of the cultural configuration of forces in the early 1930s. It is to read as Leavis reads while criticising his method of reading. What Leavis's reading overlooks is criticism's complicity with a professional ethic which marginalises that sense of 'the human' he is trying to promote. It is important to stress the uncertainty surrounding the sense of 'the human'. It arises from the tension between criticism and scientific management. As criticism is increasingly institutionalised, however, the tension disappears with criticism itself banishing 'the human' to the periphery. This is evident in the slow transformation of literary criticism into critical theory or, of practical criticism into critical practice.[57] Criticism, in other words, has so absorbed the professional ethic that it has 'translated' the latter's 'anti-humanism' into its own specialised discourse. It is no accident that theory, in the guise of structuralism, first became an issue in the late 1960s when '[l]iterary criticism ... needed ... to grow theoretical and professionalized, for so many were coming into the profession; criticism was for tenure'.[58]

Commentators such as Wright repeat Leavis's reading of the situation of criticism in the early 1930s by sharing his assumption that criticism is a transcendent activity that should or should not be allied with Marxism depending on the point of view of the critic. But though criticism may have a certain autonomy, that autonomy cannot be gauged until the extent to which criticism is determined is itself assessed. To be unaware of how the principles of scientific management impinge on criticism is to be unaware of a crucial moment in the history of criticism, when the conception of 'the human' and a method of procedure were finely balanced. The cost of this unawareness is a critical theory which imagines it has progressed beyond humanism when in fact it is a sign of the triumph of the professional society whose achievement has been to moralise technology while denying the moral significance of non-technical issues.[59] A re-examination of Leavis represents an opportunity to recover an oppositional force in criticism which, as some commentators have argued, has been decidedly uncritical in recent years.[60]

## THE PROBLEM OF CULTURAL AUTONOMY

As remarked, Leavis's dispute with the Marxists is over the autonomy of culture. Leavis is prepared to acknowledge that 'there is a sense in which economic problems are prior' (*MCC*, p. 33) but this does not mean that, by attending only to economic problems, all others are thereby dissolved. Quite the contrary for, according to Leavis, to insist on 'the dogma of the priority of economic conditions ... means a complete disregard for – or rather, a hostility towards – the function represented by *Scrutiny*' (*UWKB*, p. 39). That function can be understood as specifying what is distinctive about the cultural realm. For Leavis, it is a concern with the problem of valuation (*MCC*, p. 34) which separates culture from economics. In the former, valuation is a matter of quality, in the latter it is a matter of quantity.

The problem, as was evident from the analysis of the metaphor of the gold standard in 'Mass Civilisation and Minority Culture', is that Leavis is dependent on economic metaphors to advance the cause of culture. This suggests that there is a relation between culture and economics. Leavis, however, seems unaware of the interdependence of these terms in his argument, with the result that what he says is contradicted by how he says it. This is ironic, given the quality of attention that Leavis demands be given to language. Consciousness, it seems, overlooks as much as it looks over its object.

Indeed, even at the conscious level there are disparities between Leavis's claims about culture and economics. On the one hand, Leavis maintains that the two realms should be considered separately, on the other he concedes that culture does bear 'a close relation to the "methods of production"' (*UWKB*, p. 40). This is not necessarily a contradiction in his thinking for the separation of culture and economics is asserted in the face of what Leavis considers to be the Marxist *dogma* of the priority of economic conditions, which means that culture can only be viewed in passive terms, as an effect or symptom. Consequently, the concept is deprived of the force and energy it needs if it is to be mobilised in a critical way against civilisation.

Nevertheless, the two views do seem incompatible. This is because of the ambiguous conception of labour at the heart of Leavis's criticism. In part this ambiguity is constituted by a craft-based notion of labour and in part by one based on the principles of scientific management. The former posits a continuity between the economy and culture while the latter, in the interests of the division of labour, asserts a discontinuity between them. It is the proximity of these opposing positions in Leavis's criticism that causes him to be inconsistent on the question of the relation between culture and economics.

For Leavis, a harmonious relation between the different levels of society exists only in the past. The organic community offers one such relation, Shakespeare's England another. With regard to the latter, Leavis distinguishes between literature and art, popular culture and the economic base before describing the relation between them.

The tradition of literature and art, he writes, which

represents the finer consciousness of the race and provides the currency of finer living – can be in a healthy state only if [it] is in living relation with a real culture shared by the people at large. (*UWKB*, p. 40)

Leavis continues:

And when England had a popular culture, the structure, the framework of it was a stylization so to speak of economic necessities based ... on the 'methods of production'. (p. 40)

The relations between culture and economics are not particularly clarified by this description. It is both vague and ambiguous and this has to be seen as a fault in an article which attacks Marxism because of its reductiveness, conceptual incoherence and failure 'to be vigilant and scrupulous about the relation between words and the concrete'

(*UWKB*, p. 43). Leavis, when broaching the same question of the relation between culture and economics unwittingly reproduces the sort of abstraction he attributes to his opponents.

The vagueness is apparent in such phrases as the 'living relation' which purports to describe how literature and art – 'high' culture – articulates with 'popular' culture. Also, in what sense can the latter be said to be a 'stylization' of 'economic necessities ... based ... on the "methods of production"'? These imprecise notions are compounded by a number of ambiguities. For example, the use of the word 'real' in connection with 'popular' culture suggests a certain 'unreality' about 'high' culture. However, this 'reality' of popular culture is soon compromised by its being a 'stylization' of economic necessities. Indeed as 'stylization' it corresponds to one aspect of the 'literary' in the 'literature' of 'high' culture. The description of literature and art as 'finer consciousness' suggests that popular culture is a coarser version of it and, if this is the case, then what would that make the 'methods of production'?

The words Leavis uses to describe the relation between tradition, popular culture and the economy are couched in terms of consciousness and the body. Not only does this potentially transform a picture of society into an image of the individual, it also reflects a cultural preoccupation with consciousness and the body. Regarding the former, the inter-war years, according to O.L. Zangwill, were 'the period of the "schools", when psychology was torn asunder by internecine warfare'[61] between structural and functional psychology, behaviourism, gestalt psychology and psychoanalysis. Those disputes were, however, somewhat rarefied compared to the widespread interest in the body expressed in matters pertaining to health and physical fitness. As Valentine Cunningham observes, people were going off

> in search of [the] admirable physique, putting on shorts, taking all their clothes off in the new nudist camps, going in for collective physical jerks, joining the Youth Hotels Association (founded 28 May 1930), taking to the sun and the outdoors ... rambling, swimming, hiking, bicycling, eager for health from vitamins, orange juice, vegetarian diets, lots of roughage, and milk ... For the 30's was emphatically the era of the body.[62]

Leavis's recourse to the admittedly muted metaphor of the body to describe the relations between the different levels of society cannot be separated from the meanings given to the body in the popular culture of the 1930s. The metaphor is muted because Leavis is more concerned with the question of consciousness defined as a quality of attentiveness. As Leavis notes, 'It is this incapacity – this "vast and increasing inattention" that is the enemy' (*MCC*, p. 38). However, as has been seen, it is the body which disrupts the operations of consciousness in Leavis's criticism. Furthermore, Leavis's commitment to consciousness is undermined by his valuation of the organic community where the body is prioritised over consciousness.

## THE BODY IN THE 1930s: BOUNDARIES, PRODUCTION AND CONSUMPTION

The question arises as to why people in the 1930s were so obsessed with the body and with health. One answer is that the 1930s were an insecure period due to 'the rapid disintegration of moral values [and] of the pre-1914 pattern of life in post-war Europe'.[63] It was this insecurity which made the 1930s 'anxious and hungry for reassurance'[64] and which perhaps explains the varying attractions of Communism and Fascism. As W.W. Robson observes, 'Where the twenties had been indifferent to political or religious commitments, the thirties were obsessed with them.'[65]

In a time of uncertainty and disintegration, then, the preoccupation with the body can be seen as a concern for wholeness and integrity. The problem with this view is that the accent falls on the individual body when one of the main features of life in the 1930s was the massing together of bodies in both work and leisure. The development of the corporate economy, as it were, absorbed individual bodies into the larger social one.

This can be seen in the rationalisation of smaller companies into large combines. As John Stevenson notes, 'Out of the mergers of the twenties and thirties emerged industrial giants like ICI, EMI, Unilver, Courtauld's and Royal Dutch Shell.'[66] It was also evident in the mass production and assembly-line methods of the new industries such as motor manufacture and in the rise of mass consumer markets which saw almost a thousand new chain stores built in the inter-war period. 'By the outbreak of the Second World War,' writes Stevenson, 'Marks and Spencer, Lipton's, Sainsbury's and Woolworth's had become household names in almost every medium sized town.'[67]

Leisure too saw the massing together of bodies in dance halls, cinemas, holiday resorts such as Blackpool and holiday camps such as Butlins. The growth of these and other leisure activities were, according to Stevenson, 'part of the development of a more uniform and homogeneous society'.[68] Even the unemployed were perceived as a mass rather than as individuals. Wherever we went, writes J.B. Priestly, 'there were men hanging about, not scores of them but hundreds and thousands of them'.[69] The most dramatic expression of this mass was, of course, the hunger march which, observes A.J.P. Taylor, 'displayed the failure of capitalism in a way that mere figures or literary description could not'.[70] In this instance the perception of a mass was fleetingly allied to a sense of the concrete since, in witnessing the marches, '[m]iddle class people felt the call of conscience, they set up soup kitchens for the marchers and accommodated them in local schools'.[71]

Although there can be no doubt about the growth of a more uniform society in the 1930s it is important to emphasise the existence of certain tensions. In the first place, there was an acute awareness of class and in the second there was the isolation of the consumer. In 1937, G.D.H. and M.I. Cole concluded their survey, *The Condition of Britain*[72] by claiming that the country was still essentially 'two nations', a view backed up by John Hilton in *Rich Man, Poor Man*.[73] The consciousness of class differences was also apparent in the guilt that some writers felt at their own privileged background. They tried to deal with this by producing an oppositional literature. R.D. Charques, writing in 1933, claimed that any other sort of literature implied a submission to the prevailing social and economic order.[74] It is clear from Leavis's reaction to Marxism that the early 1930s and beyond was a period when thinkers, writers and artists were required to declare themselves. Indeed, in 1934 *New Verse* conducted a poll of poets to establish political allegiances.[75] Such pressures to declare one's position points to a sense of class polarisation that calls into question the claim that there was an 'increasing absorption of the working class into a pattern of life set by the middle classes'.[76]

The gist of this observation is that consumerism was blurring class boundaries, though this did not become fully apparent until after 1945. A key characteristic of what, in 1937, Edgell Rickword called the 'shift[] from joy in production to joy in consumption'[77] was the growing isolation of the consumer. Mass consumerism, according to Gary Cross, 'free[s] the individual from others'[78], representing, in Falk's words, a change 'of emphasis from social identity to the individual one'.[79] Instead of being orientated to others, individuals are orientated to goods.[80] This, suggests Cross, enables and encourages individuals to '"read[]" each other through the surface sign of goods'.[81] As Brian Massumi expresses it, '[t]he commodity endows us with identifiable qualities. It registers our gender, social status and character traits … [t]he commodity stands (in) for our existence'.[82] Massumi makes this claim in 1993, 49 years after Adorno noted that 'personality scarcely signifies anything more than shining white teeth and freedom from body odour and emotions'[83] and 60 years after Leavis posited a 'possible relation between the standardization of commodities and standardization of persons' (*CE*, p. 32).

Falk argues that defining individuals in terms of consumer goods problematises the boundaries of what is internal and external to a person.[84] Falk's discussion of boundaries is nothing new. It is found in both Leavis and Adorno. This is hardly surprising when it is remembered that Simmel characterised modernity itself in terms of the problem of boundaries:

> For grasping the full significance of 'boundaries' in our existence, however, this property of determinancy forms only the point of departure. For although the boundary as such is necessary, every single determinate boundary can be stepped over … and every such act, of course, finds or creates a new boundary.[85]

If the consumer's relation to the commodity represents one example of the shifting nature of boundaries, the worker's relation to the machine represents another.

Machinery dictates the pace of work and also brings into play only that part of the body which is useful from the point of view of production. A part of the body is thus emphasised at the expense of the whole and this part is coupled with a machine, creating what Mark Seltzer calls 'the body–machine complex'.[86] This is characterised by the reduction of the body to the physicality of the function of its parts, for example the speed of the hands on an assembly line. At the same time, this reduction to a part of the body is also an abstraction of the rest of it resulting, argues Seltzer, in a double discourse of the body. On the one hand there is 'the insistence on the *materiality* or *physicality* of persons, representations, and actions in naturalist discourse' while on the other there is the equally 'insistent *abstraction* of persons, bodies and motions to models, numbers, maps, charts and diagrammatic representations'.[87]

In a very schematic way, both these traits are apparent in the discourses of scientific management and Mass Observation. The former has an abstract notion of the worker in as much as it considers him or her only in relation to their productive capacities and how these can be materially improved. As Taylor so memorably put it: 'The task before us ... narrowed itself down to getting Schmidt to handle 47 tons of pig iron and making him glad to do it.'[88] Mass Observation, founded in 1937, appears to have a much greater sense of the individual's whole life, committed as it was to describing daily routines and 'everyday things'.[89] However, there was a certain ambiguity: on the one hand, the observers were 'encouraged to apply the methods of science to the complexity of modern culture'[90], on the other they were required to be 'more than mere recording instruments'.[91] Mass Observation wavered between an attention to concrete detail and an attempt to extrapolate from such details general trends in society.

Seltzer's main contention is that 'the body–machine complex' was part of a response to a desire for 'an abstract and disembodied "FORCE"'.[92] It is possible to argue that such a desire is also discernible in Leavis, whose preference for D.H. Lawrence over T.S. Eliot was based on the former's art being 'the manifest potency of life'.[93] Furthermore, in another context, Leavis writes that 'life ... doesn't need to be incorporated to be "there"',[94] showing that it is a force which transcends any of its particular manifestations. To draw attention to this similarity is to suggest that what Leavis values most in literature can be explained in terms of a cultural dynamics of force bound up with the body's relation to the machine. Criticism, in other words, simply reinscribes a cultural imperative, thereby undermining its claim to be oppositional.

Seltzer identifies this desire for force with production. Again a similar equation is found in Leavis where the admiration of 'potency' in Lawrence is expressed in a critical discourse which has, at its heart, the idea of a productive worker. Seltzer explains this promotion of force in terms of a male anxiety about·female generative power. As he observes:

> Such a capitalizing on force as a counter to female generativity in particular and to anxieties about generation and production in

general may help to explain, at least in part, the appeals to highly abstract conceptions of force.[95]

Leavis's notion of force is certainly associated with maleness, specifically male writers. In addition, his critical discourse rooted in a conception of productivity – the aim of reading is to 'establish the poem'[96] – is propelled by a vocabulary of force. That term itself, together with other related ones such as 'drive', 'emphasis' and 'insist' recur frequently in Leavis's criticism.[97] This criticism can, moreover, be seen in opposition to the feminine. It will be recalled that part of Leavis's project was 'to turn literary education into a manly profession'.[98] Further, as was also argued in the previous chapter, Leavis conceives of criticism and literature in opposition to a mass culture that reveals itself to have certain feminine characteristics.

There are, then, certain parallels between Seltzer's account of force and Leavis's literary criticism. Of course there are differences. In particular, Seltzer is writing about the end of the nineteenth and the beginning of the twentieth century in America, whereas Leavis's criticism takes shape in 1930s Britain. Nevertheless, both Seltzer and Leavis are interested in the impact of the machine in modern society and in the problems of force, maleness and femininity. And, as Leavis claims in 'Mass Civilisation and Minority Culture', the same processes that are at work in America are also at work in England (*MC & MC*, p. 17). What these similarities show, once again, is that the discourse of criticism is shaped along the lines of cultural configurations and issues that, superficially at least, have nothing to do with evaluating a literary text. Criticism seems to be amalgamated into the dominant discourse of work rather as smaller firms are merged into giant corporations. In the process, criticism seems to enact a trend of modern society rather than re-create a literary work's enactment of experience.

The double attitude to the body in production can also be said to characterise the view of the body in consumption. Put simply, the image of the body in advertising is usually an ideal body against which the 'real' one is perceived as inadequate. The body in advertising rarely admits to disease, age or 'natural' functions, and so these are felt to be 'faults' in the 'real' one. Where 'natural' functions are portrayed, as in eating or suggested, as in sexual activity, they are stylised so that the physical processes involved are as much suppressed as communicated. The 'natural' body, in short, is aestheticised in market culture. It is present to the extent that it is there to be improved, and absent to the extent that the ideal body with which consumers are encouraged to identify is always just out of reach.

The body of production and the body of consumption thus seem to complement one another and this seems to militate against the notion of cultural autonomy. Far from being autonomous, as Leavis claims, literary criticism underwrites an ideology of production and, as was seen in the last chapter, consumption, too. It does this specifically through a notion of the body. Despite Leavis's commitment to consciousness, he declares that he is one who reads 'by the body'.[99] But what he understands by the body – the body of the organic community – is not the same as the body as it is understood in the culture of early 1930s Britain. Moreover, Leavis's metaphor of the individual as society shows this. That is to say, the body is elided in that metaphor so that there is a gap between what Leavis claims and what his rhetoric reveals. No wonder, then, that Leavis distrusts metaphor. For Leavis, metaphor plays down life but it also brings to light the truth of which he is unaware: that the image of the body in his early work is determined more by its role in modern production and consumption than by its place in the organic community.


## MODERNITY: DISEMBODIMENT AND DESIRE

Leavis's conception of the relation between the different levels of society in 'Bezonian' is paradoxical. In the first place, the energy of the essay comes from Leavis's attack on what he sees as the Marxist preoccupation with class in the analysis of society. And yet the model that Leavis offers in its place is also a class-based one, since he distinguishes between 'finer consciousness' and the 'culture' of the 'people' (*UWKB*, p. 40). The apparently unified organic community is as divided as the class society to which it is opposed. Leavis, in other words, accepts class as a governing principle of society despite his espousal of 'a point of view above classes' (*MCC*, p. 35). That is, he approves of class harmony, not class conflict. The second paradox is that the account of the social formation in terms of the relations between consciousness and the body both reveals and conceals the social organisation. Conceals because the relations between consciousness and the body are a poor analogy for complex social processes, and reveals because the recourse to consciousness and the body says something about how society is imagined and how consciousness and the body are placed within it.

Leavis's metaphor marks the end of a long tradition of presenting society in terms of the body.[100] The labouring body stands at the heart of the organic community but the emphasis on discipline and training in Leavis's criticism transforms that body into the efficient operative of scientific management. This worker, compared to the labourer in the organic community, is 'bodiless', a condition registered in Leavis's metaphor by an emphasis on consciousness. It is easy to condemn Leavis's metaphor of society as being simplistic but, if it is read against the grain, it suggests that modernity is a problem of consciousness arising out of a process of disembodiment.

If this is the case, then how is it possible to discuss desire in Leavis? Here it needs to be stressed that the process of disembodiment is not to be understood – indeed, how can it? – in any literal sense. It is rather a question of how modernity imagines the body. One form of this imagining is the ideal body projected by advertising. Consequently, desire is as much *for* the body as *from* it. The 'derealisation' of the body in advertising is paralleled in psychoanalysis, which locates desire less in the body than in the transactions between consciousness and the unconscious. In Lacan particularly, desire is tangential to the body, being understood instead in relation to language, where it is seen as its motive force without ever being 'embodied' by it.

This framework provides a context for understanding two aspects of Leavis's work. The first is the vocabulary of 'force' and the second is the persistent concern with the concrete. Force, in the guise of 'life' is 'disembodied' to the extent that it transcends its various manifestations. By contrast, the concern for the concrete can be read as a desire for some form of incorporation, evident in Leavis's preference for works that present 'significant particularities of sensation, perception and feeling'[101] which criticism, in its aim to be 'a fuller bodied response',[102] can 'feel into' or 'become' (*C & P*, p. 212). Leavis's work, in other words, bears witness to a process of disembodiment by virtue of the fact that one of its most constant features is a desire for embodiment. This desire therefore puts in question the whole notion of literature as the means by which 'the stuff of experience is presented to speak and act for itself'.[103] Instead the vocabulary of force represents a surplus, something which can neither be incorporated nor represented. In this respect it seems to provide that 'something more' which Leavis desiderates. In fact, however, the desire for 'something more' is not so much satisfied as replaced by another desire. That is to say, the desire for 'something more' appears to be answered by a vocabulary of force which itself turns out to be a desire for embodiment.

This dialectic can be seen in terms of the recurrent problem of boundaries in Leavis, which has at least three different forms. The first is that general blurring of boundaries discussed in 'Mass Civilisation and Minority Culture', the second concerns literary criticism whose 'boundaries cannot be drawn'[104] yet which needs a 'determinate ... field or aim'[105] if it is to be a discipline, and the third concerns the body, whose boundaries are being changed by new work practices and the emerging culture of consumption. It is these last which create a crisis of desire: what is it, where is it located and how is it to be satisfied? These questions are aggravated by a system of advertising which constantly stimulates desire beyond any capacity to satisfy it. Consumer society, in other words, if it is to survive, must continually persuade its members not only of the desirability but also the necessity of purchase. That is why, in the early years of the century, the character of advertising changed from the presentation of information to the psychology of persuasion. Hence Roy Johnson, 'father of the "impressionistic principle" of advertising',[106] suggested that its principle ought to be 'the comfort or profit which results from the use of the product, or the dissatisfaction, embarrassment or loss which follows from its absence'.[107]

## LACANIAN PSYCHOANALYSIS, LEAVISIAN CRITICISM AND THE CONTRACT

It may be no accident that psychoanalysis develops with the rise of consumer culture. Both, after all, are concerned with desire, and psychoanalysis can even be regarded as the rationalisation for the non-satisfaction of desire in consumer culture. Since criticism also appears with consumer culture it is not surprising that it should have certain similarities to psychoanalysis. One such similarity is the importance both attach to recognition. In Lacanian psycholanalysis, recognition is considered in relation to desire.

What is important is not the satisfaction of desire but its recognition. 'It is not a question of the satisfaction of desire ... but ... of the recognition of desire'.[108] The purpose of 'authentic' speech in the early Lacan is to win recognition for desire:

Speech is that dimension through which the desire of the subject is authentically integrated on to the symbolic plane. It is only once it is formulated, named in the presence of the other, that desire, whatever it is, is recognised in the full sense of the term.[109]

Leavis also places a high value on speech, using it as a touchstone for authentic literature. It will be remembered that when asked to examine a particularly 'literary' advert in *Culture and Environment* the reader is instructed to '[m]ark the expressions in it that you would not use in speaking' (*CE*, p. 52). Similarly, 'Wordsworth's genius' is in part due to his 'power of bringing [into his poetry] the natural speaking voice' (*ROP*, p. 262). It is precisely its quality as speech that enables the critic to win for the creative writer 'what recognition [s]he gets'(*SC*, p. 246). Moreover, the desire for recognition is implicit in what is, for Leavis, the central question of criticism: 'This is so, isn't it?' (*VC*, p. 277 and *passim* throughout Leavis's work).

Both Leavis and Lacan define speech in relation to other forms of language which are less authentic. Leavis contrasts the 'blanketing use of essential terms' (*UWKB*, p. 39) with 'the duty and difficulty of using words precisely' (p. 42), while in *Culture and Environment* he bemoans the 'debasement' of speech by advertising and the popular press. For Lacan, 'The problem is that of the relations between speech and language in the subject.'[110] Lacan draws attention to how '[a]s language becomes more functional, it becomes improper for speech'.[111] What Lacan means by language becoming more functional is the way it moves 'closer to information'[112] and this observation parallels Leavis's in 'Mass Civilisation and Minority Culture', where he complains that language is being reduced to a technique (*MCMC*, pp. 40–3). Lacan fears that psychoanalysis will 'degenerate' into a 'technique' unless 'we [can] get back to the meaning of its experience'[113] – a recurrent term in Leavis's vocabulary. Similarly both Leavis and Lacan think of language not in terms of information or manipulation, which is how they each see it being used in society, but as 'something more' (Leavis) or 'evocation' (Lacan).[114]

It may be argued, and with some justification, that recognition in Lacanian psychoanalysis and Leavis's literary criticism cannot be compared because they each have different objects. In the former it is desire which is recognised, in the latter it is the value of a literary work. However, it is possible to see the latter in terms of desire, specifically the desire for embodiment. Furthermore, both Leavis and Lacan are sensitive and alert to 'the power of words'[115] and lay great stress on the intersubjective process of recognition. For Leavis

> [t]he implicit form of a judgement is: This is so, isn't it? The question is an appeal for confirmation that the thing *is* so; implicitly that, though expecting an answer, characteristically, an answer in the form, 'yes but –' 'but' standing for qualifications, reserves, corrections. Here we have a diagram of the collaborative–creative process in which the poem comes to be established as something 'out there' of common access in what is in some sense a public world.[116]

For Lacan the intersubjective process of recognition lies in the

> assumption of his [her] history by the subject, insofar as it is constituted by the Word addressed to the other, which makes up the fundamental principle ... of psychoanalysis ... [w]hen the subject commits himself [herself] to analysis he [she] accepts a position ... of interlocution.[117]

Again, there are obvious differences, Leavis's 'collaborative creative process' establishes 'the poem' whereas psychoanalysis endeavours to heal the divide between the subject's past and present. But it is precisely this last which connects psychoanalysis with Leavisian criticism since one of the principle objects of the latter is to close the gap between past and present by creating a tradition, a cultural continuity. Tradition can only fulfil this function if the authority of the succession of male authors is recognised (*MC & MC*, p. 15). The Oedipal overtones of this were discussed in the previous chapter and they are important in this context because, in the words of Lacan, 'No resolution of an analysis is possible ... if it does not end by knotting itself around this legal, legalising co-ordinate which is called the Oedipus complex.'[118] In other words, tradition and analysis aim to restore continuity to the culture and the subject respectively by securing recognition of paternal authority.

Leavis's literary criticism and Lacan's psychoanalysis can, then, be seen as specific but similar responses to modernity, understood as a rent in history. Gaining recognition depends on a process of negotiation either through creative collaboration or the analytic situation. This points to the ungrounded nature of both disciplines.

Neither unfold a pre-given truth which guarantees their utterances. In this respect they represent that aspect of modernity which Thomas Haskell has characterised as the 'growing reliance on mutual promises, or contractual relations, in lieu of relations based on status, custom, or traditional authority'.[119] Literary criticism and psychoanalysis, with their stress on intersubjective relations, exist somewhere between tradition and the contract. The concern of both Leavis and Lacan with tradition – Lacan, after all, advocates a 'return to the work of Freud'[120] – testifies to the loss of tradition while the professionalisation of both disciplines is consistent with a society based on the contractual relation.

It is this ambiguous position which makes both disciplines reproduce and resist the social formation. According to Seltzer, the society based on contract necessitates a new characterisation of the individual, one defined by a radical freedom of will that

> contractual promises presuppose ('I will') and by a power over circumstances and over temporal and physical distance, a standing security for the future delivery on one's will, that the making and keeping of promises requires ('I must').[121]

It is precisely this model of individuality, Seltzer argues, which is the prop of capitalism.

Leavis's criticism can be seen to underwrite this model by its affinities with scientific management, its assumption of the autonomous reader and by tradition's conservation of 'picked experience[s]'. Similarly, psychoanalysis can be regarded as a way of adapting the individual to the demands of the system. But Leavis also criticises the values of consumer capitalism as Lacan criticises the reduction of psychoanalysis to a technique designed to produce conformity.

Complicity and critical impulse should not, however, be seen as cancelling each other out. They derive from different levels within the one discourse. In Leavis, complicity with capitalism stems from diction, metaphors and a reading relation, all of which constitute the 'unconscious' of his criticism in contrast to his overt condemnation of the values of capitalism. This means that there is a tension in his work which may or may not be productive, depending on how and under what conditions it is read.

Leavis's metaphor of society as the relation between consciousness and the body is not, then, as straightforward as it appears. The emphasis on consciousness invites a psychoanalytic reading which would reveal the hidden desire of Leavis's criticism. For example, much might be made of how its unconscious aspects are consistent with the values Leavis consciously criticises and hence his criticism becomes an illustration of Lacan's notion that 'the unconscious is the discourse of the other'.[122]

This, however, is to privilege psychoanalysis over literary criticism. A better approach is to try and understand how the similarities between the two discourses are a result of, and a response to, modernity. By this means, Leavis's metaphor speaks of the loss of tradition and the rise of the contract. In an uncanny fashion, this illustrates Leavis's remark that metaphor 'plays down' life (*TM & S*, p. 289) but only because 'life' itself has somehow been diminished. It is the relative absence of the body in Leavis's metaphor which points to the loss of tradition while the emphasis on consciousness chimes with the notions of will and intent implicit in the promissory note and the contract.

This suspension between tradition and contract gives a more concrete sense of how desire is configured in Leavis's metaphor. Arising out of the loss of tradition, or the body, desire is desire for tradition or the body. The only form of 'embodiment' available, however, is the abstract, legal relation which desire resists. Desire survives in Leavis's vocabulary of 'force', which can thus be viewed as a protest against the confinements of modernity, one of which is the atomistic individual, necessitated by the contractual relation, yet which is precisely Leavis's metaphor for society itself. It is this atomistic character of the individual that Leavis is trying to break away from in his notion of collaborative criticism.

## LITERATURE AND SOCIETY: REPRESENTATION, EXPRESSION AND ENACTMENT

Leavis discusses society in terms of consciousness and health, which encourages the reader to view it less as a complex structure than as a well balanced individual. Leavis deploys this vocabulary to show how the different levels of society were integrated in the past. This is in contrast to the present, 1932, when society is divided, a division accentuated by the Marxist emphasis on class. Leavis's solution to this condition is to argue for 'a point of view above classes' (*MCC*, p. 35) represented particularly by literature. The relation between literature and society thus seems to be twofold. In earlier societies, such as Shakespeare's England (*UWKB*, p. 40) literature is integrated into the social formation, while in modern Britain it is a means of healing divisions within society. What is noticeable about these formulations is that the position of literature varies according to the state of society which would suggest, *contra* Leavis, that, at some level, society does have a determining role in respect of literature.

Further, the very existence of literature in Shakespeare's England presents problems for the idea of the organic community. That is to say, in Leavis's most sustained presentation of this notion, through the work of Sturt, literature has no place. In the organic community of Elizabethan England, however, the opposite is the case, literature *is* a central part of the culture. The conflicting claims concerning the relation between literature and the organic community are matched by the different dates Leavis attributes to the latter's demise. The organic community first disappears between the seventeenth and eighteenth centuries, between, that is, Bunyan and Defoe, then it is Wordsworth's death which signals that 'the traditional culture of the people was no longer there'.[123] Finally, the writings of Sturt are enlisted to show that the organic community vanished between the end of the nineteenth and beginning of the twentieth centuries.

This has implications for Leavis's discussion of the place of literature in the organic community. Its function there is to be representative. Leavis deploys the notion of literature's representativeness against what he considers to be the reductions of Marxist analysis. An example of this can be found in his essay 'Bunyan Through Modern Eyes'[124] which is, in part, directed against Jack Lindsay's Marxist study, *John Bunyan: Maker of Myths*.[125]

Leavis criticises Lindsay's study because, he believes, it reduces Bunyan's '"religious pre-occupations" ..... to explanations in terms of class relations and methods of production' (*BTME*, p. 208). This omits, for Leavis, Bunyan's qualities of 'vividness', 'vigour' and 'vitality' (pp. 206–7). *The Pilgrim's Progress* is 'the expression', not of 'class relations and methods of production' but of 'a vigorous, humane culture ..... an art of social living with its mature habits of valuation' (p. 208). Bunyan's prose was continuous with the 'free idiomatic range and vividness [that he used] in preaching, [with] the language he spoke with jailers and fellow prisoners, [and] with wife and children and friends at home'[126] and it is this 'representativeness' which gives *The Pilgrim's Progress* 'the vitality and significance of major art' (*PP*, pp. 34, 33).

'Representativeness' is, however, a problematic term because it entails a certain amount of generalisation. Representativeness is thus potentially inimical to that sense of the concrete and the particular which, for Leavis, marks off the literary from other kinds of discourse. What the representativeness of *The Pilgrim's Progress* excludes is, according to Leavis, Puritan theology. This seems paradoxical but Leavis negotiates the paradox by distinguishing between religion and theology (*PP*, p. 38). The 'paradoxical truth,' he claims, 'is that one's sense of a religious depth in the book prevails with such potency that particular theological intentions ... don't get much recognition for what they doctrinally are or, if noticed and judged to be incongruous with this basic response, don't really tell' (p. 38). Similarly, 'the creative power' of *The Pilgrim's Progress* is 'so compelling' as to render the reader 'virtually unconscious of the particular theology' (p. 37). Both these remarks are interesting in the light of Leavis's view that reading should aim at full conscious recognition of a text since they argue for a kind of unconsciousness of disruptive elements within it. Whatever threatens a coherent reading of the work should be seen as irrelevant, for it has no bearing on what constitutes the work's greatness.

Representativeness, then, entails a repression and in this it has affinities with expression. Literature expresses society in a concentrated form. Thus the style of *The Pilgrim's Progress* 'concentrat[es] the life of popular idiom, is the expression of popular habit – the expression of a vigorous, humane culture' (*BTME*, p. 208). This process elides the relations between the different elements which constitute society and in this it is akin to condensation in the dream work which dispenses with the grammar that spatialises and sustains the dream thoughts in their difference. This similarity suggests that the 'finer consciousness' represented by literature is subject to unconscious processes. Once this is conceded then the text can no longer be regarded as self-evident, as something to be recognised rather than interpreted.

Representation and expression point to an unconscious dimension of the relation between literature and society, hence the relation between the two is no longer as transparent as Leavis suggests. In fact it seems to approximate to that between the conscious and the unconscious, for literature is a 'finer consciousness' in comparison to that found in other areas of the social formation. This would point to a psychological model of the relation between literature and society rather than an historical one.

Leavis thus differentiates himself from the Marxists but at the cost of society disappearing from his argument. Yet, ironically, this same argument restores the sense of society, since it has some affinities with Lukács' account of this problem. First, the terms 'immediacy',[127] 'concrete',[128] 'sensuous',[129] 'organic',[130] 'maturity'[131] and 'life'[132] recur frequently in the criticism of both Leavis and Lukács; moreover, they are used in similar ways. Second, both thinkers believe that the best art has a profoundly impersonal character.[133] Third, each argues that art has an essential ethical component.[134] Fourth, each stresses the importance of tradition[135] and, finally, both Leavis and Lukács value art which is representative, that is, an art which, in Lukács' words, presents 'life' as 'structured and ordered more richly and strictly than ordinary life experience'.[136] Leavis detects this quality in *The Pilgrim's Progress* which, he claims, gives a 'sense ... of there being, in the order of reality in which this history is enacted, a dimension over and above those of the common sense world' (*PP*, p. 44).

Of course, there are also profound differences between the two thinkers, what Lukács ultimately means by a representative art is a work which reveals the underlying patterns of contradiction in the social order. It is the job of criticism to comprehend these patterns, which are 'the necessary developmental tendencies of the epoch' and to 'struggle for their realization'.[137] Lukács, in other words, conceives of art in terms of class struggle. Leavis, by contrast, sees the representativeness of art in terms of its ability to portray 'life' which 'can't be convincingly imagined in terms of a final cause vindicated in an achieved ultimate good, for livingness is creativity and creativity manifests itself in emerging newness'.[138] The vagueness of this phrasing should not deter the reader from the import of the remark, which is that Leavis sees art as open ended unlike Lukács who views it in terms of the transcendent signified of the class struggle. This is not to say that one type of criticism is superior to the other, rather that there is more to Leavis's work than an 'effort [] at closure and composure'.[139]

Despite the fact that Leavis and Lukács mean different things by representativeness, they are both agreed that the term implies a certain focusing on the most typical features of the social order. As noted above, this can mean eclipsing others. However, in general terms a representative work implies that society is transparent, that what is hidden can eventually be brought to view. This sense of representative is complemented by Leavis's claim that *The Pilgrim's Progress* is an 'expression' (*BTME*, p. 208) of its society. Obviously there

are differences between the two terms. In general, representativeness
connotates an 'objective' view of society whereas expression
connotates the subjective impressions of its inhabitants. However,
what both terms have in common is the assumption that the invisible
can be made visible.

The context in which Leavis uses them suggests that the nature of
society is made manifest through literature. Hence *The Pilgrim's
Progress* 'bring[s] home' to the reader that 'there is behind the literature
a social culture and an art of living' (*L & S*, p. 190). It is through
literature, in fact, that the *essential* nature of society is revealed.

> If, for instance, we want to go further than the mere constatation
> that a century and a half ago the family counted for much more than
> it does now, if we want some notion of the difference involved in
> day to day living – in the sense of life and its dimension and in its
> emotional and moral accenting ... we may profitably start trying
> to form it from the novels of Jane Austen. But only if we are capable
> of appreciating shade, tone, implication and essential structure.
> (*S & L*, p. 203)

Leavis differs from his Marxist contemporaries by claiming that
literature actively gives an insight into the nature of society whereas
they would claim that it passively reflects it. But, again, this difference
is more apparent than real for, in both cases, what is distinctively
literary threatens to disappear. That is to say, in both Leavisian and
Marxist criticism literature appears to be consumed in the act of
delivering 'knowledge' of society. If this is the case then Leavis's
position comes perilously close to that of the Marxists from whom
he is trying to distance himself. This, however, should not be surprising
when it is remembered that Leavis himself has diagnosed the problem
of the age as the dissolution of boundaries.

If there is a convergence between Leavis and Marxism then how
does he avoid the charge of reduction which he levels at the Marxists?
The answer seems to rest on Leavis's conception of language as

> more than such phrases as 'means of expression' or 'instrument of
> communication' [would] suggest; it is a vehicle of collective wisdom
> and basic assumptions, a currency of criteria and valuations col-
> laboratively determined; ... entail[ing] on the user a large measure
> of accepting participation in the culture of which it is the active living
> presence. (*PP*, p. 41)

Literature is irreducible because language itself is irreducible. The problem then becomes how to distinguish literary from other sorts of language; and it is imperative that Leavis should do so since otherwise his argument against the Marxists, which rests on the autonomy of literature, is in danger of collapsing.

What makes his case problematic is the ambiguity surrounding the term 'expression'. It seems to have two meanings, one in relation to language, the other in relation to literature. To view language in terms of expression is reductive since this gives no sense of the 'wisdom, 'values' or 'assumptions' which give a culture its resonance, and yet literature as 'the most complete use of language' (*TM & S*, p. 287) is highly valued precisely because it *is* the expression of a culture. Expression is thus, simultaneously, the lowest and highest form of language, suggesting that language is *nothing but* expression. The idea of language as being more than a 'means of expression' is not borne out by literature which appears to be only a 'means of expression'. Far from being 'something more' than a 'means of expression' literature seems to be *nothing* more than that. Consequently, it cannot have that independence which Leavis claims for it and which he uses to distinguish his position from that of the Marxists.

The centrality which Leavis accords the notion of literature as expression is at odds with his repeated description of it as a form of enactment of 'exploratory creation'.[140] Literature, he writes, is 'not … a medium in which to put "previously definite" ideas but [one of] exploratory creation' (*T & M*, p. 130). This seems to flatly contradict the idea of expression which does imply the presentation, in a more or less faithful manner, of that which already exists. Expression is therefore more 'a matter of saying' than of 'being and enacting' (p. 130). This points to a temporal delay in expression which is absent from enactment, connotating, as it does, qualities of immediacy and simultaneity.

Although they differ from one another, Leavis uses the notions of expression and enactment to articulate literature's autonomy against the Marxist view of it as a symptom of the social formation. As has been seen, this does not work in the case of expression and nor does it in the case of enactment. The enactments of literature, described by Leavis as the process whereby 'the stuff of experience is presented to speak and act for itself' (*JA*, p. 110), resemble nothing so much as the spontaneously lived ideological experience. Ideology, in the words of Eagleton, 'is a matter of how reality "strikes" us in the form of apparently spontaneous experience'.[141] It is, he continues, a language which forgets the essentially contingent, accidental relations between itself and the world, and comes instead to mistake itself as having some kind of organic, inevitable bond with what it represents.[142]

Leavis's notion of literature as enactment thus seems to affirm the ideological experience not least because he has no conception of experience as ideological. Once more, Leavis's claim that literature is more than a reflection of society is called into question.

The logic of expression and enactment can be read in at least two ways. First, the notion of literature as an autonomous realm is severely compromised by expression and enactment which reproduce and reinforce the social structure. Literature disappears into society, its concerns indistinguishable from those of the social function of which it is a part. But, second, if literature vanishes into society so, it could be argued, does society vanish into literature, and the correlation between the organic community and the literary work is a relevant consideration here. Society is 'textualised' through the *literary* mechanisms of expression and enactment. Moreover, Leavis claims that unless society is approached *as literature*, 'the thinking that attends social and political studies will not have the edge and force it should' (*L & S*, p. 194). As literature, society takes on a novelistic structure, that is, it is 'a closely organized whole'[143] whose chief characteristic is transparency, hence reading society is like reading literature; its truth is 'obvious' and 'compels itself' (p. 189) on the reader. This again draws attention to the conservative character of reading. As a recognition of the obvious it discounts what is not obvious or self-evidently there and, in terms of society, this means an alternative view of the social formation and how it could develop.

The fact that Leavis insists on the obvious truth of a work is, of course, a sign that this truth is far from obvious. Leavis himself acknowledges this when he writes that, though 'this truth compels itself, others seem to miss it' (*L & S*, p. 189). Thus, if literature is not self-evidently there then neither, by extension, is society. Both are in excess of the obvious and this undermines the implied project of reading, which is to ratify what is already in place, namely the hierarchial organisations of both literature and society.

The continuity between literary and social structure can, however, be read in another way, namely as drawing attention to the constructed nature of social reality. If Leavis conceives of society in terms of novelistic structure then it is, as it were, 'fictionalised', drained of the arresting force of the 'real'. As fiction, it demands a special kind of attention, which is for Leavis a focusing of the relation between the part and the whole, on how something is put together and this inevitably raises the possibility that it could be arranged differently.

Expression and enactment do not articulate a relation between literature and society so much as problematise the two terms. There is no clear relation between them, suggesting that any configuration is only of a provisional or strategic nature. This seems to provide the basis for a more democratic criticism than the one explicitly described by Leavis: 'a critical judgement has the form "This is so, isn't it?" [but] though my judgement asks to be confirmed … the response I expect at last will be of the form "Yes, but –" (*VC*, p. 277). There is, without doubt, a dialogic dimension to this which has not been sufficiently emphasised but the accent falls on agreement not disagreement – as is to be expected for Leavis always considers the significance of any given work to be 'obvious'. It would seem, then, that the radical potential of Leavis's criticism comes from attending to how his key terms operate in specific contexts and in this the reader is being guided by Leavis himself who notes that 'one must rely on the context to define key words' (*TL & O*, p. 34).

This attentiveness itself is also an attempt to act on Leavis's advice to be more conscious even if what is revealed are aspects of Leavis's work of which he himself was not conscious. This is something he perhaps anticipated for, despite his endeavour to be fully conscious, he was aware that 'consciousness can't eliminate the unconscious' (*TM & S*, p. 295). Such a remark legitimises the effort to draw out and develop the images, relations and logic in which he couches his arguments, for these can then lead to a reassessment of those arguments, particularly ones concerning the relation of literature and society.

This seems a pertinent issue now when the specificity of literature is ignored as in the following remark by Antony Easthope: 'Both literary and popular cultural texts operate through a system of signs … so both can be analysed in common terms.'[144] This is true but only at a basic level. It evades questions of aesthetics and ethics which Leavis confronted and which cannot be summarised so patly. Despite Leavis's claim that he has 'little use' for the word '[a]esthetic'[145] it is nevertheless the case that ethics and aesthetics are deeply entwined in his work. Hence Leavis's declaration that 'works of art *act* their moral judgement' (*JAP*, p. 118). Both converge on language. Aesthetics is a matter of how the values, distinctions, potentialities and

recognitions present in the literary tradition – which 'preserves the
full range of the English language' (*TL & O*, p. 52) – are realised and
developed through the qualities of sensuous apprehension, significant
relatedness and so forth. The ethical dimension of literature 'entail[s]
the full and firm recognition that words "mean" because individual
human being have meant the meaning' (*TL & O*, p. 58). This
foregrounds the question of responsibility in using words; a
responsibility that is all the more difficult to assume because, as
Leavis points out, 'intentions in art are nothing except as realized'.[146]
There is a difference, he argues, between 'that which has been willed
and put there ... and that which grows from a deep centre of life' (*HJ &
TFOC*, p. 225).

The word 'life' is crucial to what Leavis means by ethics. The ethical
nature of literature does not reside in 'subscribing to and applying
some ethical theory or scheme' (*VC*, p. 280) but in generating a sense
of 'a manifest potency of life' (*TL & O*, p. 49). Leavis admits to the
vagueness of such formulations[147] but claims that 'what is
inexpressible in terms of logic and clarity, the unstatable, must not
be excluded from thought' (p. 43). Thus, although the word 'life'
cannot, in any significant sense, be formulated abstractly; 'it is "there"
... in individual lives, it *is* there and its *being* there marks them live'
(p. 43). It is important to insist on the transcendence of life since, for
Leavis, 'the malady of technologico-industrial civilisation' (*TM & S*,
p. 289) lies in its inability to recognise this fact. Life as 'a necessary
word' (p. 289) challenges the 'clichés' and 'blank incuria' of this
civilisation (*EU & C*, p. 103). 'Significant art', Leavis adds in another
context, 'challenges us in the most disturbing and inescapable way
to a radical pondering, a new profound realization, of the grounds
of our most important determinations and choices' (*VC*, p. 281),
making clear, once again, the ethical force of a work depends upon
its aesthetic qualities.

The ethical nature of Leavis's criticism is surely relevant given the
revival of interest in this subject.[148] His specific contribution lies in
how ethics is related to aesthetics in the English tradition. His notion
of 'life' as a transcendent force is consistent with his view of literature
as 'a point of view above classes' and while these views may be
sociologically naive they nevertheless offer positions from which, at
least in principle, society can be viewed as a whole. The idea of
wholeness is important because it is inclusive and the value of
inclusion needs to be emphasised in a society such as ours which
marginalises and even criminalises those who do not conform 'to the

schema which it has fabricated'.[149] To discount Leavis on the basis of a petrified caricature of his work is to deprive ourselves of a nuanced vocabulary of responsibility, value and continuity, terms which, some would argue, post-structuralism has already done much to undermine.[150]

However, Leavis's contribution to a consideration of these questions cannot be truly assessed until it is clear how far the unconscious aspects of his criticism are complicit with the social order he criticises. Such an exercise is valuable not just because it directs attention specifically to those aspects of his work which do offer alternatives to the existing system but also to how all criticism which deems itself oppositional may in fact underpin the social formation, including certain brands of post-structuralism which either refer to Leavis dismissively or else pass over him in contemptuous silence. If they are indeed complicitous with the existing order then their repression of Leavis might be part of that complicity, not, of course, at the level of intention, but at the deeper one of cultural logic.

## LITERATURE AND SOCIETY: LEAVIS AND BATESON

It should be clear from the previous discussion that Leavis does not dwell on the relation between literature and society. For him, the nature of this relation, 'expression' or 'representativeness', is as obvious as the meaning of a literary work. Leavis's unwillingness to enquire more deeply into it is exemplified in his dispute with F.W. Bateson about four lines from Marvell's 'A Dialogue Between the Soul and the Body'. Essentially the disagreement is over whether the poem can be understood independently of the social context in which it was produced. Bateson's argument is that 'a work of literature cannot be properly understood or appreciated except in terms of the social context in which it originated'.[151] Leavis's argument is that it is impossible 'to arrive at this final inclusive context, the establishment of which puts the poem back in "its original historical setting"' (*RC*, p. 196). Although Leavis is quite right to point out that this context can never be reconstructed in its totality, this is not the same as saying that what is known of a particular period has no explanatory value at all.

But in any case, Leavis seems to contradict himself since he has no difficulty in conceiving of the context that produced *The Pilgrim's*

*Progress*. His confidence in this matter is evident in such pronouncements as his remark that 'the place of religion in the culture is obvious enough' (*BTME*, p. 207). Also, he has no trouble in distinguishing between the reader's *idea* of seventeenth-century puritanism and its reality: 'Puritanism considered in the context of English life from which in the concrete it was inseparable looks very different from an abstracted Puritanism, in our sense of which an account of its theological characteristics predominates' (*PP*, p. 38). Leavis then goes on to describe that 'reality' (pp. 38–9). Thus, contrary to what he asserts against Bateson, Leavis does believe that 'the social context' of a work can be articulated. The literary work expresses that context and is itself an effect of it: 'There would have been … no Bunyan if … there had not been living in the daily life of the people a positive culture' (*BTME*, p. 208). The inseparability of a work from its context is a theme that recurs throughout Leavis's writing. '[A] real literary interest, he observes, is an interest in [wo]man, society and civilization, and its boundaries cannot be drawn' (*S & L*, p. 200).

Such a remark would suggest that Leavis's position is similar to Bateson's and yet this is clearly not the case. The difference between them can be expressed by saying that Bateson wants to explain Marvell's poem whereas Leavis wants to evaluate it and this evaluation comes out of 'one's experience' (*RC*, p. 198).

> One judges a poem by Marvell not by persuading a hypothetical seventeenth-century 'context', or any 'social context' to take the responsibility, but, as one alone can, out of one's personal living. (*RC*, p. 198)

Hence Leavis has grave misgivings about '[t]he accumulation of scholarship … about and around the great things of literature' since these may prove 'the reverse of an aid and an encouragement to humane education'.[152]

Thus the apparent contradiction over the question of context seems to be resolved: Leavis is concerned with value judgements, Bateson with gathering facts. The former is to do with 'inwardness' (*S & L*, p. 200) the latter with 'external information' (p. 203). But, of course, these distinctions cannot be maintained. Literature cannot be understood as a process of valuation unless it values *something*. Leavis's contention, noted earlier, that the novels of Jane Austen make the reader feel, through a process of 'emotional and moral accenting' the force of 'the mere constatation that a century and a half ago the family counted for much more than it does now' (*S & L*, p. 203) may well be true but part of what the reader understands by this historical 'family' are its differences from the modern one. Hence 'external' features such as the patriarchal structure of the family, the position of women, the rules of social engagement, dress, codes of behaviour and leisure pursuits are important. Indeed, Leavis admits as much when he writes: 'The extra-literary knowledge the student whose main study is English Literature acquires ... will be part of a human meaning.'[153] Context, it would seem, is important. Why else would Leavis feel it necessary to give historical information in his account of *The Pilgrim's Progress* (*PP*, p. 39)? There is, in short, no evaluation that it is not context bound. In Leavis's own words, 'nothing important can really be said simply ... it takes a context to do that' (*TW & C*, p. 122).

What these remarks show is that there can be no clear demarcation between a work and its social context or, in respect of judgement, between social context and 'one's experience'. The notion of context blurs the boundaries between the work and the society in which it was produced. Consequently, Leavis cannot argue, *contra* Bateson that the poem 'is a determinate thing; it is there' (*RC*, p. 197). Leavis needs to assert this if he is to prevent literature in general, and the poem in particular, from collapsing back into the social context. However, elsewhere in his writings, Leavis shows that the poem is not 'there' in the sense that it exists prior to criticism. On the contrary, the poem 'is there *for* discussion only in so far as the discussers have each for himself recreated it ... The discussion in fact, is an effort to establish the poem' (*VC*, p. 278). If the poem is something to be created then Leavis cannot oppose it to Bateson's notion of a social context. It is rather the case that this social context is one of the elements of the discussion that establishes the poem. Incidentally, the idea that the poem is not already 'there' but has to be created contradicts Leavis's claim that the peculiar significance of a work is 'apparent at once without analysis (*RC*, p. 193). Reading is less a matter of recognition than of production, an idea implicit in the image of the labourer/worker at the heart of Leavis's criticism.

It is apparent, then, that Leavis's remarks on the relation between literature and society, between a work and its context are at best confused and at worst contradictory. On the one hand he claims that a work and its context are separate, on the other that they continuous. These mutually exclusive assertions are present in Leavis's dispute with Bateson. At the level of explicit statement, Leavis argues that the

extract from Marvell is not context-dependent but the logic of his
argument calls this into question. At this point it is necessary to recall
that Leavis believes literature is associated with 'inwardness' whereas
the details of social context are mere 'external' information. This
division corresponds to that found in *Culture and Environment* between
consciousness and the body. Hence it may be argued that Leavis, by
insisting on the incommensurability between a poem and its social
context, is reproducing that very division between consciousness
and the body which his view of literature and literary criticism is
intended to overcome.

This division between internal and external parallels that between
the soul and the body in Marvell's poem. Leavis's dispute with
Bateson is over how to understand the following lines:

> O who shall from this Dungeon, raise
> A soul inslav'd so many wayes?
> With bolts of Bones, that fetter'd stands
> In Feet, and manacled in Hands.

Bateson claims that they are best understood in terms of the Emblem
Books of the early seventeenth century. Their influence, according to
Bateson, was to make Marvell write in a type of 'picture language'
which enabled the reader to visualise clearly what is being described.
Leavis's response is to ask, 'Can he [Bateson] suggest what picture
*could* be drawn of the soul "inslav'd" in the dungeon of the body in
*any* of the "many ways" against which it protests?' (*RC*, p. 188). His
argument is that the poem 'defies visualization' (p. 188). Reading is
not about picturing what is described but about being attentive to the
poem's 'theme', namely the '*difficulty* of the distinction' (p. 191)
between soul and body, a distinction Bateson believes the
poem reinforces.

What is important is that the position of each has been reversed.
In arguing that soul and body are not easily distinguishable Leavis
can be read, because of the association of soul with 'inwardness' and
the body with what is 'external', as implying that a poem and its
context are also not so easily distinguishable. By the same logic,
Bateson, whose claim is that a poem only makes sense within its
social context, is driven to mean the opposite by his insistence on the
separability of the soul and the body. In short, the logic of the
terminology of the dispute seems to press for a contrary meaning to
the one which constitutes the explicit ground of disagreement.

Leavis's claim that soul and body are hard to separate in Marvell's poem is symptomatic of his desire to escape the constraints of binary thought – 'the Cartesian Newtonian dualism must be exorcised from the Western mind' (*TL & O*, p. 31). This is because the most important kind of thought, 'involv[ing] a consciousness of one's full human responsibility, purpose, and the whole range of human valuations ... def[ies] the rationality of either/or' (pp. 21, 37). Thus, in his criticism, Leavis resists the idea that a work has a single meaning. For example, he takes issue with M.R. Ridley, the editor of the Arden edition of *Antony and Cleopatra*, over the meaning of the image of 'the swan's down feather' in relation to Octavia (III. ii). Ridley notes that the image is 'not clear' and Leavis's retort is as follows

'It is not clear'. It ought to be clear; that is the implication. The implied criterion, 'clarity' entails an 'either/or': does the image mean *this* or *that*. The reductive absurdity of the conception of language behind the criterion thus brought up is surely plain ... the image has *both* meanings. (*J & A*, p. 102)

If meaning is undecidable at the local level then the totality of the work itself cannot be readily summarised. Thus Leavis notes of his criticism of D.H. Lawrence's *The Rainbow*: 'I have been exemplifying how impossible it is, in an attempted expository treatment of Lawrence's thought, to achieve an expository ordering' (*TW & C*, p. 131) though it should be noted that it is precisely this inability to totalise the work that 'bear[s] involuntary testimony to [its] wholeness [and] organic unity' (p. 131). That the ultimately incomplete nature of a response should not rule out the wholeness of that which is responded to is not, it will be remembered, an argument that Leavis grants to Bateson over the matter of social context. Leavis discounts social context precisely because it can never be reconstituted in its entirety.

It is tempting to see the anti-dualistic stance of Leavis's thought as a prelude to deconstruction. For instance, the relation between a poem (inwardness) and its context (external) may have some bearing on the problematic nature of meaning as understood by Derrida: 'The presumed interiority of meaning is always worked upon by its own exteriority. It is always carried outside itself. It already differs (from itself) before any act of expression.'[154] Or again, Leavis's commitment to a type of thought which avoids 'either/or' is loosely suggestive of the deconstructive project, if it can be so termed, 'to

overturn the hierarchy ... of dual oppositions'.[155] That word 'loosely',
however, registers the enormous differences between Leavis's criticism
and Derrida's deconstruction. Derrida's concern with meaning is
expressed in the form of the following questions:

> What is 'meaning' what are its historical relationships to what is
> purportedly identified under the rubric 'voice' as a value of
> presence, presence of the object, presence of meaning to
> consciousness, self-presence in so called living speech and in self-
> consciousness?[156]

These questions problematise Leavis's basic notions of consciousness
and literature as a form of enactment by querying whether
consciousness can ever be completely present to itself and by
suggesting that immediacy, which is intrinsic to the concept of
enactment, is derived.

Furthermore the common goal of thinking beyond binary
oppositions is conceived differently by the two thinkers. For Leavis,
to be rid of an 'either/or' type of thought is to apprehend the plenitude
of meaning which characterises the organic unity of a work. For
Derrida, by contrast, the overturning of a binary opposition discloses
the radical instability of meaning, 'releas[ing]' a 'dissonance' and
'disorganizing' the order or system which it upheld.[157] More generally,
as Christopher Norris has pointed out, '[d]econstruction ... has to do
with strictly *transcendental* modes of reasoning, those which raise
first order questions about the limits and conditions of knowledge in
general'[158] and this is very different from Leavis who considers
himself 'an anti-philosopher' (*TW & C*, p. 34), someone whose 'whole
effort was to work in terms of concrete judgements and particular
analyses' (*C & P*, p. 215), someone who was not concerned, in other
words, with the epistemological foundation of philosophy.[159] The
differences between Leavis's criticism and Derrida's deconstruction
should not, however, be regarded as a reason for discounting the
possibility of any dialogue between them. That would be to assert the
existence of a barrier between literary criticism and philosophy which
Derrida's own work has challenged.

Leavis's reading of 'The Dialogue Between the Soul and the Body'
shows that it questions '"conventional concepts" and current habits
of mind' (*RC*, p. 188). If this is the case then it follows that Leavis's
view of literature as expressive or representative of its society is in
need of some modification. The ideas of expression or representa-

tiveness imply an acceptance of society as it is. They are essentially conservative, promoting the organic unity of society through the organic unity of the literary work. Any division which threatens the unity in society would also threaten the unity of the literary text, whose characteristic wholeness is a *sine qua non* of Leavis's criticism. The text cannot, in other words, express division within society without violating its own unity. It could be argued that the text avoids this problem by performing the ideological operation of resolving, at an imaginary level, the real contradictions of the social formation. This, however, means that the text exceeds its task of expressing or representing society.

But this is precisely the point: literature does exceed Leavis's description of its relation to society, and there are two ways of reading that excess. The first is the one just given, literature as resolving contradictions. The second is more progressive since it views literature as challenging and interrogating the conventions and representations of society. At this point it is important to distinguish between a conception of the text that emphasises its difference from itself and one which emphasises it as an intentional, though not necessarily self-coincident structure. The former may broadly be termed a post-structuralist stance, the latter a 'traditionalist' one. Both, in this context, view the text as oppositional to society. The difference is that in the post-structuralist conception this opposition is a consequence of the text's rhetoric, logic and imagery compelling the writer to say something other than what he or she means, whereas in the traditionalist conception it is assumed, by and large, that the writer is oppositional because he or she intends to be so – though it does not follow from this that the notion of intention is either measurable or conclusive.

The consequence of these two positions is that, for post-structuralism, opposition is accidental and for 'traditional' criticism it is intentional. Obviously this is a crude characterisation but it is at least consistent with the post-structuralist claim that the subject is an effect of language. The question then becomes not which kind of opposition is more effective but how the claims of both post-structuralist and traditional criticism on this matter can be synthesised.

## RESTRAINT, EXCESS, METAPHOR AND 'LIFE'

It was observed at the beginning of the previous section that Leavis had little to say about the relation between literature and society. This was illustrated in his dispute with Bateson where he focused on literature rather than on the relation between literature and society. However, Leavis's detailed reading of Marvell's poem showed that the stated opposition between the poem and its context, and, therefore, by implication between literature and society, was, in fact, untenable. Furthermore, it showed that literature was in excess of representativeness and expression, terms which Leavis had elsewhere used to describe its relation to society. It would seem, then, that Leavis's description of the relation between literature and society is characterised by restraint and excess. Restraint because he does not analyse this relation and excess because specific readings surpass his general view of it.

The conjunction of restraint and excess should, by now, be a familiar feature of Leavis's work. It arises out of a need to respond to the loss of boundaries and dividing lines which Leavis identifies with the advent of modernity. The blurring of distinctions leads to a condition of flux which Leavis tries to counteract by an intensification and heightening of consciousness evident in the prominence Leavis gives to such terms as 'duty', 'vigilant' and 'scrupulous' (*UWKB*, pp. 42–3). Criticism, writes Leavis, is 'the duty ... of using words precisely' (p. 42) in contrast to what he considers is their imprecise use in advertising, journalism and popular fiction. This concern for exactitude is intended to correct the excess produced by the dissolution of boundaries. But if Leavis conceives of modernity in terms of excess it is also the case that he sees it as a form of reductionism – tradition to technique – that needs to be countered by the 'something more' of literature.

Arguably, metaphor is one of the chief characteristics of the literary but it is the 'something more' of metaphor which Leavis seeks to control. Metaphor 'plays down ... life' (*TM & S*, p. 289) and is always 'susceptible of more than one translation'.[160] 'Life' is a key term in Leavis's criticism. It is, he observes, 'a large word' and to 'try and define it would be futile' (*VC*, p. 281). Given that life, like metaphor, transcends the precise use of words it is difficult to see why Leavis opposes them. His argument would be that 'one can point to life as concretely "there"' (*TL & O*, p. 42) either in a person or in a work of literature whereas metaphor, being more diffuse cannot be so readily circumscribed. In addition, the fact that metaphor is 'susceptible of more than one translation' means that it does not have that immediacy which is characteristic of life.

However, these distinctions will not hold. In the first place the notion of 'there' lacks 'life' to the extent that it is constructed not given, '[y]ou cannot point to the poem; it is "there" only in the re-creative response of individual minds to the black marks on the page' (*TC*, p. 62). In the second place the use of 'translation' in relation to metaphor draws attention to its linguistic status, as if language were somehow opposed to life but, as Leavis himself states, '[t]he nature of livingness in human life is manifest in language' (*TL & O*, p. 74). Thus despite the similarity between life and metaphor, in terms of their offering 'something more', Leavis insists on their difference though without being able to articulate what this difference is.

Leavis continues to be troubled by the instrinsic plurality of metaphor. It is a reminder of the fact that no matter how scrupulous the critic is in the use of the words there is always going to be an element of imprecision suggestive of other meanings and other uses. As such metaphor, with its excess and multiplicity, is the 'other' of consciousness identified as vigilance, exactitude and precision. Paradoxically, these very qualities are themselves given metaphoric expression in the form of the gold standard which is the prop of Leavis's argument in 'Mass Civilisation and Minority Culture'. The plurality of meaning is thus understood as a form of inflation. Leavis located the source of this inflation in the Bloomsbury group who, he considered, substituted the 'currency' of 'social personal values for the relevant ones'[161] thus enacting 'a stultifying confusion of values' (*KS & CV*, p. 195). Leavis's critique of Bloomsbury and the language in which it was couched touch on the sterling crisis of 1931 and Britain's consequent abandonment of the gold standard. His metaphor, in short, is rooted in history, and it is perhaps as 'history' that metaphor is ultimately opposed to 'life'. Leavis, it would seem, is suspicious of metaphor because it is life *as history* and that is one 'incorporation', or 'embodiment' or 'thereness' of life to which he cannot admit.

Leavis avoids the plurality of meaning entailed by metaphor through an appeal to the 'obvious'. In his dispute with Bateson, Leavis claims that the 'felicity' of Marvell's words 'is surely apparent at once, without analysis' (*RC*, p. 193). At a more general level, Leavis's criticism is populated with such phrases as 'there is hardly any need to illustrate'', 'need it be said?' (*RFC*, p. 50) and 'hardly needs elaborating' (*MCC*, p. 34). It will be noted that two of these are taken from one page and that in itself should give some indication of the frequency with which these sorts of expression recur in Leavis's writing. But this appeal to the obvious exists in some tension with

Leavis's advocacy of heightened consciousness, scrupulousness, vigilance and precision: the obvious does not need the kind of detailed scrutiny implied by these terms. What this suggests is that the 'obvious' is very far from obvious. Leavis himself asserts that 'the difficulty' of criticism lies 'in deciding what kind of thing it is one has before one' (*L & S*, p. 187) and the 'obvious' is rendered even less 'obvious' when it is recalled that the work is not simply there 'before one' but has to be *produced* through creative *collaboration*. Leavis cannot, then, appeal to the 'obvious' to check the plurality of meaning associated with metaphor. On the contrary, the appeal to the 'obvious' merely demonstrates its problematic nature thereby showing that it too, like metaphor, is potentially polysemous.

Criticism, conceived as a 'discipline for relevance in dealing with created works' (*RC*, p. 200) instead of correcting the excess produced by the blurring of boundaries merely generates its own. Hence criticism is part of the condition it is intended to cure. This excess, however, is intended to counter the limitations of mass civilisation. Thus both culture and civilisation are simultaneously conceived as limit and excess, smudging the dividing line that Leavis draws between them. The consequence of this is not so much inflation but conflation, a profound disorganisation of spatial relations. It is therefore not surprising that Leavis should prove so reticent on the question of the relation between literature and society – specifically a work and its context – since to do more than assert the independent existence of a work is to run the risk of discovering that it is not so easily separable from its context, thereby undermining its identity as a unique phenomenon.

## NEGATION AND THE BODY

Leavis's reluctance to explain the relationship between literature and society can be viewed as a kind of restraint, and this feature of his work is consistent with another which may be described as litotes. Litotes comes from the Greek *litós* meaning 'single', 'simple' or 'meagre'. This is frequently used to denote a negative statement expressing something positive, for example, 'not bad' meaning 'very good'. It is a trope found throughout Leavis's work. Standards 'can best [be] describe[d]', he writes, 'in this negative kind of way' (*SC*, p. 244). Writing about poetry, Leavis observes, 'I revert [ ] to antithesis by way of making my point clear' (*ROP*, p. 258). Not only are Leavis's central ideas concerning the nature of criticism conveyed, at least in part, by recourse to litotes but so too are his views on other critics and writers. Hence he notes of Wyndham Lewis that 'no-one could with less injustice be said to be destitute of humility' (*EWL & L*, p. 245).

Litotes is not equivalent to but it is logically consistent with Leavis's appeals to the 'obvious'. Both are symptomatic of an unwillingness to expand or elaborate a point or position. Together, they suggest that Leavis's literary judgements are, at least in part, characterised by a certain negativity. Freud notes that '[a] negative judgement is the intellectual substitute for repression'.[162] Freud is referring to judgements of outright rejection and these are certainly found in Leavis, for example in his views on journalism and popular fiction. These, it has been argued, display qualities that Leavis desires for criticism, thus illustrating the psychoanalytic commonplace that what is fiercely resisted is secretly desired. But Freud's remark may also have a limited applicability to the negative *form* in which Leavis presents his favourable judgements. This means that there would be an element of repression even where approval is most strong.

The question then arises as to what it is that is repressed. It has been shown, on the basis of previous discussions, that it is not possible to identify any specific desire, so it might be more useful to consider, in this context, the general character of desire. For Lacan, it is 'paradoxical, deviant, erratic, eccentric [and] scandalous'[163] while Lyotard notes that it 'does not speak' but 'does violence to the order of utterance'.[164] In short desire, like modernity, has little respect for boundaries and dividing lines.

If the disruption of unity is a mark of desire then its presence is very much a feature of Leavis's work. What he looks for in a work is a 'significant' or 'comprehensive "relatedness"' (*AK*, pp. 18, 32) a quality, in other words, of wholeness. Yet Leavis's criticism can also be said to violate this wholeness. His discussion of Marvell's poem shows an inability to distinguish between the parts, soul and body, with the result that there is no sense of that relatedness essential to a perception of the whole.

This is all the more significant given that Leavis wants to articulate a relation between soul and body in contrast to Bateson's presentation of them, in his reading of the poem, as an antithesis. Ultimately, the emphasis in Leavis's analysis of this poem falls more on the body than on the soul. This is evident first in his endorsement of 'concrete experience' compared to Bateson's 'picture language' (*RC*, p. 191) and second in the way he finds the sufferings of the soul realised in bodily terms but not the sufferings of the body realised in soul terms (pp. 191–2).

This filtering out of the soul, despite Leavis's claim that it is 'indistinguishable' (*RC*, p. 190) from the body parallels his filtering out the theology from *The Pilgrim's Progress.:* 'It is possible to read *The Pilgrim's Progress* without any thought of its theological intention' (*PP*, p. 33); 'through reading after reading, one remains virtually unconscious of the particular theology' (p. 37); and 'while the doctrinal pre-occupation … sharpened Bunyan's observation of character and gave vivacity to his analysis, what strikes one is the rendered observation, its life and truth and depth' (p. 42). What is immediately noticeable about these quotations is that they flatly contradict some of Leavis's most deeply held views about reading.

First, it is strange that Leavis can be 'virtually unconscious' of the theology of *The Pilgrim's Progress* when he continually advocates the importance of being fully conscious of what one reads. Second, the function of criticism is in part 'to determine what is actually *there* in the work of art' (*HJ & TFOC*, p. 225) and so it is difficult to see how he can read *The Pilgrim's Progress* 'without any thought of its theological intention'. Third, although Leavis regards the notion of intention as problematic, he nevertheless maintains 'that words "mean" because individual human beings have meant the meaning' (*TL & O*, p. 58) and so it is again surprising that so little thought can be given to Bunyan's 'intention'. Fourth, the very element which Leavis regards as so inconsequential to the text is nevertheless partly responsible for its vivacity, and, finally, Leavis's claim that literature cannot be used for 'evidence' (*S & L*, pp. 195, 198) appears to be contradicted, or at least problematised, by the suggestion that Bunyan gives an in-depth and truthful rendering of his society.

Important though these points are, the relevant one for present purposes is that Leavis's marginalisation of the theology of *The Pilgrim's Progress* is necessary to his claim that the text has a positive view of the body and its place in puritan culture, manifest in 'music, dancing and the social pleasures of the table' (*PP*, p. 38). It is a work, he writes, of 'the whole man' (p. 38). Leavis has to sideline puritan theology because it repudiates the body he values. Christian, talking of his 'carnal cogitations' remarks that they 'are my Grief'.[165] Prudence, his interlocutor at this point, talks of 'vanquish[ing]'[166] the carnal, showing that, in puritan theology, the promptings of the body are harmful to the soul and must be overcome. What Leavis does, then, is to write warmly of puritan culture as it appears in *The Pilgrim's*

*Progress* but at the expense of discounting the very thing that *makes* that culture puritan – the repression of the body. In this instance, reading is less a form of recognition than a negation. Yet, ironically, Leavis's reading of *The Pilgrim's Progress* in negating its theology repeats, in an inverted form, puritan culture's negation of the body.

'Negation,' writes Freud, 'is a way of taking cognizance of what is repressed' and, he continues, '[w]e can see in this how the intellectual function is separated from the affective process'.[167] A similar separation is discernible in Leavis's discussions of 'A Dialogue Between the Soul and the Body' and *The Pilgrim's Progress* though, of course, this depends on reading these discussions in a certain way. This separation belies one of the aims Leavis attributes to reading, namely the apprehension of unity, a unity located in the image of the body. In Leavis's readings of Marvell and Bunyan, however, the body appears less as an image of unity than as one term of the binary opposition between body and soul. This echoes the division between consciousness and the body which Leavis identified, in *Culture and Environment*, as part of the condition of the modern world. Consciousness thus has to be continually on the defensive against the appeal of popular culture with its promise of immediate gratification. But, as was argued in the previous section, this characteristic of modernity is prefigured in the organic community where there is a clear separation between the body and the mind. In using the model of the organic community as the basis of his criticism, therefore, Leavis would seem to be complicit with the forces of popular culture which he claims drive a wedge between consciousness and the body.

## THE BODY IN PIECES

Furthermore, the interaction between the reading body and the body of the text seems to generate a process of sensory dissociation. This is most evident in the split between the faculties of seeing and hearing. As recognition, Leavis understands reading in terms of seeing. The literary judgements of Edmund Gosse, for example, reveal an 'inability to see what is in front of him'.[168] And, though Leavis takes Bateson to task for assuming that the imagery in 'A Dialogue Between Soul and Body' can be visualised – '[o]f its very nature it eludes, defies and transcends visualization' (*RC*, p. 188) – he later chastises Bateson over a passage from Pope's *The Dunciad* charging that 'anyone who *reads* the passage can *see*' (*RC*, p. 194). Seeing is thus a complex term.

Elements of the poem cannot be visualised and yet the sense of the poem is something seen.

In addition to being 'seen', the text is also heard. Literature, it will be remembered, is a substitute for the speech of the organic community. Donne is praised precisely because he brings into poetry 'the living spoken language, the speaking voice, and the attendant sensitive command of rhythm, tone and inflection' (*TSE & EL*, p. 138), elements to which the critic must be attuned. Literature is thus both seen and heard but the two terms do not complement one another. Though literature, but particularly poetry, is presented as a voice, it is apprehended in terms of sight. In short, it is seen but not heard. Thus there is always a part of it which escapes the conscious attention of the critic, creating a residue which can function as that elusive 'something more'. By definition, this 'something more' belongs to the unconscious, which as Lacan notes *'speaks ... where it is least expected'*.[169] Poetry too 'speaks', indeed that is what is expected of it, but only to those who can see it and that is why it is never 'heard'.

The body, then, Leavis's favoured image of unity, is itself divided. Unity seems unattainable and Leavis himself seems to disregard the principle of it at crucial moments in his exposition of the art of criticism. The emphasis on literary criticism is on the local particulars of a poem or a novel, '[p]utting a finger on this and that in the text, and moving tactically from point to point'.[170] The result is that 'there is no need' (*MN*, p. 190) to make an assertion about the value of a whole work. Or, as Leavis writes in another context, the procedure of moving from part to part meant that 'there [was] hardly any need for the critical summing up; the case was made' (*TM & S*, p. 288).

If disorder, as Lacan and Lyotard suggest, is a sign of desire, then desire would seem to be present in Leavis's work through the decentred relation between criticism and its object, in criticism lending an eye rather than an ear to the voice(s) of the text. This has parallels with Lacan's account of how desire so conditions the structure of language that the subject can never be the source of meaning, rather, as Lacan puts it, 'I think where I am not, therefore I am where I do not think'.[171] In both cases, 'truth' comes from elsewhere. This reading of Leavis reverses the terms of Freud's argument. He claims that negative judgements allow the repressed idea into consciousness but not its accompanying affect.[172] In Leavis there is a strong sense of the affect but not of the idea. This difference can be accounted for by the fact that Freud's interest is in the *content* of negative judgements while the focus here is on the negative *form* of Leavis's judgements.

Again, what is at issue is not the identity of desire but rather how Leavis's writing stages the problem of desire in the modern world. As was argued earlier, desire is a problem because the body, suspended between production and consumption, is being constantly redefined in Britain from the 1930s onwards.

## SIGHTLINES: LEAVISIAN CRITICISM AND CONSUMERISM

A significant change in the 1930s is the growth of discourses of observation. The documentary film unit under John Grierson at the GPO aimed to bring to public attention previously 'invisible' areas of British life,[173] and the narrator of Christopher Isherwood's novel *Goodbye to Berlin*, declares, 'I am a camera.'[174] Time and motion studies are increasingly important in the sphere of production[175] while the dynamics of consumerism situate subjects as spectators of the world of commodities. Finally, looking and being looked at are brought together in the phenomenon of Mass Observation.[176] It may be no coincidence that arguably the most politically aware decade of the century also sees the institutionalisation of various practices of surveillance.[177]

Leavisian criticism is also part of the procedures and mechanisms of observation and, as such, it is related to both production and consumption. The former has already been discussed and it only remains to emphasise that criticism oversees the work with a view to it producing 'something more' to compensate for the loss of community. A consideration of the relation of criticism to consumption is important because it helps to illuminate the problem of desire. This has also been raised but needs further comment. Briefly, consumerism associates desire with looking. 'Modern Consumerism,' writes Robert Bocock, 'operates ... through the image, by attracting the eye.'[178] And, because looking is what characterises criticism's relation to the text and also because of the similarity, mentioned in the previous chapter, between the reader and the consumer, it is possible to claim that the relation between criticism and literature is like the relation between the consumer and the commodity; it is a relation, in short, of desire. One of the elements of consumption is imitation, the desire to be like someone else, to reduce the difference between self and other.[179] This too is apparent in criticism, specifically in Leavis's idea that criticism should be 'more than ordinar[ily] faithful[ ]' to the text, that it should 'recreat[e]' (*VC*, p. 278) it rather than assert its own distinctiveness by offering to explain it.

More generally, Leavis's account of literature as a substitute for the organic community is similar to the standard analysis of consumer society[180] which, incidentally, recalls Lacan's account of the relation between need, demand and desire discussed in the last chapter. This analysis states that 'real' needs are substituted for 'artificial' desires, and whereas 'real' needs are attached to and can be satisfied by 'real' objects neither of these conditions applies to 'artificial' desires. These are constantly stimulated by advertising and so can never be satisfied by any particular object. Thus they are always in excess of any particular expression of them, making them consistent with the nature of desire in Leavis's writing.

Consumerism and criticism converge on desire. Both the commodity and literature are presumed to satisfy desire but they only perpetuate it. They do so because, as substitutes, they can never fill the place of that which they have replaced and hence they are a mark of emptiness.[181] This confers a negative character on desire which chimes with the negative form of Leavis's judgements. Leavis's call for 'something more' to be provided by literature, opens an endless series of additions that exist in a paradoxical relationship with that part of his criticism which insists on control and precision; a juxtaposition that mirrors the nature of consumer society itself as at once 'scarcity and abundance'.[182]

On this analysis, Leavis's conception of reading seems to be thoroughly implicated in the logic of consumerism. This impression is confimed when that other element of Leavis's criticism is considered, namely reading as a form of seeing, a form of bringing into focus, through terms like 'clarity' and 'discrimination', what is there in the work. This suggests that reading is part of that operation of mass culture whereby 'visibility is thrust upon everything'.[183] This idea is also implicit in Leavis's view of mass civilisation as a process of 'standardisation' and 'levelling down'.

However, this emphasis on seeing in Leavis's criticism, which appears to be in accord with the consumerist display of commodities, exists in some tension with the driving force of desire that escapes expression and resists representation. This opens up the possibility of understanding desire in a more positive way. First, it is in conflict with the transparency and visibility of modern society and, as such, introduces notions of complexity, depth and obscurity. And second, the fact that desire is never manifest in concrete form means that it can be construed as a utopian impulse, propelled beyond the confines of the perpetual present.

Whether this understanding of desire can also be applied to consumer society is a moot point. Leavisian criticism makes possible this reading of desire because of its likeness and unlikeness to that society. One aspect of that unlikeness is a concern for the past, specifically how to bridge the gap between the past and the present. This is also a concern of early Freudian psychoanalysis[184] and, like psychoanalysis, Leavisian criticism aims to do this by the process of a 'full conscious recognition' (*VC*, p. 278) of the past, specifically in the form of how tradition is present in new works. What this very schematic parallel between Leavis's conception of criticism and the early Freud suggests is that criticism, though it may be an instance of the working of desire in consumer culture, also has the potential to be distanced from it partly because of its discourse of restraint and value, and partly because of the suggestive connections between the logic of that discourse and that of early psychoanalysis. It is therefore able to offer an understanding of desire in contrast to consumer society, which merely promotes and perpetuates it.

## PUBLIC AND PRIVATE: THE PROBLEM OF INWARDNESS

It has been argued that desire is a problem of the body being redefined in mid-century Britain. Suspended between production and consumption it is both visible and invisible in contrast to the increasing visibility of the body of the corporate state. The ambiguity surrounding the body is mirrored in the ambiguity of the 'body' of the literary text. This 'body' is at once 'obvious' and something of which the critic has to become fully conscious. It is therefore both 'there' and not 'there'. The redefinition of the body has implications for the relation between consciousness and the body, between, that is, what is internal and what is external. These changes must be considered in the context of the transformation of the public and private spheres, and the demarcation between these domains in the 1930s. This transformation, according to John Thompson, was due to 'the development of mass communication'.[185] His argument is that this rendered obsolete the old public–private dichotomy whereby what was public was 'open or available to the public' and what was private was 'hidden from view'.[186] From now on there was to be little distinction between – and in the context of this argument his terms are highly relevant – a 'visibl[e]' public sphere and an 'invisibl[e]'[187] private one. With the advent of the newsreel, the radio and mass circulation newspapers both public and private events could equally be brought before the 'public' gaze.

This trend was accentuated by the move to greater state intervention into areas normally considered outside its control, for example private economic activity and personal relations, a trend which was to reach its climax in the legislative programme of the Labour government of 1945.[188] The intrusion of the state was greatly resented in some quarters, particularly by the unemployed, who faced the humiliation of the means test men who had access to their homes and personal records. This led, according to Cross, to a highly protective attitude towards the home and the private sphere.[189] Thus at the very moment that the distinction between the public and the private begins to break down there is an insistence, in some quarters, on the separateness and integrity of the latter.

Such an insistence can be found in Leavis's work. First, he invests in the notion of an 'inner human nature' (*RC*, p. 52) which transcends class (*MCC*, p. 35). Second, literature is 'an intimate study of the complexities, potentialities and essential conditions of human nature' (*L & S*, p. 184). Third, Leavis conceives of reading as, in part, the creation of an inward space. The literary critic must have 'an inward acquaintance with the work (*S & L*, p. 195). A 'living critical inwardness with literature' (p. 200), he continues, is a mark of 'be[ing] able in the fullest sense, to read' (p. 203). And fourth, consistent with these ideas of an inner human nature and reading as a mode of inwardness with literature, is Leavis's claim that a judgement 'must be personal and sincere' (*VC*, p. 277). This investment in what is inward, personal and sincere helps to explain his dispute with Bateson over whether a poem is self-sufficient or needs to be seen in its context.

However, just as Leavis cannot maintain an absolute separation between a poem and its context so too do his notions of inwardness break down. His claim concerning an inner human nature hovers between an implied individual essence and a collective cultural experience. This is made plain by his footnoting of the phrase 'inner human nature', whose problematic status is already indicated by Leavis enclosing it in quotation marks. The footnote acknowledges Leavis's sense of the inadequacy of the phrase: 'Some readers, of course, will demand more at this point, appealing to the judgements of the experience of the race' (*RC*, p. 52). Thus an inner human nature is relativised in terms of national character. Leavis's assertion that literature is a study of human nature is immediately followed by the disclaimer that that 'is too large a proposition to take us anywhere' (*L & S*, p. 184) and he therefore contextualises it in terms of tradition which stresses 'the *social* aspect of creative achievement' (p. 185, italics added). He then goes on to argue that 'the literary critic's interest in literature leads to a new recognition of the essentially social nature of the individual' (p. 187). It seems that a concern with inner human nature inevitably leads to a consideration of its social determinations; what is inner is inscribed on society's surface. Or as Leavis puts it, 'You can't contemplate the nature of literature without enquiring some inhibition in respect of that antithesis "the individual and society"' (p. 185).

The same point can be made in regard to reading an 'inwardness with literature' (*S & L*, p. 200). This inwardness is a sensitivity to the 'sense of life and its dimensions ... its emotional and moral accenting [its] tone and essential structure' (p. 203). Inwardness is partly expressed through the metaphor of voice, 'accent[]' and 'tone'. The assumption is that what is inward can be externalised by the voice. This suggests that the true destiny of the inner lies on the outside and this undermines its status as a privileged category in Leavis's aesthetic. Moreover – and somewhat ironically – Leavis's assumption of a connection between inner thought and vocal expression belongs at the heart of the philosophical tradition from which he is trying to distance himself. According to Derrida this tradition devalues writing as only an 'imitation ... of the living voice or present *logos*'.[190] Although Leavis would not subscribe to this view, it is nevertheless implicit in his claim that literature is a substitute for the speech of the organic community, which seems to be a particular instance of the more general view found in Plato that, in the words of Derrida, '[t]he book ... stands as a substitute for (so-called) living (so-called) dialogue'.[191] Literature cannot give a *sense* of life precisely because it is a substitute for *sense* itself.

The 'voice' of literature does not expect a response in the same way as does the sincere and personal judgement illustrated in Leavis's question 'This is so, isn't it?' Here too, what is inward requires validation by something outside itself. What is personal and sincere is not in itself sufficient, but must be authenticated by others. In this instance other readers or critics whose interaction is institutionalised through the whole apparatus of higher education: lectures, seminars, tutorials, conferences, journals and so on, some of which offer an opportunity for a more immediate exchange of views than others. Once more this emphasises how the inner always manifests itself through social forms. This is not to say that there is no distinction between the two; rather it is to underline how Leavis's literary criticism is less a means of conserving interiority than an instance of the general realignment between inner and outer, mind and body that was characteristic of certain changes in society when he was writing.

### FREUD, LEAVIS AND JUDGEMENT

This blurring of the boundary between inner and outer also has a psychoanalytic explanation. In his essay 'On Negation', Freud observes that

> [j]udging is a continuation, along lines of expediency, of the original process by which the ego took things into itself or expelled them from itself, according to the pleasure principle.[192]

That is, the origins of judgement are found in the oral stage which gives a peculiar aptness to that aspect of Leavis's criticism which responds to literature as 'speech' or 'voice'. The next stage in the development of judgement, according to Freud, is to check 'whether something which is in the ego as a presentation can be rediscovered in perception (reality) as well'.[193] And, in keeping with the first stage of judgement, this too is 'a question of *external* and *internal*'.[194] It is a matter, Freud writes, of re-finding an object which 'once brought real satisfaction' but has since 'been lost'.[195] Putting this in terms of Leavis's criticism it could be argued, albeit crudely, that 'judgement' is the process of rediscovering in literature the lost body of the organic community.

A further way in which Freud's analysis of judgement may illuminate the role of judgement in Leavis's criticism concerns his remark that affirmative judgements, as 'substitute[s] for uniting, belong[] to Eros', while negative ones, the 'successor[s] to expulsion, belong[] the instinct of destruction'.[196] It is the connection between negative judgements and the death instinct that is important here. In 'Beyond the Pleasure Principle' the death instinct is used to explain the compulsion to repeat. This is conceived as a '"daemonic" force', an energy that defies rationalisation except in terms of the death instinct.[197] Negative judgements thus come to be representative of a force, a desire for death. This analysis has some applicability to Leavis since his criticism contains judgements expressed in a negative form and a mechanics of force, though this is not to say that they are related.

This force has already been explained in terms of the body and the machine and male anxiety over production. The fact that it is also associated with 'life' gives it a transcendent quality which means it constitutes that 'something more' which Leavis requires of criticism and literature. At the same time it is also the very opposite of what Leavis requires since, precisely because it is transcendent, it cannot be contained by the boundary lines which Leavis is trying to establish through a vocabulary of 'relevance' and 'precision'. Force, in short, threatens to dissolve the dividing lines that are necessary for literary criticism to exercise its function. Thus, in desiring 'something more', Leavisian criticism 'desires' its own dissolution.

There are, then, a number of parallels between Freud's account of judgement and the nature of judgement in Leavisian criticism. Both are part of – and negotiate – wider changes in society. Their mutual concern with the nature of interiority, though expressed in different ways, suggests a reaction to common developments. One aspect of this development was the growth of scientific management which renders the notion of 'the human' redundant. This makes Leavis's criticism appear anachronistic and so it cannot function to preserve a notion of 'the human', understood as a form of privileged inwardness. Psychoanalysis, by contrast, is more successful in preserving a notion of interiority but at the cost of pathologising it.

## READING AND THE NATURE OF CRITICISM

In any case, Leavis's literary criticism is hampered in its task of apprehending the inner because its model of literature is founded on the labouring body of the organic community which precludes interiority by being 'unaware'. This means that Leavis's conception of the body is similar to that found in consumerism. In effect, Leavisian literary criticism inadvertently underwrites consumerism's emptying out of the body's interiority. Once more it is a question of recognising literary criticism's unwitting complicity with various social forces in order to better assess its oppositional value; or even whether it can be oppositional since that very term implies a basic dualism that this analysis has tried to show is untenable.

It would not be too much to claim that literary criticism actually assists in the process of emptying out interiority. This is evident in a certain violent orientation of criticism towards literature. Intelligence should be trained so that it can have 'a real inward grasp of English literature'.[198] That word 'grasp' suggests less a 'delicate receptivity' (*RFC*, p. 47) to a work than an invasion of it. This is supported by Leavis's claim that to analyse a poem or a novel or a play is to 'tak[e] possession' (*VC*, p. 279) of it and Lawrence's criticism is praised precisely because it is 'extraordinarily penetrating'.[199] Again, this calls into question the idea of reading as recognition. In this context, it seems more like a form of appropriation.

The intrusive character of reading is consistent with that increased state intervention and diminution of the private sphere noted earlier. Its desire to 'penetrate', 'grasp' and 'possess' the work further suggests an aggressive male sexuality in relation to a 'female' text and this reflects criticism's masculine ambitions and anxieties noted earlier. The desire to dominate the text also recalls Adorno's characterisation of the Enlightenment as the perversion of reason into a tool of domination. Some of the many consequences of this are '[t]he restriction of thought to organisation and administration';[200] 'the execution of the particular';[201] the 'negation of ... immediacy'[202] and the 'atroph[y]' of 'imagination'.[203] These are all things to which Leavis is opposed and he, like Adorno, identifies them with the Enlightenment which 'confounds thought and mathematics',[204] and reduces thinking 'to logical formalism'.[205] In Leavis's words, 'since the triumph of *la raison* in the seventeenth century philosophy has assumed ... that it has ... the exclusive right to be called "thought"' (*TM & S*, p. 292). Leavis argues for a different kind of thought, one which apprehends the immediate and is sensitive to the particular. Nevertheless, there is a dimension to his criticism which disregards these principles, showing that it is as much a part of as opposed to the tradition of Enlightenment. As Derrida notes, 'We can pronounce not a single destructive proposition which has not already had to slip into the form, the logic and the implicit postulations of precisely what it seeks to contest'.[206]

As a form of appropriation, reading does not respect the integrity of the unique text. Far from displaying the qualities of a 'delicately receptive responsiveness' (*ROP*, p. 257) it trespasses on the work thereby confounding the problem of borders that it is supposed to resolve. The 'thereness' of the poem on which Leavis insists thus seems to invite violation as well as a 'deliberate following through of that process of creation in response to the poet's words ... ensur[ing] a more than ordinary faithfulness and fitness' (*VC*, p. 278).

The poem can only be 'possessed' or 'penetrated' if it is 'there' to be so treated. Leavis appears to have little doubt that the poem is 'there' otherwise he would not be able to assert *à propos* of Bateson, that 'anyone who *reads* the passage can see' (*RC*, p. 194). This comment shows that the 'thereness' of the poem is bound up with the 'obviousness' of its meaning. Both reinforce one another: the poem's being 'there' is a guarantee of its meaning just as the meaning is a guarantee of the poem's being there. Furthermore, the obviousness of the meaning removes any need to interpret the poem. As Michael Bell has noted, Leavis's characteristic concern is not interpretative, rather 'it is to give an adequacy of attention to the self-evident'.[207]

However, as was noted earlier, there is a contradiction between Leavis's practice of criticism, which takes for granted that the poem is 'there' and his metacritical claim that the poem is '"there" only when it's realized in separate minds' (*VC*, p. 278). Critical discussion, in fact, is not so much *about* the poem as 'an effort to establish [it]' (p. 278). Leavis sees this endeavour in terms of fidelity to the poem but how is it possible to be faithful to something which is yet to be established? If the poem is not 'there' except 'in so far as the discussers have each for [themselves] recreated it' (p. 278) then it makes no sense to talk about being faithful to it as this assumes that it already exists. Moreover, the fact that the poem only exists in the re-creations of those who are discussing it suggests that there is no such thing as 'the poem' only different 'versions' of it.

The term re-creation implies that there is an original poem which is re-created. But since the poem only exists in its re-creations, without which it is only 'the black marks on the paper' (*VC*, p. 278) this original remains at the level of a postulate. This postulate, since it can never be realised, shows that criticism always re-creates the poem as other or different from itself and hence criticism can never be 'faithful' to the poem. What criticism does therefore is to create rather than re-create 'the poem' and Leavis himself hints at this when he refers to criticism as a '*creative* or recreative process' (p. 278, italics added).

Leavis explains what he means by creativity in his essay 'Justifying One's Valuation of Blake'[208] where he notes that it is 'heuristic; it is concerned with discovery or new realization ... with apprehensions and intuitions that of their nature can't be *stated*' (*JOVB*, p. 14). If criticism is creative then it can never really be 'faithful' to 'the poem' – it can only *add* to it though a process of 'discovery'. The fact that

there are aspects of 'the poem' to be discovered undermines any idea
that it is 'obvious'. Since 'the poem' is not 'obvious' then it is difficult
to know what exactly it is that criticism is being 'faithful' to. Criticism
adds to 'the poem' but, because this 'poem' is never concretely 'there',
these additions become 'the poem'. To put this in terms of the general
argument there is never 'the poem', there is only 'something more'.
Criticism thus fails to coincide with its object and instead replaces it.

The logic of Leavis's argument – though he would deny it – would
seem to be that criticism is a substitute for literature in the same way
that literature is a substitute for the organic community. Furthermore,
the language of criticism, in so far as it is creative rather than diagnostic
cannot, of its nature, make *statements* about 'the poem' or indeed
literature generally, rather it 'enacts' works as literature 'enacts'
experience. Criticism, that is to say, is more a matter of ontology than
of epistemology, and a failure to fully appreciate this may lie behind
disagreements with Leavis's reading of particular works. The putative
ontological character of criticism arises from the hesitancy surrounding
whether the poem is 'there' or not. If it is, then criticism approximates
to epistemology since it can make verifiable statements about 'the
poem'. If, however, 'the poem' is not 'there' but is the creation of
criticism then criticism has a strong ontological component to its
character. This same hesitancy over whether the poem is 'there' and
whether, therefore, criticism is more ontological than epistemological also has a bearing on whether the accent of Leavis's writing falls
finally on a work's meaning or its significance. Although these are
ultimately inseparable, Leavis rarely discusses them together and, on
different occasions, characterises the study of English either in terms
of meaning or significance. 'To be intelligent about meaning,' he
writes, 'is central to "English" as a discipline of thought' (*TL & O*, p. 57).
While in another context he observes that the critic, when confronted
with a work, should ask him or herself the following questions

> How, as we come to appreciate it and to realize its significance, does
> it affect our sense of the things that have determining significance
> for us? How does it affect our total sense of relative value, our sense
> of direction, our sense of life? (*SC*, p. 247)

Meaning is, in general, something that is verifiable and therefore is
a matter of epistemology. Significance, however, cannot be verified
or even defined. It is associated with 'life'[209] and 'being' (*EU & C*,
p. 110) with, in short, ontology.

The discontinuity between meaning and significance – terms which will be discussed again in the next chapter – may have some bearing on those other pairings already examined, for example, consciousness and the body, and the work and its context. The fact that the opposition between these terms proved to be, at the very least, problematic suggests that it may be possible to reconcile meaning and significance. Moreover, this reconciliation may bring about a fresh understanding of the ethical component of Leavis's criticism, which for too long has been dismissed as 'righteous moralising'.[210]

Leavis's failure – if that is the right word – to bring meaning and significance into some sort of explicit relation fissures a text along the lines of either meaning or significance. This helps to 'de-realise' literature in much the same way that the creative aspect of criticism de-realises it. That is, by assuming the poem is yet to be established, criticism deprives it of that concrete particularity and sensuous apprehension which gives it the vivid immediacy of 'life in the living' (*TM & S*, p. 292). The institution of criticism de-realises literature by producing it through discussion instead of being compelled by the sheer presence of literature to recognise it as already 'there'.

It could be argued that, in this way, criticism is complicit with the abstractions and reductions of mass civilisation, transforming the immediacy of the text into a generalised mediation.[211] Criticism in seeking to oppose this process, dissolves literature in the very moment it declares its authenticity. It seems that criticism is creative only to the extent that it negates literature. This, however, is a somewhat despairing view and depends on assumption of the *a priori* existence of literature before the destructive intervention of criticism. It is more useful to highlight how criticism produces literature. This offers a potentially more democratic view of Leavis's criticism than is evident in his insistence on the 'obvious', whose transparency permits no discussion.

Furthermore, the indeterminate relationship between meaning and significance raises issues which are not always adequately addressed by the post-structuralist promotion of the plurality of meaning. For example, why is the plurality of meaning in itself desirable? Are all the meanings found in a text equally admissible, prominent or valid? And, finally, isn't the ethic of a multiplicity of meanings itself founded on the attribution of a *single* meaning to the works of critics such as Leavis?[212] In other words, a consideration of the possible relations between meaning and significance in Leavis introduces questions of value – both aesthetic and ethical – into post-structuralist accounts of meaning, where they seem to exist only implicitly, if at all.

The next chapter will consider in more detail the idea that criticism establishes 'the poem'. It will consider, that is, what Leavis calls 'the third realm' and the different ways in which this can be understood.

# 4

# The 'Third Realm'

The 'third realm'[1] is a way of conceiving the poem as being both independently 'there' and 'there' as a product of discussion. The 'third realm' is what distinguishes 'literary–critical analysis' from mathematics, scientific … philosophico–logical [or] biographical, psychological descriptions'.[2] Leavis expands his idea of literary critical analysis as follows:

> Analysis … in so far as it aims at establishing a favourable judgement, is the process of justifying the assumption that a poem which we take to be a real poem stands between us in what is in some sense a public world. Minds can meet in it and there is so essential a measure of concurrence as to its nature and constitution that there can be intelligent – that is, profitable – differing about what precisely it is. It is neither merely private, nor public in the sense that it can be brought into a laboratory, quantified, tripped over, or even pointed to – the only way to point to particulars in it is to put one's finger on given spots in the assemblage of black marks on the page – and that assemblage is not the poem. The poem is a product and, in any experienced actual existence, a phenomenon, of human creativity the essentially collaborative nature of which it exemplifies in diverse distinguishable modes. And yet it is real.
> (*TL & O*, p. 36)

Analysis seems to be a combination of aesthetics and epistemology; the former because it is concerned to establish 'a *judgement*' and the latter because it is concerned to establish the *reality* of the poem and how the reader comes to know that reality. Literary criticism, on this definition, is an attempt to synthesise the various faculties that have been separated by the advent of modernity.

However, there are a number of problems with Leavis's description of the 'third realm'. One of these has already been mentioned and concerns the ambiguity of the poem being 'there' and not 'there'. Logically, the poem would have to exist prior to minds meeting in it and this is implied by the fact that the poem is 'real' and 'stands between' readers in 'a public world'. At the same time this is clearly not the case because the poem is a 'product' of 'human creativity'.

The poem's ambiguous status is further underlined by its not being identified with the 'black marks on the page'. These have to be converted into a poem through an act of creation. The 'poem' thus has a 'double' existence as 'raw material' and 'finished product', an analogy which again highlights the notion of productive labour at the heart of Leavis's criticism. The existence of 'black marks on the page' also gives the 'poem' a 'thing' like quality which is at odds with the view of the 'third realm' as 'the collaboratively created *human* world'[3] (italics added). In the former capacity, the 'poem' presents the reader with 'the difficulty ... [of] deciding what kind of thing it is',[4] a different process from establishing it through creative collaboration. The 'poem's' status is thus rendered even more ambiguous; it is at once something 'there' but alien and something that does not yet exist.

As something 'there', the 'poem' is 'seen' – that is how Leavis is able to describe it as 'black marks on a page'. But the collaboration that establishes the poem is, of its nature, an ongoing process and so the 'poem' is never sufficiently 'there' to be 'seen'. It is discussed, apprehended and, ideally, realised but it is not 'seen'. Nevertheless, in his disputes with other critics Leavis resorts to metaphors of sight to establish his case. Thus, a key term in Leavis's criticism refers more to the 'black marks on the page' than to the critical act of converting them into a 'poem'. The analogy of sight for reading was something he himself was uneasy about.

> It will be noted by the way how inevitably we slip into the visual analogy, the type and model of objectivity being the thing seen ... and, further, that there is the significant linguistic usage by which to 'see' is to understand ('I see!').[5]

Criticism never quite succeeds in establishing the poem for although there is 'a measure of concurrence' about it there is also a 'differing about what precisely it is'. Another aspect of the poem's 'double' existence is evident here. Simultaneously, it is identical and non-identical to itself, raising the question of how minds can 'meet in' a poem if they disagree 'about what precisely it is'. This disagreement ensures that the 'poem' has no final, definitive existence; it is continuously deferred. The fact that the poem is deferred means that it is always in excess of any particular discussion which 'establishes' it. This excess is produced by the critical act, but not recognised by it, hence it continues to desire 'something more'. Criticism seems to produce the very thing it desires but without realising that it does so.

Another example of Leavisian criticism's failure to be fully conscious of itself occurs in the use of words which contradict its project. This may broadly be described as the problem of valuation. Leavis persistently rejects the idea that valuation has anything to do with 'the standards in the Weights and Measures Office'[6] or that it can be understood 'in terms of money'.[7] Yet, in the extract given at the beginning of this section, he maintains that it is 'essential' that there is 'a *measure* of concurrence' about the 'nature' and 'constitution', in other words the value of the poem. Moreover, this 'measure of concurrence' is precisely what allows '*profitable*' discussion to occur.

The word 'profitable' is the monetary equivalent of 'something more'. This highlights how Leavisian criticism, in its pursuit of 'something more', underwrites the profit motive of capitalism. Furthermore, profit is bound up with considerations of productivity which lie at the heart of Leavis's writing. The term 'profitable' shows, once again, how despite trying to think beyond the values of 'technologico–Benthamite civilisation' Leavis is unable to do so. This is because he is constrained to use the language of – and therefore the ideology of – that civilisation with the result that he endorses as much as criticises it. Language, it may be said, catches Leavis out.

## THE 'THIRD REALM' AND *DIFFÉRANCE*

The problems in Leavis's description of the 'third realm' are both temporal and spatial. Temporal because of the difficulty of deciding whether 'minds' come before the poem or the poem before 'minds' or whether it would be better, as Leavis implies, to banish the idea of chronological sequence altogether and imagine the complex relations between 'minds' and poem simultaneously. Spatial because of *where* 'minds' meet and because the very term 'minds' recalls the problematic relation of mind and body, of how they are situated towards one another in a culture which is busy realigning and re-imagining them.

The temporal and spatial aspects of the 'third realm' suggest parallels with Derrida's discussion of *différance*, which is both 'temporization' and 'spacing'.[8] The term is made up of the verbs to differ and to defer. '[T]o differ,' writes Derrida, is 'discernibility, distinction, separation, diastem, *spacing*' while 'to defer' is 'detour, relay, reserve, *temporization*'.[9] Both these characteristics belong to the 'third realm'. 'Spacing' may be said to refer to the fundamental separation of the 'poem' from the 'black marks on the page' while 'temporization' would seem to apply to the way the poem is deferred and never quite established. Derrida is at pains to point out that 'temporization' and 'spacing' are 'joined',[10] that they are co-existent with one another and hence their 'different' meanings are contained in the one term. Similarly, there is no real distinction between 'temporization' and 'spacing' in the 'third realm': the fact that the poem is yet to be established simultaneously opens a space between it and the 'black marks on the page'.

Derrida's analysis of *différance* is, of course, far removed from the concerns of the 'third realm'. Derrida is trying to show how *différance* is what enables signification to take place. It is, writes Derrida, 'The play which makes possible nominal effects.'[11] This is crucial to Derrida's argument, which is directed against the Western philosophical tradition. Simplifying drastically, this tradition states that truth exists in a transcendent realm to which the proper exercise of reason gives access. Truth is thus something which already exists and is therefore to be discovered rather than created. Derrida's point is that truth, and its various correlates such as being, consciousness and presence, 'are produced effects ... which do not find their cause in a subject or a substance, in a thing in general ... [but] in the play of *différance*'.[12] One consequence of this is that the meaning of these terms is never self-evidently 'there' but dispersed in the discourses that produce them. In addition, the mention of each term, for example truth, is partly conditioned by a sense of other contexts in which it has appeared and those in which it may appear. Bearing within itself 'the mark of the past element, and already letting itself be vitiated by the mark of its relation to the future element'[13] truth is divided both from its present and self-presence.

The very different concerns of Derrida and Leavis mean that his notion of *différance* cannot be mapped exactly on to the 'third realm'. Nevertheless, Derrida does not confine *différance* to the philosophical tradition.

We will designate as *différance* the movement according to which language, or any code, any system of referral in general, is constituted 'historically' by a weave of differences.[14]

This provides a licence to extend the application of the term to criticism – a 'system' which 'refers' to literature[15] – though with the proviso that it cannot mean the same in that context as it does in the philosophical one.

*Différance* draws attention to how a concept, such as 'truth' or 'being', is produced through a movement of 'spacing' and 'temporization'. As noted, a similar movement is discernible in the 'third realm'. However, where *différance* is 'about' the possibility of signification and refers to nothing material, there is, in the 'third realm', a strong sense of the materiality of signification evident in the perception of the 'black marks on the page'. As such, these 'black marks' are probably better understood in terms of Lacan's description of the signifier which is 'material'[16] and which, as a part of the signifying chain, produces meaning though is never equivalent to it. The same might be said of the 'black marks on the page' since Leavis is quite emphatic that they are not 'the poem' though 'the poem' has no existence without them. This similarity perhaps creates a parallel between 'the poem' and desire since both seem to be 'there' in respect of language.

The comparison with Lacan complements Derrida's claim that the movement of *différance* 'puts into question the authority of presence [and] its simple, symmetrical opposite, absence or lack'.[17] Consequently meaning can never be regarded as being simply 'there'. Lacan makes a similar point when he notes that the bar separating the signifier and the signified is 'a barrier resisting signification',[18] and that the action of the signifying chain is such that 'the ring of meaning flees from our grasp along the verbal thread'.[19] The operation of the 'third realm' too means that the 'poem' is never quite established, partly because there will always be 'differ[ences] about what precisely it is' and partly because there is an ambiguity in analysis itself. On the one hand 'it aims at establishing a favourable *judgement*', implying that the poem is already 'there' while on the other it aims at establishing the poem, implying that it is not.

The 'poem', in being neither simply present or absent seems to be an illustration of the effect of *différance*. *Différance*, writes Derrida, 'exceeds the alternative of presence and absence'.[20] It is 'the very opening of a space in which philosophy [but it could equally be

poetry] produces its system and its history ... inscribing it and
exceeding it without return'.[21] The 'poem', in being beyond presence
and absence, is identified with excess and this is at odds with Leavis's
view of poetry as 'embodiment' or 'enactment'. As excess, the' poem'
constitutes that 'something more' desired by Leavisian criticism but
at the cost of the dissolution of the 'body' of the 'poem'.

'Something more' is here an effect, but another understanding of
the term is possible through its affinities to *différance*. Specifically,
'something more' involves temporisation – disagreement about the
'poem' means that there is always more to say about it and therefore
the 'poem' is deferred – and spatialisation – because the poem is
distinct from the 'black marks on the page'. 'Something more' can thus
be seen as a movement which precipitates the poem into existence.
Hence, the very thing which is desired for literature is the very thing
which makes it appear.

In this respect, 'something more' is the philosophical counterpart
of the dissolution of boundaries which defines Leavis's critical project.
Thus the *desire* for 'something more' contradicts the critical project
since it is a desire to return to that state of flux that criticism was called
upon to remedy. Once more, the desire for 'something more' can be
seen as similar to the death drive. As a desire to return to an earlier
state it negates Leavis's claim in *Culture and Environment* that 'there
can be no ... going back' (*CE*, p. 96) but it is consistent with the
metaphor of the wheelwright's craft for literary criticism since a
wheel indicates cyclical returns.

'Something more' which, in 'Mass Civilisation and Minority
Culture', was seen as a solution to the problem of the lack of commonly
accepted definitions, itself turns out to be the purest expression of that
problem. In other words, it is precisely because of the loss of
distinctions and dividing lines that there are no commonly accepted
definitions. To supplement existing ones is merely to add to the
excess which has created the problem in the first place.

Another connection between *différance* and 'something more' in
Leavis lies in Derrida's claim that *différance* means that 'we necessarily
misconstrue'[22] our relationship to being, truth, or in this case poetry.
Briefly, critical commentary assumes that 'the poem' is 'there', whereas
the spatialising and temporising movement of the 'third realm' –
whose essence is 'something more' – shows that 'the poem' exceeds
presence or absence. The implication is that 'the poem' is consistently
misrecognised. Such a view would seem to be borne out by those
instances in Leavis's criticism where, despite his commitment to

consciousness, other meanings of which he seems unaware obtrude themselves. Furthermore, the misrecognition[23] of 'the poem' or indeed any object of criticism, makes fraught with irony Leavis's claim that 'the poem' cannot be 'tripped over'. On the contrary, it is precisely because 'the poem' is misrecognised that it can indeed be 'tripped over'. The basis of this misrecognition becomes clear when it is remembered that the dominant metaphor for *understanding* 'the poem' is 'seeing' while a key one for 'the poem' is 'voice'.

The existence of 'the poem' beyond presence or absence brings out a further aspect of *différance* which may usefully be applied to Leavis. 'A certain alterity,' writes Derrida, 'is definitively exempt from every process of presentation.'[24] This appears to mean that the movement of *différance* dissolves the idea of substantial oppositions. Oppositions cannot confront one another as fixed presences because *différance* calls the notion of oppositions, for example presence and absence, into question.[25] This has some bearing on Leavis's dispute with Bateson since it gives some theoretical support to the argument, advanced earlier, that a poem and its context cannot be opposed to one another as two distinct and self-sustaining entities. More importantly, it may be used to focus Leavis's apparently contrary claim that 'literary inquiry ... cannot be intelligently pursued except as an inquiry into ... civilization'.[26] This acknowledges that a poem and its context have no substantial existence apart from one another. The words of a poem have had and will have deployment in other contexts and this constitutes an excess, a 'something more', that disrupts it as a self-enclosed entity.[27] The same reasoning would also apply to the idea of a separate context, whose own 'borders' would be no more secure than those of 'the poem'.

Derrida's 'definition' of *différance* as 'neither a word nor a concept'[28] recalls Leavis's use of litotes and negative presentation, which were discussed in the previous chapter. It thus serves to further underline the affinities between aspects of his work and Leavis's conception of the 'third realm'. This seems to mimic the work of *différance*, and *différance* also seems to provide a context for understanding the notion of 'something more' in Leavis. Both Leavis and Derrida show, in their different ways, that there is a connection between a sense of lack and a desire for 'something more'. However, this connection is not always clear in Leavis and so a comparison with Derrida helps to focus it. The difference is that whereas Derrida shows this connection to be a function of language as a *system*[29] of which human intention, identity and agency are mere effects, Leavis shows it to be the essence of human creativity and communication.

Leavis's notion of the 'third realm', though similar to Derrida's *différance*, is about purposive collaboration. It is also a recognition that, though language resists the shaping power of intention and though, even at its most critically charged, language is incorrigibly ambiguous, this nevertheless does not excuse speakers from being responsible in their use of it. Indeed it is because language is ineradicably plural that human beings have to struggle to make it mean in the way they want it to mean. The accent of Leavis's work, in the context of the comparison of the 'third realm' with *différance*, falls on this necessary struggle with language rather than on language as an autonomous structure that hollows out being and shows purpose and intention to be no more than fond humanist illusions.

The argument, in short, is that Leavis's work, because of its similarities to and differences from certain aspects of post-structuralist thought, can help to restore a sense of 'the human'[30] to the latter. The point is not to oppose Leavis to post-structuralism, or vice versa, but to try to find a way of articulating two strands of thought that are both part of British cultural life in order to generate new insights into it.

It is not clear what the implications of Derrida's notion of *différance* are for an analysis of society and this is partly because *différance* is not grounded in any specific social practice. Leavis's notion of the 'third realm' is, however, clearly tied to the institutions and practices of criticism. This, like the 'black marks on the page' highlights its material character. This materiality is not immediately apparent in Leavis's negative presentation of the 'third realm' as 'neither merely private nor public', though that negative presentation is reinforced by the affinity with Derrida's negative 'definition' of *différance*. Both, however, are given a material and critical edge by a comparison with Adorno's concept of negative dialectics.

## NEGATIVE DIALECTICS AND THE 'THIRD REALM'

Negative dialectics is a form of thought which Adorno opposes to 'identitarian thinking'.[31] This latter 'says what something comes under, what it exemplifies or represents'.[32] In other words, it ignores or represses what is particular and it does this is the interests of conformity. Identity thinking, observes Adorno, is 'a doctrine of adjustment'.[33] As such, it is associated with ideology and the clearest example of ideology is the 'culture industry' which 'impresses the same stamp upon everything'.[34] The individual, writes Adorno, 'is tolerated only so long as his [her] complete identification with the generality is unquestioned'.[35] In being opposed to identity thinking, negative dialectics can be seen as a form of ideology critique.[36]

Negative dialectics aims to redeem the particular from identity thinking. It does this by noting, 'to begin with, ... that objects do not go into their concepts without leaving a remainder'.[37] This 'more' is what has been 'pushed out'[38] of the object by identity thinking. In Adorno's words: 'The innermost core of the object proves to be simultaneously extraneous to it, the phenomenon of its exclusion, the reflex of an identifying stabilizing procedure'.[39] An example of how identity thinking can squeeze out inwardness is the operation of exchange value 'which *a priori* keeps ... subjects from being subjects and degrades subjectivity itself to a mere object'.[40]

Having shown that there is always a disparity between an object and its concept, negative dialectics then addresses itself to the task of 'say[ing] what something is'.[41] The details of this process are not relevant here but the following points are in order. First, negative dialectics endeavours to generate more than one concept for an object, bringing them into a 'constellation' which would illuminate that side of the object 'which to a classifying procedure is either a matter of indifference or a burden'.[42] Second, negative dialectics, by drawing attention to the gap between a concept and its object, promotes an awareness of 'the contradiction between what things are and what they claim to be'.[43] Third, negative dialectics tries to take account of the role of the body in cognition, '[t]he somatic moment as the not purely cognitive part of cognition is irreducible'.[44] Somatic processes cannot be wholly equated with cognition and thus the body itself becomes an analogy of 'the remainder' that is 'left over' by objects not going into their concepts.

Adorno's negative dialectics provides a framework for understanding negative presentation in Leavis. To begin with, both Adorno and Leavis formulate their thought against what they perceive to be the limitations of traditional philosophy. Each believes that that philosophy is concerned with definitions which take no account of the complexity of experience.[45] Negative dialectics tries to acknowledge this complexity by critically reflecting on 'its own motion'[46] in contrast to philosophy's 'deficient self-reflection'.[47] Leavis tries to acknowledge it by a mode of thought 'that brings in consciously ... the un-Cartesian reality underlying language and implicit in it; [that is] what is inexpressible in terms of logic and clarity' (*TL & O*, p. 43).

More generally, negative dialectics and Leavisian criticism are committed to non-definition; 'the most important words', writes Leavis, 'are incapable of definition'[48] in contrast to what Adorno terms identity thinking and what Leavis refers to as 'the Cartesian–Newtonian dualism' (*TL & O*, p. 31).

Neither negative dialectics nor Leavisian criticism impose an identity on their respective objects. Leavis describes the critic's task as *not* 'measuring' a work with 'a norm ... applie[d] from the outside'.[49] At the same time, just as negative dialectics is concerned 'to say what something is'[50] so too is Leavisian criticism since it focuses on a work's 'precise thisness of meaning'.[51] Another way of making this connection is to note that both Adorno and Leavis are committed to the particular and the concrete, not the abstract and general. 'Philosophical thinking', observes Adorno, 'crystallizes in the particular,'[52] and Leavis describes his 'whole effort' as one of 'work[ing] in terms of concrete judgements and particular analyses' (*C & P*, p. 215).

The concern for the particular in negative dialectics and Leavisian criticism can be interpreted as a concern with inwardness. As noted earlier, it is '[t]he innermost core of the object'[53] which is extracted by identity thinking and Leavisian criticism's concern with the particular is dependent on a notion of reading as 'inwardness' (*TM & S*, p. 288). The difference between negative dialectics and Leavisian criticism is that Adorno recognises that inwardness is under siege in modern culture and is therefore a problematic term whereas Leavis takes it for granted. For Leavis, inwardness is the chief characteristic of a form of thought which is 'conceived as profoundly other than philosophical' (p. 288). It is therefore part of a binary opposition which structures his writing. This is ironic given that Leavis claims his work is an attempt to move beyond 'the rationality of either/or' (*TL & O*, p. 37). If Leavis regards the notion of inwardness as unproblematic, however, his work, as previously discussed, demonstrates that it is anything but.

Adorno regards inwardness in terms of 'something more' thus providing another context for understanding that notion in Leavis. 'What is', writes Adorno, 'is more than it is. This "more" ... has been pushed out of [the object].'[54] It is important to remember at this point that the word 'object', as used by Adorno, refers to the condition of subjects in capitalist society – 'the subject is an object'[55] precisely because subjectivity, in the sense of inward particularity, has been repressed by identity thinking in the interests of conformity. 'Something more' may, then, be associated with inwardness, but the very fact that it is 'something more', and therefore not integrated, points to a problem in the relations between inner and outer, mind and body. 'The innermost core of the object [subject] is simultaneously extraneous to it',[56] an observation that sharpens the earlier claim concerning how inwardness in Leavisian criticism is always externalised.

But if 'something more' is associated with inwardness, it could equally be associated with the body.[57] Adorno claims that the somatic moment is in excess of the cognitive one. For Leavis, the body is the basis of reading (*ROP*, p. 268) but it is also a dangerous excess – that is why, in *Culture and Environment*, it has to be suppressed. Further, the *body* of a text like *Culture and Environment* (*CE*, p. 10) means far more than Leavis says it does. And finally, that particular text constructs its reader as both male and female thus transgressing the boundaries of the sexed body.

'Something more' is, then, related to both mind and body. By referring to both, it offers itself as a solution to the problem of how to join them together. 'Something more', a phrase which connotates excess, comes to represent the promise of unity in a society where '[t]he separation of feeling and understanding hypostasizes the dismemberment of man into functions'.[58] This society tries to disguise the consequences of that separation by the false unity of the culture industry,[59] false because it is imposed from without. 'Every detail,' argues Adorno, 'is ... stamped with sameness'.[60] The formula has replaced the work, with the result that '[t]he whole and the parts are alike; there is no antithesis and no connection'.[61] The unity of 'something more', by contrast, has no such pre-arranged harmony. The fact that it is 'more' already means that it has escaped the integrative drive of the culture industry. Its unity is specific to itself and is marked by a tension between part and whole. At the same time, it has a negative character because the content of 'something more' remains to be determined. True, it refers to body and mind but their unity is a formal achievement predicated on their being 'something more'; something extraneous to how they are represented in the culture industry.

## ADORNO AND LEAVIS: TRADITION AND NEGATIVE PRESENTATION

In all these ways 'something more' offers itself as a critique of the culture industry, and it therefore holds out the hope of true fulfilment and reconciliation. Adorno argues that one way of achieving this is through an encounter with artistic tradition. This tradition, he claims, is a history of styles which 'represent[] a promise in every work of art'.[62] This promise states that the particular 'will be reconciled ... with the idea of true generality',[63] an expression which shows that even Adorno's work is not free from the abstractions he associates with the culture industry. This promise appears in the organisation of the work of art where part and whole exist in a balanced and necessary relationship. However, this amounts to no more than 'lending new shape to conventional social forms'[64] thereby ratifying and holding them in place. But, continues Adorno, it is the very failure of art to keep its promise which means that, unlike philosophy, it can express suffering[65] as well as show that reconciliation has to be sought beyond the existing social framework.

This argument provides another rationale for Leavis's valuation of tradition. It will be remembered that Leavis identifies tradition with language which is conserved, renewed and added to by literature. Language 'embodies values, constatations, distinctions, promptings, recognitions of potentiality [none of which] dictat[e] an ideal comprehensive conclusion' (*TL & O*, p. 49). The very nature of tradition means that it offers alternative ways of constructing experience and valuing community and so it can be deployed against the existing order. It is, writes Adorno, 'a vital force ... against ossification'.[66] It introduces a sense of history into 'the abstract present';[67] it is a mark of otherness in a culture of sameness and it is not programmatic in a culture that demands conformity. Whether it follows from this that Leavis's conception of art includes the notion of suffering is another matter. The important point is that Adorno's view of tradition provides a positive understanding of Leavis's use of the term.

There are, then, various ways in which Adorno's negative dialectics can be brought to bear in a general fashion on the element of negative presentation in Leavis's criticism, thereby highlighting its potentially emancipatory possibilities. One final similarity concerns language. Both Adorno and Leavis write in a peculiarly concentrated and difficult way. In the case of Adorno this is a deliberate manoeuvre to prevent his thought from being assimilated to the existing order. To write in a transparent manner is to collude with a culture where 'visibility is thrust upon everything that can be seen'.[68] This investment in seeing is, argues Mark Seltzer, 'a policing of the real',[69] but it is precisely 'the real', as constructed by the culture industry, from which Adorno is trying to disengage himself. Hence he writes in a manner which 'challenges signification and [which] by its very distance from meaning revolts in advance against [the] subordination of meaning'.[70]

Although Leavis provides no rationale for his mode of writing, described by John Carey as 'a style that keeps clarity so sternly at bay'[71] reasons for its alleged 'cumbrous[ness], uncouth[ness] clums[iness]' 'rebarbative[ness]' and 'inelegan[ce]'[72] are not hard to find. In the first place it is Leavis's task, as a critic, to identify and win recognition for 'the creatively original writer' (*SC*, p. 246). What would distinguish such a writer from his or her contemporaries would be a certain distance from and challenge to the conventional norms and expressions of the culture in which he or she writes. '[I]ts significance' Leavis writes, 'will be in some measure a matter of its defeating and correcting habit' (p. 247). As such, the really 'new work of art' (p. 247) will not be immediately accessible and will therefore require an effort of readjustment, a break with the established patterns of thought and valuation. The unfamiliar nature of this work – a 'sign[]' of genuine new life' (p. 245) will in part be reflected in the critic's commentary on it, since it is part of his or her aim to 'make you feel what it is like to read an author'.[73]

One way of accounting for the difficulty of Leavis's style is, then, that he was trying to win recognition for works, the most obvious examples would be those of T.S. Eliot and Lawrence, whose significance was not immediately apparent in the existing cultural framework. Another, related to the first, is that Leavis was trying to promote a type of thought that was distinct from philosophy. This thought is best exemplified by literature which, as previously noted, is not bound by the logic of either/or as Leavis believes is the case with Cartesian philosophy. His argument is that philosophical discourse is too categorical, too concerned with fixed definitions to register the transformations and subtle movements of language over time. It is, in short, 'restrictive' (*TL & O*, p. 26), confining language to 'a means of expression' when in fact it is

> the precipitate of immemorial human living, and embodies values, distinctions, identifications, conclusions, promptings, cartographical hints and tested potentialities. It exemplifies the truth that life is growth and growth change, and the condition of these is continuity. (*TL & O*, p. 44)

The organic metaphor of growth elides complex and discontinuous histories yet it also makes provision for them by the emphasis on growth and change. Furthermore, the idea that language is more than 'a means of expression' – all its possibilities are not immediately apparent – suggests it can resist the cultural imperative that everything be visible. This connects Leavis's use of language with Adorno's. Both are writing in opposition to the dominant modes of expression and this is reflected in their respective styles which are judged 'difficult' against it.

Leavis not only urges the adoption of a more comprehensive thought than can be found in philosophy, he also pits this thought against the logic of 'technologico–Benthamite' civilisation which confines 'human ends' solely to a 'rising standard of living' (*TIOC*, p. 91).

> [I]t won't do to make a rising material standard of living the self sufficient aim on the confident assumption that we needn't admit any other kind of consideration, any more adequate recognition of human nature and human need, into the incitement and direction of our thinking and our effort; technological and material advance and fair distribution – it's enough, it's the only true responsibility, to concentrate on them; that's the attitude I confront (*TIOC*, p. 78)

Leavis is *not* arguing that technology, material growth and equitable distribution are undesirable, simply that they are not enough; 'something more' is required. This relates to questions of significance, people have 'a need to feel life significant' (*TIOC*, p. 92) but this word cannot be easily defined. It therefore has a negative quality that prevents it from being too easily assimilated to the ends of the 'culture industry'. Furthermore, the lack of a ready answer to the question 'What is significance?' (p. 92) within the terms of the 'culture industry' challenges the latter's claim to encompass and comprehend all experience.

By situating such 'negative definitions' in the context of Adorno's work Leavis's writing can be rescued from the charges of mystification and obscurantism.[74] Indeed, these charges themselves reflect the belief that everything can be made visible and thus they accuse in the name of the dominant order. But if Leavis's style resists making terms like 'significance' visible, if it thickens language to the point where it is no longer transparent it is also the case that it feels the pull toward visibility and transparency. 'The "seeing" elements of our inner experience as clearly defined objects, involve ... something we naturally call thought. And it will be noted ... how inevitably we slip into that analogy' (*J & A*, p. 90). Although Leavis tries to guard against the careless use of 'the visual analogy' it is nevertheless the case that the optical metaphor[75] pervades his notion of reading, 'anyone who reads can see' (*RC*, p. 194).

The struggle to establish that 'reality' is not wholly identifiable with its appearance is therefore internal to Leavis's criticism, making it difficult to oppose it to the 'culture industry' in any simplistic way. Leavis's idea that reading is a matter of perceiving the 'obvious' dovetails with the 'culture industry's' requirement that everything be made visible. But the fact that Leavis's style of writing renders his meaning far from obvious suggests that there is more to 'reality' than its appearance.

Leavis's 'convoluted and parenthetical'[76] style can, then, be regarded as interfering with normal signifying practices. Just as the 'third realm' delays the 'poem' and draws attention to how it is constructed, so does Leavis's style perform the same function in relation to meaning. As such, it poses a challenge to the ideology of the 'culture industry' which first states that meaning is spontaneously 'there', and then repeats it. In short, Leavis's rebarbative style can be interpreted in a positive way and this is made especially clear by a comparison with Adorno.

A similar defence of Derrida's style has been made by Christopher Norris. John Harwood accuses Derrida of being 'impenetrable and interminable'.[77] But by what criteria? Norris notes that terms like *différance* 'exceed[] and disturb[] the classical economy of language and representation',[78] implying that these cannot be used as a standard by which to judge Derrida since his work is a critique of the assumptions on which they are based. Norris's argument is particularly relevant in this context because the 'third realm' acts in a manner analogous to *différance*. Consequently it lends further support to the points already made regarding both the idea of the 'third realm' and Leavis's style.

## LEAVIS AND WITTGENSTEIN

It has been argued that the 'third realm' has affinities with Derrida's *différance* and, to a lesser extent, Adorno's negative dialectics. There are clear differences between these thinkers but there are also similarities or, what Wittgenstein terms in another context, 'family resemblances'.[79] It is doubtful whether Leavis himself would have approved of these comparisons, for Derrida and Adorno are philosophers and Leavis sought to distance himself from philosophy. However, as previously noted, Derrida problematises the border between philosophy and literature and literary criticism and a similar case could be made for Adorno. It will be remembered that Leavis himself hesitates over where to draw the dividing line, for while '[t]he presence of philosophy in the university should be important for "English"' this does not mean 'seminars on Wittgenstein for literary students' (*TL & O*, p. 28).

The mention of Wittgenstein is important. Leavis usually equates philosophy with Cartesianism and this may be because he half recognises that it is easier to distance his thought from the rationalist tradition than from Wittgenstein's thinking about language. This deserves a study in its own right but one or two points can be made here.

First, Wittgenstein argues that words do not have essential definitions, rather they are defined by their 'use'[80] in particular 'language games'.[81] This resembles Leavis's notion that words 'must rely on the context to define [them]' (*TL & O*, p. 34). Second, Wittgenstein characterises philosophy as 'a battle against the bewitchment of our intelligence by means of language'[82] and Leavis conceives of literary criticism at least partly in the same terms. This is evident not only in the attacks on advertisements but also on poetry which 'work[s] so insidious a spell', is an 'enchantment', is 'dreamy' or 'hypnotic'.[83] Leavis identifies these qualities with Victorian Romanticism, a tradition he denigrates in favour of a poetry of 'the actual working world' (*NB*, p. 36). Third, John Casey has suggested that, in Leavis's criticism, '[i]nner states are essentially expressed by and judged in term of objective qualities; there is no room for essentially private emotions, subjective responses'.[84] This resembles Wittgenstein's claim that emotions, mental states or sensations are always 'recognised and measured by outward criteria – by people's activity and behaviour and, therefore, far from being inner or private to the mental life of the individual, [they] exist out in the open, in the public domain'.[85] Moreover, it should be stressed that in making this point, Wittgenstein is attacking the Cartesian tradition that says we can be directly acquainted with our mental states, the very tradition that Leavis himself attacks though for different reasons.

These similarities are compounded by what Leavis himself says of Wittgenstein. In 'Memories of Wittgenstein'[86] Leavis notes that after the altercation which characterised their first meeting Wittgenstein put his hand on Leavis's shoulder and said, 'We must know one another' (*MOW*, p. 132). This is ambiguous – 'we must get to know one another' and/or 'surely we already know each other' – and it is matched by an uncertainty as to who has which attributes.

> This might perhaps seem to indicate that any arrogance there might be was mine. Actually, I think it would be a misleading word to use of either of us, though it seems to me to apply, if at all, to Wittgenstein rather than to me. (*MOW*, p. 130)

Furthermore, if this essay frequently shows how Leavis and Wittgenstein resemble one another it also fails to distinguish the literary critic's approach to a work from that of the philosopher. After Leavis has read Empson's poem 'Legal Fictions' to Wittgenstein, the latter persistently presses Leavis to explain it. Leavis tries but keeps being interrupted.

> At the third or fourth interruption of the same kind I shut the book and said, 'I'm not playing.' 'It's perfectly plain you don't understand the poem in the least,' he said. 'Give me the book.' I complied, and, sure enough, without any difficulty, he went through the poem, explaining the analogical structure that I should have explained myself, if he had allowed me. (*MOW*, p. 145)

Finally, at the close of 'Mutually Necessary', in which Leavis takes issue with Michael Tanner over the nature of value judgements and whether poetry can be discussed in terms of philosophy, Leavis turns to Wittgenstein to support his point that language is more than logic. '[W]hat is the use of studying philosophy,' writes Wittgenstein, 'if all that it does for you is to enable you to talk with some plausibility about some abstruse questions of logic, etc.?'[87] What it should do, continues Wittgenstein, is 'improve your thinking about the important questions of everyday life'[88] – which is precisely Leavis's point about literature.

The similarities between aspects of Leavis and parts of Wittgenstein's thought once more show that the concerns of Leavisian criticism cannot, despite Leavis's assertions to the contrary, be entirely separated from those of philosophy. Leavis is able to maintain his stance as an 'anti-philosopher' only because he had a narrow conception of philosophy as a form of enquiry dominated by pre-occupations with analytical method, by questions about the relationship between investigative procedure and objects of attention, by considerations of what could be identified as real in language and what was the result of subjective misconception and what was not.[89]

Such a view prevented Leavis from appreciating that the boundary between literary criticism and philosophy was even more fluid than his own, by no means clear, pronouncements on the matter suggest.

## THE 'THIRD REALM': BOUNDARIES AND THE SPACE OF READING

Leavis's description of the 'third realm' can also be discussed in terms of borders, specifically those of public and private. Literary criticism belongs to 'the realm of that which is neither public in the ordinary sense, nor merely private' (*TL & O*, p. 36). Here the notion of border is seen as a limitation and this reverses Leavis's position in 'Mass Civilisation and Minority Culture' where he deplored the loss of boundaries and dividing lines. Indeed, the 'third realm' seems to approximate to that condition since there are no clear demarcations between public and private. It would appear that the condition criticism set out to correct has become the sphere of its operation. The 'third realm' thus seems continuous with, rather than critical of, the 'borderless' condition of modernity. The same might also be said of the 'third realm's' negation of public and private since, as was discussed in the previous chapter, the development of mass communications has made the distinctions between the two terms far from clear. In both these instances, Leavisian criticism seems to testify to a process of homogenisation. Conceived in opposition to 'civilisation' it now merely seems to reflect and reproduce it. Even the very name, the 'third *realm*' suggests a model or mirror image of the state itself.

The 'third realm' is a paradox. It simultaneously respects and rejects the principle of boundaries. That is to say, it marks out the territory of literary criticism by redrawing the boundaries of public and private. Its announcement that it transcends boundaries constitutes its own boundary. This boundary is intended by Leavis to distinguish literary criticism from other discourses. They belong either to the public or to the private sphere. By contrast the object of criticism, here 'the poem', 'is neither merely private, nor public in the sense that it can be brought into a laboratory, quantified, tripped over or even pointed to' (*TL & O*, p. 36). The question is whether Leavis succeeds in demonstrating that 'the poem' straddles the public/private divide.

In the first instance it should be noted that Leavis fails to illustrate how a poem is not 'merely private', only how it is not public. But in showing how a poem is *not* public he seems to imply that it *is* just that. A poem, he explains, is not public because it *'can* be brought into a laboratory, quantified, tripped over or even pointed to'. The sense is that a poem is not public because it *can* be brought into a laboratory but this is *not* what Leavis means. He intends the opposite, that a poem is not public because it cannot be brought into a laboratory and scrutinised in an impersonal manner.

The fact that Leavis appears to write the opposite of what he means would seem to bear out his claim that language isn't adapted to discussing the 'third realm' (*TM & S*, p. 288). In trying to show how a poem transcends the divide between public and private, Leavis's syntax suggests that it inclines more toward the former state. However, 'the meaning' of the single word 'laboratory' can be construed as simultaneously denoting what is both private and public. Private because of the confidential nature of research – particularly if it is to do with the military – and public because of its accountability to government bodies as well as from the fact that the results of a great deal of research are published and available in magazines such as *Nature* and *New Scientist*.

The significance of this is that 'laboratory' cannot be used, as Leavis intends it be used, to distinguish between literary critical and scientific thinking since the term reveals itself as both public *and* private which is exactly the characteristic of poetry; 'neither merely private, nor public', implying that it is a combination of both. This suggests that language in general is already both public and private or 'neither merely private, nor public'. And, if so, then the 'third realm' is a repetition of what is already the case, it is the essence of what is and, far from breaking new ground, it ratifies the old one. It is therefore conservative, the more so perhaps because it presents the old as the new, which is precisely one of the ways in which Adorno characterises the 'culture industry'.[90]

The convergence of distinct cultural spaces points to a loss of 'the poem'. A poem, writes Leavis, 'cannot be pointed to as a distinct entity but it is possible to point[] to particulars in it' (*TL & O*, p. 36). The particulars of the poem presuppose the existence of the whole but this is denied by Leavis since the poem cannot be pointed to in its entirety. This would seem to undermine Leavis's commitment to unity and wholeness, to 'significant' or 'comprehensive "relatedness"'.[91] The 'absence' of the whole means that there is no organising framework for its various details. Consequently they are dispersed, existing as fragments rather than constitutive parts of an 'organic' whole; the space of 'the poem' has disappeared and so these parts are potentially available for deployment in other discourses. They are free floating, not fixed in the unique hierarchy of 'the poem'. It is 'the poem' as a whole which locates its parts in varying degrees of surface and depth and so its dissolution entails a loss of perspective in the art of reading.

This is apparent in Leavis's equation of 'in' with 'on'. '[T]he only way of pointing to particulars *in* it is to put one's finger *on* given spots in the assemblage of black marks on the page' (*TL & O*, p. 36, italics added). 'In' implies depth, 'on' implies surface. Here, however, to put a finger 'on' the surface of a poem is simultaneously to perceive its depth. Furthermore, the spots which are identified with surface of the poem in contrast to the particulars 'in it' could themselves be viewed in terms of depth since they are '*in* the assemblage of black marks' which themselves are '*on* the page'. Finally, the surface is usually encountered before the depth but, in Leavis's sentence, the particulars *in* the poem are mentioned *before* the 'spots' on which the critic places his or her finger. All this problematises surface and depth as distinct categories.

The 'third realm' sees the loss of spatial barriers between public and private and surface and depth. In place of separate spheres there is a generalised space without perspective or dimension and that is why it cannot be described as surface. It is a medium in which objects are juxtaposed rather than ordered and so it confers equality, or rather sameness, on whatever appears in it. It is the space not of hierarchy but collage. In its disregard of boundaries it approximates to the space of mass culture where, as was noted earlier, 'the borderline between culture and empirical reality becomes more and more indistinct'.[92] And, in its flatness, it corresponds to that 'depthlessness' which Frederic Jameson claims is post-modernism's 'supreme formal feature'.[93] This space, moreover, cannot be divorced from the spread of Western capitalism which, through investment, production and markets pays scant respect to national or even regional barriers. Hans Berten, for example, observes that 'the nation state has lost its relevance' due to the 'homogenizing force' of international capitalism.[94]

The spatial characteristics of the 'third realm' have certain consequences for Leavis's notion of reading. The absence of distinct spatial barriers helps criticism to refer 'sensitively, faithfully and closely'[95] to the work. Criticism, it will be remembered, aims to 're-create' 'the poem' and so reduce the distance between itself and the work. In addition, the depthlessness of the 'third realm' dovetails with Leavis's repeated idea that a work is 'obvious'; that it has no hidden depths since everything that is important about it is immediately apparent.

But this 'depthlessness' causes problems for tradition, which is central to Leavis's idea of reading. Tradition is *something more* than an assemblage of ... separate authors' (italics added).[96] As such when dealing with a new work, the critic asks

> explicitly and implicitly: 'Where does this come? How does it stand in relation to ... ? How relatively important does it seem?' And the organization into which it settles as a constituent in becoming 'placed' is an organization of similarly 'placed' things. (*C & P*, p. 213)

This description of tradition implies the sort of depth which is lacking in the 'third realm'. There, as was argued above, works are juxtaposed rather than related and this gives no sense of their 'relative importance' as conveyed by tradition. On the contrary, the space of the 'third realm', like that of the 'culture industry', reveals a capacity of combining together dissimilar objects, artifacts and persons in a relationship of equivalence. This complements the exchange relation of capitalism and therefore counters the role of tradition in trying to apprehend the unique value of each work. The 'third realm' thus inhibits as well as facilitates what Leavis means by reading.

The depthlessness of the 'third realm' also supports and subverts the self-evidence of a work. This self-evidence depends on the metaphor of sight. That Hopkins's 'religious interests' are bound up with 'a vigour of mind' is 'something that can be seen ... at once'.[97] Such a statement implies a transcendent view of a work. It implies, in other words, ideas of distance and perspective that the 'third realm' has called into question. The challenge to spatial barriers and the play between 'in' and 'on' indicates the fluidity of locations and positions including that of the reader. To put the matter another way, the instability of the prepositions 'in' and 'on' problematises the *pre* position of the reader as someone outside the text and able to view it as a whole.

There are, in any case, intrinsic problems with what may be termed Leavis's empiricist aesthetics. The idea that seeing a poem is equivalent to understanding it plays down the importance of 'the mediating influence of pre-reflective judgements and inferences which are themselves the consequences of previous reflections'.[98] As Leavis himself notes, 'without some relevant predisposition, we can't really perceive' (*SC*, p. 247). Furthermore, there is the fact that, in his discussion of the 'third realm', Leavis speaks only of the parts of a poem, not the whole. This is symptomatic of how, in empiricism, 'attention is inevitably, inextricably linked to inattention'.[99] In the words of Jules David Law, 'While perceiving, we are led from one sign to another; one sign slips out of focus as another sign passes into focus.'[100]

The 'depthlessness' of the 'third realm', together with the tensions in empiricism itself destabilise the notion of the transcendent reader. He or she no longer occupies a secure position in relation to the text because of the dissolution of the spatial co-ordinates on which that position depends. In these circumstances reading is less the certainty of immediate apprehension and more the possibility of vertigo. No longer outside the work, the reader is in danger of being absorbed into it. This is another and perhaps rather extreme way of expressing what Leavis himself says about the act of criticism. On the one hand the critic has the work 'before' (*L & S*, p. 187) or 'in front of' (*MN*, p. 199) him or herself while, on the other, an 'inner response ... take[s] possession of the created work' (*VC*, p. 279). The critic, in other words, is both 'outside' and 'inside' the work.

## SURVEYING THE BODY: PRODUCTION, CRITICISM AND CONSUMPTION

This unresolved dialectic between transcendence and immanence in the act of reading is analogous to the dual action of modernity in respect of embodiment and disembodiment. Both these processes are at work in production and consumption. In the former, the 'natural' body is replaced by the 'body–machine complex' and in the latter 'natural' identities are replaced with 'volunteer' ones.[101] Seltzer describes scientific management's 'disarticulation of natural bodies', its 'mapping of the body onto the machine' and its 're-embodiment of individuals as the "head" and "hands" of a new corporate whole'.[102] He also shows how consumption disavows the 'natural' body through the creation of artificial wants. He sees this 'relative disembodiment' as one of the signs of the '*aestheticization* of the natural body in market culture' and this aestheticization itself as 'the achievement of personation through practices of consumption'.[103]

These transformations, though accented differently are also negotiated in Leavisian criticism. The loss of the 'natural' body of the organic community, for example, is something to be regretted. Yet its disappearance is partly the effect of the diction of scientific management which can be found in Leavis's early criticism. The programme of scientific management was to remake human beings in accordance with the needs of production and profit. By being divided into types appropriate for the various stages of the production process the worker was seen as an extension of the machine and was therefore defined in purely physical terms. His or her human qualities and idiosyncrasies were viewed as sites of uncertainty, conflict and error which had to be eliminated in the interests of efficiency.[104]

Leavis's work, with its emphasis on human creativity (see, for example, *PC & SH*, pp. 186–7) can be seen to define itself against the pragmatic instrumentality of figures like Taylor whose system, in seeking to make human beings more 'manageable' and predictable, left little room for them to create themselves. Furthermore, Leavis's general emphasis on consciousness offers itself as a corrective to scientific management's reduction of human beings to their working bodies.

At the same time, Leavis's work also underwrites the principles of scientific management. In order to ensure the success of its programme, scientific management constantly had to monitor workers' progress. The chief means of doing this was the time and motion study. Scientific management, in short, was a mechanism of surveillance. It would be too much to say that Leavisian criticism surveyed the work in the disciplinary way that scientific management surveyed workers but both are committed to the principle of observation. What is required of 'modernist' bodies, according to Seltzer, is that they be seen. Technologies of the body, such as those represented by scientific management, and also those of the survey, statistics and market research,[105] are examples of the imperative to 'mak[e] everything, including interior states, visible, legible and governable'.[106]

Leavis's view of the work as 'obvious' is one manifestation of this. Where it differs is in its conception of the body. The re-embodiments of modernity are based on a rejection of the 'natural' body whereas Leavis reconfigures English Literature precisely in terms of the 'natural' body as exemplified by the labourer of the organic community. *Revaluation*, for example, with its 'surveying eye',[107] sees the representative poetry of the present as descended not from the 'dream world' (*NB*, p. 14) of nineteenth-century verse but from that of 'the sinew and living nerve' (*R*, p. 19) of seventeenth-century poetry.

This 'body', though 'natural' and 'whole' compared to the engineered body of the worker, is nevertheless a *seen* body. And it is so because of the optical metaphor that underpins the act of reading. Furthermore, this 'body' is a body without an interior for, it will be remembered, the labourer of the organic community is presented as having no inner life. To that extent he – there are no women in *The Wheelwright's Shop* – resembles those whose humanity is subtly redefined by scientific management 'as purely physical, excluding them from the exercise of the mind'.[108]

There is a relation between the visual and the corporeal. The demand that 'everything be made visible'[109] produces a body that can be viewed in its entirety. By being available to inspection this body can be controlled and measured. Both these are apparent in the production process. The worker is controlled through a battery of procedures and regulations governing everything from clothing to 'clocking on' while his or her performance is measured against production targets.[110] More generally, Mark Seltzer has argued that the imperative to measure, evident in the consumer survey and market sample, registers a change in what it means to be 'representative'.[111] They articulate a mean, an average which correlates persons and measure. They 'individualize individuals' producing 'not the individual universal (the "type" of Lukácsian realism) but the statistical person [the consumer] as the typical'.[112]

The assumption behind the sample and the survey is that there is an equivalence between human wants and the market. As Seltzer puts it, 'The logic of the market projects a fantasy of perfect reciprocity ... wants are thus inseparable from the measures, models and standards of consumer culture.'[113] The latter create 'wants' underlining the fact, already evident from scientific management, that 'the individual is something that can be made'.[114] Put simply, he or she identifies with a particular representation which then becomes the basis of his or her 'interior'. The individual is, at it were, 'formed from the outside in'.[115]

The character of this culture is such that value is equated with visibility; it works to eliminate the difference between the appearance of things and their reality. Money is one expression of this. It is the common measure in the exchange of goods, each product displaying its price. Money makes visible the worth of a commodity in relation to others on the market. It posits and appears to guarantee a relationship between symbol and thing. Leavis himself unwittingly testifies to this aspect of money through his analogy of the gold standard for the evaluation of literary works.

Leavis's currency metaphor, like his metaphor of the literary text promotes the principle of visibility. At the level of metaphor, in other words, Leavisian criticism helps to sustain and reproduce a culture of surveillance and measurement, a culture where the equivalence between the market and human wants ultimately 'makes persons into things [and] things ... into persons'.[116] Aspects of Leavis's rhetoric therefore appear to be profoundly at odds with his critique of the measurable and material ends of 'technologico–Benthamite civilisation', increased productivity, more leisure and a rising standard of living.[117]

The word 'appear' is used because it is important to stress that Leavis is *not* opposed to these ends. His argument is only that they 'need to be accompanied by another, and quite different, devotion of purpose and energy, another sustained collaborative effort of creative intelligence' (*TIOC*, p. 95) which would address itself to questions of value, significance and creativity. And '[t]o point out these things', Leavis remarks, 'is not be a Luddite' (p. 95).

The metaphors of currency and the body do not contradict Leavis's main points against 'technologico–Benthamite civilisation', rather they strengthen that element in his argument which acknowledges and accepts it. As such they detract from the emphasis that Leavis wants to give to those ends which do not lend themselves to 'statistical measuration'.[118] This is a different process from Leavis's use of the diction of scientific management; the deployment of words like 'discipline', 'training', 'relevance' and 'organization' and 'control' are actively promoted by Leavis as a programme of reading whereas, as has been seen, there is an air of anxiety, even apology about metaphor since it 'plays down ... life' (*TM & S*, p. 289).

The discourse of scientific management is designed to improve production and, to that end, it reinvents the body of the worker.

Leavis's criticism is implicated in both these to the extent that it utilises the vocabulary of scientific management. It produces, for example, a particular conception of literature, expressed by a notion of tradition as 'something more' (*AB*, p. 49 and *L & S*, p. 184). This 'something more' is used to counter the reduction of human significance to the ends of 'technologico–Benthamite civilisation'. At the same time, however, it serves those ends since tradition is, among other things, 'something more than individual'.[119] That is to say, it has an impersonal character which parallels the disregard of the individual which can be found in surveys and statistics as well as in scientific management, where the aim is to submerge the worker 'into the generalized culture of the corporate "family"'.[120]

Leavisian criticism is also engaged in the production of a particular type of reader. This is evident from *Culture and Environment*. Such a reader would display, among other qualities in their response to works, those of 'maturity', 'intelligence', 'perception', 'sensitivity', 'relevance' and 'delicacy'. As these terms can also describe works of literature[121] it can be argued that a particular type of reader is being produced for a particular type of literature. This too is consistent with scientific management which aims to train the worker for one particular task and no other. But the training of readers is also bound up with the creation of a minority, an educated elite and thus it helps both to rationalise and justify the divisions of class society.[122] Leavisian criticism, in other words, can be said to enact and negotiate the rival claims of class and corporatism for understanding British society.

Since the vocabulary of scientific management produces a new conception of the human body – which might be expressed by saying that the part is greater than the whole – its presence in Leavis's criticism exists in some tension with the metaphor of the 'natural' body. In this respect, Leavis's writing represents one aspect of that process of disembodiment and re-embodiment described earlier. It participates in the process of disembodiment not just through its unwitting alliance with the values of scientific management but also through its rejection of the body associated with the pleasures of mass culture (*CE*, p. 3). It is more difficult to say how Leavis's criticism contributes to the process of re-embodiment in modernity since it resurrects the very body that modernity has disavowed. In any case, such a body can only exist in the analogical form of the novel, poetry being understood more in terms of voice. But, bearing in mind these reservations it is still the case that the 'return' of the 'natural' body in Leavis's writing can act as a check on and critique of the 'part' body of scientific management.

The 'natural' body may be anachronistic from the point of view of production but not from that of consumption, with which it has a much more ambiguous relationship. As Seltzer has noted, the paradox of consumption

> is the manner in which a style of life characterized by its excessiveness or gratuitousness – by its exceeding or disavowing material, and natural and bodily needs – is yet understood on the model of the natural body and its needs, that is, on the model of hunger and eating.[123]

Consumerism simultaneously affirms and denies the 'natural' body in a continuous process of disembodiment and re-embodiment.

Disembodiment is intrinsic to the term 'consumption' itself which, in the nineteenth century, was a synonym for tuberculosis, a disease 'in which the body was consumed'.[124] It is important to stress the link between consumption and disease since Leavis's criticism of the culture of consumption was conducted partly through a metaphor of health (see, for example, *CE*, p. 4) which itself reflected the concerns of the social hygiene movement. This movement proposed a whole series of reforms 'involving medical inspection, control, regulation, and increasingly institutionalisation'[125] and so it was as committed to the principle of visibility as Leavisian criticism, therefore making the metaphor of health an appropriate part of its rhetoric. In addition, the ultimate concern of the social hygiene movement – one of whose main targets, incidentally, was tuberculosis[126] – was to increase economic efficiency.[127] Leavis's metaphor of health thus serves the interests of production at the same time that it critiques consumption.

Seltzer has described 'the move from an ethos of production to a culture of consumption' in terms of 'a replacement of the natural body by its substitutes or representations'.[128] A simple example of this would be the desire to model oneself on the image of the perfect body found in advertisements. Hence, according to Mike Featherstone, advertising creates a world 'in which individuals are made to become emotionally vulnerable, constantly monitoring themselves for bodily imperfections'.[129] More generally, Robert Bocock argues that consumption is a process in which a purchaser of an item 'is actively engaged in trying to create and maintain *a sense of identity* through the display of purchased goods'.[130] What is important here is the image of the item rather than the item itself. This image signifies the kind of person someone is both to themselves and others. Consumption is concerned with signs and symbols rather than things and objects, with representations of the body rather than the 'natural' body itself.

Seltzer's account of the rise of consumer society matches Leavis's description of the transition from the relations of the organic community to the contiguities of civilisation. Seltzer claims that the 'natural' body is replaced by its 'substitutes', Leavis that the organic community is replaced by the 'substitute' of literature. More particularly, Leavis understands the organic community in terms of a body which is reconfigured in the 'body' of the literary work. This, however, while showing that the same imagery is used to illustrate the rise of literary criticism and consumerism, also shows that the organic community is itself already a representation since it is apprehended through a metaphor of the 'natural' body. Such an observation seriously challenges the explanation of the rise of both literary criticism and consumerism as the replacement of the 'natural' body by its representations. It would be more correct to say that there are only representations and it is these which change with the development of a culture of consumerism.

While it is important not to collapse the differences between Leavis and Seltzer – one is concerned with the maintenance of tradition, the other with 'the rival determinations of the individuality of the individual in consumer society'[131] – it is also important to note the similarities between them. What is implicit in Leavis's rhetoric and imagery – modernity as a process of disembodiment and re-embodiment – is explored by Seltzer. A comparison of the two helps to account for why literary criticism and consumerism appeared *together* in a *pronounced* form in the early 1930s. One reason is that criticism provides consumerism with that model of the 'natural' body whose 'return' consumer culture constantly demands.[132]

A key similarity is that the embodiments of criticism and consumerism are both couched in a rhetoric of freedom whose nature it seems necessary to demonstrate by measuring it against the embodiments of class and gender.[133] Leavis, in his debate with Marxism stressed the autonomy of the human spirit and its freedom from determination but this is accompanied, at least in *Culture and Environment*, by a strong sense of mass culture as a body that is by turns both female and working class (see *CE*, pp. 17, 49, 57, 91). The implication is that the emphatic physicality of these embodiments is due to their being determined, the corollary being that freedom from determination is associated with a state of relative disembodiment. Consequently, while Leavisian criticism may provide a means of transcending the determinations of the 'immediate environment' (p. 4) that form women and the working class, it does so at the cost of a diminished sense of its own particular version of embodiment.

## THE LANGUAGE OF CRITICISM AND THE PROBLEM OF READING: TRADITION AND ADVERTISING

It is clear from the above that Leavisian criticism is deeply entangled with the logic and rhetoric of production and consumption. As such, it enacts the contradiction between the two which Seltzer has described as 'an ascetics of production (self-discipline)' versus 'an aesthetic of consumption (self-aggrandizement)'.[134] The former is evident in Leavis's use of words like 'discipline', 'precision', 'discrimination', 'relevance' and 'delimitation' which are used to 'produce' a specific discourse, literary criticism, whose function is to articulate and sustain a concept of tradition based on a notion of literature as read by trained practitioners. The latter is apparent in the problem of 'something more' which, as has been shown, takes many different forms in Leavis's work. Among other things, it supplements definitions, combats the reductions of civilisation, is the excess of metaphor and the transcendence of tradition.

This 'something more' can be regarded as the literary critical expression of the imperative 'to consume more and more'.[135] Just as 'something more' cannot finally be explained by any one of its manifestations neither can the desire to consume be satisfied by any one commodity. As argued earlier, this is because consumption is directed less at the object than at what it stands for, prestige, sophistication, poise and so on. These cannot be purchased and so possession of the object is always going to fuel rather than satisfy desire.

Baudrillard claims that this situation leads to 'a frustrated desire for totality'[136] and again there is a parallel with Leavis's work. Specifically, Leavis is concerned with the unity of a work and the organisation of tradition, however, as has been shown, he has difficulty in building the parts of a work into a whole. Tradition is problematic because, like 'life', 'the only way in which one can point to [it] as concretely "there" is to point to an individual [work]' (*TL & O*, p. 42) and yet, at the same time, it 'doesn't need to be incorporated to be "there"', (*TM & S*, p. 289) because it is 'something more than an assemblage of individual masterpieces' (*AB*, p. 49). It is such contrary formulations which give rise to and perpetuate the problem of 'something more' in Leavis's work.

The contradiction between production and consumption affects the conception of the body in Leavis's criticism. The 'natural' and 'whole' body of the craftsman co-exists with the 'artificial' and 'part' body of the worker required by scientific management. The 'part' body serves the desire for 'something more' while the 'natural' body underwrites the way the body is made conspicuous in consumer culture to compensate for its being filtered out of the proliferating discourses of administration and social regulation. Leavisian criticism, in other words, through its entanglement with the discourses of production and consumption, enacts the disembodiments and re-embodiments characteristic of modernity. This explains the ambiguity of 'the poem' being 'there' and not 'there'. By being conceived as a body, 'the poem' is inevitably caught up in the dialectic of disembodiment and re-embodiment that structures the notion of the body in Leavis's work. True, 'the poem' is most often presented in terms of voice but in the 'third realm' it is equated with a body through Leavis's phrase that minds meet in 'the poem'. The notion of mind instantly conjures up its opposite term, body, and the ultimate suggestion is that minds are embodied in 'the poem' in the same way that literary works embody 'experience'.

The contradiction between production and consumption, between restraint and excess constitutes the act of reading. On the one hand criticism should respond 'sensitively and with precise discrimination to the words on the page' (*TSOC*, p. 228). On the other hand there is the question of how these particular words combine with others to create that distinctive whole which is the work. There is also the matter of how these works are selected and combined to form a tradition which is conceived as 'something more' than an 'accumulation of separate works' (*L & S*, p. 184).

As a discipline of relevance and the production of 'something more', reading is a problem of organisation. How do the parts of a work build into the whole and where does this whole fit into 'the' tradition? As has been seen, the parts do not always cohere to form a unity. In the 'third realm', for example, 'the poem' is a collection of particulars which are never resolved into a final form. Similarly, tradition can never be grasped as a whole because it is only ever perceived in individual instances, whose existence in any case, following the logic of the last sentence, is in doubt.

Despite the pursuit of unity therefore, Leavisian criticism rarely seems to achieve it. This need not be viewed negatively for it challenges the unity of the 'culture industry' by calling into question the very possibility of closure. However, it could be argued that the 'culture industry' itself rejects the idea of closure through the promotion of consumerism which stimulates desire without ever satisfying it. In this context, the failure to achieve unity in Leavis merely reinforces the openness of consumer culture. What this ignores, though, is the signifying system of consumerism. As Baudrillard has observed, there is no real difference between commodities because they all promote the desirability of the 'life style'[137] of advanced capitalism. As such, consumer culture is closed. In the words of Baudrillard, consumption 'is a complete set of values, with all that the term implies concerning group integration and social control'.[138]

Advertising is of crucial importance to this process. Baudrillard claims that it is 'a system of signification but not language, for it lacks an active syntax'.[139] Advertising, argues Baudrillard, 'has the simplicity and effectiveness of a code'.[140] He continues:

> It does not structure the personality; it designates and classifies it. It does not structure social relations: it demarcates them in a hierarchical repertoire. It is formalized in a universal system of recognition of social statuses: a code of 'social standing'.[141]

This is a familiar point, the commodity as the criterion which defines social being. But what Baudrillard is anxious to emphasise is that it is rapidly becoming the only means of identifying someone's 'social standing'. Baudrillard acknowledges that commodities, or what he calls 'objects', have always constituted a system of recognition 'but in conjunction with, and often in addition to, other systems (gestural, ritual, ceremonial, language, birth status, code of moral values, etc.).[142] What is distinctive about consumer capitalism, he continues, is that 'other systems of recognition are progressively withdrawing'.[143]

Baudrillard's analysis of advertising is strikingly similar to Leavis's. Baudrillard claims that advertising classifies the personality, a claim borne out by Leavis's analysis of selected advertisements in *Culture and Environment* (*CE*, pp. 11–25). Further, both Baudrillard and Leavis are in agreement about the condition of language in consumer culture. For Baudrillard, advertising squeezes out other means of recognition, evaluation and relation while for Leavis, advertising 'debas[es] ... important words' as well as 'our emotional vocabulary' (p. 53) and therefore its potential to 'structure' personality, leaving advertising free to 'classify' it. The differences between Baudrillard and Leavis are first that Leavisian criticism participates in the very process it criticises. For example, it too, like advertising, classifies people. 'What kind of person', writes Leavis, 'can you imagine as responding to such an appeal as this last?' (p. 51). Second, Leavis, unlike Baudrillard, actively promotes the maintenance of tradition through literature as a means of resisting the depredations of advertising.

The key difference between advertising and tradition is that in the former every object means the same, in the latter, every work is different. This affects the signifying structure of advertising and tradition respectively. Baudrillard has claimed that advertising 'lacks an active syntax', whereas Leavis claims that tradition provides 'a cultural grammar and syntax' to deal with the 'tropical profusion of topics and vocabularies' which characterise 'mass civilisation'.[144] Advertising's lack of syntax means that it does not distinguish between goods, they all signify the same thing and therefore the best way for advertising to get its message across is to present these goods *en masse*.

The grammar of tradition, by contrast, so places each work as to make manifest its unique value. It can only do this by operating on a principle of selection. The criteria for selection, for example 'representativeness', highlight what certain works have in common without making them equivalent. This preserves a principle of differentiation to counteract the drive of advertising to reduce everything to the same meaning. Tradition selects and combines to create an order in which works are meaningfully related to one another. Advertising neither selects nor combines, it is 'strictly asyntactic: diverse brands follow one another, are juxtaposed and substituted for one another without articulation or transition'.[145] Compared to tradition therefore, advertising is an 'impoverished language[]: full of signification and empty of meaning'.[146]

But, as mentioned earlier, Leavisian criticism can operate in the manner of advertising. Juxtaposition, for example, is one of its favoured modes of procedure (*CE*, p. 51). Such parallels render ambiguous its notions of order and hierarchy. A similar ambiguity afflicts key Leavisian terms such as 'representativeness' and 'standard'. The ambiguity of these derives from the transition from a *laissez-faire* to a corporate economy. To put it schematically, the individual is the important category of the former and the citizen of the latter. The individual is defined by his or her difference and autonomy, the citizen by his or her sameness and conformity.[147] This changes the meaning of 'representative' and 'standard'.

## TERMS AND TRANSCENDENCE

For Leavis, *The Pilgrim's Progress* is 'a representative product'[148] of puritan culture. Its 'human significance' (*PP*, p. 35) is due to it being 'a vehicle of collective wisdom and basic assumptions, a currency of criteria and valuations collaboratively determined' (p. 41). 'Representative' here concerns the linguistic resources of the culture but in the modern world it is defined as conformity to a model such as that provided by the consumer survey and marketing sample. Leavis uses 'representative' to refer to the creative potential of language as it is manifested through the literature of any given period but, for modernity, the term means measuring human beings against a statistical average.

Leavis himself is not able to banish the notion of measurement entirely from valuation (*MN*, p. 190) hence it is an element of 'representative' since part of the process of valuation is to determine exactly which works are 'representative'. The work that is 'representative' becomes a measure of the culture. The very word encourages the reader to view a culture as homogeneous instead of as a collection of diverse practices. The 'representative' work establishes a hierarchy of what is acceptable, normal and approved, thereby compelling different activities to submit to a common measure. This is to state the case extremely. The point is that the term 'representative' in Leavis's writing means both creativity and measurement and this reflects the tension between the categories of individual and citizen.

The same is true of the term 'standard'. The difference between *laissez-faire* individualism and corporate citizenship is registered in the difference between the notion of the standard as personal, 'ideal and extraordinary ... and the notion of the standard as the normal, the average and the measurable'.[149] This difference can be found in the two uses of the term 'standard' in Leavis's criticism. In the first place it refers to standards of literature, in the second place to a process of standardisation. The first sense is inseparable from the notion of judgement. The critic appeals to 'standards' on the basis of his or her judgements. '[S]tandards are "there",' writes Leavis, 'for the critic to appeal to only in so far as there is [an educated public]; one capable of responding when appealed to, and of making its responses felt' (*SC*, p. 244). Judgements 'must be personal and sincere,' as Leavis puts it, 'I cannot have my judging done for me by someone else. Either I judge for myself or there is no judging' (*VC*, p. 277). The second sense of 'standard' concerns the 'relation between the standardization of commodities and standardization of persons' (*CE*, p. 32). In this context the 'standard' is what is average not what is authentic.

Although Leavis opposes the personal 'standard' against the standardisations of mass culture there is a blurring of the two terms. That is to say, the personal standard involves an element of impersonality. An understanding of tradition, for example, means that 'a good critic, or a cultivated person of sure judgement … exhibit[s] more than merely individual taste' (*CE*, p. 82). This detracts from the notion of the personal judgement as does the fact that this judgement itself requires approval – 'This is so, isn't it?' – which suggests a potential deficiency in the genuinely personal response. The determining influence of tradition in this response and the desire to match it with the response of others begins to blur the boundary between the personal standard and the standard as the measurable and the mean.

One way in which Leavis guards against the merger of the two meanings is by arguing that the standards to which the literary critic appeals are implicit. This was discussed in some detail in relation to 'Mass Civilisation and Minority Culture'. The points to note here are first, that the notion of implicit standards undermines the drive to visibility which is such a strong feature of Leavis's work. And, in the process it separates out 'standard' from 'standardization' since the latter term is implicated in the transparencies of 'mass culture': to standardise is to make available a common measure that is visible everywhere. The second point is that the notion of an *implicit* standard helps to conserve the idea of authenticity. As Simmel expresses it, 'The attraction of the "genuine", in all its contexts, consists in its being more than its immediate appearance.'[150] By keeping standards implicit, Leavis is endeavouring to protect notions of the 'genuine' and the 'authentic' from the standardisations of 'mass culture', though how successful he is is another matter.

The mingling of meanings in a single word runs alongside a cluster of terms referring to 'character' and 'personality' respectively. Warren Susman has suggested that the nineteenth century was concerned with character, the twentieth with personality.[151] According to Mike Featherstone, words associated with character include 'discipline' and 'self-denial' and those associated with personality include 'dominant', 'creative' and 'forceful'.[152] It would be too much to say that Leavis's criticism is structured around these terms but it is nevertheless the case that the words 'discipline', 'creative' and 'force' do occupy prominent positions in his vocabulary. Furthermore, 'self-denial' could be applied to Leavis's attitude towards the pleasures of the body in 'mass culture' while the notion of 'dominant' could be used to describe criticism's violent appropriation of the text.

The co-presence of these terms or the ideas associated with them suggests that Leavis's criticism reflects the shift in emphasis from 'character' to 'personality'. This is simply a different way of expressing an earlier point, namely that Leavisian criticism negotiates the changing relationship between body and mind in consumer culture; the move from 'character' to 'personality' capturing, in schematic form, the growing importance of the body at the expense of the mind.

The complex transformations between body and mind are bound up with changes in the nature of production and consumption. These are enacted through Leavis's vocabulary, his image of the body and his concern with inwardness. Since the purpose of his criticism is to teach reading, the act of reading itself becomes entangled with the transactions between body and mind, production and consumption. Ideally, each act of reading presents an opportunity to resolve these tensions; in practice, however, they seem merely to reproduce them. The fact that Leavisian criticism describes certain problems, such as the loss of boundaries, suggests its distance from them, a distance which allows it to see these problems clearly. But this appears to be no more than an illusion when it is remembered how Leavisian criticism also enacts, and thereby perpetuates, these very same problems.

The above considerations cast doubt on the critic's ability 'to realize as sensitively and completely as possible this or that which claims his [or her] attention' (C & P, p. 213). Since the work needs to be realised, it cannot be described as 'obvious'. In realising the work, criticism behaves in a manner akin to psychoanalysis; it makes manifest what is latent. This implies that criticism has a transcendent view of the work, a transcendence which is based on an imitation of it since Leavis claims that criticism also seeks to 're-create' the work. But even if criticism can be supposed to transcend the work it cannot transcend

itself. This is evident in its blindness to the import of its own
vocabulary, imagery metaphors, logic and rhetoric, all of which
depend on another discourse to 'realise' them in much the same way
as 'literature' depends on criticism to 'realise' it as 'literature'.

Not being able to read itself casts doubt on criticism's claim to
read literature. Instead of focusing on the work, criticism seems
caught up in the play of tensions between production and
consumption without being aware that that is what it is doing. Such
unawareness means that criticism cannot transcend itself, which
suggests, paradoxically, the existence of boundaries whose loss it
otherwise enacts. This particular boundary is a form of unconsciousness regarding the significance of its own textuality which is
highly ironic since criticism is viewed as the ability to respond
'sensitively and with precise discrimination to the words on the page'
(*TSOC*, p. 228). Confined within its own boundary, criticism becomes
a distorted mirror for the atomisation of the consumer.[153]


## READING BY THE BODY

The contradiction between production and consumption centres on
the body, that problematic term in Leavis's criticism. Leavis claims
to read 'with the ear and by the body, as one reads or should read
Shakespeare [and] all poets that matter' (*ROP*, p. 268). But there is an
altogether more tactile quality to his description of reading in the 'third
realm': 'the only way of pointing to particulars in [the poem] is put
one's fingers on given spots in the assemblage of black marks on the
page' (*TL & O*, p. 36). To touch a 'spot' is somehow to transform it
into a 'particular' but, though the body is credited with this, it cannot
piece these particulars together to form a whole.

One reason for this is that the body itself is not a whole, being
divorced from the mind. This is implicit in Leavis's claim that 'minds
meet in [a poem]' (*TL & O*, p. 36) as if prior to that meeting they existed
in some disembodied state. Another reason why reading by the body
does not unify the parts of a poem into a whole has to do with the
changed meaning of the body in consumer culture. As Featherstone
observes, 'the progressive expansion of the market ... discredit[ed]
and unhing[ed] long held meanings which were firmly grounded in
social relationships and cultural objects'.[154] One consequence of this
is that the body loses its relation to history and 'liv[es] only for the
moment'.[155] It therefore cannot read with that due sense of tradition

which Leavis regards as a vital element in the apprehension of a literary work. Tradition provides a notion of wholeness since it is only by being placed in relation to other works that a particular work acquires its distinctive unity. The suggestion that reading is tactile gives it a sense of immediacy but not wholeness since the particulars remain particulars. As such, Leavis's discussion of the 'third realm' endorses, albeit inadvertently, the new hedonistic body of consumer culture.

This body is a body 'of pleasure'.[156] One of its pleasures, according to Seltzer, is that of a 'corporeal absorption'[157] in what it sees. This forms a dialectic with the power of seeing which depends on distance. A transparent society, one whose members '*see* [themselves] continually on the videoscreen of statistics'[158] is one where

> the power of seeing is quickly disrupted by the pleasures of seeing: the very absorption in, even intoxication with, seeing opens up the possibility of violent loss of balance or *dis*empowerment.[159]

This seems to describe that tension between transcendence and immanence which characterises the Leavisian reader who simultaneously appears to be outside and inside the work.

Leavis continually asserts that criticism is a matter of inwardness both with the self and with the work: '[t]he process ... of inner response and discipline by which we take possession of the created work' (*VC*, p. 279). The loss of the transcendent position in relation to the work, however, makes this inwardness the result of a 'fall' into the work rather a controlled exploration of it. But, as was discussed earlier, the 'third realm' subverts conventional notions of space such as inside and outside, surface and depth, thus rendering the usual notion of inwardness untenable. In its place is a condition of depthlessness which corresponds to the body as 'surface'; the 'body' of the poem as 'read' by the 'body' of the reader, neither of them having the 'depth' that conventionally comes from 'inwardness'.

Such a consideration pushes into the background the question of consciousness and into the foreground the body and its pleasures. As such, it recalls Barthes's analysis of the pleasure of the text as that moment 'when my body pursues its own ideas, for my body does not have the same ideas as I do'.[160] This was discussed earlier in relation to *Culture and Environment*. The relevant point here is Barthes's identification of pleasure with excess,[161] with the text, 'in the form of a body split ... into erotic sites'[162] by the body of the reader so that it is 'outside any imaginable finality' – *even that of pleasure.*[163]

Seltzer and Barthes provide a new perspective on Leavisian criticism's concern with embodiment. Specifically, embodiment appears to be as much an accidental as a deliberate feature of the reading process understood as a desire to be 'inward' with the work. This is due to the destabilising of the transcendent reading position which 'topples' the reader into the work. Instead of surveying it, he or she is drawn into it. Seltzer and Barthes bring out the element of pleasure involved in this absorption, locating it in the body, arguably at the expense of consciousness. This bodily pleasure, which in its extreme form shades into bliss and so resists expression,[164] explains why Leavis does not believe language is adapted to discussing the 'third realm' (*TM & S*, p. 288).

The main point, however, is that pleasure prevents unity. It does so in two ways. First because its very existence seems to depend on the undermining of that transcendent position which sustains the reader's consciousness, thereby allowing him or her to realise the text by seeing it as a whole, and second because pleasure, according to Barthes, is associated with excess and transgression. This makes it a perfect complement for the 'third realm', which is founded on the blurring of boundaries.

## LEAVIS, DERRIDA AND 'FORCE'

If pleasure is a form of excess then it parallels the nature of 'force' in Leavisian criticism. This too militates against the principles of wholeness and unity. There are many different terms and meanings to do with 'force' in Leavisian criticism. It is related to production and to the unsettling resonances of metaphor. It is related to life, particularly Leavis's appreciation of Lawrence, whose 'vitality of ... thought is one with his extraordinary power of living'[165] but it is also analogous to the 'death instinct' because it drives beyond those boundaries upon whose existence Leavisian criticism depends. Since it seems to stand for so many meanings, some of which, like the last two, are flatly opposed to one another, 'force' can be understood as a process that problematises meaning. This is also evident from its role in Leavis's rhetoric. Terms like 'insist', 'emphasise' and 'enforce' are deployed to make the obvious 'obvious': 'I need ... to enforce my point, which, obvious as it is, is so important as to demand full critical recognition' (*TW & C*, p. 43). But to insist on the 'obvious' is, of course, to call the 'obvious' into question. Finally, force can be said to characterise criticism's relationship to the work, in that it 'penetrates', 'grasps' and 'possesses' it. All these verbs suggest less a respect for meaning than an appropriation of it for other purposes.

Derrida's discussion of force helps to clarify Leavis's use of the term. According to Derrida any attempt to articulate meaning as a unity 'necessarily' forms a

> restricted passageway ... against which all possible meanings push each other, preventing each other's emergence ... but calling upon each other ... in a kind of autonomous over assemblage of meanings'.[166]

The endeavour to express wholeness creates a pressure, a force that dissipates it. This would seem to be relevant to Leavisian criticism with the value it attaches to relatedness, unity and wholeness. It is here that Leavis can be seen to differ from Derrida since the latter believes that totality is impossible because language – and therefore, by implication, literature – 'excludes totalization'.[167] Language, Derrida continues, is a field of play

> that is to say, a field of infinite substitutions only because it is finite, that is to say, because instead of being an inexhaustible field ... instead of being too large, there is something missing from it: a center which arrests and grounds the play of substitutions.[168]

Although Leavisian criticism can be described in terms of substitution – the literary work for the organic community – and although it is cognisant of its own ungrounded nature due to the dissolution of a common culture, it is nevertheless committed to establishing, quite literally, a 'centre' (*LS*, p. 210) in the form of an English school that will promote a form of thought that overcomes 'the dualism[s] of subject and object, fact and value' (*TW & C*, p. 45). Were it not for this holistic ambition, Leavis's work might prove more of an exception to Derrida's claim that 'literary criticism is structuralist in every age'[169] than it already is. For example, Leavis's criticism does not separate itself from force nor from the work so that the latter, 'divested of its forces', can be 'more clearly perceived'.[170]

What Leavisian criticism tries to do instead is to marry force and totality, something which Derrida claims is impossible.

Force in whatever form – and it has to be said that Derrida's characterisation of it is highly abstract – is inimical to the notions of wholeness, unity and totality. Another factor which militates against these qualities is 'space' itself. Leavis notes that 'any suggestion of the spatial misrepresents the Third Realm' (*TM & S*, p. 289). The problematising of space in the 'third realm' has consequences for the notions of shape and form. If the 'third realm' precludes any hint of the spatial then it is not a medium in which it is possible to conceive of a whole work since this depends precisely on those qualities of shape and form that are not just dependent upon but which help to define the spatial itself. Furthermore, the 'wholeness' of the work can only truly emerge from an act of 'placing valuation' (*MN*, p. 200) but no such act is possible where there is no space for works to be so 'placed'.

Leavis does not explain what he means when he dissociates any notion of the spatial from the 'third realm'. His claim that it is 'neither merely private nor public' (*TL & O*, p. 36) does not help because this implies a different conception of space rather than no space at all. This absence of space not only makes it difficult to conceive of the work as a unity but, more radically, throws its very existence into doubt. Derrida accounts for there being 'no *space* of the work'[171] by arguing that it is impossible for the work ever to be '*present*' in the sense of being 'summarized by some absolute simultaneity or instantaneousness'.[172] This may throw some light on the 'spacelessness' of the 'third realm' because as 'the poem' is never fully present then it cannot be précised.

Since 'the poem' is never quite established, it cannot be said to occupy space. And yet this hardly seems satisfactory, for how can a poem, which is to be a 'living reality in the present',[173] possibly fulfil that expectation, unless it enters the space of that present? It may be better to see 'the poem' as producing its own space which is contrary to that of the 'culture industry' where everything is the same because it is visible and where everything is controlled because it is surveyed. The fact that 'the poem' is always deferred, means that it resists visibility and therefore control. Not being fully 'there', it can never be made transparent by summary. 'The poem's' space, like 'the poem' itself, is always provisional, never definitive. Such freedom, however, excludes unity.

The lack of unity is not just a product of the special characteristics of space, force or the body, it is something that is inherent in Leavis's criticism through his emphasis on sensuous particularity. This inclines his criticism away from unity, wholeness and relatedness despite his attachment to these principles. Hence Leavisian criticism is always in danger of perceiving the work as a collection of particulars rather than as an organic unity. And, if this is the case, then 'the work' cannot be considered as 'representative' of society since such a relation rests on a notion of wholeness which 'the work', as a mess of fragments, confounds. If a work is to be representative, there must be a unity that it can be representative of, and, if it is to be representative of that unity, then it follows that 'the work' itself must be one.

Unless properly understood, fragmentation can appear as a species of unity. For example, a fragmented work can be representative of a fragmented society, the fragmented condition of each being redeemed by the homologous relation between them. What has to be stressed is that there is no work as such; the fragments remain fragments, they do not build into a whole that is identifiable as 'the work'. 'The work' has no borders and no space and it cannot therefore be representative. This is an extreme conception of 'the work' but it is consistent with Leavis's concern with the concrete and with the fact that, in the 'third realm' the particulars never progress to a poem. Leavisian criticism thus seems to deny the idea of relation even as it upholds it; this denial perhaps constituting a critique of the term in a society where all relation, according to Adorno, is domination.[174]

## THE PROBLEM OF INTENTION AND THE 'THIRD REALM'

The notion of intention is important to Leavis's understanding of the 'third realm'. Criticism, in the 'third realm' is 'essentially the process by which we "meet" in a meaning; the poem stands there before us and we "meet" in it' (*TM & S*, p. 288). The poem, it will be noted, is equated with a single meaning rather than with a number of meanings, a view that supports Leavis's assertion that there is a 'correct reading of the poem'.[175] This meaning is the product of intention.

Thought about language should entail the full and firm recognition that words 'mean' because individual human beings have meant the meaning, and that there is no meaning unless individual human beings can meet in it, the completing of the element of 'intend' being represented by the responding someone's certitude that the last condition obtains. (*TL & O*, p. 58)

Like E.D. Hirsch,[176] Leavis identifies the meaning of a work with what the author intended. The role of the critic is to recognise the meaning of the work as intended, thereby endorsing the connection between intention and meaning.

This account, however, does not do justice to the complexity of the 'third realm'. In the first place, to identify 'the poem' with a meaning is to give it a presence and a transparency that is at odds with Leavis's claim that 'the poem' has yet to be established. Secondly, the purpose of the 'third realm' is to make manifest the special kind of thought that attaches to the study of literature, but the equation of 'the poem' with the author's meaning fails to differentiate this thought from 'ordinary' kinds of thought. That is to say, literature cannot be regarded as distinct from other discourses on the grounds that its meanings are intended, as this would apply to most forms of exchange. Furthermore, to see 'the poem' as the expression of the author's intended meaning echoes the very view of language that Leavis consistently repudiates, namely that it is 'a method of symbolising human thought'.[177] Leavis want to show that language, particularly literary language, is 'more' than that and he locates this 'more' in tradition – 'my point is that language is more than a "means of expression": it embodies values, constatations, distinctions, promptings, recognitions of potentiality' (*TL & O*, p. 49). Since language is more than a means of expression, the poem cannot be entirely accounted for in terms of it being the expression of its author's meaning.

Indeed, it is hard to know what sense to make of the idea that 'words "mean" because individual human beings have meant the meaning', in the light of the distinction, derived from Blake, that Leavis makes between 'identity' and 'selfhood'.

The individual as 'selfhood' wills egotistically, from his [her] own enclosed centre, and is implicitly intent on asserting possession. As creative identity, the individual is the agent of life and 'knows he does not belong to himself'. He serves something that is quite other than his [her] selfhood, which is blind and blank to it. (*PC & SH*, p. 172)

This distinction, which problematises the notion of agency, would seem to correspond to another that Leavis makes in respect of intention, namely that 'the deep animating intention ... is something very different from the intention the author would declare'.[178]

What follows from this is that 'real' meaning appears to come less from the individual's self than from tradition which, moreover, constitutes his or her true identity. This is a very different understanding of the relationship between meaning and intention from the one Leavis gives in his account of the 'third realm'. There he clearly implies that the author's intention determines the poem's meaning. Now it seems intention is the effect of the individual's identity which itself is the product of tradition.

Meaning not only emanates from tradition but from deep within the body as well. Words are 'servants of an inner impulse ... imperiously commanded and controlled from an inner centre'.[179] Meaning is first decentered from intention to tradition and then from consciousness to the body, where the vocabulary of force is again in evidence. This vocabulary describes how language is shaped by impulse, which suggests an analogy between 'force' and unconscious processes such as the return of the repressed. Leavis's description that 'it is the burden to be delivered, the precise and urgent command from within that determines expression' (*J & TRW*, p. 121) hints at the existence of an inner compulsion that subordinates language to its own ends. Meaning seems to be the product of 'impulse' as well as intention and, in this respect, Leavis demonstrates, albeit unwittingly, Lacan's point that '[b]ehind what a discourse says, there is what it means, and behind what it means, there is again another intended meaning, and nothing will ever be exhausted by that'.[180]

A final problem concerning the source and therefore the status of meaning has to do with the critic. Leavis claims that 'the poem' has a particular meaning because that is the one intended by the author. But then Leavis uses the author's work as an expression of his own meaning. 'In expounding Lawrence,' he writes, 'I express my own thoughts' (*MN*, p. 195). A work's meaning is therefore intended by the critic as well as the author.

## LEAVIS, LACAN AND 'RECOGNITION'

This use of literary by critical discourse is similar to what Lacan calls 'interlineation',[181] the process whereby the discourse of the unconscious 'takes possession'[182] of another discourse in order to win recognition for the subject's desire. It is interesting that Lacan sees the unconscious as taking possession of another discourse for this corresponds to the critic's 'first concern', which is 'to enter into possession of the given poem' (*C & P*, p. 213). Furthermore, the critic's 'constant concern is never to lose his [her] completeness of possession' (p. 213.)

What is at stake in this possession of 'the given poem' is the desire for recognition. The key question of Leavisian criticism is 'This is so, isn't it?'. Recognition is also central to psychoanalysis: 'That the subject should come to recognise and to name his [her] desire, that is the efficacious action of analysis.'[183] That recognition should be central to Leavisian criticism and Lacanian psychoanalysis can be explained by the rise of consumerism which, as Baudrillard has argued, means a withdrawal of all forms of recognition other than that conferred by the object. Consumerism removes a number of different grounds for social belief and action, replacing them with the single one of the commodity.

This alters the perceptions of persons. Simplifying drastically, they are no longer recognised in relation to their place in a community but according to how well, in the new emphasis on personality, they can win and hold attention. And in the culture of consumerism the best way to do this is through the ownership and display of goods. But it is not only consumerism that changes the ways of seeing people, so too does bureaucracy. As Max Weber has noted:

> Its specific character, which is welcomed by capitalism, develops the more completely the more the bureaucracy is 'dehumanised', the more completely it succeeds in eliminating ... love, hatred, and all purely personal, irrational and emotional elements which escape calculation.[184]

Both consumerism and bureaucracy change the meaning of what it is to be a person. No longer is anyone recognised in terms of autonomy and creativity but by what he or she consumes and by how far he or she conforms to rationally calculable principles.

Leavisian criticism and Lacanian psychoanalysis face problems of grounding in this culture because each wants to maintain a different notion of what it means to be a person. The problem of grounding has already been discussed in relation to 'Mass Civilisation and

Minority Culture', when Leavis complained that certain terms needed supplementing because they could no longer be taken for granted and, in the case of Lacan, it is sufficient to note his anxiety over whether psychoanalysis could be established on a secure footing.[185] Nor is it necessary to go into detail regarding each discipline's respective notion of what it is that constitutes a person. It is enough to observe that, for Leavis, a person is defined through the qualities of 'consciousness', 'sensitivity', 'maturity', 'delicacy', 'complexity' and so forth. These can be ranged in defiant opposition to the superficialities of the consumer. The subject of Lacanian psychoanalysis, however, has an altogether more ambiguous relationship with the consumer in as much as it partly validates the 'non-being' on which consumerism depends.

If criticism 'possesses' literature in order to win recognition, what exactly is it seeking recognition for? The 'meaning' of a poem? The 'creatively original writer'? The astuteness of the critic? (*SC*, p. 246) or the claim that it alone is the truly professional criticism compared to the *belle lettres* of Bloomsbury or the social and personal values of the London literary scene? To ask this question is to assume that recognition is being sought for a specific thing and, in a sense, this is true: Leavis does want recognition for his specific practice of criticism and for his claim that certain writers are more important than others. This, however, takes no real account of the highly complex relations between desire and recognition as described by Lacan.

The relevant consideration here is Lacan's claim that 'man's desire finds its meaning in the desire of the other ... because the first object of desire is to be recognized by the other'.[186] Being brutally reductive, this means that the subject wins recognition by naming his or her desires in language, what in his early writings Lacan calls the 'symbolic system' and in his later ones 'the other'. In naming his or her desires in language, the subject names them as 'other' to him or herself. And, although this implies that the subject has 'true' desires which languages cannot express, this is not in fact the case. What happens instead, according to Lacan, is that

> something of the subject's becomes detached in the very symbolic world [language] that he [she] is engaged in integrating. From then on it will no longer be something belonging to the subject. The subject will no longer speak it, no longer integrate it. Nevertheless, it will remain there, somewhere, spoken, if one can put it in this way, by something the subject does not control.[187]

In other words, for the subject to identify with his or her desire, as it is named in language, constitutes a misrecognition. It is a failure to understand that, as Lacan puts it, 'I is another'[188] and this 'I' is distinct from the ego which is the source of misidentifications. It is important to stress that this 'I' is not the site of the subject's 'true' desire. Desire, it will be remembered, represents the difference between need and demand, between, that is, bodily processes and linguistic expression. It is what is left out as the former is 'translated' into the latter. Desire therefore 'is the desire for nothing nameable'.[189] It is, as Lacan writes in another context, the 'desire for nothing'.[190]

The subject's failure to recognise this means that he or she will not be able to escape the captivations of the imaginary. That is, the subject will continue to assume that lack of fulfilment and a false sense of being are the result of identifying with the wrongly named desire; something that can be remedied by renaming it correctly. But this still means that the subject is identifying with the desire of the other, with, that is, the image of him or herself that language has, through the channels of the family, the school, the workplace and the community, provided. The subject, says Lacan, 'exhausts him[her]self in pursuing the desire of the other' because he or she does not realise that his or her 'own desire is the desire of the other'.[191] That is to say, the subject does not realise that he or she is 'another' to him or herself. It is the aim of analysis to make the subject recognise this, to realise that his or her

> being has never been anything more than his [her] construct in the Imaginary and that this construct disappoints all his [her] certitudes. For in this labour [analysis] which he [she] undertakes to reconstruct this construct *for another* he [she] finds again the fundamental alienation which made him [her] construct it *like another one*, and which has always destined it to be stripped from him [her] by another.[192]

This highly compressed account of recognition in Lacan has some relevance to an understanding of the relation of Leavisian criticism to literature. Specifically, that relation can be seen as one of misrecognition based on imaginary captivation. In trying to 're-create' the given work, in trying to be faithful to it, in trying, in short, to imitate it, Leavisian criticism can be said to be like the subject who bases his or her desire on the desire of the other. On this model it is not criticism which 'recognises' and so names literature but literature which recognises and so names criticism. Literature is the 'other' through which criticism comes to exist. Moreover, just as the subject identifies the other's desire as his or her own, so too does Leavis claim, in the case of Lawrence, that literature expresses his thoughts.

But the main way in which Leavisian criticism exemplifies the imaginary fixation on the text is through the use of that word 'possess'. It will be remembered that, in his remarks on Blake, Leavis characterised 'selfhood' and 'egotism' as 'intent on asserting possession', as opposed to 'creative identity' where 'the individual … "knows he [she] does not belong to him[her]self"' (*PC & SH*, p. 172). If, as Leavis says, criticism's relation to the text is one of possession then criticism reveals itself as belonging to the misrecognitions of the ego. By seeing itself, through its identification with the work as 'creative identity' Leavisian criticism fails to see what it 'really' is, a species of 'selfhood'.

Since Leavisian criticism is not made in the image of literature as it imagines itself to be, then how is this notion of desire as desire of the other to be understood? Here again, the word 'possess' is important. It is a key term in consumerism which, at the time Leavis was writing, was in the process of redefining subjectivity in terms of *possessions*. It would seem, then, that criticism's desire really is the desire of the – or at any rate its – 'other'; namely consumerism's desire to possess. And the fact that there is no awareness of this in Leavisian criticism merely illustrates Lacan's observation that the

> unconscious is made up of what the subject essentially fails to recognise in his [her] structuring image, in the image of his ego – namely those captivations by imaginary fixations which were unassimiliable to the symbolic development of his [her] history.[193]

The 'unconscious' of Leavisian criticism is not only the result of its opposition to consumerism, it *is*, at least in part, this consumerism. This 'unconscious' makes its presence felt in the commentary on literature, colonising that discourse for its own purposes. And, in so far as it escapes Leavis's attention, this 'unconscious' constitutes an excess, a 'something more' which is not only what Leavisian criticism 'desires', but it is also the very nature of consumerism itself.

It would be wrong to conclude from this that the consumerist desire to possess is the 'real' desire of Leavisian criticism, that its desire for 'recognition' for the significance of a particular work or for itself as criticism resolves into the wants and preferences of consumerism. This would be to ignore Lacan's claim that desire is a lack which has

nothing specific for its object – unless recognition can be counted as
that object. Lacan claims that the aim of 'speech' is 'the recognition
of desire'[194] but he gives no examples of what that desire may be,
noting only that there is a confusion between 'the recognition of
desire' and 'the desire for recognition'.[195]

To repeat, the important point is that desire can never be recognised
in the sense of being named, because it is extraneous to language. It
is therefore not 'there' to be named and this is what the subject must
recognise. The subject must also recognise that he or she desires to
be recognised but this can never be achieved as long as the subject
desires as an other. What the subject must realise is that he or she is
already an other to him or herself and it is recognition of this which
'creates, brings forth a new presence in the world',[196] a 'non being'
that has 'come to be'.[197]

It is this aspect of recognition which can be most usefully applied
to Leavisian criticism. In the first place, it provides an account of how
criticism can be 'other' to itself by misrecognising itself in literature.
And, in the second place, the Lacanian understanding of recognition
shifts the focus away from the 'obviousness' of the work by
underlining the fact that it is yet to be established. This view of
recognition means that Leavisian criticism can be seen as counteracting
the seductions of presence apparent in the commodity and as pushing
beyond the perpetual present of the 'culture industry'.

In order for recognition to work in the way Lacan claims it should,
the subject has to understand that what he or she is or will 'be' is what
he or she always 'was'. The action of analysis is such that 'the subject
becomes at each stage what he [she] was before and announces
him[her]self – he [she] will have been – only in the future perfect
tense'.[198] The subject, in other words, comes to terms with his or her
'non being' and this involves a reconceptualisation of his or her past.
A parallel process occurs in Leavisian criticism where the significance
of a work only becomes apparent through its relation to tradition (SC,
p. 246). It is therefore tempting to see Leavis's tradition as analogous
to the unconscious, a temptation that is strengthened by the following
considerations.

First Lacan notes that one of the places where the unconscious is
'written down' is 'in traditions',[199] second, Lacan claims that the
unconscious is structured like a language[200] while Leavis notes that
tradition is 'a grammar and a syntax' (WWWC, p. 86) and, third,
Lacan's remark that the unconscious is 'transindividual'[201] matches
Leavis's assertion that tradition transcends the individual.

Furthermore, Lacan is as concerned to 'recover' the unconscious as Leavis is to recover tradition and, in both cases, this recovery is necessary to restore a sense of continuity.[202] There are, however, some obvious differences between tradition and the unconscious. For example, tradition is primarily a matter of content – what is it that constitutes a or 'the' tradition? – whereas the unconscious is primarily a process. As content, tradition belongs to the realm of consciousness whereas the unconscious is, of course, unconscious. Even if certain aspects of tradition are forgotten they can, in principle, be recovered and so tradition belongs more to the preconscious than to the unconscious. It is accessible whereas the unconscious is not.[203] Moreover, tradition ideally testifies to the existence of a community and its culture whereas the unconscious denotes the non-existence, or non-being of the single subject. Tradition, that is, is what has and may yet still exist whereas the unconscious is what is yet to be.

Thus, although it is possible to read the Leavisian understanding of tradition in a positive way – the concern with community, for example, as a corrective to the atomistic individualism of consumerism – the final emphasis falls on continuity, on what has been. This view of tradition entails a conservative interpretation of the claim that the poem is yet to be established. That is to say, if literature preserves 'the subtlest and finest use of language' as a way of 'keeping in touch with our spiritual tradition' (*CE*, p. 82) then 'the poem' is, in a sense, already established. No matter what its unique particularity it functions to perpetuate tradition and, as such, represents a return, not a new direction.

This is not to dismiss the Leavisian conception of tradition, it is simply to note that although it has certain affinities with Lacan's understanding of the unconscious, it cannot be read, as can the latter, in terms of a 'coming to be'. True, both tradition and the unconscious involve a redefinition of the past in relation to the present but recognition of tradition is very different from the recognition of the unconscious. In the former case, recognition is always of what was consciously or preconsciously known. Tradition therefore involves a 'misrecognition' in contrast to the 'true' recognition in relation to the unconscious and because misrecognition always characterises the relationship to tradition, it cannot be appropriated in a new or radical way.

Unless, that is, Lacan's understanding of recognition is exploited in relation to Leavis's understanding of that term. This has the effect of presenting the 'familiar' in an 'unfamiliar' way as well as highlighting the notion that 'the poem' is yet to be established. Lacan's concept of recognition, in short, prevents tradition from repeating itself. The accent is less on criticism securing agreement about the 'obviousness' of a work – 'This is so, isn't it?' – and more on the collaborative effort involved in bringing it into existence. In this guise, criticism comes close to Derrida's description of writing as 'inaugural'. That is, '[i]t does not know where it is going, no knowledge can keep it from the essential precipitation to the meaning which it constitutes and that is, primarily, its future'.[204]

## MEANING AND SIGNIFICANCE

The orientation towards the future depends on a relation to the past and one of the reasons why Leavis's work is valuable is because it endeavours to engage with and articulate a notion of the past through tradition. Tradition is one example of what Leavis means by 'significance', a key term in his vocabulary. The stress he gives it is one of the ways of differentiating his work from post-structuralist criticism which is more concerned with meaning though it is, of course, difficult to separate terms so closely related. E.D. Hirsch has tried to distinguish between them as follows:

> *Meaning* is that which is represented by a text; it is what the author meant by his use of a particular sign sequence; it is what the signs represent. *Significance*, on the other hand, names a relationship between that meaning and a person, or a conception, or a situation or indeed anything imaginable'.[205]

This is different from post-structuralist understandings of meaning. In general these assert that the work is not so much the expression of the author's meaning as an ideological construct or a site of conflicting meanings, or a site for the production of meaning.[206] These, and other aspects of post-structuralist criticism provide new and valuable ways of looking at works, but they tend to characterise earlier forms of criticism as having a simplistic understanding of the relation between meaning and intention. Belsey, for example, claims that Leavis views literature 'as a revelation of the qualities of mind of ... individual authors'[207] which is entirely contrary to his repeated claim that 'language is more than a "means of expression"' (*TL & O*, p. 49).

The fact is that Leavis's views on meaning are too complex to allow of summary dismissal. He is aware of how 'a climate of assumptions and habits of which it is unconscious determines our awareness or unawareness'[208] and of how 'words and syntactical conventions ... dictate thought and disguise or transmute basic intention, perception and apprehension'.[209] He is, in other words, aware of how language structures thought, though not in any focused way. He has no conception, for example, of how ideology interpellates individuals and positions them as subjects. Nevertheless, it should be acknowledged that Leavis is aware of the determinations of language and that he believes these determinations can be resisted if one is conscious of them. By endeavouring to transcend them a writer, a critic or a speaker is exercising responsibility and trying to achieve sincerity.

What needs to be recognised is the difficulty of this process. Intention is not easily realisable when there are so many contrary forces acting upon it. It is something precarious and hard won, something clawed back from the gravitational pull of language that would otherwise align it with convention and orthodox opinion. It does not, in Leavis's view, totalise the work or make it transparent.

The broad post-structuralist claim that traditional criticism is based on the assumption that literature is essentially the expression of the author's meaning is, as Peter Washington has shown, untenable.[210] Not only does it ignore the complexity of intention, but it also has a contradictory relation to it. That is to say, while discounting the notion of intention as the mirage of traditional criticism, post-structuralist criticism still relies on it to make good its claim that meanings can be altered in accordance with a politically progressive agenda. Intention is thus absent and present, marginal and central, dismissed and deployed in the logic of post-structuralist criticism. The consequence of this is that certain issues which intention raises such as choice, responsibility, valuation and action can either be occluded or presumed to be axiomatic. Leavis, by contrast, confronts these issues of responsibility and valuation directly, and choice and action indirectly, through his belief that literary criticism, properly conceived, 'carries with it the ... realization that a serious interest in literature leads inevitably outwards into other than literary–critical interests'.[211]

Hirsch restricts meaning to what the author intended, Leavis does not for, as he puts it, '[u]nless someone means and someone else takes the meaning, there is no meaning' (*TM & S*, p. 285). Meaning, in other words, is relational and this links it to Hirsch's definition of significance as a 'relationship', thus underlining the affinity between the two terms. This is further reinforced by Leavis's association of significance with relatedness. The quality he values in the literary tradition is, for example, 'significant relatedness in an organic whole'.[212]

This closeness of meaning and significance makes it difficult to distinguish the two terms from one another, especially when Leavis 'insist[s]' that 'essential meaning should be recognized [as] ... significance' (*I*, p. 31). However, it is possible to discriminate between meaning and significance in Leavis's work on the grounds that meaning is 'obvious' and therefore something which can be expressed whereas significance cannot. 'If one is challenged to ... say what "significance" is ... it is hardly possible to answer convincingly at the level of the challenge' (*TIOC*, p. 92). Significance is one of those 'most important words ... [that] are incapable of definition' (*PC & SH*, p. 163). And they are 'incapable of definition' because 'in any vital use they will *live*, even disconcertingly: there lies their importance for thought' (p. 163). This links significance with life – 'a necessary word' (*TW & C*, p. 123) which also does not admit of a ready definition. Neither, of course, does value, (see *TM & S*, p. 288 and *MN*, pp. 189–91), hence it too is related to significance. '[V]alue,' writes Leavis, 'is inextricably bound up with significance'.[213] And, as 'value judgements are made in genuine personal self commitment' (*EU & C*, p. 109), the significance is associated with what is personal, genuine and sincere.

It might be possible to discriminate between meaning and significance on the basis that valuation is a process of finding some meanings more significant than others. However, it should be stressed that any differences between meaning and significance are matters of degree rather than substance for, just as meaning can be immediate, so too can the apprehension of significance.

> The nearest the perceptively thinking individual gets to the certainty that he [she] is in direct possession of significance itself, unmediated, is in the certitude that he [she] has taken possession of the basic major perceptions, intuitions, and realizations communicated with consummate delicacy to the reader in the mastering of the creative work of a great writer. (*MN*, p. 192)

This quotation can be juxtaposed with one from Barthes which brings out succinctly what Leavis envisaged as the relationship between meaning and significance. 'What is significance?' asks Barthes, 'It is meaning *in so far as it is sensually produced.*'[214] Leavis would agree, believing that meaning and significance converge when there is no divorce between sensibility and intelligence, thinking and feeling. However he would not relate this to an erotics of reading as Barthes does although, as has been seen, his work has the potential to be viewed in this way.

It will be remembered that Leavis equates significance with relatedness. The task of criticism, he notes, is 'to make us see certain essential facts in significant relation' (*TP & TP*, p. 73). This concern with relatedness stems from the problem of borders, that dissolution of dividing lines which initiates Leavis's critical project. The question of relation cannot be separated from the high value placed on unity with regard to the body, the individual literary work and tradition. '[T]he scrutiny of the parts', writes Leavis, 'must be at the same time an effort towards a fuller realization of the whole'[215] because 'significance … is conveyed by the whole' (*AK*, p. 31). Leavis does not enquire too deeply into the relation of parts and whole and so evades the problem of the hermeneutic circle – how is it possible to recognise the parts without first identifying the whole and vice versa.

## LEAVIS AND ADORNO: THE PROBLEM OF FORM AND THE 'MEANING' OF SIGNIFICANCE

Leavis's failure to consider in greater detail the relation between part and whole means that he has a somewhat naive view of artistic form. Literature, for him, is a matter of 'sensuous concreteness',[216] a phenomenological enactment of experience not a description of it. There is little sense of the mediated nature of experience, indeed it is the mark of great literature that it is 'unmediated', that it 'makes the immediate experience irresistibly real' (*MN*, p. 192). Leavis was hostile to the notion of form because he felt that it was opposed to 'the values and interests of general living'.[217] Accordingly he found it difficult to develop an idea of form that would account for the effect of sensuous concreteness. This, in fact, seemed to be the result of transcending form rather than of form itself: 'the verse has such life and body that we hardly seem to be reading arrangements of words' (*J & A*, p. 108). The question of form is, as it were, dissolved into life, '[i]s there any great novelist whose preoccupation with "form" is not a matter of his [her] responsibility towards a rich human interest?' (*GT*, p. 40).

Without a notion of form, it is difficult for Leavis to discuss the unity – and hence the significance – of a work. This problem is subliminally registered in the 'third realm' where the assemblage of black marks never quite converts into a whole poem. But if the lack of form inhibits the quest for unity it is also, as has been seen, bound up with, for reasons not entirely clear, the vivid intensity that characterises 'sensuous concreteness'. The value Leavis puts on this can be read as a critique of technologico–Benthamite civilisation's tendency to reduce what is unique and particular to that common measure, the standard of living. Although the commitment to the particular can be viewed in this way there is the danger that what Adorno calls the 'postulate of particularization' will have 'the negative effect of serving to reduce aesthetic distance, thus aligning itself with the existing order'.[218] Leavis's work, in other words, seems to underwrite that operation of mass culture where, through a process of 'sensuous individuation',[219] the particular is made to appear absolutely unique when, in reality, this simply serves to disguise its 'participat[ion] in the infinite nature of production'[220] which has shrunk 'the world [to] abstractness and self-sameness'.[221]

In this way, mass culture eliminates the tension between part and whole, and Leavis's criticism seems to reflect this. Unless, that is, the reader focuses on the ambiguity of the work's being 'there', the contrast between it being a 'highly organized pattern' (*GT*, p. 211) and a mere 'assemblage of black marks on the page'. This would go some way to restoring a sense of difference between part and whole which is otherwise dissolved in 'a kind of reverent openness before life' (p. 17).

Some of Adorno's ideas on form may be relevant here, particularly because he, like Leavis, sees culture in terms of language. Art, he writes, is 'similar to language'[222] but, unlike Leavis, he takes this notion a step further claiming that '[l]inguisticality is the true subject of art'.[223] Adorno claims that '[l]anguage is both hostile to the particular and concerned with its redemption'[224] and that the best way to achieve this is through art. Art can only do this if it fashions the relation between the particular and what Adorno calls the 'universal' according to 'its own needs'[225] rather than the needs of the culture industry. Adorno argues that although art is orientated towards the particular, the particular is transcended in virtue of art's orientation toward it. The linguistic nature of art is important here. Just as a sentence presupposes the existence of the whole of the language of which it is a part so does the existence of the artistic particular presuppose the existence of the whole of the art work of which it is a part and vice versa. As Adorno puts it, art 'approximates [to] language most closely ... where it enunciates something that transcends here and now by being enunciated'.[226]

Art, however, is a concentration and a deliberate shaping of that relation between part and whole which characterises language as a whole. This shaping is governed by the paradoxical task with which art is faced: 'to attest to the lack of concord while at the same time working to abolish discordance'.[227] Hence the relation between the parts and the whole is best described as dialectical, but in the negative sense that Adorno gives to the term, which is, to put it at its most reductive, thesis and antithesis with only the future possibility of synthesis.

It is Leavis's conception of the relation between the work and tradition which most lends itself to Adorno's account of the relation between the particular and the universal. Without the particular work there would be no tradition but it is tradition which gives the work its significance. Tradition may transcend the work but at the same time the work has played a part in determining the nature of that tradition which now defines it. This relation is not entirely reciprocal since it is characterised by a number of tensions. For example, the work seems to have an immediate impact that tradition lacks and yet part of the effect of the work comes from it being *mediated* through tradition. Moreover the unity of the work seems easier to apprehend than that of tradition until it is recalled that the problem of relation which characterises tradition is precisely that of 'the work' for it is never clear how it resolves itself into a unity from the 'assemblage of black marks on the page'.

These tensions show that the relations between the work and tradition resist as much as reciprocate one another. They therefore never take a final form. The relation between the work and tradition is never closed. And for this reason, neither the work nor tradition can ever be regarded as being present. The tensions, connections and antitheses both between and within them prevent them from achieving that unity which would make them fully and completely present. By never being closed and by never being present, the relation between the work and tradition checks the impulse of the 'culture industry' towards closure and total visibility. The relation between part and whole in the 'culture industry' is one of domination, the part reflects and is subservient to the whole. This is not the case in the relation between the work and tradition precisely because this relation poses the very notion of relation as problematic. In doing so it respects the separate but related claim of part and whole and so keeps alive the principle of unity in an age of fragmentation.

The view of art as language confers upon it a certain quality of impersonality which parallels Leavis's view of tradition. Art, writes Adorno, 'speaks the language of a "We"'[228] and the same might be said of tradition, first because it is conceived in terms of language and second because it transcends the individual. Adorno further claims that the 'We' of art is not continuous with 'ordinary communicative language'.[229] Hence it cannot be reduced to a specific political, class, ethnic or gender position. If it were, then it would simply be part of the objectified expressions against which it is a protest.

The 'collaborative creativity' (*TL & O*, p. 49) of Leavis's tradition gives language a communal basis that approximates to Adorno's notion of 'We'. Moreover, that fact that language is 'more than a "means of expression"' embodying, as it does, 'values, constatations, distinctions, promptings [and] recognitions of potentiality' (p. 49) shows that, like Adorno's 'We' it too goes beyond 'ordinary communicative language': negating the objectifications of institutionalised language, it gestures towards the future when its potentialities might be realised. And, just as the relation between the work and tradition holds out the possibility of true harmony as opposed to the false harmony of the 'culture industry' so too do Adorno's 'We' and Leavis's tradition anticipate 'a real social whole' and '[a] subject to go with [it]'.[230]

These connections with Adorno show how Leavis can be read as a challenge to the 'culture industry' and this would constitute one aspect of what he means by 'significance'. It is, he writes, 'a matter of defeating and correcting habit' (*SC*, p. 247), habit which, Leavis argues, comes from the 'immediate environment' as does 'taste ... preconception, attitude and quality of living' (*CE*, p. 5). The impact of 'significant art' he elsewhere notes, lies in its 'challeng[ing] us in the most disturbing and inescapable way to a radical pondering, a new profound realization, of the grounds of our most important determinations and choices' (*VC*, p. 281). Significant art jolts the reader into an awareness of his or her responsibilities towards that 'we' implicit in the notion of tradition, as represented by the literary work. It compels readers to a committed re-evaluation of themselves but in relation to a notion of community. This community is defined through its 'creative collaboration' in respect of language and it confronts readers with their responsibility for ensuring the continuity of tradition and the advancement of creative thought.

It is an essential responsibility because '[i]n creating language human beings create the world they live in' (*TM & S*, p. 285). This is not to be understood in any literal sense, but rather it points to a depth, range and resonance in language use that offers a far greater potential for the possibility, range and quality of experience than is available in the discourses of management, consumerism or 'mediaspeak'.[231] What is at stake is the creation of a sensibility (*TL & O*, p. 53) which resists lazy or evasive linguistic practice, which respects complexity and which is committed to the enlarging, sharpening, focusing and better ordering of our perceptions, responses and judgements.[232]

The collaboration which creates this sensibility 'entails, vitally and essentially, disagreements' (*TL & O*, p. 49) and 'difference[s] without which there could be no completely human humanity' (*TW & C*, p. 142). These disagreements and differences are needed 'to strengthen the ... grasp of a significance ... that will inform and guide creativity' (*TL & O*, p. 68). This can be contrasted with the 'culture industry' which seeks the suppression of difference and the promotion of conformity. As a result, it takes no account of 'the need to feel life significant' (*TIOC*, p. 92) being concerned only with what can be 'measured, aggregated and averaged' (*TSE & EL*, p. 142).

Because it stands in contradistinction to the standardisations of the 'culture industry' and because it stimulates the individual into an exploration of the meaning of community as well as into a sense of his or her relation to it, significance can be said to have an ethical dimension. It militates against consumerist isolation, encouraging an awareness of responsibility towards others through a focus on the material effects of language use.

The weakness of this position is that it shows little cognisance of how these otherwise admirable principles can be translated into practical terms. True, Leavis argues in some detail what literary criticism can be expected to achieve but this ignores how, as an institution, literary criticism is implicated in the reproduction of the structures and values to which it is opposed. More importantly there is the whole question of how individuals separated along class, gender, race and cultural lines can possibly see themselves first as part of the same language community and second as having equal power or interest in regard to that language. Nevertheless, this does not rule out the possibility of some action through literary criticism but there

can be no literary criticism – or indeed literary theory – without
literature, which is today losing its status as a separate subject as it
is absorbed into media and cultural studies.

Significance has an aesthetic as well as an ethical aspect, and the
two are closely interwoven. In great art there is, writes Leavis,

> the concern, intense and profound, for what, talking loosely, as we
> *have* to talk (for no precision is possible), we speak of as the 'meaning
> of life'. Such a concern, felt as the question 'What for – what
> ultimately for?' is implicitly asked in all the greatest art, from which
> we get not what we are likely to call an 'answer' but the confirmation
> of a felt significance; something that confirms our sense of life as
> more than a mere linear succession of days, a matter of time as
> measured by the clock – 'tomorrow and tomorrow and tomorrow'.
> (*PP*, p. 46)

The ethical aspect lies in the involvement with ultimate questions
which are not covered by the formulae, conventions and judgements
of mass culture. These questions carry the individual beyond the
impulses and interests of the ego towards, Leavis believes, the deeper
'individuality of the individual', towards a state of 'achieved
singleness', a condition of 'whole unified being' (*TW & C*, p. 68)
towards, in short, that impersonal identity which is the consequence
of the 'proper' relation to tradition. That art can transport the
individual in this way is a function of its 'urgent creative exploring'
(*TC*, p. 56) which impacts simultaneously on the reader's intellect,
imagination and senses. It is this simultaneous play on the different
faculties that constitutes one aspect of a work's aesthetic. Another is
the concern with relation, with how parts relate to form a whole.

This concern is evident in all areas of Leavis's work, with reader
and author over the question of meaning; with critic and educated
public; with part and whole and with how works relate to form a
tradition. Relation is necessary for unity and unity for significance but,
as Leavis's characterisations of criticism show, nothing can remain
sealed within its own province. Hence there can be no essence to a
literary work, it is always relational; that is why Leavis can claim that
'English literature must be different for every age' (*I*, p. 8) it changes
according to the needs of the present. Viewed from this perspective,
there is little difference between Leavis's position and that of a post-
structuralist like Antony Easthope who also believes that literary

value is relational, claiming that 'good texts are not always the same, but always significantly different'.[233]

This description of relation, however, gives little sense of the problem of relation in Leavis for it implies that these are entities which can be related. And yet, as has been seen, the existence of such an entity as 'the poem' is highly dubious because of the difficulty of converting those 'black marks' into a sensible whole.

This disarticulation is mirrored in the decline of the category of the aesthetic to which Leavis himself contributed (see *TW & C*, p. 34). Adorno observes that, in the 'culture industry', '[t]ragedy is reduced to the threat to destroy anyone who does not co-operate'[234] while Lacan claims that society is 'more and more losing the sense of tragedy'.[235] The ultimate consequence of this, argues Lacan, will be the dissolution of the Oedipus complex. The authority of the father will not be recognised, precipitating a crisis in symbolic relations which are held in place by that initial recognition. Leavis's work which, due to the absence of an educated public, is structured round the problems of recognition and relation, would seem to suggest that what Lacan predicted has indeed occurred.

The above considerations make it difficult to see significance as the corollary of unity. If relation is problematised to the extent that unity is jeopardised then so too is significance. The ethical and the aesthetic aspects of significance converge on the problem of relation, the former is in part to do with transforming the linearity of days into a pattern, the latter with shaping 'black marks' into a whole. However, these undertakings are never complete and so the sense of 'significance' is never realised. It exists beyond the sense-making apparatus of the 'culture industry' but eludes the grasp of art. It gestures towards a better future, and it escapes the relentless drive to visibility which is perhaps the chief characteristic of the culture industry.

It is here that the value of significance resides. In connection with standards it will be remembered that the genuine was that which was more than its appearance. In the case of jewellery, argues Simmel, 'this "more than appearance" is its *value*, which cannot be guessed by being looked at, but is something that ... is added to the appearance'.[236] The difference between appearance and 'more than appearance' can only be confirmed by taking 'possession'[237] of the jewellery. What Leavisian criticism does is to problematise this basic relation of capitalism while seeming to imitate it in urging the critic to 'possess' the work so as to realise what is not immediately apparent about it.

At the same time, however, the work is felt to be 'obvious' so that 'anyone who reads ... can see' (*RC*, p. 194). This suggests that there is no 'more than appearance' and this is in fact the case in the economic relation where the apparent difference between appearance and 'more than appearance' disappears with the price paid to possess the object. By contrast, the literary critical endeavour to 'possess' the work fails to make what is 'obvious' about it coincide with its significance because it cannot quite apprehend or convey that related unity of parts and whole on which the sense of significance depends.

Significance is what is not realisable and thus it gives a more durable and resonant quality to value than is implied in Simmel's use of the term. The impossibility of criticism ever fully realising the significance of the work keeps open the gap between appearance and 'more than appearance'; a space in which other possibilities, relations and values pertaining to what it is to be human in the millennium can be sounded. It is for this reason that capitalism wants to appropriate this distinction wholly for itself, exploiting it as a seductive ploy of advertising while in reality triumphing as the difference between the appearance and reality of goods vanishes with every act of purchase.

# Conclusion

There is no one conclusion that can be drawn from the different approaches I have taken to Leavis. Indeed, my aim has been to show that there can be no single reading of his work because it is far more diverse and ambivalent than has usually been recognised. To this end, I have approached Leavis from a broadly post-structuralist perspective since such a perspective views any given text, ostensibly at any rate, as inherently plural. In doing so, I hope to have shown that there are affinities between certain aspects of Leavis's work and parts of post-structuralist thought, though without collapsing the two together.

The central tension of Leavis's writing is between the desire to be precise and the recognition of the inevitability of imprecision. This, of course, is a tension in language generally, but it takes different forms in different discourses. The concern with relevance and exactitude is uppermost in scientific management, whereas advertising is most effective when it plays on several different registers at once. In the discourse of bureaucracy, as in Leavisian criticism, the tension between, to use the technical terms, denotation and connotation, is more pronounced. Bureaucracy, with its rules, procedures and strictly defined spheres of operation is highly specific, yet always applies the general rule to the particular case. By contrast, Leavisian criticism has a profound commitment to sensuous particularity but, at the same time, it invests heavily in a notion of tradition which is general to the extent that it is characterised by 'representativeness'.

The fact that bureaucracy and Leavisian criticism are both structured around the same problematic of the relation between the particular and the general suggests that they are connected. And this is hardly surprising when it is remembered that the very existence of literary criticism *as a profession* is a result of that demand for *specialist* education which occurred due to bureaucratic expansion. But literary criticism, specifically Leavisian criticism, is not just the consequence of bureaucracy but also its complement. That is to say, one of the major tasks of bureaucracy is to articulate and administer *corporate* society, balancing and harmonising its different interests which would otherwise be expressed as class antagonism. This is very close to the practice of Leavisian criticism which constructs the literary text as a *body* and which endeavours to establish a consensus among the different responses it provokes. The central tension of Leavisian criticism and bureaucracy, the tension that is between the particular and the general, is contained but not resolved in each discourse by an image of the body. Once a certain level of bureaucratic organisation has been reached then literary criticism, at least the Leavisian kind, becomes, in principle, dispensable.

If one of the reasons for the ambiguity of Leavis's criticism is its relation to bureaucracy, another is the way its diction, logic and rhetoric are implicated in those of scientific management and consumerism. This compromises its claim to be oppositional since it helps to reproduce the very things to which it is opposed. By the same token, Leavisian criticism reacts back on these discourses unsettling their assumptions as much as they unsettle its own. For example, the interplay between scientific management with its single objective and Leavisian criticism with its varied ones destabilises the meaning of shared terms such as 'discipline' and 'control'. These retain a notion of the necessity of ends but raise questions concerning their nature and the means used to fulfil them. In short, the intercalation of Leavisian criticism with other discourses precipitates a re-evaluation of their shared terms and assumptions with a view to expanding them beyond the cultural imperatives to consume and conform.

Leavisian criticism raises the issue of valuation directly as well as indirectly. One of Leavis's constant themes is that there are no ultimate grounds for a value judgement since, in order to be authentic, it must be personal and sincere. However, personal responses can be guided by implicit standards and a due sense of significance, both of which are imparted by tradition. But tradition cannot be regarded as a guarantee of value since it is constantly being modified.

Despite there being no final court of appeal in the arbitration of value judgements we are not, Leavis believes, excused from making them. Value judgements are therefore bound up with an existential sense that meaning and significance have to be more made than found. They call for the careful exercise of thought – in the Leavisian sense of the term – and a due consciousness of the responsibility involved in making them. At the very least this requires being clear about the reasons for making one kind of judgement rather than another. Although it is commonly accepted – despite evidence to the contrary – that Leavis did not explicate the basis of his criticism, it seems to me that he is a good deal more forthcoming in this area than some post-structuralist thinkers.[1]

The valuation of literature cannot be separated from the valuation of 'life'. '[A] serious interest in literature', writes Leavis, 'leads inevitably outwards into other than literary–critical interests'.[2] 'Literary study', Leavis continues,

> gives an incomparable initiation into the idea of tradition. And the perception of relations with other works goes, of course, with a perception of relations with things and conditions outside the literary order. (*LD*, p. 175)

This can be interpreted as a defence of class divisions and hierarchies but that would hardly do justice to what Leavis is struggling to articulate.

Another approach to the problem is to look at what Leavis means by a literary critical judgement that has 'a moral significance'.[3] This does not mean 'subscribing to and applying some ethical theory or scheme – something other than [the] critical sensibility ... that takes over the function of critical judgement' (*VC*, p. 280) rather it is a case of whether a work 'makes *for* life or against it' (p. 281). 'Life', of course, 'is a large word' and to 'try and define it would be futile' (*VC*, p. 281). Some may regard this as evasive but it is no more so than Derrida's claim that *différance* is 'neither a word not a concept'.[4] Both writers are trying to give, in their different ways, a sense of something that disturbs and exceeds the conventional forms of expression and this cannot be done by sweeping general statements, only by the sensitive exploration of particular issues.

What Leavis seems to mean by a work that 'makes for life' is one which irresistibly challenges the reader's habits, perceptions and valuations, provoking him or her to a creative re-evaluation of all he or she takes for granted. Viewed in this way, the training of a literary sensibility is not consistent with a desire to uphold the status quo. On the contrary, it is a means of critiquing and moving beyond it. This becomes more clear when it is realised that thought about 'life' cannot be separated from thought about language.[5] It therefore follows that great literature, in extending thought about language, also extends it about 'life'. This is simply a different way of stating Leavis's familiar claim that the conditions, possibilities and potential quality of experience, and the capacity for profound and feeling comprehension, are in part determined by the linguistic resources of a culture as represented by its literary tradition.

Of course there are any number of objections to this position. Who constructs this tradition, who has access to it and is it really the case that the quality of life depends upon a just appreciation of literature? These criticisms, however, have a reflex air about them for they do not really attempt to engage with what Leavis is saying or why. His basic claim is that there is a connection between language and life, a proposition that can hardly be denied. He also claims that literature stimulates the reader to a greater awareness of the depths, complexities and resonances of 'life' than does, for example, popular journalism which mostly seeks to instil and reinforce knee-jerk judgements instead of overcoming them.

Leavis, in short, tries to maintain a vital and living connection between language and experience that other aspects of the culture seem intent on severing. The slogans, headlines and soundbites of consumer culture rarely address its deepest problems and neither, it can be argued, do the concerns of post-structuralism. Its specialised – even fetishised – vocabulary seems, at times, to promote plurality rather as advertising does choice: only to enforce its own particular orthodoxies on subjectivity, language and meaning.

None of this is to say that Leavis should be read uncritically, simply that he should be *read*. In conceiving of a continuity of valuation from literature to 'life' Leavis implicitly poses the question of the relation between aesthetics and ethics. The recent revival of interest in this problem takes account of the shift from a foundationalist to a pragmatist view of meaning, something which is partially registered in Leavis's claims regarding the disintegration of a common culture. This shift, according to David Parker, 'involves a turn to literature and the arts as sites of the culture's deepest moral questioning'.[6] Leavis understood literature in precisely this way and for that reason his contribution to the debate cannot be ignored.

To assess that contribution would require a separate study. Among the things on which it would have to focus are the following: how, in a fragmented society of equally fragmented subjects, Leavis poses the question of unity as at once impossible but necessary. How, in a society dominated not just by the exchange relation but also by administration, where the individual case submits to the general rule, Leavis forges a language for recovering and attending to sensuous concreteness. How, in a society of surveillance where what is not visible is somehow suspect, Leavis maintains a sense of inwardness as essential. How, in a consumer society encouraging egotism and competition, Leavis articulates a notion of tradition that gives a different sense of identity and relation to others. How, in a society of the perpetual present, Leavis finds in tradition the pulse of history. How, in a society of planned obsolescence, Leavis sees tradition as an expression of the principle that there are perceptions, apprehensions, intuitions and values that are worth preserving. How, in a society which dissolves the distinctions between 'high' and 'popular' culture, Leavis offers a model of how they can be mutually sustaining, developing in the process a vocabulary which enables aesthetic experience to be discussed in a discriminating but by no means final manner. And how, in a society of distractions, Leavis advocates the virtues of attentiveness and sustained concentration.

And how, finally, in a society of means and averages, Leavis tries to uphold a notion of valuation centring on openness, responsiveness and 'significance'. Consequently art should not be approached merely to confirm one's ideas, thoughts and values but to have them probed, tested and challenged. Such self-transcendence creates the possibility for other sorts of transcendence so that individuals need not be confined within their own 'phrase regimes'[7] or cultural *cul de sacs*. Such ideas, as a great part of the history of the criticism of Leavis has shown, are easy to caricature but difficult to comprehend.

# Notes

## INTRODUCTION

1. See 'Critical Mass', Antithesis, *The Times Higher Education Supplement*, 7 February 1992, p. 2.
2. Ian MacKillop, *F.R. Leavis: A Life in Criticism* (Harmondsworth: Allen Lane/Penguin, 1995).
3. Francis Mulhern, *The Moment of 'Scrutiny'* (London: Verso, 1979/1981) p. 328.
4. Garry Watson, *The Leavises, the 'Social' and the Left* (Swansea: Brynmill, 1977).
5. See, for example, Malcolm Bradbury, 'Whatever Happened to F.R. Leavis?' in *The Sunday Times*, 9 July 1995, pp. 10–11. Note particularly the section 'How To Be a Leavisite' which neatly summarises the ingredients of the Leavis myth.
6. See, for example, Geoffrey Wheatcroft, 'Dr Jargon's Little List', Magazine Section, *Daily Telegraph*, 15 July 1995, p. 14; Nigel Williams, 'The Mystery of Dr Leavis', Weekend Section *The Independent*, 15 July 1995, p. 6; Nigel Spivey, 'Embattled Preacher with a Cult Following', Weekend Section Three, *Financial Times*, 16 July 1995, p. 13; and Christopher Hawtree, 'Criticism and Feuds' in *The Times Education Supplement*, 28 July 1995, p. 17. See, for one of the few reviews which attempts to engage with Leavis's critical ideas, Dan Jacobson 'A Reader for Life', *The Times Literary Supplement*, 4 August 1995, pp. 3–4.
7. Ronald Hayman, *Leavis* (London: Heinemann, 1976).
8. William Walsh, *F.R. Leavis* (London: Chatto & Windus, 1980).
9. R.P. Bilan, *The Literary Criticism of F.R. Leavis* (Cambridge: Cambridge University Press, 1979).
10. Robert B. Boyers, *F.R. Leavis: Judgement and the Discipline of Thought* (Columbia: University of Missouri Press, 1978).
11. John Casey, 'Object, Feeling and Judgement: F.R. Leavis' in John Casey, *The Language of Criticism*, (London: Methuen, 1966) pp. 153–78.
12. Michael Tanner, 'Literature and Philosophy', *New Universities Quarterly* 30:1, Winter 1975, pp. 54–64 and '"Mutually Necessary": A Rejoinder', *New Universities Quarterly* 30:3, Summer 1976, pp. 313–23. See also Tanner's review of Casey's *The Language of Criticism* in *Oxford Review* 4:2, 1967, pp. 58–71.
13. Fred Inglis, 'Resistance and Social Decline', in Fred Inglis, *Radical Earnestness: English Social Theory 1880–1980* (Oxford: Martin Robertson, 1982) pp. 91–108.
14. Lesley Johnson, 'F.R. Leavis', in Lesley Johnson, *The Cultural Critics: From Matthew Arnold to Raymond Williams* (London: Routledge and Kegan Paul 1979), pp. 93–115.

15. Elizabeth and Tom Burns, 'Introduction', in Elizabeth and Tom Burns (eds) *The Sociology of Literature and Drama: Selected Readings* (Harmondsworth: Penguin, 1973) pp. 9–30.

16. Chris Baldick, 'The Leavises: Armed Against the Herd', in Chris Baldick, *The Social Mission of English 1848–1932* (Oxford: Clarendon Press, 1983/1987), pp. 162–95.

17. Bernard Bergonzi, 'Leavis, Lewis, and Other Oppositions', in Bernard Bergonzi, *Exploding English: Criticism, Theory and Culture* (Oxford: Clarendon Press, 1990) pp. 40–70.

18. An indispensable guide both to Leavis's work and to criticism of Leavis is M.B. Kinch, William Baker and John Kimber, *F.R. Leavis and Q.D. Leavis: An Annotated Bibliography* (New York: Garland, 1989).

19. Michael Bell, *F.R. Leavis* (London: Routledge, 1988).

20. Catherine Belsey, *Critical Practice* (London: Methuen, 1980) p. 38.

21. Ibid.

22. This opposition is often more stated or implied rather than carefully argued. See Belsey, *Critical Practice*, pp. 11–13, 14 and Antony Easthope, *British Post-structuralism Since 1968* (London: Routledge, 1988/1991) pp. 11, 134, 141, 154, 172. In defining itself in opposition to Leavis, post-structuralist criticism ironically reinforces the sort of binary thinking which it otherwise seeks to challenge. The general Marxist view of Leavis has been aptly summarised by Tony Bennett who claims that Leavis is the last in a line of critics who have 'been concerned to reinforce a class differentiation at the level of language', Tony Bennett, *Formalism and Marxism* (London: Methuen, 1979) p. 161.

    Such negative assessments are contrary to the call from a number of the contributors to Peter Widdowson (ed.) *Re-reading English* (London: Methuen, 1982) for a fresh engagement with Leavis. This was prompted by a sense of crisis in English studies to which the solutions proposed were mainly Marxist or post-structuralist. Nevertheless there seemed to be an understanding that it would be difficult to proceed with these until they were situated in relation to Leavis's legacy. See John Hoyles, 'Radical Critical Theory and English', John Oakley and Elizabeth Owen '"English" and the Council for National Academic Awards' and David Craig and Michael Egan, 'Historicist Criticism', all in ibid., pp. 40–60, 105–18, 207–22.

    That call, however, went unheeded. Not only has there been no reappraisal of Leavis but also the potential alliance between post-structuralism and Marxism failed to materialise. Literary criticism is the poorer on all these counts.

23. Catherine Belsey, 'Re-reading the Great Tradition' in Widdowson, *Re-reading English*, pp. 121–35.

24. Christopher Norris, 'Post-structuralist Shakespeare: Text and Ideology', in John Drakakis (ed.) *Alternative Shakespeares* (London: Methuen, 1985) 47–66, esp. 58–66.

25. Antony Easthope, *Literary into Cultural Studies* (London: Routledge, 1991) p. 71. See also pp. 65–71.

26. On intention see F.R. Leavis, 'Henry James and the Function of Criticism' in F.R. Leavis, *The Common Pursuit* (Harmondsworth:

Penguin/Chatto & Windus, 1962/1993) pp. 221–32, 225; on the dynamic nature of English Literature see F.R. Leavis, 'The Present and the Past', in F.R. Leavis, *English Literature in Our Time and the University* (Cambridge: Cambridge University Press, 1969/1979) pp. 63–82, 77; and on reality as an effect of language see F.R. Leavis, 'Thought, Meaning and Sensibility: The Problem of Value Judgement' in F.R. Leavis, *Valuation in Criticism and Other Essays*, ed. G. Singh (Cambridge: Cambridge University Press, 1986) pp. 285–297, 285. These ideas occur throughout Leavis's work; they may even be said to inform it.

27.  I discuss Belsey's treatment of Leavis in 'F.R. Leavis and Post-structuralism', in Ian MacKillop and Richard Storer (eds) *F.R. Leavis: Essays and Documents* (Sheffield: Sheffield Academic Press, 1995) pp. 154–69.

28.  See John Needham, 'Leavis and the Post-Saussureans', in *English* 34: 150, Autumn 1985, pp. 235–50.

29.  Steven Connor, *Theory and Cultural Value* (Oxford: Basil Blackwell, 1992) p. 14. See also John Frow, *Cultural Studies and Cultural Value* (Oxford: Clarendon Press, 1995). It is worth noting that although Frow's position is very different from Leavis's he nevertheless uses the same framework as Leavis, namely 'that there is no longer a stable hierarchy of value' (ibid., p. 1) to analyse the problem of value. This framework seems to be offered as new each time it is used. Leavis, for example, seems to have forgotten that Mill used it in 'Civilization'. See John Stuart Mill, 'Civilization', in Peter Keating (ed.), *The Victorian Prophets* (London: Fontana, 1981) pp. 70–103, esp. 92–3. This 'forgetting', this starting each time from the same place prevents the sort of cumulative analysis that follows from the perception of continuity. For another expression of this problem see Gillian Rose, 'Architecture to Philosophy: The Postmodern Complicity', *Theory, Culture and Society* 5:2–3, pp. 357–72, esp. 368.

30.  See, for example, A.T. Nuyen, 'Adorno and the French Post-Structuralist: On the Other of Reason', *Journal of Speculative Philosophy* 4:4, 1990, pp. 310–22.

31.  Scientific Management in the form of Taylorism '[was] imported from America between the wars ... Taylorism ... was not unknown here even in 1914 ... but it was not until the 1930s that it made any noticeable progress'. Eric Hopkins, *The Rise and Decline of the English Working Classes 1918–1990: A Social History* (London: Weidenfeld & Nicolson, 1991) p. 19.

There is some dispute about when the phrase mass consumerism can be used accurately in respect of Britain. John Stevenson argues that the mass consumer market appeared in the 1930s. See John Stevenson, *British Society 1914–45* (Harmondsworth: Penguin, 1984) pp. 113, 116 & 126–9. Evidence to support his view comes from Hopkins who notes that consumer spending, among the employed, increased by 23 per cent from 1914 to 1938. Furthermore, a contemporary commentator, Edgell Rickword, makes the point that 'the traditional attitude to labour has become obscured, the emphasis has shifted from joy in production to joy in consumption', Edgell

Rickword, 'Culture, Progress and English Tradition', in Edgell Rickword, *Literature in Society:* Essays and Opinions II 1931–1978, ed. A. Young (Manchester: Carcanet, 1978) p. 93. Robert Bocock, however, makes the point that mass consumption did not develop in Britain until the 1950s. See Robert Bocock, *Consumption* (London: Routledge, 1993) p. 21.

    For the purposes of this discussion I take the position that the conditions for the emergence of mass consumerism, increased spending power, the progress of advertising, mail order schemes, the development of the chain store, the ready availability of credit facilities and so on, began to appear on a large scale in the 1930s though it was not until the middle 1950s that *most* of the population could be said to have benefited from them.

32.    Pasi Falk, *The Consuming Body* (London: Sage, 1994) p. 158.

33.    F.R. Leavis, *How To Teach Reading: A Primer for Ezra Pound* (Cambridge: Minority Press, 1932) p. 73. Hereafter *HTTR* with page references given in the text.

34.    Jean Baudrillard, 'Consumer Society', in Jean Baudrillard, *Selected Writings,* ed. Mark Poster (Cambridge/Oxford: Polity Press/Basil Blackwell, 1988) pp. 29–56, p. 30.

35.    Ibid.

36.    F.R. Leavis, 'What's Wrong with Criticism?' in F.R. Leavis, *For Continuity* (Cambridge: Minority Press, 1933) pp. 68–90, 69. Hereafter *WWWC*, with page references given in the text.

37.    Frederick Winslow Taylor, *The Principles of Scientific Management* (London: Harper Row, 1911/1947). One of Taylor's aims is to 'show the enormous gains which [will] result from the substitution by our workmen of scientific for rule-of-thumb methods', p. 16.

38.    'The principal object of management should be to secure the maximum prosperity for the employer, coupled with the maximum prosperity for each employee', ibid., p. 9. For examples of 'Taylorism' in Britain see Oliver Sheldon, *The Philosophy of Management* (London: Pitman, 1923) and B. Seebohm Rowntree, *Industrial Unrest: A Way Out* (London: Longman, 1922).

39.    F.R. Leavis, 'Mass Civilisation and Minority Culture' in Leavis, *For Continuity*, pp. 13–46, 31. Hereafter *MC & MC* with page references given in the text.

40.    F.R. Leavis, 'Introductory', in Leavis, *English Literature in Our Time and the University*, pp. 1–35, 17.

41.    F.R. Leavis, *New Bearings in English Poetry* (Harmondsworth: Penguin, 1932) p. 42. Hereafter *NB* with page references given in the text.

42.    F.R. Leavis, *Revaluation: Tradition and Development in English Poetry* (Harmondsworth: Penguin/Chatto & Windus, 1936/1967) p. 44. Hereafter *R* with page references given in the text.

43.    Mike Featherstone, 'The Body in Consumer Culture' in Mike Featherstone, Mike Hepworth and Bryan S. Turner, *The Body: Social Process and Cultural Theory* (London: Sage, 1991) pp. 170–96, 177.

44.    Ibid., p. 172.

45.    See ibid., p.187–8.

46.  F.R. Leavis, 'Eliot's "Axe To Grind" and the Nature of Great Criticism' in Leavis, *English Literature in Our Time and the University*, pp. 85–108, 90.

47.  Sigmund Freud, *Civilization and Its Discontents*, trans. Joan Riviere, revised and edited by James Strachey (London: Hogarth, 1930/1979) p. 62; see also p. 73. It is worth noting that *Civilization and Its Discontents* appeared in the same year as 'Mass Civilisation and Minority Culture', the latter first being published, in pamphlet form, by Gordon Fraser's Minority Press in 1930.

48.  F.R. Leavis, *The Critic As Anti-Philosopher: Essays and Papers*, ed. G. Singh, (London: Chatto & Windus, 1982) and F.R. Leavis,*Valuation in Criticism and Other Essays*, ed. G. Singh (Cambridge: Cambridge University Press, 1986).

49.  F.R. Leavis and Denys Thompson, *Culture and Environment: The Training of Critical Awareness* (London: Chatto & Windus, 1933/1964). Although Thompson is down as co-author he said that his part 'was to advise on school conditions and possibilities; that the book was essentially Leavis's in conception', Hayman, *Leavis*, p. 22. MacKillop, by contrast, claims that Leavis and Thompson 'had so much help' from Queenie Leavis 'that it is surprising her name did not appear on the title page', MacKillop, *F.R. Leavis: A Life In Criticism*, p. 208. MacKillop goes on to suggest that '[t]here was probably more of Q.D.L. than F.R.L. in *Culture and Environment*' (p. 209). This is certainly true in terms of material, much of which came from Q.D. Leavis, *Fiction and the Reading Public* (London: Chatto & Windus, 1932) but the thought and purpose of the book is recognisably Leavis's own.

50.  This dispute, which will be discussed in Chapter 3, was over the nature of criticism. The relevant articles are F.W. Bateson, 'The Function of Criticism at the Present Time', in *Essays in Criticism* 3:1, 1933, pp. 1–27 and F.R. Leavis, 'The Responsible Critic: or the Function of Criticism At Any Time' in *Scrutiny* 19:3, 1953, pp. 162–83.

## CHAPTER 1: 'MASS CIVILISATION AND MINORITY CULTURE'

1.  F.R. Leavis, 'Mass Civilisation and Minority Culture', in F.R. Leavis, *For Continuity* (Cambridge: Minority Press, 1933) pp. 13–46. Henceforth referred to as *MC & MC* with page references given in the text.

2.  Francis Mulhern, *The Moment of 'Scrutiny'* (London: Verso, 1981) p. 50. Mulhern's seems to be the representative view. See for example Chris Baldick, *The Social Mission of English Criticism 1848–1932* (Oxford: Clarendon Press, 1987) pp. 165–8; John Carey, *The Intellectuals and the Masses: Pride and Prejudice among the Literary Intelligentsia* (London: Faber, 1992) pp. 9–10; Pamela McCallum, *Literature and Method: Towards a Critique of I.A. Richards, T.S. Eliot and F.R. Leavis* (Dublin: Gill and Macmillan, 1983) pp. 153–77, esp. 155–6; Anne Samson, *F.R. Leavis* (New York: Harvester Wheatsheaf, 1992) pp. 36–61, esp. 40–2;

and Raymond Williams, *Culture and Society 1780–1950* (Harmondsworth: Penguin/Chatto & Windus, 1975) pp. 246–57, esp. 247–8.

3. One of the obstacles to a sympathetic understanding of Leavis is precisely this opposition between 'culture' and 'civilisation'. Leavis uses 'culture' to refer to a positive body of achievements and habits, expressed as a mode of living superior to 'civilisation'. Today 'culture' is no longer in opposition to 'civilisation'. It stands by itself and broadly refers to the ensemble of different cultural practices which constitute the way of life of a society. This widening of the term does, however, make it difficult to distinguish qualitatively between different cultural practices. All of them seem to be of equal value, thus there are no ultimate aesthetic grounds for distinguishing between Barbara Cartland and Shakespeare.

    The ultra-relativist case, of which this is an extreme example, is found in Barbara Herrnstein Smith, *Contingencies of Value: Alternative Perspectives for Critical Theory* (Cambridge, Mass.: Harvard University Press, 1988). For the evolution of the term 'culture' see Williams, *Culture and Society*. For a brief overview of the two terms see Raymond Williams, *Keywords: A Vocabulary of Culture and Society* (London: Fontana, 1983) pp. 57–60, 87–93. For a clear guide to the term 'culture' in current thought see Rachel Billington, Sheelagh Strawbridge, Lenore Greensides and Annette Fitzsimons, *Culture and Society* (London: Macmillan, 1991).

4. One of the aims of this and subsequent chapters is to challenge the generally accepted view of Leavis's criticism as the 'means [whereby] a ruling élite provides itself with a sensibility which is the source of and guarantee of its right to control and administer experience', Catherine Belsey, 'Re-reading the great tradition' in Peter Widdowson (ed.) *Re-reading English* (London: Methuen, 1982) pp. 121–35, 129.

    Belsey's view is based, in part, on the following quotation: there is 'a necessary relationship between the quality of the individual's response to art and his general fitness for a humane existence' (p. 129). The quotation is given in Mulhern, *The Moment of 'Scrutiny'*, p. 48. The context in which Belsey places the quotation implies that she attributes it to Leavis. '[T]he judgement of relative value is not purely a matter of literary appreciation. It is implicit throughout *The Great Tradition*, and explicit elsewhere, that there is a "necessary relationship between the quality of the individual's response to art and his general fitness for a human existence"' (ibid.). The quotation, however, does not come from Leavis. It is, as Mulhern makes clear, from the editors, Donald Culver and L.C. Knights, of the first issue of *Scrutiny* (*The Moment of 'Scrutiny'*, p. 48). This appeared in May 1932 and Leavis did not join the editorial board until September 1932. (See Mulhern, *The Moment of 'Scrutiny'*, pp. 3–48 and L.C. Knights 'Scrutiny and F.R.L.: A Personal Memoir', in Denys Thompson (ed.), *The Leavises: Recollections and Impressions* (Cambridge: Cambridge University Press, 1984) pp. 70–81.

It is this sort of misrepresentation of Leavis that contributes to the perception of him as an elitist. Garry Watson has made a detailed study of what he considers to be a systematic distortion of Leavis's criticism in his book *The Leavises, the Social and the Left* (Swansea: Brynmill, 1977). Variations of Belsey's view of Leavis can be found in the Literature and Society Group 1972–3, 'Literature/Society: Mapping the Field' in *Culture, Media and Language*, (London: Hutchinson/Centre for Contemporary Cultural Studies, University of Birmingham, 1980) pp. 227–34, esp. 229; and in Paul Lawford, 'Conservative Empricism in Literary Theory: A Scrutiny of the Work of F.R. Leavis', Part 1, *Red Letters*, 1:1, pp. 12–15; Part 2, *Red Letters*, 2:2, pp. 9–11.

5. J.B. Watson regarded himself as the founder of behaviourist psychology. For a brief overview of his work see O.L. Zangwill, 'Psychology', in C.B. Cox and A.E. Dyson (eds), *The Twentieth Century Mind: History, Ideas and Literature in Britain 2:,1918–1945* (Oxford: Oxford University Press, 1972) pp. 171–95, esp. 174–6.

6. See Michel Foucault, *Discipline and Punish: The Birth of the Prison*, trans. Alan Sheridan (Harmondsworth: Penguin, 1991).

7. Foucault's claim in *The History of Sexuality Volume 1: An Introduction*, trans. R. Hurley (Harmondsworth: Penguin, 1990) that '[w]here there is power, there is resistance' (p. 95) is at odds with his analysis which shows how subjects are so enmeshed in the power/knowledge nexus that compels them to speak of their sexuality that they cannot resist it. Christopher Norris makes a similar point when he writes that by 'reducing "reason" to its lowest common denominator (instrumental rationality) Foucault in effect closes off any prospect of progressive or emancipatory change', Christopher Norris, *Truth and the Ethics of Criticism* (Manchester: Manchester University Press, 1994) p. 42.

8. Some would dispute Foucault's historical sense: 'Unfortunately, most of Foucault's bold historical points are far from ... accurate', J.C. Merquior, *Foucault* (London: Fontana, 1985) p. 57.

9. R. Paget, *Babel* (London: Kegan Paul, 1930), p. 18, quoted by Leavis in *MC & MC*, p. 42.

10. Ibid.

11. T.W. Adorno 'The Schema of Mass Culture', in T.W. Adorno, *The Culture Industry: Selected Essays on Mass Culture*, ed. J.M. Bernstein (London: Routledge, 1991), pp. 53–84, 71.

12. Ibid.

13. Ibid., p. 76.

14. Ibid., p. 80.

15. Ibid., p. 61.

16. Ibid., p. 60. On the notion of time in consumer society see John Berger, *Ways of Seeing* (London: BBC/Penguin, 1972) pp. 144–9; Brian Massumi, 'Everywhere You Want To Be: Introduction to Fear', in Brian Massumi (ed.) *The Politics of Everyday Fear* (Minneapolis: University of Minnesota Press, 1993) pp. 3–40, esp. 8–9; and Frederic Jameson, 'Postmodernism and Consumer Society' in Hal Foster (ed.) *Postmodern Culture* (London: Pluto, 1985), pp. 111–25.

17. Adorno, 'The Schema of Mass Culture', p. 57.

18.  Ibid., p. 72.
19.  Ibid., p. 74.
20.  Ibid., p. 71.
21.  T.S. Eliot quoted by Leavis in *MC & MC*, p. 31. Leavis gives no reference for the quotation.
22.  Adorno, 'The Schema of Mass Culture', p. 75.
23.  Ibid., p. 79.
24.  Pierre Macherey, *A Theory of Literary Production*, trans. G. Wall (London: Routledge and Kegan Paul, 1978) p. 61.
25.  For details see C.L. Mowat, *Britain Between the Wars* (London: Methuen, 1950) pp. 199–200, 267–8, 384–5, 390, 403–6 and Malcolm Smith, *British Politics, Society and the State Since the Late Nineteenth Century* (London: Macmillan, 1990) pp. 94, 96.
26.  The fact that Leavis seems to regard the meaning of his metaphor as self-evident is reminiscent of Derrida's remark that what is sought in metaphor is 'the return of the same'. Derrida's observation arises in the course of a long discussion of the relation between metaphor and philosophy, hence it is not strictly relevant to literary criticism. Nevertheless, there is much in Derrida's essay that could be usefully applied to an understanding of Leavis's treatment of metaphor. See Jacques Derrida, "White Mythology', in Jacques Derrida, *Margins of Philosophy*, trans. Alan Bass (New York: Harvester Wheatsheaf, 1982) pp. 209–71, 266.
27.  I.A. Richards *Principles of Literary Criticism* (London: Routledge and Kegan Paul, 1924/1959) p. 61, quoted by Leavis in *MC & MC*, p. 14.
28.  Ibid.
29.  The claim is made by Greta Jones, *Social Hygiene in Twentieth Century Britain* (London: Croom Helm, 1986) p. 18. See also Stuart Hall and Bill Schwarz 'State and Society 1880–1930' in Mary Langan and Bill Schwarz (eds) *Crisis in the British State 1880–1930* (London: Hutchinson/Centre for Contemporary Cultural Studies, University of Birmingham, 1985), pp. 7–33.
30.  Jones, *Social Hygiene in Twentieth Century Britain*, p. 6.
31.  Ibid., pp. 30, 35.
32.  Ibid., p. 31.
33.  Ibid., p. 10.
34.  Ibid., p. 18.
35.  T.W. Adorno, *Minima Moralia: Reflections from Damaged Life*, trans. E.F.N. Jephcott (London: Verso, 1993) p. 154. According to Adorno, the requirement that people 'should be wholly and entirely' (p. 153) what they are, in other words that they should be genuinely themselves, is simply society's way of encouraging its members to identify with and so perpetuate 'the monadological form which social oppression imposes on [them] (p. 154). Adorno takes issue with Heidegger on the question of authenticity (see T.W. Adorno, *The Jargon of Authenticity*, trans. K. Tarnowski and F. Will (London: Routledge and Kegan Paul, 1973) which makes him relevant to a consideration of this issue in Leavis, since as Michael Bell has pointed out, Heidegger is 'the nearest philosophical model for Leavis's

conception of [poetic] language'. Michael Bell, *F.R. Leavis* (London: Routledge, 1988) pp. 36–54.

36. Adorno, *Minima Moralia: Reflections from Damaged Life*, p. 155.
37. Ibid.
38. As the following quotation indicates, without language there is no consciousness. '[A] language', writes Leavis

> is more than an instrument of expression; it registers the consequences of many generations of creative response to living: implicit valuations, interpretive constructions, ordering moulds and frames, basic assumptions. (F.R. Leavis, 'Pluralism, Compassion and Social Hope', in F.R. Leavis *Nor Shall My Sword: Discourses on Pluralism, Compassion and Social Hope* (London: Chatto & Windus, 1972) pp. 163–98, 184.)

Leavis makes a similar point when he remarks that the critic 'ought to realize vividly ... that he [or she] is (or should be) contemplating the basic condition of thought when he turns his [or her] mind on the nature of language'. F.R. Leavis 'Thought, Language and Objectivity', in *The Living Principle: English As a Discipline of Thought* (London: Chatto & Windus, 1975) pp. 19–69, 57. More succinct is the claim that '[t]here [can] be no developed thought of the most important kind without language'. F.R. Leavis, *Thought, Words and Creativity: Art and Thought in Lawrence* (London: Chatto & Windus, 1976) p. 20.

What emerges from these quotations is a view of language as the basis of thought and also that the quality of thought is dependent on the quality of the language. Hence Leavis's claim that

> Modern English ... represents drastic impoverishment; the assumptions implicit in it eliminate from thought, and from the valuations and tested judgements that play so essential a part in thought, very important elements of human experience – elements that linguistic continuity once made available. ('Thought, Language and Objectivity', p. 67)

Leavis does not distinguish between thought and consciousness. Indeed, his use of the two terms suggests their meanings are similar. 'The *thought* in question for us, vindicators of "English", ... involves a *consciousness* of one's full human responsibility, purpose, and the whole range of human valuations' (ibid., p. 21, italics added). Compare this to Leavis's view of consciousness in 'Mass Civilisation and Minority Culture' as a

> capacity [that] does not belong merely to an isolated aesthetic realm: it implies responsiveness to theory as well as to art, to science and philosophy in so far as these may affect the sense of the human situation and of the nature of life. (*MC & MC*, p. 15)

Nevertheless, it is possible to distinguish between the two terms. While language gives rise to both consciousness and thought, the former seems to have a broader range of meanings than the latter. To begin with, the relation between language and consciousness implies, in phrases such as language being 'more than an instrument of expression' (Thought, Language and Objectivity', p. 67) that there is an unconscious dimension to language in Leavis. This paves the way for a psychoanalytic approach to the relation between consciousness and language in his work, as does the fact that consciousness is seen in terms of the body and its desires.

These issues will be discussed in the following chapters, as will the fact that consciousness is bound up with the notion of recognition, a key term in the early psychoanalytic writings of Lacan. Thought, by contrast, is concerned with the problem of continuity in cultural life, creativity, valuation, judgement and significance. Its project is the 'creative reality of human significances, values and non-measurable ends which our technologico–Benthamite civilization ignores and progressively impoverishes, thus threatening human existence'. (F.R. Leavis, '"English", Unrest and Continuity', in Leavis, *Nor Shall My Sword: Discourses on Pluralism, Compassion and Social Hope*, pp. 103–33, 110.)

Ultimately, it is impossible to disentangle consciousness and thought in Leavis's work, if only because he tends to use the terms interchangeably. However, as I have suggested, there is a distinction to be made. My main concern will be with 'consciousness'.

39. See note 21.
40. For an account of the relation between metaphor and money see Allen Hoey, 'The Name on the Coin: Metaphor, Metonymy and Money', *Diacritics* 18:2, Summer 1988, pp. 26–37. See also Marc Shell, *The Economy of Literature* (Baltimore: Johns Hopkins University Press, 1978).
41. See, for example, F.R. Leavis 'Mutually Necessary', in F.R. Leavis *The Critic As Anti-Philosopher*, ed. G. Singh (London: Chatto & Windus, 1982) pp. 186–208, esp. 189–90. See also F.R. Leavis, 'Standards of Criticism' in F.R. Leavis, *Valuation in Criticism and Other Essays*, ed. G. Singh (Cambridge: Cambridge University Press, 1986) pp. 244–52, esp. 244.
42. See F.R. Leavis, '"Under Which King, Bezonian?"', 'Marxism and Cultural Continuity' and 'Restatements for Critics', in Leavis, *Valuation in Criticism and Other Essays*, pp. 38–45, 31–7 and 46–53 respectively. Leavis's relation to Marxism is discussed in Chapter 3.
43. Norman Angell, *The Press and the Organisation of Society* (Cambridge: Minority Press, 1922) p. 17, quoted by Leavis in *MC & MC*, p. 19.
44. See Sigmund Freud, *The Interpretation of Dreams*, trans. J. Strachey. Edited James Strachey and A. Tyson, revised Angela Richards (London: Pelican, 1976) pp. 628–51. For one account of what Freud means by the conscious and unconscious see Sigmund Freud, 'Conscious and Unconscious' in Sigmund Freud, *On Metapsychology:*

*The Theory of Psychoanalysis*, trans. James Strachey. Edited by Angela Richards (Harmondsworth: Penguin, 1991) pp. 351–6.

45. Angell, *The Press and the Organisation of Society*, p. 27, quoted by Leavis in *MC & MC*, p. 20.

46. See, for example, the long quotations from J.B. Watson which Leavis gives in *MC & MC*, pp. 40–1. The quotations from J.B. Watson, *The Ways of Behaviourism* (London: Kegan Paul, 1925) are pp. 48, 60–1, 63, 86 and 111 respectively. Further examples that Leavis gives of the instrumental mentality are Major Leonard Darwin, who believes 'that human excellence may, for practical Eugenic purposes, be measured by earning capacity' and Sir Richard Paget, who argues that 'it is time English was deliberately and scientifically standardised as a language of thought' (*MC & MC*, p. 42).

47. Samson, *F.R. Leavis*, p. 30.

48. Ibid., p. 29.

49. Ibid., p. 61.

50. T.W. Adorno and Max Horkheimer, 'The Culture Industry: Enlightenment as Mass Deception' in T.W. Adorno and M. Horkheimer, *Dialectic of Enlightenment*, trans. J. Cumming (London: Verso, 1992) pp. 120–67, 120.

51. T.W. Adorno, 'Culture Industry Reconsidered', in Adorno, *The Culture Industry: Selected Essays on Mass Culture*, pp. 85–92, 85.

52. Ibid.

53. See Adorno, 'The Schema of Mass Culture', p. 56.

54. Adorno and Horkheimer, 'The Culture Industry: Enlightenment as Mass Deception', p. 126.

55. Adorno, 'The Schema of Mass Culture', p. 79.

56. F.R. Leavis, 'Eliot's "Axe To Grind" and the Nature of Great Criticism', in F.R. Leavis, *English Literature in Our Time and the University* (Cambridge: Cambridge University Press, 1969) pp. 85–108, 97.

57. F.R. Leavis, 'Tragedy and the "Medium": A Note on Mr. Santayana's "Tragic Philosophy"', in F.R. Leavis, *The Common Pursuit* (Harmondsworth: Penguin/Chatto & Windus, 1962/1993) pp. 121–35, 130.

58. T.W. Adorno, 'Letters to Walter Benjamin', in T.W. Adorno, W. Benjamin, E. Black, B. Brecht and G. Lukacs, *Aesthetics and Politics*, ed. R. Taylor (London: Verso, 1990) pp. 110–33, 123.

59. For an example of Leavis's more detailed discussion of value see F.R. Leavis 'Mutually Necessary'; 'Valuation in Criticism' and 'Thought, Meaning and Sensibility', in F.R. Leavis *Valuation in Criticism and Other Essays*, pp. 276–84 and pp. 285–7 respectively. In these essays Leavis rejects the idea that valuation is a process of 'putting a price on a work' ('Valuation in Criticism', p. 279) which of course undermines, albeit retrospectively, the economic metaphor in 'Mass Civilisation and Minority Culture'. In 'Mutually Necessary', however, he does admit that it is very difficult to separate value from price,

the word 'value' as we have it in 'value judgement' brings together in a treacherous confusingness two very different things. The sense that everyone takes seriously is the same the word has when we talk of the value of an article in terms of money'. ('Mutually Necessary', p. 190)

Leavis does not make clear what the other 'thing' is. The implication, in a long passage (ibid.), is that it is the opposite of price, or indeed of any process of mathematical or scientific quantification.

This lack of definition is consistent with Leavis's claim 'that the most important words ... are incapable of definition' ('Pluralism, Compassion and Social Hope', p. 163). This is not an evasion, rather a recognition that the meanings and connotations of words are always socially formed. The use of a term is the product of, among other things, the speaker's intention, the receiver's expectation and the context in which it is uttered. Understood in this way, it is possible to see how Leavis can be used to critique Saussure, who saw language primarily as a system of 'differences *without positive terms*'. Ferdinard de Saussure, *Course in General Linguistics*, trans. W. Baskin (London: Fontana, 1974) p. 120. Leavis seems to acknowledge that meaning is something that individuals and groups struggle over in concrete situations whereas Saussure seems to imply that it arises merely as a function of the internal structure of language alone.

It is this 'difference' between Leavis and Saussure that may account for the hostility of post-structuralist critics to Leavis. But, if there are differences between Leavis and Saussure, there are also similarities. For example, Saussure's description of value as something not fixed in itself but determined by its environment or surroundings (Saussure, *Course in General Linguistics*, pp. 111–12) is echoed in Leavis's notion of 'placing valuation' ('Mutually Necessary', p. 200), that is, how a new work is placed in 'an organization of similarly "placed" things that have found their bearing with regard to one another', F.R. Leavis, 'Criticism and Philosophy', in Leavis, *The Common Pursuit*, pp. 211–22, 213.

The main point is that Leavis argues for the relative nature of a work's value *and this is precisely what makes it an economic term*. The structure of tradition is, indeed, analogous to that of an economy where the value of a work constantly shifts in relation to other works as the value of money is modified according to the movement of currency. Leavis cannot, therefore, separate value from price despite his insistence on their non-commensurability. That is his first problem. His second is that the economic nature of value means that it can never be absolute or unchanging, a characteristic suggested by the notion of implicit standards. What is not seen can be fantasised as secure, fixed and permanent.

60.   The difficulty of the concept of culture is occluded in models such as that proposed by John Fiske, who claims that society can be understood in terms of the subordinate group resisting the attempts of the dominant one to impose its values upon it. See John Fiske, *Understanding Popular Culture* (London: Unwin Hyman, 1989). This account irons out the differences between one cultural pursuit and

another, as does Fiske's use of the term pleasure which, he claims, characterises the experience of popular culture. Pleasure, in conferring a spurious democracy on different activities, consequently evades questions of ethics and aesthetics: it sanctions badger baiting as much as reading a Jane Austen novel.

Fiske's approach to culture reflects an age when relativistic thought has come more and more to the fore. One problem with relativistic thought is that it assumes all cultural practices are of *equal* value. But, if this is the case, then what sense can be made of the term relative since it implies that all things are *different*? There thus seems to be something paradoxical in the relativist's position. Another problem with relativistic thought is its attitude towards 'high culture' which it sees as standing for 'universal value standards', Anthony Giddens, David Held, Dan Hubert, Steve Lloyd, Debbie Seymour and John Thompson, 'Some Theoretical Considerations', in A. Giddens et al. *The Polity Reader in Cultural Theory* (Cambridge/Oxford: Polity Press/Blackwell, 1994), pp. 15–23, 21. What this ignores is that 'high' culture is produced only in relation to 'mass' or 'popular' culture. It is therefore of its nature relativistic.

All these terms, 'high', 'mass' or 'popular' culture are extremely complex and need to be approached with care. The aim should be to find better and more productive ways of discussing them; something which is not achieved by dismissing the challenges and claims of 'high' culture as something irrelevant or outmoded. Ironically, the argument against 'high' culture is conducted in the idiom developed by high culture, that is the language of value. What this ignores is how culture, whether 'high', 'mass' or 'popular' is coming to be seen increasingly in terms of technology. For a good overview of this approach see Gretchen Bender and Timothy Druckery (eds) *Culture on the Brink: Ideologies of Technology* (Seattle: Bay Press, 1994).

61.  J.A. Cuddon, *The Penguin Dictionary of Literary Terms and Literary Criticism* (Harmondsworth: Penguin, 1991) p. 545.
62.  This, in fact, is Leavis's position throughout most of his later work. '[L]anguage', he writes,

> gives us so much more than a felicitous analogy. A language *is* a life, and life involves change that is continual renewal. A language has its life in use – use that, of its nature, is a creative human response to changing conditions, so that in a living language we have a manifestation of continuous collaborative creativity. (F.R. Leavis, 'Pluralism, Compassion and Social Hope', in Leavis, *Nor Shall My Sword: Discourses on Pluralism, Compassion and Social Hope*, pp. 163–98, 183.)

63.  See Roman Jakobson, 'Two Types of Language and Two Types of Aphasia Disturbance', in Roman Jakobson and Morris Halle, *Fundamentals of Language* (New York: Moulton, 1956) pp. 69–76.
64.  On the difficulty of distinguishing metaphor from metonymy see David Lodge, 'Metaphor and Metonymy', in David Lodge, *The Modes*

*of Modern Writing* (London: Edward Arnold, 1977) pp. 73–124, pp. 75–6; 81 n., 100 and 111. For a general discussion of the relation of metaphor to thought see Andrew Ortony (ed.) *Metaphor and Thought* (Cambridge: Cambridge University Press, 1979).

65.  See Richard Rorty, *Contingency, Irony and Solidarity* (Cambridge: Cambridge University Press, 1989). See also Stanley Fish, *Doing What Comes Naturally: Change, Rhetoric and the Practice of Theory in Literary and Legal Studies* (Oxford: Clarendon Press, 1989).

66.  I am grateful to Christopher Norris for the observation that an anti-fundamentalist's argument would be that criteria, standards and cultural values could still be invoked as long as these were understood as relativised to a given cultural place and time.

67.  See, for example, F.R. Leavis, 'Élites, Oligarchies and an Educated Public', in Leavis, *Nor Shall My Sword: Discourses on Pluralism, Compassion and Social Hope*, pp. 201–28, 205.

68.  T.W. Adorno, 'Culture and Administration', in Adorno, *The Culture Industry: Selected Essays on Mass Culture*, pp. 93–113, 93.

69.  Ibid., p. 111.

70.  Ibid., p. 101.

71.  Jacques Lacan, *Speech and Language in Psychoanalysis*, trans. Anthony Wilden (Baltimore and London: Johns Hopkins University Press, 1994) p. 31. It should be noted that this idea can be interpreted in a number of different ways, not least because, as William J. Richardson has pointed out, Lacan has repeated the claim in a number of different contexts. See William J. Richardson, 'Psychoanalysis and the Being-Question', in Joseph H. Smith and William Kerrigan (eds) *Interpreting Lacan* (New Haven: Yale University Press, 1983) pp. 139–59, 153. On the difficulty of this question in Lacan see Anika Lemaire, *Jacques Lacan*, trans. David Macey (London: Routledge and Kegan Paul, 1977) p. 170 and Malcolm Bowie, 'Jacques Lacan', in John Sturrock (ed.) *Structuralism and Since: From Levi Strauss to Derrida* (Oxford: Oxford University Press, 1979) pp. 117–53, 135–6.

72.  '*The Book Guild* cater[s] for the *ordinary intelligent reader* not for the highbrows – [it is] an organisation which realise[s] that – *a book can have a good story and a popular appeal and yet be good literature*'. *Book Guild* publicity leaflet, quoted by Leavis in *MC & MC*, p. 33. Leavis gives no reference for the quotation. For an ideological account of book clubs in the 1930s and beyond see Janice Radway, 'Mail-Order Culture and Its Critics: The Book-of-the-Month Club, Commodification and Consumption', in Lawrence Grossberg, Gary Nelson and Paula Treichler (eds) *Cultural Studies* (London: Routledge, 1992) pp. 512–30.

73.  Leavis took this idea from Q.D. Leavis, *Fiction and the Reading Public* (London: Chatto & Windus, 1932). See esp. pp. 83–96.

74.  Gilbert Russell, *Advertisement Writing* (London: Earnest Benn, 1927) p. 34, quoted by Leavis in *MC & MC*, p. 35.

75.  Sigmund Freud, 'Beyond the Pleasure Principle', in Freud, *On Metapsychology: The Theory of Psychoanalysis*, pp. 275–338, esp. 308.

76.  Robert and Helen Lynd, *Middletown* (New York: Constable, 1929).

77. In connection with this 'something more', it is worth noting that America was perceived, in the inter-war years, in terms of consumption, as indeed the land of 'something more'. See Gary Cross, *Time and Money: The Making of Consumer Culture* (London: Routledge, 1993) p. 15.

78. Lynd, *Middletown*, p. 204, quoted by Leavis in *MC & MC*, p. 17.

79. The notion of 'something more' also draws freely on Derrida's essay, 'That Dangerous Supplement', in Jacques Derrida, *Of Grammatology*, trans. Gayatri Chakravorty Spivak (Baltimore: Johns Hopkins University Press, 1976) pp. 141–64.

80. Here, as with all translations, caution is necessary. However, even if allowances are made for flexibility in the translation of specific words, the ideas are sufficiently similar as to warrant comparison. See Adorno, 'The Schema of Mass Culture', p. 53, and 'Culture and Administration', pp. 101, 104, 106.

81. It would be possible to extend and refine these remarks in the context of Derrida's notion of *différance*. See Jacques Derrida, 'Différance', in Derrida, *Margins of Philosophy*, pp. 3–27.

82. Derrida, 'That Dangerous Supplement', p. 158.

83. Ibid.

84. Adorno, 'Culture and Administration', p. 113.

85. Ibid.

86. Ibid.

87. Adorno, 'How To Look at Television', in Adorno, *The Culture Industry: Selected Essays on Mass Culture*, pp. 136–53, 138.

88. Leavis, *Thought, Words and Creativity: Art and Thought in Lawrence*, p. 148.

89. I.A. Richards, *Practical Criticism* (London: Kegan Paul, 1929), pp. 319–20, quoted by Leavis, *MC & MC*, p. 30.

90. See, for example, Steven Connor, *Theory and Cultural Value* (Oxford: Basil Blackwell, 1992), Antony Easthope, 'The Question of Literary Value', *Textual Practice* 4:3, 1990, pp. 376–89, and John Frowe, *Cultural Studies and Cultural Value* (Oxford: Clarendon Press, 1995).

## CHAPTER 2: *CULTURE AND ENVIRONMENT*

1. F.R. Leavis and Denys Thompson, *Culture and Environment: The Training of Critical Awareness* (London: Chatto & Windus, 1933/1964). Hereafter *CE* with page references given in the text.

2. Raymond Williams, *Culture and Society 1780–1950* (Harmondsworth: Penguin/Chatto & Windus, 1958/1975) pp. 246–57. Williams makes two main points about the organic community; first that 'it has always gone' and second that Leavis's account of it ignored 'the penury, the petty tyranny, the disease and mortality, the ignorance and frustrated intelligence which were also among its ingredients' (Williams, *Culture and Society*, pp. 252, 253). This criticism is only partly justified because

it glosses over the complexity of Leavis's attitude to the question of texts as evidence of the life of past societies.

At first, this attitude seems straightforward; literature should not be used as evidence. '[L]iterature,' Leavis writes, 'isn't so much material lying there to be turned over from the outside, and drawn on, for reference and exemplification.' F.R. Leavis, 'Sociology and Literature', in F.R. Leavis, *The Common Pursuit* (Harmondsworth: Penguin/Chatto & Windus, 1962/1993) pp. 195–203, 198. Later, however, Leavis argues that literature is a special kind of evidence, one that historians or sociologists fail to grasp if they treat it as simply one more archive without paying attention to its special qualities as language. As Leavis consistently argues 'language is a cultural life, a living, creative continuity'. F.R. Leavis, 'Four Quartets', in F.R. Leavis, *The Living Principle: 'English As a Discipline of Thought'* (London: Chatto & Windus, 1975) pp. 155–264, 197. That is, the grammar, the syntax, the vocabulary, the idioms, the phrasing and the rhythm of the language suggest an attitude to life that is as much evidence about the past as any facts it may convey. This point applies not only to literature but also to social history. Hence it is as important to be attuned to the language of social history, which incorporates values, distinctions, identifications and conclusions as it is to be attuned to these same things in literary language.

Social history, observes Leavis, only has 'shape and significance' when it is 'informed by the life and pressure of ... questions' such as

> What, as civilisation to live in and be of, did England offer at such a time? As we pass from now to then, what light is thrown on human possibilities – on the potentialities and desirabilities of civilised life? In what respects might it be better to live then than now? What tentative conception of ideal civilisation are we prompted towards by the links we gather from history? Leavis, 'Sociology and Literature', p. 202.)

It is with such questions in mind that Leavis read Sturt.

> The attention we aimed at promoting was to the present, and our emphasis was on the need to understand the nature of the accelerating and inevitable change that was transforming our civilisation. The wheelwright's business ... didn't merely provide him [Sturt] with a satisfying craft that entailed the use of a diversity of skills; it contained a full human meaning in itself – it kept a human significance always present. (F.R. Leavis, 'Luddites? Or Is There One Culture', in F.R. Leavis, *Nor Shall My Sword: Discourses on Pluralism, Compassion and Social Hope* (London: Chatto & Windus, 1972) pp. 77–99, 85.)

Thus Williams is only partially correct to criticise Leavis on the grounds that he ignored factual evidence since Leavis was not reading Sturt only in factual terms.

However, it is true that Leavis occasionally invites such criticism by remarks like the following: '*The Wheelwright's Shop* forms part of the documentation adduced to bring home the truth that there was once an organic community'. F.R. Leavis, 'The Organic Community', letter to *The Spectator*, 10 May 1963, in F.R. Leavis, *Letters in Criticism*, ed. John Tasker (London: Chatto & Windus, 1974) pp. 100–1, 100. Then there is the problem of Leavis's seeming to give more importance to factual issues than evaluative ones, apparent in his criticism of the historian J.H. Plumb, who supported C.P. Snow's point in his Rede lecture that the agricultural poor 'in any country where they have had the chance ... have walked off the land into the factories as fast as the factories could take them'. Snow, quoted by F.R. Leavis in 'Pluralism, Compassion and Social Hope', in Leavis *Nor Shall My Sword: Discourses on Pluralism, Compassion and Social Hope*, pp. 163–98, 187. The quotation comes from C.P. Snow, *The Two Cultures* (Cambridge: Cambridge University Press, 1959/1993) p. 26. Ironically, one of the sources from which Leavis draws these facts are the novels of Thomas Hardy (ibid., p. 188). Thus Leavis uses literature in precisely the manner in which he said it should not be used.

In any case, Leavis was perfectly aware of the dreadful conditions endured by many in the past. These however – and it is here that his position may be found objectionable – were not his main concern; that was art and the creativity it represented.

Because one is grateful for Dickens and the past conditions that made him possible one is not to be taken as blind to the miseries, squalors and inhumanities his art records. What matters, the supreme significance, is the art and the general human creativity it represents, and it is a genocidal illusion that indifference to art and the conditions of it, even though indifference presents itself as zeal for social reform, will improve the lot of humanity. (F.R. Leavis, 'Élites, Oligarchies and an Educated Public', in Leavis, *Nor Shall My Sword: Discourses on Pluralism, Compassion and Social Hope*, pp. 201–28, 207.)

Those who find this unpalatable may do so because it implies that suffering is justified if it produces art. But this ignores the point that a condition of 'inhumanit[y]' is *ultimately* incompatible with '*human* creativity' and, of course, the very notion of 'humanity' itself. What Leavis is trying to do is to focus attention on what art can contribute to humanity that a social welfare programme cannot. He is not arguing that one excludes the other. If he appears to be making that claim it is for two reasons. First, the myth of Leavis as an elitist conditions a response to his work which looks for such a reading and, second, Leavis has to give art more prominence to counter the way he believes it is devalued in the culture generally.

Leavis's attitude to the question of historical evidence is, then, at the very least, problematic. As he himself writes, 'How does one get access to the "historical past"? – that, surely, is the great problem.'

F.R. Leavis, 'The Radical Wing of Cambridge English', letter to *The Listener*, 3 November 1960 in Leavis, *Letters in Criticism*, 75–7, 76.

It is important to appreciate this since the organic community – over which the question of evidence arises – forms the basis of Leavis's view of literature. To misunderstand his attitude towards that is therefore to risk misunderstanding his entire position. Williams encourages such a misunderstanding by his concentration on the matter of evidence and it is this approach which has influenced later assessments of Leavis's analysis of not just the organic community but society at large. See, for example, Chris Baldick, *The Social Mission of English Criticism 1848–1932* (Oxford: Clarendon Press, 1987) pp. 192–3; Paul Filmer, 'The Literary Imagination and the Explanation of Socio-cultural Change in Modern Britain', *The European Journal of Sociology* 10:2, 1969, pp. 271–91; Ralph Freadman and S.R. Millar, 'Three Views of Literary Theory', *Poetics: International Review for the Theory of Literature* 17:1–2, 1988, pp. 9–24; Ian Gregor, 'English, Leavis and Social Order', *Twentieth Century Studies* 9, September 1973, pp. 22–31; Lesley Johnson, 'F.R. Leavis' in Lesley Johnson, *The Cultural Critics* (London: Routledge & Kegan Paul, 1979) pp. 93–115; Paul Lawford, 'Conservative Empiricism in Literary Theory: A Scrutiny of the Work of F.R. Leavis' in *Red Letters* 1:1, 1976, pp. 12–15, and 'F.R. Leavis: A Scrutiny' in *Red Letters* 2:2, pp. 9–11; Francis Mulhern, *The Moment of 'Scrutiny'* (London: Verso, 1979) pp. 58–63, 72–6; Andrew Milner, 'Leavis and English Literary Criticism', *Praxis* 1:2, 1976, pp. 91–106; Anne Samson, *F.R. Leavis* (New York: Harvester Wheatsheaf, 1992) pp. 52–5; David Sampson, 'Literature Versus Society? Recent Trends in Literary Criticism', *Southern Review* 12:3, 1979, pp. 268–84.

For an early critique of the organic community see Austin Duncan-Jones, 'The Organic Community', *Cambridge Review*, 26 May 1933, pp. 432–3.

For more sympathetic views of the organic community see R.P. Bilan, *The Literary Criticism of F.R. Leavis*, (Cambridge: Cambridge University Press, 1979) pp. 14–18; Eugene Goodheart, *The Failure of Criticism* (Cambridge, Mass.: Harvard University Press, 1978) pp. 69–83; and Fred Inglis, 'Resistance and Social Decline', in Fred Inglis, *Radical Earnestness: English Social Theory, 1880–1980* (Oxford: Martin Robertson, 1982) pp. 91–108, esp. 104–8.

For a broadly similar but left-wing analysis of history to that which Leavis provided see Edgell Rickword, 'Culture, Progress, and English Tradition', in Edgell Rickwood, *Literature in Society: Essays and Opinions II, 1931–1978*, ed. A. Young (Manchester: Carcanet, 1978) pp. 93–104. For first hand accounts of *an* organic community, see George Ewart Evans, *The Days That We Have Seen* (London: Faber, 1975) esp. p. 71. For George Sturt's account of the organic community see David Gervais, 'Late Witness: George Sturt and Village England' in *Cambridge Quarterly* 20, 1991, pp. 21–44.

For a brief contextualisation of Leavis's thought within the English tradition see Pamela McCallum, *Literature and Method: Towards a*

*Critique of I.A. Richards, T.S. Eliot and F.R. Leavis* (Dublin: Gill & Macmillan, 1983) pp. 153–67, 178–82.

3.  Michael Bell, *F.R. Leavis* (London: Routledge, 1988) p. 116. Bell's own perceptive comments on the organic community can be found on pp. 115–20.

4.  Williams, *Culture and Society* p. 252.

5.  Ibid., p. 250.

6.  It is worth pointing out that Leavis's ideas of rational recreation belong firmly in the tradition of English socialism. For the response of socialists to leisure and free time in the nineteenth and early twentieth century see Chris Waters, *British Socialists and the Politics of Popular Culture 1884–1914* (Manchester: Manchester University Press, 1990).

7.  Constance Harris, *The Use of Leisure in Bethnal Green*, preface L.P. Jacks (London: Lindsey Press, 1927).

8.  Gary Cross, *Time and Money: The Making of Consumer Culture* (London: Routledge, 1993) p. 22. This superb study contains an excellent bibliography covering many of the issues discussed here.

9.  Thorstein Veblen, *The Theory of the Leisure Class* (New York: Dover, 1899/1994) pp. 43–62.

10.  Rexford Tugwell, *Industry's Coming of Age* (New York: Harcourt Brace, 1927) pp. 258–9.

11.  T.W. Adorno 'Free Time', in T.W. Adorno, *The Culture Industry: Selected Essays on Mass Culture*, ed. J.M. Bernstein (London: Routledge, 1991) pp. 162–70, 164.

12.  Ibid., p. 168.

13.  Ibid., p. 167.

14.  Cross, *Time and Money: The Making of Consumer Culture*, p. 75.

15.  Henry Overstreet, *A Guide to Civilized Leisure* (New York: Books for Libraries Press, 1934) p. 246.

16.  E.B. Castles, *The Coming of Leisure* (London: New Education Foundation, 1935) p. 18. See also Lancelot Hogben, *Education for an Age of Plenty* (London: Life and Leisure Pamphlets 7, 1937).

17.  Leavis cited folk dancing as one of the characteristics of the organic community (*CE*, p. 1). For details of the emphasis on community see Cross, *Time and Money: The Making of Consumer Culture*, pp. 105, 113.

18.  Ibid., p. 163.

19.  W.D. Scott, quoted by Cross, ibid., p. 157. Cross does not give the source of the quotation.

20.  George Orwell, *The Road to Wigan Pier* (Harmondsworth: Penguin, 1937/1989 ) p. 83.

21.  Cross, *Time and Money: The Making of Consumer Culture*, p. 100.

22.  Ibid., p. 109.

23.  Ibid., p. 114.

24.  'The view that mechanisation released the libido from work discipline and produced passive and bored leisure presumed the conservative psychological models of Ortega, Freud, Adorno and other defenders of classical high culture', ibid., p. 55.

25.  Evans, *The Days That We Have Seen*, p. 71.

26. E.P. Thompson, introduction to George Sturt, *The Wheelwright's Shop* (Cambridge: Cambridge University Press, 1923/1993) p. xiv.

27. John Stevenson, *British Society 1914–1945* (Harmondsworth: Penguin, 1984) p. 108.

28. Ibid., p. 114.

29. For a detailed account of this process see Harold Perkin, *The Rise of Professional Society: England Since 1800* (London: Routledge, 1989).

30. Evans, *The Days That We Have Seen*, p. 71.

31. Colin Crouch, 'Research on Corporatism in Britain'. Discussion paper at the Conference on Organizational Participation and Public Policy, Princeton University, September 1981, quoted by Perkin, *The Rise of Professional Society: England Since 1880*, p. 287.

32. Perkin, *The Rise of Professional Society: England Since 1880*, p. 288.

33. Brian Doyle, *English and Englishness* (London: Routledge, 1989). See esp. pp. 20, 79–80, 84, 87, 91, 92.

34. See Mulhern, *The Moment of 'Scrutiny'*, p. 32.

35. Sturt, *The Wheelwright's Shop*, p. 74, quoted by Leavis, *CE*, p. 79.

36. D.H. Lawrence quoted by Leavis, *CE*, p. 97. Leavis gives no source for the quotation. For a slightly later but largely similar view of 'the machine' see Orwell, *The Road to Wigan Pier*, pp. 183–4.

37. T.W. Adorno and Max Horkheimer, 'The Culture Industry: Enlightenment as Mass Deception', in T.W. Adorno and Max Horkheimer, *Dialectic of Enlightenment*, trans. John Cumming (London: Verso, 1944/1992) pp. 120–37, 164.

38. Ibid.

39. Guy Debord, *The Society of the Spectacle*, trans. Donald Nicholson-Smith (New York: Zone Books, 1967/1994) p. 76.

40. Ibid., p. 12.

41. Ibid., p. 29.

42. Ibid., p. 12.

43. Ibid., p. 23.

44. Ibid., p. 16.

45. Norman Angell, *The Press and the Organization of Society* (Cambridge: Minority Press, 1922) p. 62, quoted by Leavis, *CE*, p. 37.

46. Q.D. Leavis, *Fiction and the Reading Public* (London: Bellew Publishing, 1932/1990) pp. 197–8, quoted by Leavis, *CE*, pp. 53–4.

47. T.W. Adorno, 'Culture Industry Reconsidered', in Adorno, *The Culture Industry: Selected Essays on Mass Culture*, pp. 85–92, 90.

48. See note 35.

49. Sturt, *The Wheelwright's Shop*, p. 140, quoted by Leavis, *CE*, p. 80.

50. See note 36.

51. See note 49.

52. Sturt, *The Wheelwright's Shop*, p. 54, quoted by Leavis, *CE*, p. 84.

53. F.R. Leavis, 'Towards Standards of Criticism', in F.R. Leavis, *Anna Karenina and Other Essays* (London: Chatto & Windus, 1973) pp. 219–34, 221.

54. Sturt, *The Wheelwright's Shop*, p. 36.

55. Ibid., p. 44.

56. Ibid., p. 53.

57. Frederick Winslow Taylor, *The Principles of Scientific Management* (London: Harper Row, 1911/1964) pp. 15, 20.
58. Sturt, *The Wheelwright's Shop*, p. 54. It is worth noting that one of the motifs of *The Wheelwright's Shop* is Sturt's sense of himself as a poor manager, 'under my ignorant management the men had grown not so much lazy as leisurely. I know this but too well; but I did not know how to mend the matter' (p. 200).

   History shows that scientific management proves to be the remedy for this type of problem in industry. It is a solution which Sturt rejects – though there is an air of ambiguity about that rejection. 'Are we not taking industry too seriously to be sensible about it?' he writes at the end of *The Wheelwright's Shop*. 'Reading of "Scientific Management" I recall something quite different from that ... which reached down to my time from an older England' (pp. 202–3). Sturt then relates an anecdote about an apprentice being sent to ask him for a straight hook. The anecdote is intended to illustrate the 'friendly, jolly' (p. 202) character of the labour relations of old England. But Sturt also raises the problem of 'time wasting' and loss of 'profit' (p. 203) which were the very questions to which scientific management addressed itself. The importance of scientific management to Leavis's criticism will be discussed more fully in the next chapter.
59. Taylor, *The Principles of Scientific Management*, p. 9.
60. Ibid., p. 16. Contrast Sturt, '"[r]ule-of-thumb" was my guide', *The Wheelwright's Shop*, p. 60.
61. See note 35.
62. See F.R. Leavis, 'Joyce and "The Revolution of the Word"', in F.R. Leavis, *The Critic As Anti-Philosopher*, ed. G. Singh (London: Chatto & Windus, 1982) pp. 121–8. This article was written in 1933, the year that *Culture and Environment* was published.
63. Georg Simmel, 'The Metropolis and Mental Life', in Georg Simmel, *On Individuality and Social Forms*, ed. Donald N. Levine (Chicago: The University of Chicago Press, 1971) pp. 324–39.
64. Ibid., p. 325.
65. Ibid., p. 326.
66. Ibid.
67. Ibid., p. 325.
68. Ibid.
69. Walter Benjamin 'On Some Motifs in Baudelaire', in Walter Benjamin, *Illuminations*, ed. Hannah Arendt, trans. Harry Zohn (London: Fontana, 1973/1992) pp. 152–96, 159.
70. Ibid., see pp. 154–7.
71. Simmel, 'The Metropolis and Mental Life', p. 325.
72. Leavis may be committed to more consciousness in *Culture and Environment*, but he has reservations about being too conscious. 'There are', he writes, 'ways in which it is possible to be too conscious; and to be so is ... one of the troubles of the present age'. F.R. Leavis, *New Bearings in English Poetry* (Harmondsworth: Penguin/Chatto & Windus, 1932/1973) p. 73. Hereafter *NB*, with page references given in the text. Ian MacKillop has noted that, 'in his first book' – *New*

*Bearings in English Poetry* – Leavis was 'more enthusiastic about issues of consciousness than culture', Ian MacKillop, *F.R. Leavis, A Life in Criticism* (Harmondsworth: Allen Lane/Penguin, 1995) p. 137. Consciousness and culture soon merge for Leavis but that does not lessen the problem of consciousness in his work.

73. See note 52.
74. See note 35.
75. Jean-François Lyotard and Jean-Loup Thébaud, *Just Gaming*, trans. Wlad Godzich (Manchester: Manchester University Press, 1985) p. 34.
76. Ibid., p. 33.
77. Ibid., p. 32.
78. Ibid., p. 33.
79. Ibid.
80. F.R. Leavis, 'Justifying One's Valuation of Blake', in Leavis, *The Critic As Anti-Philosopher*, pp. 1–23, 23. Hereafter referred to as *JOVB* with page references in the text. See also Leavis, 'Pluralism, Compassion and Social Hope', p. 172 and 'The Pilgrim's Progress', in Leavis, *Anna Karenina and Other Essays*, pp. 33–48, p. 45.
81. Lyotard and Thébaud, *Just Gaming*, p. 33.
82. Ibid., p. 34.
83. Ibid.
84. T.W. Adorno, 'The Schema of Mass Culture' in Adorno, *The Culture Industry: Selected Essays on Mass Culture*, pp. 53–84, 60.
85. Debord, *The Society of the Spectacle*, p. 76.
86. F.R. Leavis, 'T. S. Eliot and English Literature', in F.R. Leavis, *Valuation in Criticism and Other Essays*, ed. G. Singh (Cambridge: Cambridge University Press, 1986) pp. 129–48, 130.
87. Terry Eagleton, *Literary Theory*, (Oxford: Basil Blackwell, 1985) p. 37.
88. See, for example, George Watson, *The Literary Critics: A Study of English Descriptive Criticism* (London: Woburn Press, 1973) pp. 198–207. Watson points out that Leavis's *The Great Tradition* is only one tradition, that of 'serious moral concern' (p. 202) and that there are others. See also Edward Greenwood, *F.R. Leavis* (London: Longman, 1978) p. 44.
89. George Sturt, *Change in the Village* (London: Duckworth, 1912/1959) p. 141 quoted by Leavis, *CE*, p. 69.
90. See note 25 and also the discussion of the term 'organic' in Raymond Williams, *Keywords* (London: Fontana, 1976/1988) pp. 227–9.
91. F.R. Leavis, 'Gerard Manley Hopkins: Reflections After Fifty Years' in Leavis, *The Critic As Anti-Philosopher*, pp. 76–97, 84.
92. F.R. Leavis, *Revaluation: Tradition and Development in English Poetry* (Harmondsworth: Penguin/Chatto & Windus, 1936/1967) p. 202. Hereafter referred to as *R*, with page references given in the text.
93. See note 73.
94. Sturt, *The Wheelwright's Shop*, p. 32, quoted by Leavis, *CE*, p. 85.
95. Sturt, *The Wheelwright's Shop*, p. 154, quoted by Leavis, *CE*, p. 88.
96. Sturt, *The Wheelwright's Shop*, p. 202, quoted by Leavis, *CE*, p. 90.
97. Ibid.
98. Ibid.
99. Ibid.

100. Sturt, *Change in the Village* p. 143, quoted by Leavis, *CE*, p. 70.
101. Adorno, 'The Schema of Mass Culture', p. 71.
102. 'Simulation threatens the difference between "true" and "false", between "real" and "imaginary"', Jean Baudrillard, *Simulations*, trans. Paul Foss et al. (New York: Semiotext(e), 1983) p. 5.
103. Sturt, *The Wheelwright's Shop*, p. 16–17, quoted by Leavis, *CE*, p. 77.
104. Sturt, *The Wheelwright's Shop*, p. 54–5, quoted by Leavis, *CE*, p. 84.
105. See note 73.
106. Sturt, *The Wheelwright's Shop*, pp. 17, quoted by Leavis, *CE*, pp. 74–5. Later, Sturt writes '"The men", though still my friends ... became machine "hands"', p. 201.
107. See note 49.
108. Sturt, *The Wheelwright's Shop*, p. 201, quoted by Leavis, *CE*, p. 89.
109. Ibid.
110. F.R. Leavis, 'Literary Criticism and Philosophy', in Leavis, *The Common Pursuit*, pp. 211–22, 212–13.
111. T.W. Adorno, 'Culture Criticism and Society', in Paul Connerton, ed. *Critical Sociology: Selected Readings* (Harmondsworth: Penguin, 1976) pp. 19–34.
112. Sturt, *Change in the Village*, p. 148, quoted by Leavis, *CE*, p. 73.
113. Ibid.
114. See note 35.
115. See note 112.
116. See note 35.
117. Sturt, *The Wheelwright's Shop*, p. 19, quoted by Leavis, *CE*, p. 78.
118. I.A. Richards, *Practical Criticism* (London: Routledge & Kegan Paul, 1929) pp. 320–1, quoted in Leavis, *CE*, p. 81.
119. See note 35.
120. See note 73.
121. Sturt, *The Wheelwright's Shop*, p. 140–1, quoted by Leavis, *CE*, p. 79–80.
122. Sturt, *The Wheelwright's Shop*, p. 154, quoted by Leavis, *CE*, p. 88.
123. See note 35.
124. F.R. Leavis, 'Valuation in Criticism' in Leavis, *Valuation in Criticism and Other Essays*, pp. 278–84, 281. Hereafter *VC* with page references given in the text.
125. See Perkin, *The Rise of Professional Society: England Since 1880*, pp. 112–13, 177, 298. Lyndall Urwick was the main exponent of scientific management in the inter-war years in Britain and, during the 1930s, was an important influence on industrial administration. Ibid., pp. 298, 304. See also Harold Pollard, *Development in Management Thought* (London: Heinemann, 1974) and James Burnham, *The Management Revolution* (Harmondsworth: Penguin, 1945).
126. See note 35.
127. See note 36.
128. See note 94.
129. Jacques Lacan, *Écrits: A Selection*, trans. Alan Sheridan (London: Tavistock Publications, 1977) pp. 148–78, 157. Anne Samson draws attention to a possible parallel between Leavis's description of the loss of the organic community and Lacan's account of the transition from

the mirror stage of development to the symbolic of language but she does not expand upon it. See Samson, *F.R. Leavis*, pp. 52–3.

130. Jacques Lacan, *The Seminars of Jacques Lacan: Book I Freud's Papers on Technique 1953–1954*, trans. John Forrester (Cambridge: Cambridge University Press, 1988) p. 192.
131. Lacan, *Écrits: A Selection*, p. 200.
132. For Lacan's account of this dialectic see ibid., pp. 285–7.
133. Ibid., p. 104.
134. Ibid., p. 302.
135. Ibid., p. 200.
136. Ibid.
137. Although there is an argument that the mass market was in place before the First World War, see W. Hamish Fraser, *The Coming of the Mass Market 1850–1914* (London: Macmillan, 1981) it is nevertheless the case that the culture of consumerism began to take shape in the inter-war years. See, for example, Cross, *Time and Money: the Making of Consumer Culture*, and Stevenson, *British Society 1914–1945*, esp. pp. 112–15, 125–9. See also Robert Bocock, *Consumption*, (London: Routledge, 1993) for a brief history and analysis of consumerism.
138. See Stuart Hall and Bill Schwarz, 'State and Society 1880–1930', in Mary Langan and Bill Schwarz (eds) *Crises in the British State 1880–1930* (London: Hutchinson/Centre for Contemporary Cultural Studies, University of Birmingham, 1985) pp. 7–33.
139. Language 'is a subtle body, but body it is. Words are trapped in all the corporeal images that captivate the subject', Lacan, *Écrits: A Selection*, p. 87. What Lacan means by this could be explored in relation to Leavis's notion of language as embodiment.
140. Lacan, *Écrits: A Selection*, p. 287.
141. Ibid., p. 88.
142. Jacques Lacan, *The Four Fundamental Concepts of Psychoanalysis*, trans. Alan Sheridan (Harmondsworth: Penguin, 1977) p. 108.
143. Lacan, *Écrits: A Selection*, p. 167.
144. F.R. Leavis, 'Tragedy and the Medium', in Leavis, *The Common Pursuit*, pp. 121–35, 130.
145. Sturt, *The Wheelwright's Shop*, pp. 17, 55 and *passim*.
146. See note 135.
147. Valentine Cunningham, *British Writers of the Thirties* (Oxford: Oxford University Press, 1985) pp. 159–65.
148. Lacan, *Écrits: A Selection*, p. 36.
149. Lacan, *The Seminars of Jacques Lacan: Book I: Freud's Papers on Technique 1953–1954*, p. 104.
150. See, however, the arguments in note 2. The understanding of literature as 'evidence' takes on a new meaning when put into the context of psychoanalysis.
151. Barbara Herrnstein Smith, *Contingencies of Value: Alternative Perspectives for Critical Theory* (Cambridge Mass.: Harvard University Press, 1988) pp. 17.
152. Steven Connor, *Theory and Cultural Value* (Oxford: Basil Blackwell, 1992) p. 11.

153. Ibid., p. 14.
154. Stevenson, *British Society 1914–1945*, p. 250.
155. Connor, *Theory and Cultural Value*, p. 12. See also Steven Connor, *Postmodern Culture: An Introduction to Theories of the Contemporary* (Oxford: Basil Blackwell, 1989) pp. 14–21.
156. For one version of this argument, see Christopher Norris, *What's Wrong with Postmodernism: Critical Theory and the Ends of Philosophy* (New York: Harvester Wheatsheaf, 1990) p. 23.
157. Leavis, it might be argued, suppresses the question of aesthetics in his writing. He equates an interest in aesthetics with an interest in form which he sees as excluding 'value judgements' and the 'interests of general living'. F.R. Leavis, 'The Logic of Christian Discrimination', in Leavis, *The Common Pursuit*, pp. 248–54, 251. However, the focus on and the feel for the sensuous in his writing is itself an aesthetic. Kant, for example, believed that the category of the aesthetic 'provided the "rules of sensuousness" which provided intuitions for the Understanding', Andrew Bowie, *Aesthetics and Subjectivity: From Kant to Nietzsche* (Manchester University Press, 1990) p. 29. Furthermore, Kant's later idea of the aesthetic as 'that representation of the imagination which gives much to think about, but without any determinate thought, i.e. *concept* being able to be adequate to it, which consequently no language can completely attain and make comprehensible' (Kant, quoted by Bowie, p. 29) finds a parallel in Leavis's repeated notion that the really important words cannot be defined and that both criticism and literature are forms of enactment rather than statements about 'experience' or the work.
158. Christopher Norris is perhaps the best example here. See Christopher Norris, *The Truth About Postmodernism* (Oxford: Basil Blackwell, 1993).
159. Leavis, 'Sociology and Literature', p. 195.
160. J.B. Watson quoted by O.L. Zangwill, 'Psychology', in C.B. Cox and A.E. Dyson (eds) *The Twentieth Century Mind: History, Ideas and Literature in Britain 1918–1945* (Oxford: Oxford University Press, 1972) pp. 171–95, 174. No source is given for the quotation.
161. Ibid., p. 176.
162. T.W. Adorno, *Minima Moralia: Reflections from Damaged Life*, trans. E.F.N. Jephcott (London: Verso, 1974/1993) p. 65.
163. Pasi Falk, *The Consuming Body* (London: Sage, 1994). See also D. Frisby, *Georg Simmel* (London: Routledge, 1984) pp. 131–2.
164. Stevenson, *British Social History 1914–1945*, p. 289.
165. See note 36.
166. Lacan, *The Seminars of Jacques Lacan: Book I: Freud's Papers on Technique 1953–1954*, p. 271.
167. See note 35.
168. Ibid.
169. See note 112.
170. Adorno and Horkheimer, 'The Culture Industry: Enlightenment As Mass Deception', p. 167.
171. Sinclair Lewis, *Babbit* (New York: Harcourt Brace, 1992) p. 86, quoted by Leavis, *CE*, p. 32.

172. Falk, *The Consuming Body*, p. 175.
173. Ibid., p. 156.
174. Ibid, pp. 151, 154.
175. See, for example, Fraser, *The Coming of the Mass Market 1850–1914*, pp. 134–46 and Raymond Williams, 'Advertising: The Magic System', in Raymond Williams, *Problems in Materialism and Culture* (London: Verso, 1980) pp. 170–95.
176. Falk, *The Consuming Body*, p. 156.
177. See T.J. Jackson Lears, *Some Versions of Fantasy: Towards a Cultural History of American Advertising* (Cambridge: Cambridge University Press, 1984) p. 370.
178. Falk, *The Consuming Body*, p. 160. For a discussion of Lacan and advertising see Falk, p. 176 and also Bocock, *Consumption*, pp. 83–4, 86–94.
179. Falk, *The Consuming Body*, p. 168.
180. Karl Marx, 'The Fetishism of the Commodity' in Connerton (ed.) *Critical Sociology: Selected Readings*, pp. 73–89, 74.
181. F.R. Leavis 'Marxism and Cultural Continuity', in Leavis, *Valuation in Criticism and Other Essays*, pp. 31–7, 35.
182. See Eagleton, *Literary Theory*, pp. 79–80.
183. Jean Baudrillard, 'Consumer Society', in Jean Baudrillard, *Selected Writings*, ed. Mark Poster (Cambridge/Oxford: Polity Press/Basil Blackwell, 1988) pp. 29–56, 53.
184. Ibid.
185. Ibid., p. 54.
186. Falk, *The Consuming Body*, p. 55.
187. Adorno, 'Cultural Criticism and Society', p. 33.
188. T.W. Adorno, 'Culture and Administration' in Adorno, *The Culture Industry: Selected Essays on Mass Culture*, pp. 93–118, 98.
189. G.H.L.F. Pitt-Rivers, *The Clash of Culture and the Contact of Races*, (London: Routledge, 1927) p. 215, quoted by Leavis, *CE*, p. 30..
190. Sturt, *The Wheelwright's Shop*, p. 19, quoted by Leavis, *CE*, p. 78.
191. Ibid.
192. Michael Joseph quoted by Leavis *CE*, p. 38. The quotation comes from Michael Joseph, *Journalism for Profit* (London: Hutchinson, 1924). I have been unable to find the original page reference.
193. *The Concise Oxford Dictionary* (Oxford: Oxford University Press, 1976).
194. Ibid.
195. Walter Benjamin, *One Way Street and Other Writings*, trans. Edmund Jephcott and Kingsley Shorter (London: Verso, 1979/1992) p. 89.
196. Ibid. Compare Baudrillard, '[w]e are witnessing the end of perspective and panoptic space', *Simulations*, p. 54.
197. Benjamin, *One Way Street and Other Writings*, p. 89.
198. Sturt, *The Wheelwright's Shop*, pp. 19–20, quoted by Leavis, *CE*, p.78.
199. See note 35.
200. See Sturt, *The Wheelwright's Shop*, pp. 24, 26, 54. On these pages Sturt extols the virtues of folk lore and intuitive knowledge yet his description of Turner as someone who 'knows, or thinks he knows, why certain late bearing apple trees have fruit only every other year'

(Sturt, *Change in the Village*, p. 144, quoted in *CE*, p. 70) suggests the opposite: a superior attitude towards country superstition. This reflects Sturt's ambiguous attitude towards scientific management, mentioned in note 58.

201.  Sturt, *Change in the Village*, p.137, quoted by Leavis, *CE*, p.67.

202.  Extract from *Your Money's Worth*, quoted by Leavis, *CE*, p. 49. Leavis gives no details of the source.

203.  Extract quoted by Leavis, *CE*, p. 57. No details of the source.

204.  Extract from 'The Commercial Side of Literature', quoted by Leavis, *CE*, p. 99. No details of the source.

205.  F.R. Leavis, 'Introduction', *Mill on Bentham and Coleridge* (London: Chatto & Windus, 1950) pp. 1–38, 3. Hereafter *MB & C* with page references given in the text.

206.  Sturt, *The Wheelwright's Shop*, p. 32, quoted by Leavis, *CE*, p. 85.

207.  Doyle, *English and Englishness*, pp. 70–1.

208.  Roland Barthes, *The Pleasure of the Text*, trans. Richard Millar (Oxford: Basil Blackwell, 1975/1990) p. 21.

209.  Ibid., p. 51.

210.  Ibid., p. 14. Compare to 'significant art challenges us in the most disturbing and inescapable way to a radical pondering, a new profound realization, of the grounds of our most important determinations and choices'. Leavis, 'Valuation in Criticism', p. 281. The difference is that art, for Leavis, would not be seen as bringing to a crisis the reader's relation to language. Nevertheless, that possibility is inherent in his work since civilisation has 'uprooted' and 'displaced' language. Furthermore, the fact that Leavis, like Barthes, sees literature as unsettling, opens his criticism to a reading in terms of bliss which would radicalise his notion of the sensuous.

211.  Barthes, *Pleasure of the Text*, p. 51.

212.  Ibid.

213.  Ibid., p. 52.

214.  Ibid.

215.  Ibid., p. 51.

216.  Ibid., p. 20.

217.  Ibid., p. 17.

218.  Ibid., p. 16.

219.  Ibid., p. 51.

220.  Ibid., p. 220.

221.  See, for example, C.K. Stead, *The New Poetic: Yeats to Eliot* (London: Hutchinson, 1964/1983) esp. pp. 148–86.

## CHAPTER 3: LITERATURE AND SOCIETY

1.  F.R. Leavis, 'Marxism and Cultural Continuity', preface to *For Continuity* (Cambridge: Minority Press, 1933) pp. 7–12; 'Under Which King Bezonian?', *Scrutiny* 1:3, December 1932, pp. 202–15; and 'Restatement for Critics', *Scrutiny* 1:4, March 1933, pp. 315–23. All

reprinted in F.R. Leavis, *Valuation in Criticism and Other Essays*, ed. G. Singh (Cambridge: Cambridge University Press, 1986) pp. 31–7; 38–45 and 46–53 respectively. Hereafter *MCC*, *UWKB* and *RFC* with page references – from *Valuation in Criticism* – given in the text. Strictly speaking 'Restatement for Critics' is, as Ian MacKillop notes, more to do with 'the impact made upon Leavis by the appearance of Lawrence's letters' (edited by Huxley) which Leavis had reviewed in December 1932, Ian MacKillop, *F.R. Leavis: A Life in Criticism* (Harmondsworth: Allen Lane/Penguin, 1995) p. 190. For further details see M.B. Kinch, William Baker and John Kimber, *F.R. Leavis and Q.D. Leavis: An Annotated Bibliography* (New York: Garland Publishing, 1989) p.42. Nevertheless, Leavis's comments on Marxism in that article, together with the date of it justify its being grouped with the other two. Another article that could be included on the same basis is 'Towards Standards of Criticism' in F.R. Leavis *Anna Karenina and Other Essays* (London: Chatto & Windus, 1967/1973) pp. 219–34, which was originally the introduction to *Towards Standards of Criticism: Selections from the Calendar of Modern Letters* (London: Wishart, 1933) pp. 1–26.

2. Francis Mulhern, *The Moment of 'Scrutiny'* (London: Verso, 1979), pp. 79–80. The words are Mulhern's. Compare Leavis, 'the inevitability (and desirability) of drastic social change makes an active concern for cultural continuity the more essential', F.R. Leavis, 'Towards Standards of Criticism', pp. 225–6.

3. Mulhern, *The Moment of Scrutiny*, p. 73 note 103. This is a task which still needs to be undertaken.

4. A.L. Morton, 'Culture and Leisure' in *Scrutiny* 1:4, March 1933, pp. 324–6, 324.

5. Iain Wright, 'F.R. Leavis: The Scrutiny Movement and the Crisis' in Jon Clark, Margot Heinemann, David Margolies and Carol Snee (eds) *Culture and Crisis in Britain in the Thirties* (London: Lawrence & Wishart, 1979) pp. 37–65, 55.

6. David Margolies *'Left Review* and Left Literary Theory' in ibid., pp. 67–82, 68. See also Valentine Cunningham, who comments that the most typical understanding of the Marxist throughout the 1930s was of someone 'prompt in sliding the analysis from one kind of crisis to another, from economics to the imagination, to the threat of war without once letting the argument falter', Valentine Cunningham, *British Writers of the Thirties* (Oxford: Oxford University press, 1989) p. 42.

7. Wright, 'F.R. Leavis: The Scrutiny Movement and the Crisis' p. 54. Wright implies Butterfield was a Marxist but this is debatable. In *The Whig Interpretation of History* (New York: Norton, 1931/1965) Butterfield had attacked historians like Macaulay and Trevelyan for interpreting the past according to the needs of the present. The implication was that the present could not be explained as determined by the past, which was precisely the Marxist view: the contemporary crisis as determined by the history of class struggle. As B.J. Atkinson observes, 'Butterfield, at this time, conceived of history as a means

not of solving problems but of making people realize how complicated they were', B.J. Atkinson 'Historiography' in C.B. Cox and A.E. Dyson (eds) *The Twentieth Century Mind: History, Ideas and Literature in Britain 2: 1918–1945* (Oxford: Oxford University Press, 1972) pp. 57–67, 62. As Butterfield himself noted, '[t]he last word of the historian is not some fine, firm general statement; it is a piece of detailed research', *The Whig Interpretation of History*, p. 73. This accent on the concrete matches Leavis's own and so there is less difference between them than Wright implies.

8. H. Butterfield, 'History and the Marxian Method' in *Scrutiny* 1:4, March 1933, pp. 339–55. This is, of course, the same issue which contains 'Restatement for Critics'.

9. Wright, 'F.R. Leavis: The Scrutiny Movement and the Crisis', p. 56.

10. Perry Anderson, 'Components of the National Culture', *New Left Review* 50, July–August 1968, pp. 3–57, 53.

11. F.R. Leavis, 'The Marxian Analysis: A Review of *The Mind in Chains*, ed. C. Day Lewis (London: Muller, 1937) and *Capitalist and Socialist* by Beryl Pring (London: Methuen, 1937) in *Scrutiny* 6:2, September 1937, pp. 201–4, 203. Hereafter *TMA* with page references given in the text. For an account of middle-class writers and Marxism see Cunningham, *British Writers of the Thirties*, pp. 211–14.

12. The question of Leavis and class deserves more attention than can be given here not least because class itself is such a notoriously difficult term to define, a fact not helped by its having been eclipsed in recent years by considerations of gender, sexuality and ethnicity. For accounts of Leavis and class see Noël Annan, 'Bloomsbury and the Leavises', in Jane Marcus (ed.) *Virginia Woolf and Bloomsbury: A Centenary Celebration* (London: Macmillan, 1987) pp. 23–38 and F.W. Bateson, 'The *Scrutiny* Phenomenon' in *Sewanee Review* 85:1, January–March 1977, pp. 144–52. Neither of these is particularly satisfactory, not least because they each assume a 'classless' position against which Leavis can seem petty and resentful.

13. Francis Mulhern (ed.) *Contemporary Marxist Literary Criticism* (London: Longman, 1992) pp. 12–13.

14. The relevant essays here would be 'Contradiction and Overdetermination' and 'On the Materialist Dialectic', both in Louis Althusser, *For Marx*, trans. Ben Brewster (London: New Left Books, 1977) pp. 89–128, 163–218. See also 'A Letter on Art' in Louis Althusser, *Lenin and Philosophy and Other Essays*, trans. Ben Brewster (London: New Left Books, 1977) pp. 221–7.

15. It is perfectly possible to interpret this statement in an altogether different way. Leavis's emphasis on a discriminating minority and his equation of literature with order and hierarchy means that it can function in schools and universities as a way of reproducing and reinforcing the class divisions of capitalist society and hence it cannot so easily be seen as a means of resistance to that society. This claim has been made by John Willinsky who writes that Leavis's work 'could serve as what has been described as the school's legitimating role in the reproduction of social stratification'. John Willinsky, 'Leavis,

Literary Theory and Public Education', *Mosaic* 21: 2–3, 1988, pp. 165–77, 173. On the relationship between education and ideology see Louis Althusser, 'Ideology and Ideological State Apparatuses', in *Lenin and Philosophy and Other Essays*, pp. 127–86. On the use of literature in education see Pierre Macherey and Etienne Balibar, 'On Literature as an Ideological Form', in Mulhern *Contemporary Marxist Literary Criticism*, pp. 34–54.

16. Althusser, 'Ideology and Ideological State Apparatuses', p. 164.
17. See Antony Easthope, *British Post-Structuralism Since 1968* (London: Routledge, 1988) pp. 19, 20.
18. Jean Baudrillard 'The Mirror of Production', in Jean Baudrillard, *Selected Writings*, ed. Mark Poster (Oxford/Cambridge: Polity Press/Basil Blackwell, 1988) pp. 98–118, 102.
19. Ibid., p. 103.
20. For an account of the relationship between literature and scientific management see James F. Knapp, *Literary Modernism and the Transformation of Work* (Evanston: Northwestern University Press, 1988) esp. pp. 1–18.
21. 'The fundamental assumption behind [scientific management] was that all work, whether physical, intellectual, or artistic was amenable to "scientific" re-organization for the purpose of achieving roughly equivalent increases in productivity', ibid., p. 10.
22. Frederick Winslow Taylor, *The Principles of Scientific Management* (London: Harper Row, 1911/1964) p. 74.
23. F.R. Leavis, 'Standards of Criticism', in Leavis, *Valuation in Criticism and Other Essays*, pp. 244–52, 252. Hereafter *SC* with page references given in the text.
24. F.R. Leavis, 'Judgement and Analysis', in *The Living Principle: 'English' as a Discipline of Thought* (London: Chatto & Windus, 1975) pp. 71–154, 108. Hereafter *J & A* with page references given in the text.
25. See Chapter 2, note 112.
26. See Chapter 2, note 206.
27. Taylor, *The Principles of Scientific Management*, p. 59.
28. George Sturt implies this in his comparative valuations of the sawyers and the wheelwrights. See George Sturt, *The Wheelwright's Shop* (Cambridge: Cambridge University Press, 1923/1993) Chapters IV and VII.
29. Taylor, *The Principles of Scientific Management*, p. 38.
30. Ibid.
31. Ibid., p. 96.
32. See ibid., p. 24.
33. Ibid., p. 73.
34. Ibid., p. 70.
35. Sturt's relation with his employees·is far more complex than Leavis indicates. Sturt admits that he 'allowed a gulf to widen between George Cook and myself ... I to the employer's side, he to the disregarded workman's', Sturt, *The Wheelwright's Shop*, p.113. What mattered was the capitalist, not the human relation. Sturt did not attend Cook's funeral.

36. F.R. Leavis, 'Towards Standards of Criticism', p. 221. Hereafter *TSOC* with page references given in the text.

37. Taylor, *The Principles of Scientific Management*, p. 7.

38. Harold Perkin, *The Rise of Professional Society: England Since 1880* (London: Routledge, 1989). Ironically, there was a work science journal called *The Human Factor*, which was published during the late 1920s and early 1930s. See Gary Cross, *Time and Money: The Making of Consumer Culture* (London: Routledge, 1993) p. 97.

39. F.R. Leavis, 'T. S. Eliot and English Literature', in *Valuation in Criticism*, pp. 129–47, 142. Hereafter *TSE & EL* with page references given in the text.

40. T.W. Adorno, *Minima Moralia: Reflections From Damaged Life*, trans. E.F.N. Jephcott (London: Verso, 1978/1993) p. 47.

41. Henri Lefebvre, *Critique of Everyday Life*, trans. John Moore (London: Verso, 1947/1991) p. 61.

42. Ibid., p. 41.

43. Ibid., p. 56.

44. Ibid., p. 57.

45. Ibid., p. 42.

46. Ibid., p. 48.

47. Ibid., p. 49.

48. See, for example, John Fiske, *Understanding Popular Culture* (London: Unwin Hyman, 1989). For a good overview of the field of cultural studies see David Harris, *From Class Struggle to the Politics of Pleasure: The Effects of Gramscianism on Cultural Studies* (London: Routledge, 1992).

49. See Harris, *From Class Struggle to the Politics of Pleasure* and Stephen Regan (ed.) *The Politics of Pleasure: Aesthetics and Cultural Theory* (Buckingham: Open University Press/Anglia Polytechnic University, 1992). For the view that pleasure should be the sole end of criticism see Barbara Kruger, *Remote Control: Power, Cultures and the World of Appearances* (Cambridge, Mass.: MIT Press, 1993). This view should be balanced against the following remark from Adorno:

> Pleasure always means not to think about anything, to forget suffering even when it is shown. Basically it is helplessness. It is flight; not as it is asserted, flight from a wretched reality, but from the last remaining thought of resistance. The liberation which amusement promises is freedom from thought and negation. ('The Culture Industry: Enlightenment As Mass Deception', in Theodor Adorno and Max Horkheimer, *Dialectic of Enlightenment*, trans. John Cumming (London: Verso, 1944/1992) pp. 120–67, 144.)

Baudrillard makes a similar point. See Baudrillard, 'Consumer Society', in Baudrillard, *Selected Writings*, pp. 29–56, 46.

50. Georg Simmel, 'Subjective Culture', in Georg Simmel, *On Individuality and Social Forms*, ed. Donald Levine (Chicago: The University of Chicago Press, 1971) pp. 227–34, 228.

51.	T.W. Adorno, 'Culture and Administration', in T.W. Adorno, *The Culture Industry: Selected Essays on Mass Culture*, ed. J.M. Bernstein (London: Routledge, 1991) pp. 93–113, 98.

52.	Raymond Williams, *Marxism and Literature* (Oxford: Oxford University Press, 1977) p. 121.

53.	Ibid., p. 123.

54.	Ibid., p. 126.

55.	Ibid., p. 122.

56.	Cross, *Time and Money: The Making of Consumer Culture*, p. 57. See also George Lansbury, *My England* (London: Selwyn & Blount, 1934). This forms a useful complement to the works of George Sturt. See also Martin Weiner, *English Culture and the Decline of the Industrial Spirit, 1850–1980*, (Cambridge: Cambridge University Press, 1981) Chapter 4, esp. pp. 118–21; and Alun Hawkins, 'The Discovery of Rural England', in Robert Colls and Philip Dodd (eds) *Englishness: Politics and Culture* (London: Croom Helm, 1986) pp. 63–88.

57.	Catherine Belsey, *Critical Practice* (London: Methuen, 1980) provides a clear overview of this development.

58.	Malcolm Bradbury, 'The Impact of Literary Theory', in Lisa Appignanesi (ed.), *Ideas from France: The Legacy of French Theory* (London: Free Association Books, 1989) pp. 7–15, 12.

59.	See Zygmunt Bauman, *Modernity and the Holocaust* (Ithaca: Cornell University Press, 1989) p. 160.

60.	Criticism is used in its widest sense here, referring not just to literary criticism but to cultural criticism as well. In Leavis, of course, there was a close relation between the two. For an account of how 'uncritical' criticism can be see Christopher Norris, *Uncritical Theory: Postmodernism, Intellectuals and the Gulf War* (London: Lawrence & Wishart, 1992).

61.	See O.L. Zangwill, 'Psychology' in C.B. Cox and A.E. Dyson (eds), *The Twentieth Century Mind: History, Ideas and Literature in Britain 2: 1918–1945* (Oxford: Oxford University Press, 1972) pp. 171–95.

62.	Cunningham, *British Writers of the Thirties*, pp. 161–2.

63.	Arthur Koestler, 'The Initiates', Richard Crossman (ed.) *The God That Failed: Six Studies in Communism* (London: Hamish Hamilton, 1950) pp. 25–32, 30.

64.	C.L. Mowat, *Britain Between the Wars 1918–1939* (London: Methuen, 1955) p. 523.

65.	W.W. Robson, *Modern English Literature* (Oxford: Oxford University Press, 1970) p. 125.

66.	John Stevenson, *British Society 1914–1945* (Harmondsworth: Penguin, 1984/1990) p. 112.

67.	Ibid., p. 113.

68.	Ibid., p. 381. The dance hall was one place where bodies were massed together. Although they represented a kind of freedom, for example, 'greater opportunities for women to go out and enjoy themselves' they also contained the pleasures, energies, 'undisciplined steps' and 'lack of propriety in bodily movements' unleashed by the 'wild sounds of "jazz"'. (Iain Chambers, *Popular Culture: The Metropolitan Experience*

(London: Routledge, 1986) p. 135.) This containment was the work of 'a growing army of dance instructors led by Victor Sylvester, and the increasingly predictable metronome rhythms of the white dance bands' (ibid., pp. 135–6).

69. J.B. Priestly, *English Journey* (London: Heinemann, 1934/1968) p. 314.
70. A.J.P. Taylor, quoted in Norman Page, *The Thirties in Britain* (London: Macmillan, 1990) p. 30. The quotation comes from A.J.P. Taylor, *English History 1914–1945* (Harmondsworth: Penguin 1970) p. 433.
71. Ibid.
72. G.D.H. and M.I. Cole *The Condition of Britain* (London: Gollancz, 1937), mentioned in Stevenson, *British Society 1914–1945*, p. 345.
73. John Hilton, *Rich Man, Poor Man* (New York: Garland 1938/1944), mentioned in Stevenson, *British Society 1914–1945*, p. 345.
74. R.D. Charques, *Contemporary Literature and the Social Revolution* (London: Martin Secker, 1933) pp. 48–9. But see also George Orwell, 'Inside the Whale' in *Inside the Whale and Other Essays* (Harmondsworth: Penguin, 1957/1988) pp. 9–50.
75. 'An Enquiry', *New Verse* 11, 1934, pp. 2–22.
76. Stevenson, *British Society 1914–1945*, p. 166.
77. Edgell Rickword, 'Culture, Progress and English Tradition', in Edgell Rickword, *Literature in Society: Essays and Opinions II*, ed. A. Young (Manchester: Carcanet Press, 1978) pp. 93–104, 93.
78. Cross, *Time and Money: The Making of Consumer Culture*, p. 158.
79. Pasi Falk, *The Consuming Body* (London: Sage, 1994) p. 137.
80. Ibid., p. 139.
81. Cross, *Time and Money: The Making of Consumer Culture*, p. 160.
82. Brian Massumi, 'Everywhere You Want To Be: Introduction to Fear', in Brian Massumi (ed.) *The Politics of Everyday Fear* (Minneapolis: University of Minnesota Press, 1993), pp. 3–38, 7.
83. Adorno and Horkheimer, 'The Culture Industry: Enlightenment As Mass Deception', pp. 120–67, 167.
84. Falk, *The Consuming Body*, p. 136.
85. Georg Simmel, 'The Transcendent Character of Life', in Georg Simmel, *On Individuality and Social Forms*, pp. 353–74, 354.
86. Mark Seltzer, *Bodies and Machines* (London: Routledge, 1992) p. 6.
87. Ibid., p. 14.
88. Taylor, *The Principles of Scientific Management*, p. 44.
89. Humphrey Jennings and Charles Madge (eds), *Mass Observation Day-Survey: May 12 1937* (London: Faber, 1937/1987) p. iv. On Mass Observation see also Angus Calder and Dorothy Sheridan, *Speak for Yourself: A Mass Observation Anthology 1937–1949* (London: Jonathan Cape, 1984).
90. Ibid., p. iii.
91. Ibid., p. iv.
92. Seltzer, *Bodies and Machines*, p. 31.
93. F.R. Leavis, 'Thought, Language and Objectivity' in Leavis, *The Living Principle*, pp. 19–69, 49. Hereafter *TL & O* with page references given in the text.

94. F.R. Leavis, 'Thought, Meaning and Sensibility: The Problem of Value Judgement', in Leavis, *Valuation in Criticism and Other Essays*, pp. 285–97, p. 289. Hereafter *TM & S* with page references given in the text.

95. Seltzer, *Bodies and Machines*, p. 29.

96. F.R. Leavis, 'Valuation in Criticism', in Leavis, *Valuation in Criticism and Other Essays'*, pp. 276–84, 278. Hereafter *VC* with page references given in the text.

97. On one page of one essay the word 'assert' occurs three times, the word 'force' twice and the words 'drive' and 'insist' once. F.R. Leavis, 'English, "Unrest" and Continuity', in F.R. Leavis, *Nor Shall My Sword: Discourses on Pluralism, Compassion and Social Hope* (London: Chatto & Windus, 1972) pp. 103–33, 120. Hereafter referred to as *EU & C*, with page references given in the text. This should give some indication of how central to his criticism is Leavis's vocabulary of force.

98. Willinsky, 'Leavis, Literary Theory and Public Education', p. 172.

99. F.R. Leavis, 'Reading Out Poetry', in Leavis, *Valuation in Criticism and Other Essays'*, pp. 253–75, 268. Hereafter *ROP*, with page references given in the text.

100. For an overview of the role of the body in social theory see Bryan S. Turner, 'Recent Developments in the Theory of the Body', in Mike Featherstone, Mike Hepworth and Bryan S. Turner, (eds). *The Body: Social Processes and Cultural Theory* (London: Sage, 1991/1992) pp. 1–35.

101. F.R. Leavis, 'Johnson As Poet', in F.R. Leavis, *The Common Pursuit* (Harmondsworth: Penguin/Chatto & Windus, 1962/1993) pp. 116–20, 118. Hereafter *JAP* with page references given in the text.

102. F.R. Leavis, 'Literary Criticism and Philosophy', in ibid., pp. 211–22, 213. Hereafter *C & P*, with page references given in the text.

103. F.R. Leavis, 'Johnson and Augustanism', in ibid., pp. 97–115, 110. Hereafter *JA*, with page references given in the text.

104. F.R. Leavis, 'Sociology and Literature', in ibid., pp. 195–203, 200. Hereafter *S & L*, with page references given in the text.

105. F.R. Leavis, 'The Responsible Critic: Or the Function of Criticism at Any Time', in Leavis, *Valuation in Criticism and Other Essays*, pp. 194–206, 195. Hereafter *RC*, with page references given in the text.

106. Falk, *The Consuming Body*, p. 154.

107. Roy Johnson, quoted in ibid., p. 154. Falk gives the source as *Printers Ink* 75, 25 May 1911, pp. 10–11.

108. Jacques Lacan, *The Seminars of Jacques Lacan Book I: Freud's Papers on Technique 1953–1954*, trans. John Forrester, ed. Jacques Alain Miller (Cambridge: Cambridge University Press, 1988) p. 183.

109. Ibid.

110. Jacques Lacan, *Écrits: A Selection*, trans. Alan Sheridan (London: Tavistock Publications, 1977) p. 68.

111. Ibid., p. 85.

112. Ibid., p. 86.

113. Jacques Lacan, *Speech and Language in Psychoanalysis*, trans. Anthony Wilden (Baltimore: Johns Hopkins University Press, 1968/1994) p. 30.

114. 'The function of language is not to inform but to evoke', Lacan, *Écrits: A Selection*, p. 86. This description of language in not far removed from Leavis's description of literary language which should not be 'statement, exposition and reflection' but should instead capture in words and 'present[] ... to speak for themselves, significant particularities of sensation, perception and feeling, the significance coming out in complex total effects which are also left to speak for themselves', Leavis, *JAP*, p. 118.

115. Lacan, *Speech and Language in Psychoanalysis*, p. 25.

116. F.R. Leavis, *Two Cultures? The Significance of Lord Snow*, in Leavis, *Nor Shall My Sword: Discourses on Pluralism, Compassion and Social Hope*, pp. 41–74, 62. Hereafter *TC*, with page references given in the text.

117. Lacan, *Speech and Language in Psychoanalysis*, pp. 19–20.

118. Lacan, *The Seminars of Jacques Lacan Book 1: Freud's Papers on Technique 1953–1954*, p. 198.

119. Thomas Haskell, quoted in Seltzer, *Bodies and Machines*, p. 73. The quotation comes from Thomas Haskell, 'Capitalism and the Origins of Humanitarian Sensibility, Part Two', in *The American Historical Review* 90: 2, June 1985, pp. 534–63, 553. Compare Lacan, 'The human action ... is originally founded on the existence of the world of the symbol, namely on laws and contracts', Lacan, *The Seminars of Jacques Lacan Book 1: Freud's Papers on Technique 1953–1954*, p. 230.

120. Lacan, *Speech and Language in Psychoanalysis*, p. 30.

121. Seltzer, *Bodies and Machines*, p. 73.

122. Lacan, *The Seminars of Jacques Lacan Book 1: Freud's Papers on Technique 1953–1954*, p. 85.

123. F.R. Leavis, 'Literature and Society', in Leavis, *The Common Pursuit*, pp. 182–94, 192. Hereafter *L & S* with page references given in the text.

124. F.R. Leavis, 'Bunyan Through Modern Eyes', in Leavis, *The Common Pursuit*, pp. 204–10. Hereafter *BTME* with page references given in the text.

125. Jack Lindsay, *John Bunyan: Maker of Myths* (London: Methuen, 1937). Leavis also takes issue, in this essay, with William Tindall's *John Bunyan: Mechanick Preacher* (Columbia: Columbia University Press, 1934).

126. F.R. Leavis, 'The Pilgrim's Progress', in F.R. Leavis, *Anna Karenina and Other Essays* (London: Chatto & Windus, 1967/1973) pp. 33–48, 1. Hereafter *PP* with page references given in the text.

127. Notes 127–35 give quotations only from Lukács as there are numerous examples of the same features of Leavis's work throughout my argument. The 'self-contained immediacy [of] the work of art', Georg Lukács 'Art and Objective Truth' quoted in Raman Selden (ed.) *The Theory of Criticism: From Plato to the Present* (London: Longman, 1988) pp. 59–66, 60. The quotation comes from Georg Lukács, 'Art and Objective Truth', Georg Lukács, *Writer and Critic and Other Essays*, ed. and trans. Arthur Kahn (London: Merlin Press, 1970) pp. 34–43, 37.

128. 'The tremendous social power of literature consists in the fact that it depicts the human being ... in a concrete fashion not equalled by any other field of reflection of objective reality', Georg Lukács, 'Marx and

the Problem of Ideological Decay', in Georg Lukács, *Essays on Realism*, trans. David Fernbach, ed. Rodney Livingstone (London: Lawrence & Wishart, 1980) pp. 114–66, 143.

129. The novel should aim at 'sensuous representation', Georg Lukács, *The Theory of the Novel*, trans. Anna Bostock (London: Merlin Press, 1971) p. 79.
130. '[T]hat organic quality which is the aim of [the novel]', ibid., p. 77.
131. 'The novel is the art form of virile maturity', ibid., p. 71. '[T]he objectivity of the novel is the mature [person's] knowledge that meaning can never quite penetrate reality, but that, without meaning, reality would disintegrate into the nothingness of inessentiality', ibid., p. 88.
132. 'Only in the novel [can we find] the affirmative experience of the life process', ibid., p. 127.
133. Ibid., pp. 124–5, 127, 144–53.
134. 'In the novel ... the ethical intention is visible in the creation of every detail and hence is, in its most concrete content, an effective structural element of the work itself', ibid., p. 72.
135. 'Wherever the cultural heritage has a living relationship to the real life of the people it is characterized by a dynamic, progressive movement in which the active creative forces of popular tradition ... are buoyed up, preserved, transcended and further developed', Georg Lukács, 'Realism in the Balance', trans. R. Livingstone, in Theodor Adorno, Walter Benjamin, Ernest Bloch, Bertolt Brecht, Georg Lukács, *Aesthetics and Politics*, ed. Ronald Taylor (London: Verso, 1977/1990) pp. 28–59, 53–4.
136. Lukács, 'Art and Objective Truth', p. 63.
137. Georg Lukács, 'The Novels of Willi Bredel', in Lukács, *Essays on Realism*, pp. 23–32, 29.
138. F.R. Leavis, 'Introductory', in Leavis, *Nor Shall My Sword: Discourses on Pluralism, Compassion and Social Hope*, . pp. 11–37, 20.
139. Terence Hawkes, *Meaning By Shakespeare* (London: Routledge, 1992) p. 71.
140. F.R. Leavis, 'Tragedy and the Medium', in Leavis, *The Common Pursuit*, pp. 121–35, 130. Hereafter *T & M*, with page references given in the text.
141. Terry Eagleton, *Ideology: An Introduction* (London: Verso, 1991) p. 18.
142. Ibid., p. 200.
143. F.R. Leavis, 'Anna Karenina: Thought and Significance in a Great Creative Work', in *Anna Karenina and Other Essays*, pp. 9–32, 14.
144. Antony Easthope, *Literary Into Cultural Studies* (London: Routledge, 1991) p. 66.
145. F.R. Leavis, *Thought, Words and Creativity: Art and Thought in Lawrence* (London: Chatto & Windus, 1976) p. 34. Hereafter *TW & C*, with page references given in the text.
146. F.R. Leavis, 'Henry James and the Function of Criticism', in Leavis, *The Common Pursuit*, pp. 223–32, 225. Hereafter *HJ & TFOC*, with page references given in the text.

147. See F.R. Leavis, 'Pluralism, Compasion and Social Hope', in Leavis, *Nor Shall My Sword: Discourses on Pluralism, Compassion and Social Hope*, pp. 163–98, 163.

148. See, for example, *The Critical Review* 33, November 1933, which was given over to this topic.

149. T.W. Adorno, 'The Schema of Mass Culture', in Adorno, *The Culture Industry: Selected Essays on Mass Culture*, pp. 53–84, 79.

150. See, for example, Christopher Norris, *Truth and the Ethics of Criticism*, (Manchester: Manchester University Press, 1994).

151. F.W. Bateson, 'The Function of Criticism at the Present Time', *Essays in Criticism* 3:1, 1953, pp. 1–27, 8, quoted by Leavis, *RC*, p. 199.

152. F.R. Leavis, 'In Defence of Milton', in Leavis, *The Common Pursuit*, pp. 33–43, 35.

153. F.R. Leavis, 'Eliot's "Axe To Grind" and the Nature of Criticism', in F.R. Leavis, *English Literature in Our Time and the University* (Cambridge: Cambridge University Press, 1969) pp. 85–108, 95–6.

154. Jacques Derrida, 'Semiology and Grammatology: Interview with Julia Kristeva', in *Positions*, trans. Alan Bass (London: Athlone Press/University of Chicago Press, 1987) pp. 17–36, 33.

155. Jacques Derrida, 'Positions: Interview with Jean-Louis Houdebine and Guy Scarpetta', in ibid., 39–96, pp. 41–2.

156. Jacques Derrida, 'Implications: Interview with Henri Ronse', in ibid., pp. 3–14, 5.

157. Jacques Derrida, 'Positions: Interview with Jean-Louis Houdebine', in ibid., p. 42.

158. Christopher Norris, 'Derrida and Kant', in Christopher Norris, *What's Wrong with Postmodernism: Critical Theory and the Ends of Philosophy* (New York: Harvester Wheatsheaf, 1990) pp. 194–207, 195.

159. Nicholas Tredell claims that Leavis and Derrida have much in common because they are 'anti-philosophers' and, in doing so, he tends to collapse the differences between them. See Nicholas Tredell, *The Critical Decade: Culture in Crisis* (Manchester: Carcanet, 1993) pp. 1–8.

160. F.R. Leavis, 'Mr. Eliot, Mr. Wyndham Lewis and Lawrence', in Leavis, *The Common Pursuit*, pp. 240–47, 246. Hereafter *EWL & L* with page references given in the text.

161. F.R. Leavis, 'Keynes, Spender and Currency Values', in F.R. Leavis, *A Selection from Scrutiny: Volume I* (Cambridge: Cambridge University Press, 1968) pp. 185–96, 195. Hereafter *KS & CV* with page references given in the text.

162. Sigmund Freud, 'On Negation', in Sigmund Freud, *On Metapsychology: The Theory of Psychoanalysis*, trans. James Strachey, ed. Angela Richards (Harmondsworth: Penguin, 1984/1991) pp. 437–43, 438.

163. Lacan, *Écrits: A Selection*, p. 286.

164. Jean-François Lyotard, 'The Dream Work Does Not Think', in *The Lyotard Reader*, ed. Andrew Benjamin (Oxford/Cambridge MA: Basil Blackwell, 1989) pp. 19–55, 19.

165. John Bunyan, *The Pilgrim's Progress* (Belfast: Ambassador Productions, 1992) p. 50.

166. Ibid., p. 51.

167. Freud, 'On Negation', p. 438.
168. F.R. Leavis, 'What's Wrong with Criticism', in F.R. Leavis, *For Continuity* (Cambridge: Minority Press, 1933) pp. 68–90, 75.
169. Lacan, *Écrits: A Selection*, p. 125.
170. F.R. Leavis, 'Mutually Necessary' in F.R. Leavis, *The Critic As Anti-Philosopher*, ed. G. Singh (London: Chatto & Windus, 1982) pp. 186–208, 190. Hereafter *MN* with page references given in the text. It will be noted that this introduces a tactile element into the apprehension of a work which, since it is not related either to 'seeing' or 'hearing', further underlines the point about dissociation. This tactile element of reading is discussed in the next section.
171. Lacan, *Écrits: A Selection*, p. 166.
172. See Freud, 'On Negation', p. 438.
173. See Graham Murdock, 'Dilemmas of Radical Culture: Forms of Expression and Relations of Production', in Francis Barker et al., *1936: The Sociology of Literature Volume 2, Practices of Literature and Politics* (Colchester: University of Essex, 1979) pp. 21–45, 33–7.
174. Christopher Isherwood, *Goodbye to Berlin* (London: Hogarth, 1939) p. 1.
175. 'Ordinary still photography' was used for the first motion studies, then 'stereoscopic photography' then 'cine camera'. See Harold Pollard, *Development in Management Thought* (London: Heinemann, 1974) pp. 23–4.
176. See Stevenson, *British Society 1914–1945*, p. 321.
177. A Foucauldian approach to some of the phenomena I have listed here would strengthen the argument. The relevant book would be Michel Foucault, *Discipline and Punish: The Birth of the Prison*, trans. Alan Sheridan (Harmondsworth: Penguin, 1977/1991) esp. the section entitled 'Panopticism', pp. 195–228.
178. Robert Bocock, *Consumption* (London: Routledge, 1993) p. 89.
179. See Falk, *The Consuming Body*, pp.119–22.
180. See ibid., pp. 106–18.
181. Derrida's analysis of the supplement may have some bearing here. See Jacques Derrida, *Of Grammatology*, trans. Gayatri Chakravorty Spivak (Baltimore: Johns Hopkins University Press, 1976) pp. 141–64, esp. 145.
182. Falk, *The Consuming Body*, p. 108.
183. Adorno, 'The Schema of Mass Culture', p. 72.
184. See, for example, Sigmund Freud, 'Fragment of an Analysis of a Case of Hysteria (Dora)', in Sigmund Freud, *Case Histories I: 'Dora' and 'Little Hans'*, trans. Alix and James Strachey, ed. Angela Richards, (Harmondsworth: Penguin, 1977) esp. pp. 45–8.
185. John Thompson, 'Social Theory, Mass Communication and Public Life' in Antony Giddens et al., *The Polity Reader in Cultural Theory* (Cambridge/Oxford: Polity Press/Basil Blackwell, 1994) pp. 24–37, 29.
186. Ibid., p. 30.
187. Ibid.
188. For a brief account of state intervention see Stevenson, *British Society 1914–1945*, pp. 306–12.
189. See Cross, *Time and Motion: The Making of Consumer Culture*, pp. 140–1.

190. Jacques Derrida, 'The First Session', in Jacques Derrida, *Acts of Literature*, ed. Derek Attridge (London: Routledge, 1992) pp. 127–80, 133.

191. Ibid., p. 132.

192. Freud, 'On Negation', p. 441.

193. Ibid., p. 439.

194. Ibid.

195. Ibid., p. 440.

196. Ibid., p. 441.

197. Sigmund Freud, 'Beyond the Pleasure Principle', in Freud, *On Metapsychology*, pp. 275–338, 307, 311.

198. F.R. Leavis, 'Literary Studies: A Reply', in Leavis, *Valuation in Criticism and Other Essays*, pp. 207–17, 217.

199. F.R. Leavis, 'The Wild, Untutored Phoenix', in Leavis, *The Common Pursuit*, pp. 231–9, 237.

200. Theodor Adorno and Max Horkheimer, 'The Concept of Enlightenment' in Adorno and Horkheimer, *Dialectic of Enlightenment*, pp. 3–42, 36.

201. Ibid., p. 22.

202. Ibid., p. 27.

203. Ibid., p. 35.

204. Ibid., p. 25.

205. Ibid., p. 26.

206. Jacques Derrida, 'Structure, Sign and Play in the Discourse of the Human Sciences', in Jacques Derrida, *Writing and Difference*, trans. Alan Bass (London: Routledge & Kegan Paul, 1978/1990) pp. 278–93, 280–1.

207. Michael Bell, *F.R. Leavis*, (London: Routledge, 1988) p. 49.

208. F.R. Leavis, 'Justifying One's Valuation of Blake', in Leavis, *The Critic As Anti-Philosopher*, pp. 1–23. Hereafter *JOVB* with page references given in the text.

209. F.R. Leavis, 'Luddites? Or There Is Only One Culture', in Leavis, *Nor Shall My Sword: Discourses on Pluralism, Compassion and Social Hope*, pp. 77–99, 92.

210. Antony Easthope, *Literary into Cultural Studies*, p. 10.

211. It is worth noting that the generalised mediation of literature may also have something to do with the residual Oedipal structure of Leavisian criticism. As Lacan notes, the Oedipus complex is one of those moments that 'decisively tips the whole of human knowledge into mediatization', Lacan, *Écrits: A Selection*, p. 5. The whole issue of 'enactment' in Leavis needs to be looked at from the point of view of phenomenology and critiques of phenomenology.

212. Catherine Belsey would be a good example here. She sees Leavis as an 'expressive realist', Belsey, *Critical Practice*, pp. 11–14.

## CHAPTER 4: THE 'THIRD REALM'

1. F.R. Leavis, 'Thought, Language and Objectivity', in F.R. Leavis, *The Living Principle: English As a Discipline of Thought* (London: Chatto & Windus, 1975) pp. 19–69, 36. Hereafter *TL & O* with page references

given in the text. Leavis claims, though without explaining why, he 'threw out years ago' the 'formulation' of the 'third realm', nor does he explain why he feels the need to restore it here. In any case, the phrase can be found *passim* throughout his work.

2.   F.R. Leavis, 'Thought, Meaning and Sensibility: The Problem of Value Judgement', in F.R. Leavis, *Valuation in Criticism and Other Essays*, ed. G. Singh (Cambridge: Cambridge University Press, 1986) pp. 285–97, 287. Hereafter *TM & S* with page references given in the text.

3.   F.R. Leavis, 'Luddites? Or There Is Only One Culture', in F.R. Leavis, *Nor Shall My Sword: Discourses on Pluralism, Compassion and Social Hope* (London: Chatto & Windus, 1972) pp. 77–99, 98. Hereafter *TIOC* with page references given in the text. For what Leavis means by 'human' see ibid., p. 94.

4.   F.R. Leavis, 'Literature and Society' in F.R. Leavis, *The Common Pursuit* (Harmondsworth: Penguin/Chatto & Windus, 1962/1993) pp. 182–94, 187. Hereafter *L & S* with page references given in the text.

5.   F.R. Leavis, 'Judgement and Analysis', in Leavis, *The Living Principle: English As a Discipline of Thoughts*, pp. 71–154, 90. Hereafter *J & A* with page references given in the text.

6.   F.R. Leavis, 'Standards of Criticism', in Leavis, *Valuation in Criticism and Other Essays*, pp. 244–52, 244, Hereafter *SC* with page references given in the text.

7.   F.R. Leavis, 'Mutually Necessary', in F.R. Leavis, *The Critic As Anti-Philosopher*, ed. G. Singh (London: Chatto & Windus, 1982) pp. 186–208, 190. Hereafter *MN* with page references given in the text.

8.   Jacques Derrida, *'Différance'*, in Jacques Derrida, *Margins of Philosophy*, trans. Alan Bass (New York: Harvester Wheatsheaf, 1982) pp. 3, 27, 9.

9.   Ibid., p. 18.

10.  Ibid., p. 9. See also p. 13: 'An interval must separate the present from what it is not in order for the present to be itself, but this interval that constitutes it as present must, by the same token, divide the present in and of itself, thereby also dividing, along with the present, everything that is thought on the basis of the present ... every being and ... substance or the subject.'

11.  Ibid., p. 26.

12.  Ibid., p. 11.

13.  Ibid., p. 13.

14.  Ibid., p. 12.

15.  I am thinking of criticism as a 'system' in so far as it has a certain methodology. This is a clumsy term to use in respect of Leavis but it is partly justified by his demand that criticism should be disciplined, relevant and precise in order to realise what is there in the text.

16.  Jacques Lacan, *Écrits: A Selection*, trans. Alan Sheridan (London: Tavistock Publications, 1977) p. 147.

17.  Derrida, *'Différance'*, p. 10.

18.  Lacan, *Écrits: A Selection*, p. 149.

19.  Ibid., p. 166.

20.  Derrida, *'Différance'*, p. 20.

21. Ibid., p. 6.
22. Ibid., p. 20.
23. This is an important term in Lacanian psychoanalysis, where it refers to the subject's identification with an image. This image confers an imaginary unity on the subject who is, in reality, broken and split. What Lacan says about the subject may have some bearing on the Leavisian critic who hovers between a recognition of the text as a unity and as fragmented 'black marks on a page'. Leavisian criticism, in short, offers the potential to perceive the text in either an imaginary or a symbolic way. See Lacan, *Écrits: A Selection*, pp. 1–7, 34–113.
24. Derrida, *'Différance'*, p. 20.
25. See ibid., p. 16.
26. F.R. Leavis, 'Literary Studies: A Reply', in Leavis, *Valuation in Criticism and Other Essays*, pp. 207–17, 216. Hereafter *LS* with page references given in the text.
27. Derrida's comments on 'the trace' seem relevant here. See Derrida, 'Différance', p. 24.
28. Ibid., p. 3.
29. The idea of language as a system or a structure seems to be a good instance of Adorno's remark that 'the bureaucratic way of thinking has become the secret model for a thought allegedly still free', T.W. Adorno, *Negative Dialectics*, trans. E.B. Ashton (London: Routledge, 1973/1990) p. 32.
30. The notion of 'the human' seem to be making a return. See Tvetan Todorov, *On Human Diversity: Nationalism, Racism and Exoticism in French Thought* (Cambridge, Mass.: Harvard University Press, 1993).
31. Adorno, *Negative Dialectics*, p. 149.
32. Ibid.
33. Ibid., p. 148.
34. Theodor Adorno and Max Horkheimer, 'The Culture Industry or Enlightenment as Mass Deception', in Theodor Adorno and Max Horkheimer, *Dialectic of Enlightenment*, trans. John Cumming (London: Verso, 1979/1992) pp. 120–67, 120.
35. Ibid., p. 154.
36. See Adorno, *Negative Dialectics*, p. 148.
37. Ibid., p. 5.
38. Ibid., p. 161.
39. Ibid.
40. Ibid., p. 178.
41. Ibid., p. 149.
42. Ibid., p. 162.
43. Ibid., p. 167.
44. Ibid., p. 193.
45. 'Definitions are not the be all and end all of cognition', ibid., p. 165. Compare to Leavis, 'The most important words are more than ambiguous in a way that defies dictionary definition', F.R. Leavis, *Thoughts, Words and Creativity: Art and Thought in Lawrence* (London: Chatto & Windus, 1976) p. 93.
46. Adorno, *Negative Dialectics*, p. 141.

47. Ibid., p. 176.
48. F.R. Leavis, 'Pluralism, Compassion and Social Hope' in Leavis, *Nor Shall My Sword: Discourses on Pluralism, Compassion and Social Hope*, pp. 163–98, 163. Hereafter *PC & SH* with page references given in the text.
49. F.R. Leavis, 'Literary Criticism and Philosophy' in Leavis, *The Common Pursuit*, pp. 211–22, 213. Hereafter *C & P*. with page references given in the text.
50. See note 41.
51. F.R. Leavis, 'Reading Out Poetry' in Leavis, *Valuation in Criticism and Other Essays*, pp. 253–75, 260. Hereafter *ROP* with page references given in the text.
52. Adorno, *Negative Dialectics*, p. 138. But see also pp. 173–4.
53. Ibid., p. 161.
54. Ibid.
55. Ibid., p. 179. See also pp. 175, 183.
56. Ibid., p. 161.
57. See also Theodor Adorno and Max Horkheimer, 'The Importance of the Body', in Adorno and Horkheimer, *Dialectic of Enlightenment*, pp. 231–6.
58. Theodor Adorno, *Minima Moralia: Reflections from Damaged Life*, trans. E.F.N. Jephcott, (London: Verso, 1974/1993) p. 197.
59. See Adorno, 'The Culture Industry: Enlightenment As Mass Deception', pp. 121–31.
60. Ibid., p. 128.
61. Ibid., p. 126.
62. Ibid., p. 130.
63. Ibid.
64. Ibid.
65. The history of philosophy 'shows amazingly few indications of the sufferings of human kind', Adorno, *Negative Dialectics*, p. 153; and, 'it is now virtually in art alone that suffering can still find its own voice, consolation, without immediately being betrayed by it'. Theodor Adorno, 'Commitment' in Theodor Adorno, Walter Benjamin, Ernst Bloch, Bertolt Brecht and Georg Lukács, *Aesthetics and Politics*, (London: Verso, 1977/1990) pp. 177–95, 188.
66. T.W. Adorno, 'Culture and Administration', in *The Culture Industry: Selected Essays on Mass Culture*, ed. J.M. Bernstein (London: Routledge, 1991) pp. 93–113, 104.
67. T.W. Adorno, 'The Schema of Mass Culture', in Adorno, *The Culture Industry: Selected Essays on Mass Culture'*, pp. 53–84, 60.
68. Ibid., p. 72.
69. Mark Seltzer, *Bodies and Machines* (New York & London: Routledge, 1992), p. 96.
70. Adorno, 'Commitment', p. 179.
71. John Carey, 'Yours Cantankerously', *Observer*, 2 June 1974, p. 32. See Garry Watson's comments on Carey's remark in Garry Watson, *The Leavises, the Social and the Left* (Swansea: Brynmill, 1977) pp. 28–30.

72. Respectively, Stephen Spender in *Criterion*, 16 January 1937, pp. 350–3; Richard Church in *Christian Science Monitor*, 27 January 1937, p. 10; Geoffrey Tillotson in *English* 5, Spring 1944, pp. 23–4; an anonymous review in *The Listener*, 31 January 1952, p. 191. All quoted by M.B. Kinch, '"Saying Everything At Once?" The Prose Style of F.R. Leavis', in *English Studies* 73:6, 1992, pp. 517–22.

73. A. Alvarez quoted by Ian MacKillop, *F.R. Leavis: A Life in Criticism* (Harmondsworth: Allen Lane/Penguin, 1995) p. 284. MacKillop does not give the source of the quotation.

74. 'Leavis's work can ... be seen as one more example of that will to mystify the politics of criticism by fixing its sights on a long-lost age of "organic" cultural values'. Christopher Norris, 'Editor's Foreword', to Michael Bell, *F.R. Leavis* (London: Routledge, 1988) p. ix.

75. The dominance of the optical metaphor in Leavis's criticism may be accounted for by his empiricism. Traditionally,

> 'empiricist inquiry is limited by its schematic reliance on *optical* models of cognition and judgement, a reliance that leads to highly problematic analogies between language and visual perception and to the mistaken belief that interpreting a text is like 'seeing' an object. (Jules David Law, *The Rhetoric of Empiricism: Language and Perception from Locke to I.A. Richards* (Ithaca: Cornell University Press, 1993) p. 2.)

76. M.B. Kinch '"Saying Everything At Once?" The Prose Style of F.R. Leavis', p. 517.

77. John Harwood, *Eliot to Derrida: The Poverty of Interpretation*, (London: Macmillan, 1995) p. 165.

78. Christopher Norris, *Derrida* (London: Fontana, 1987) p. 15.

79. Ludwig Wittgenstein, *Philosophical Investigations*, trans. G.E.M. Anscombe (Oxford: Basil Blackwell, 1953/1991), p. 32.

80. Ibid., p. 54. Wittgenstein summarises his point in the form of a question. 'The question "What is a word really?" is analogous to "What is a piece in chess?"', ibid., p. 47.

81. Ibid., p. 11.

82. Ibid.

83. F.R. Leavis, *New Bearings in English Poetry* (London: Chatto & Windus, 1932/1976) pp. 45, 42, 36. Hereafter *NB* with page references given in the text.

84. John Casey, *The Language of Criticism* (London: Methuen, 1966) p. 177. Also useful in this context may be Cyril Barrett, 'Wittgenstein, Leavis and Literature', *New Literary History* 19:2, Winter 1988, pp. 385–401.

85. A.C. Grayling, *Wittgenstein* (Oxford: Oxford University Press, 1988) p. 77.

86. F.R. Leavis, 'Memories of Wittgenstein', in Leavis, *The Critic As Anti-Philosopher*, pp. 129–45. Hereafter *MOW* with page references given in the text. For another view of Leavis's relationship with Wittgenstein

see Terence Hawkes, *Meaning By Shakespeare* (London: Routledge, 1993) pp. 67–78.

87. Wittgenstein, quoted by Leavis in 'Mutually Necessary', p. 208. The quotation comes from Norman Malcolm's *Memoir of Wittgenstein* (Oxford: Oxford University Press, 1958) p. 39.

88. Ibid.

89. Barry Cullen, '"I thought I had provided something better" – F.R. Leavis, Literary Criticism and Anti-Philosophy', in Gary Day, *The British Critical Tradition* (London: Macmillan, 1993) pp. 188–212, 197.

90. 'What parades as progress in the culture industry, as the incessantly new which it offers up, remains the disguise for an eternal sameness'. T.W. Adorno, 'Culture Industry Reconsidered' in Adorno, *The Culture Industry: Selected Essays on Mass Culture*, pp. 85–92, 87.

91. F.R. Leavis, 'Anna Karenina: Thought and Significance in a Great Creative Work', in F.R. Leavis, *Anna Karenina and Other Essays* (London: Chatto & Windus, 1973) pp. 1–32, 18, 32. Hereafter *AK* with page references given in the text.

92. Adorno, 'The Schema of Mass Culture', p. 53.

93. Frederic Jameson, 'Postmodernism, or the Cultural Logic of Late Capitalism', *New Left Review* 146, 1984, pp. 53–92, 60.

94. Hans Berten, *The Idea of the Postmodern: A History* (London: Routledge, 1995) p. 245. See also Antony Giddens, *The Consequence of Modernity* (Cambridge: Polity Press, 1990).

95. F.R. Leavis, 'Valuation in Criticism', in Leavis, *Valuation in Criticism and Other Essays*, pp. 276–84, 281. Hereafter *VC* with page references given in the text.

96. F.R. Leavis, 'Adam Bede', in Leavis, *Anna Karenina and Other Essays*, pp. 49–58, 49. Hereafter *AB* with page references given in the text.

97. F.R. Leavis, 'Gerard Manley Hopkins' in Leavis, *The Common Pursuit*, pp. 44–58, 48.

98. Jules David Law, *The Rhetoric of Empiricism: Language and Perception from Locke to I.A. Richards*, p. 237.

99. Ibid.

100. Ibid.

101. Seltzer, *Bodies and Machines*, p. 123.

102. Ibid., p. 95.

103. Ibid., p. 124.

104. For a good summary of this process see James F. Knapp, *Literary Modernism and the Transformation of Work* (Evanston: Northwestern University Press, 1988) pp. 1–18,

105. See Seltzer, *Bodies and Machines*, pp. 82, 105, 124.

106. Ibid., p. 95.

107. F.R. Leavis, *Revaluation: Tradition and Development in English Poetry* (Harmondsworth: Penguin/Chatto & Windus, 1936/1967) p. 17.

108. Knapp, *Literary Modernism and the Transformation of Work*, p. 7.

109. See note 68.

110. In bureaucratic control, class differences are absorbed into the corporate 'family' so that 'workers owe not only a hard day's work to the corporation but also their demeanour and affections', Richard

Edwards, *Contested Terrain: The Transformation of the Work Place in the Twentieth Century* (New York: Basic Books, 1979) p. 148.

111. Seltzer, *Bodies and Machines*, p. 82.
112. Ibid., pp. 82–3.
113. Ibid., pp. 57 & 59.
114. Ibid., p. 94. See also Michel Foucault, *Discipline and Punish: The Birth of the Prison*, trans. Alan Sheridan (Harmondsworth: Penguin, 1977/1991), p. 194.
115. Seltzer, *Bodies and Machines*, p. 94.
116. Ibid., p. 86.
117. F.R. Leavis, 'Two Cultures? The Significance of Lord Snow', in Leavis, *Nor Shall My Sword: Discourses on Pluralism, Compassion and Social Hope*, pp. 41–74, 59. Hereafter *TC* with page references given in the text.
118. F.R. Leavis, '"English", Unrest and Continuity', in ibid., pp. 103–33, 123. Hereafter *EU & C* with page references given in the text.
119. F.R. Leavis, 'Towards Standards of Criticism', in Leavis, *Anna Karenina and Other Essays*, pp. 219–34, 221. Hereafter *TSOC* with page references given in the text.
120. Knapp, *Literary Modernism and the Transformation of Work*, p. 11.
121. See, for example, F.R. Leavis, *The Great Tradition* (Harmondsworth: Penguin/Chatto & Windus, 1948 & 1967) p. 67.
122. See Francis Mulhern, *The Moment of 'Scrutiny'* (London: Verso, 1979/1981), pp. 76–7 and, more generally, Pierre Macherey and Etienne Balibar 'On Literature As an Ideological Form', trans. Ian McLeod, John Whitehead and Anne Wordsworth, *Oxford Literary Review* 3, 1978, pp. 4–12.
123. Seltzer, *Bodies and Machines*, p. 121.
124. Susan Sontag, *Illness as Metaphor* (Harmondsworth: Penguin, 1977/1987) p. 15.
125. Greta Jones, *Social Hygiene in Twentieth Century Britain* (London: Croom Helm, 1986) p. 17.
126. See F. Honigsbaum, 'The Struggle for the Ministry of Health 1914–1919'. *Occasional Papers on Social Administration No. 37* (London: G. Bell & Sons, 1970) pp. 39–56.
127. See Jones, *Social Hygiene in Twentieth Century Britain*, p. 10.
128. Seltzer, *Bodies and Machines*, p. 60.
129. Mike Featherstone, 'The Body in Consumer Culture' in Mike Featherstone, Mike Hepworth and Bryan D. Turner (eds) *The Body: Social Process and Cultural Theory* (London: Sage, 1991), pp. 170–96, 175.
130. Robert Bocock, *Consumption* (London: Routledge, 1993) p. 67. See also A. Tomlinson, *Consumption Identity and Style: Marketing Meanings and the Packaging of Pleasure* (London: Routledge, 1990).
131. Seltzer, *Bodies and Machines*, p. 88.
132. Ibid., p. 60.
133. Ibid., pp. 64, 125.
134. Ibid., p. 60.

135. Jean Baudrillard, 'The System of Objects', in Jean Baudrillard, *Selected Writings*, ed. Mark Poster, (Cambridge/Oxford: Polity Press/Basil Blackwell, 1988/1990) pp. 10–28, 25.
136. Ibid.
137. See Jean Baudrillard, 'Consumer Society', in Baudrillard, *Selected Writings*, pp. 29–56, pp. 36–7.
138. Ibid., p. 49.
139. Baudrillard, 'The System of Objects', p. 19.
140. Ibid.
141. Ibid.
142. Ibid.
143. Ibid.
144. F.R. Leavis, 'What's Wrong with Criticism?' in F.R. Leavis, *For Continuity* (Cambridge: Minority Press, 1933) pp. 69–90, 88.
145. Baudrillard, 'The System of Objects', p. 17.
146. Ibid.
147. For a good overview of this see Stuart Hall and Bill Schwarz, 'State and Society 1880–1930', in Mary Langan and Bill Schwarz (eds) *Crises in the British State* (London: Hutchinson/Centre for Contemporary Critical Studies, University of Birmingham, 1985) pp. 7–33.
148. F.R. Leavis, 'The Pilgrim's Progress', in Leavis, *Anna Karenina and Other Essays*, op. cit. pp. 33–48, 35. Hereafter *PP* with page references given in the text.
149. Seltzer, *Bodies and Machines*, p. 58.
150. Georg Simmel, *The Sociology of Georg Simmel* (New York: The Free Press, 1950) pp. 328–34, 340.
151. Warren Susman, 'Personality and the Making of Twentieth Century Culture', J. Higham and P.K. Conkin (eds) *New Directions in American Intellectual History* (Baltimore: Johns Hopkins University Press, 1979) pp. 212–26.
152. Featherstone, 'The Body in Consumer Culture', p. 188.
153. See Baudrillard, 'Consumer Society', p. 53.
154. Featherstone, 'The Body in Consumer Culture', p. 173.
155. Ibid., p. 176.
156. Ibid., p. 177.
157. Seltzer, *Bodies and Machines*, p. 97.
158. Jean Baudrillard, 'The Masses', in Baudrillard, *Selected Writings*, pp. 207–19, 210.
159. Seltzer, *Bodies and Machines*, p. 97. See also Adorno, *Negative Dialectics*, pp. 31–3.
160. Roland Barthes, *The Pleasure of the Text*, trans. Richard Millar (Oxford: Basil Blackwell, 1976/1994) p. 17.
161. Ibid., p. 19.
162. Ibid., p. 56.
163. Ibid., p. 52.
164. Ibid., pp. 4, 21.
165. F.R. Leavis, *Thought Words and Creativity: Art and Thought in Lawrence* (London: Chatto & Windus, 1976) p. 28. Hereafter *TW & C* with page references given in the text.

166. Jacques Derrida, 'Force and Signification' in Jacques Derrida, *Writing and Difference*, trans. Alan Bass (London: Routledge, 1978) pp. 1–30, 9.

167. Jacques Derrida, 'Structure, Sign and Play', in ibid., pp. 278–93, 289.

168. Ibid.

169. Derrida, 'Force and Signification', p. 9.

170. Ibid.

171. Ibid., p. 14.

172. Ibid.

173. F.R. Leavis, 'T.S. Eliot and English Literature', in Leavis, *Valuation in Criticism and Other Essays*, pp. 129–48, 16. Hereafter *TSE & EL* with page references given in the text.

174. See Adorno, 'The Schema of Mass Culture', p. 65.

175. F.R. Leavis, 'The Responsible Critic: Or the Function of Criticism at the Present Time', in Leavis, *Valuation in Criticism and Other Essays*, pp. 184–206, 197.

176. '*Meaning* is that which is represented by a text; it is what the author meant by his use of a particular sign sequence; it is what the signs represent. *Significance*, on the other hand, names a relationship between that meaning and a person, or a conception or a situation or indeed anything imaginable'. (E.D. Hirsch, *The Aims of Interpretation* (Chicago: University of Chicago Press, 1976) p. 8.)

177. See Chapter 1, note 9.

178. F.R. Leavis, 'Henry James and the Function of Criticism', in Leavis, *The Common Pursuit*, pp. 223–32, 225.

179. F.R. Leavis, 'Joyce and the "Revolution of the Word"', in Leavis, *The Critic As Anti-Philosopher*, pp. 121–8, 123. Hereafter *J & TRW* with page references given in the text.

180. Jacques Lacan, *The Seminars of Jacques Lacan Book I: Freud's Papers on Technique 1953–1954*, trans. John Forrester (Cambridge: Cambridge University Press, 1988) p. 242.

181. Ibid., p. 245.

182. Ibid., p. 247.

183. Jacques Lacan, *The Seminars of Jacques Lacan Book II: The Ego in Freud's Theory and in the Technique of Psychoanalysis*, trans. Sylvana Tomaselli (Cambridge: Cambridge University Press, 1988) p. 228–9.

184. Max Weber quoted by Anthony Giddens, *Capitalism and Modern Social Theory: An Analysis of the Writings of Marx, Durkheim and Max Weber* (Cambridge: Cambridge Univerity Press, 1971/1992) p. 216. The quotation comes from Max Weber, *Economy and Society: Volume 3* (New York: Bedmaster Press, 1968) p. 975.

185. See Jacques Lacan, *Speech and Language in Psychoanalysis*, trans. Anthony Wilden (Baltimore : Johns Hopkins University Press, 1968/1994) pp. 46–7.

186. Jacques Lacan, *Écrits: A Selection*, trans. Alan Sheridan (London: Tavistock Publications, 1977) p. 58.

187. Lacan, *The Seminars of Jacques Lacan Book I: Freud's Papers on Technique 1953–1954*, p. 191.

188. Lacan, *The Seminars of Jacques Lacan Book II: The Ego in Freud's Theory and in the Technique of Psychoanalysis*, p. 9.

189. Ibid., p. 223.
190. Ibid., p. 211.
191. Lacan, *The Seminars of Jacques Lacan Book I: Freud's Papers on Technique 1953–1954,*p. 221.
192. Lacan, *Speech and Language in Psychoanalysis*, p. 11.
193. Lacan, *The Seminars of Jacques Lacan Book I: Freud's Papers on Technique 1953–1954*, p. 283.
194. Ibid., p. 183.
195. Lacan, *Écrits: A Selection*, p. 172.
196. Lacan, *The Seminars of Jacques Lacan Book II : The Ego in Freud's Theory and in the Technique of Psychoanalysis*, p. 229.
197. Ibid., p. 308.
198. Lacan, *Écrits: A Selection*, p. 306.
199. Lacan, *Speech and Language in Psychoanalysis*, p. 21.
200. See Lacan, *Écrits: A Selection*, p. 147 and *Speech and Language*, p. 19.
201. Lacan, *Speech and Language in Psychoanalysis*, p. 19.
202. See ibid., p. 20.
203. Lacan, *The Seminars of Jacques Lacan Book I: Freud's Papers on Technique 1953–1954*, p. 158.
204. Derrida, 'Force and Signification', p. 11.
205. See note 176.
206. Some of the relevant texts here are Roland Barthes, 'The Death of the Author', in Roland Barthes, *Image-Music-Text*, trans. Stephen Heath (London: Fontana/Collins, 1977) pp. 142–8; Paul de Man, 'Semiology and Rhetoric', in Josué Harari (ed.) *Textual Strategies: Perspectives in Post-Structuralist Criticism* (London: Methuen, 1980) pp. 121–40; and Tony Bennett, *Formalism and Marxism* (London: Methuen, 1979).
207. Catherine Belsey, *Critical Practice* (London: Methuen, 1980) p. 12.
208. F.R. Leavis, 'The Present and the Past: Eliot's Demonstration', in F.R. Leavis, *English Literature in Our Time and the University* (Cambridge: Cambridge University Press, 1969/1979) pp. 63–82, 81. Hereafter *TP & TP* with page references in the text.
209. F.R. Leavis, 'Why "Four Quartets" Matters in a Technologico–Benthamite Age', in ibid., pp. 111–32, 122.
210. See Peter Washington, *Fraud: Literary Theory and the End of English* (London: Fontana, 1988) pp. 29–31.
211. F.R. Leavis, 'The Literary Discipline and Liberal Education', in Leavis, *Valuation in Criticism and Other Essays*, pp. 163–83, 176.
212. F.R. Leavis, 'Introductory', in *English Literature in Our Time and the University*, pp. 1–35, 8. Hereafter *I* with page references given in the text.
213. F.R. Leavis, 'Literature and the University: The Wrong Question', in ibid., pp. 39–60, 50.
214. Barthes, *The Pleasure of the Text*, p. 61.
215. F.R. Leavis, 'Literary Studies' in F.R. Leavis, *Education and the University* (London: Chatto & Windus, 1943) pp. 66–86, 71.
216. F.R. Leavis, 'Gerard Manley Hopkins: Reflections After Fifty Years', in Leavis, *The Critic As Anti-Philosopher*, pp. 76–97.

217. F.R. Leavis, 'The Logic of Christian Discrimination', in Leavis, *The Common Pursuit*, pp. 248–55, 251.
218. Adorno, *Aesthetic Theory*, trans. Christian Lenhardt (London: Routledge, 1984) p. 291.
219. Adorno, 'The Schema of Mass Culture', p. 57.
220. Ibid., p. 55.
221. Ibid., p. 57.
222. Adorno, *Aesthetic Theory*, p. 292.
223. Ibid., p. 239.
224. Ibid., p. 292.
225. Ibid., p. 6.
226. Ibid., p. 293.
227. Ibid., p. 241.
228. Ibid., p. 240.
229. Ibid.
230. Ibid., p. 241.
231. On 'mediaspeak' see Laura Thompson, Life Magazine, *The Observer*, 8 January 1995, p. 70.
232. On this issue see Richard Hoggart, 'On Language and Literacy Today', in Richard Hoggart, *An English Temper: Essays on Education, Culture and Communications* (Oxford: Oxford University Press, 1982) pp. 94–102.
233. Antony Easthope, *Literary into Cultural Studies* (London: Routledge, 1991) p. 57.
234. Adorno, 'The Culture Industry or Enlightenment as Mass Deception', p. 152.
235. Lacan, *Écrits: A Selection*, p. 310.
236. Simmel, *The Sociology of Georg Simmel*, p. 341.
237. Seltzer, *Bodies and Machines*, p. 215.

## CHAPTER 5: CONCLUSION

1. The basic point is that much of what can be regarded as post-structuralist writing seems to assume or take for granted the reader's acquiescence, agreement and approval of its premises so that they need never be explicated or argued over. Catherine Belsey's *Critical Practice* (London: Methuen, 1980) would be a case in point, as would Antony Easthope's *Literary into Cultural Studies* (London: Routledge, 1991).
2. F.R. Leavis, 'The Literary Discipline and Liberal Education', in F.R. Leavis, *Valuation in Criticism and Other Essays*, ed. G. Singh (Cambridge: Cambridge University Press, 1986) pp. 167–83, 176. Hereafter *LD* with page references given in the text.
3. F.R. Leavis, 'Valuation in Criticism', in ibid., pp. 276–84, 280. Hereafter *VC* with page references given in the text.
4. Jacques Derrida, '*Différance*', in Jacques Derrida, *Margins of Philosophy*, trans. Alan Bass (New York: Harvester Wheatsheaf, 1982), pp. 1–27, 3.

5. Firstly, there [can] be no developed thought – thought about life – without a highly developed language. Secondly, the most complete use of the English language ... is in the major works of great creative writers. Thirdly, every creative writer of the greatest kind knows that in a major work he is developing thought – thought about life. Leavis, 'Valuation in Criticism', p. 287.

6. David Parker, 'The Turn to Ethics in the 1990s', in *The Critical Review* Vol. 33, November 1993, pp. 3–14, 13. See also Christopher Cordner, 'F.R. Leavis and the Moral in Literature', in Richard Freadman and Lloyd Rheinhart (eds) *On Literary Theory and Philosophy: A Cross Disciplinary Encounter* (London: Macmillan, 1991) pp. 60–81.

7. For a full discussion of this expression see Jean-François Lyotard, *The Differend: Phrases in Dispute*, trans. Georges Van Den Abeele (Manchester: Manchester University Press, 1988).

# Bibliography

## PRIMARY SOURCES

### Books

Leavis, F. R. *How To Teach Reading: A Primer For Ezra Pound* (Cambridge: Minority Press, 1932).
—— *New Bearings in English Poetry* (Harmondsworth: Penguin, 1932).
—— *For Continuity* (Cambridge: Minority Press, 1933).
—— *Determinations: Critical Essays* (London: Chatto and Windus, 1934).
—— *Revaluation: Tradition and Development in English Poetry* (Harmondsworth: Penguin is association with Chatto and Windus, 1936 and 1967).
—— *Education and the University* (London: Chatto and Windus, 1943).
—— 'Introduction' to *Mill on Bentham and Coleridge* (London: Chatto and Windus, 1950).
—— *D. H. Lawrence: Novelist* (Harmondsworth: Penguin, 1955 and 1968).
—— *The Common Pursuit* (Harmondsworth: Penguin in association with Chatto and Windus, 1962 and 1993).
—— *A Selection From Scrutiny Volume I* (Cambridge: Cambridge University Press, 1968).
—— *A Selection From Scrutiny Volume II* (Cambridge: Cambridge University Press, 1968).
—— *English Literature In Our Time and The University* (Cambridge: Cambridge University Press, 1969 and 1979).
—— *Nor Shall My Sword: Discourses on Pluralism, Compassion and Social Hope* (London: Chatto and Windus, 1972).
—— *Anna Karenina and Other Essays* (London: Chatto and Windus, 1973).
—— *Letters in Criticism*, ed. John Tasker (London: Chatto and Windus, 1974).
—— *The Living Principle: English As A Discipline of Thought* (London: Chatto and Windus, 1975).
—— *Thought, Words and Creativity: Art and Thought in Lawrence* (London: Chatto and Windus, 1976).
—— *The Critic As Anti-Philosopher: Essays and Papers*, ed. G. Singh (London: Chatto and Windus, 1982).
—— *Valuation in Criticism and Other Essays*, ed. G. Singh (Cambridge: Cambridge University Press, 1986).
Leavis, F. R. and Thompson, Denys, *Culture and Environment: The Training of Critical Awareness* (London: Chatto and Windus, 1933 and 1964).

### Articles

Leavis, 'Under Which King Bezonian' in F. R. Leavis, *Valuation in Criticism and Other Essays* ed. G. Singh (Cambridge: Cambridge University Press, 1986), pp. 38–45.

—— 'Restatement for Critics' in F. R. Leavis, *Valuation in Criticism and Other Essays*, op. cit. pp. 31–7.

—— 'Marxism and Cultural Continuity', in F. R. Leavis, *Valuation in Criticism and Other Essays*., op. cit. pp. 46–53.

—— 'What's Wrong With Criticism' in F. R. Leavis, *For Continuity* (Cambridge: Gordon Fraser, The Minority Press, 1933), pp. 68–90, p. 75.

—— 'Mass Civilisation and Minority Culture' In F. R. Leavis, *For Continuity*, pp. 13–46, p. 31.

—— 'The Marxian Analysis: A Review of *The Mind in Chains*, ed. C. Day Lewis (London: Muller, 1937), in *Scrutiny* 6:2 September 1937, pp. 201–4, p. 203, and Beryl Pring, *Capitalist and Socialist* (London: Methuen, 1937) in *Scrutiny* 6:2, 1937, pp. 201–4.

—— 'Literary Studies' in F. R. Leavis, *Education and the University* (London: Chatto and Windus, 1943), pp. 66–86, p. 71.

—— 'Introduction' to *Mill on Bentham and Coleridge* (London: Chatto and Windus, 1950), pp. 1–38, p. 3.

—— 'The responsible critic: or the function of criticism at any time' in *Scrutiny* 19:3 1953, pp. 162–83.

—— 'The Radical Wing of Cambridge English' Letter to *The Listener*: November 3, 1960 in F. R. Leavis, *Letters in Criticism*, op. cit. pp. 75–7, p. 76..

—— 'Tragedy and the "Medium": A Note on Mr. Santayana's "Tragic Philosophy" in *The Common Pursuit* (Harmondsworth: Penguin in association with Chatto and Windus, 1962 and 1993), pp. 121–35, p. 130.

—— 'Sociology and Literature' in F. R. Leavis, *The Common Pursuit* pp. 195–203.

—— 'Henry James and the Function of Criticism' in F. R. Leavis, *The Common Pursuit*, pp. 221–32.

—— 'The Logic of Christian Discrimination' in F. R. Leavis, *The Common Pursuit*, pp. 248–54.

—— 'Literary Criticism and Philosophy' in F. R. Leavis, *The Common Pursuit*., pp. 211–22.

—— 'Johnson as Poet' in F. R. Leavis, *The Common Pursuit*, 116–120.

—— 'Literary Criticism and Philosophy' in *The Common Pursuit*, pp. 211–22.

—— '*Johnson and Augustanism*', *The Common Pursuit*, op. cit. pp. 97–115.

—— 'Sociology and Literature', *The Common Pursuit*, op. cit. pp. 195–203.

—— 'Literature and Society' in F. R. Leavis, *The Common Pursuit*, op. cit. pp. 182–94.

—— 'Bunyan Through Modern Eyes' in F. R. Leavis, *The Common Pursuit*, pp. 204–10.

—— 'In Defence of Milton' in F. R. Leavis, *The Common Pursuit*, pp. 33–43.

—— 'The Wild, Untutored Phoenix' in F. R. Leavis, *The Common Pursuit*., pp. 231–9.

—— 'Mr. Eliot, Mr. Wyndham Lewis and Lawrence' in F. R. Leavis, *The Common Pursuit*, pp. 240–7.

—— 'Gerard Manley Hopkins' in F. R. Leavis, *The Common Pursuit*, pp. 44–58.

—— 'The Pilgrim's Progress' in F. R. Leavis, *Anna Karenina and Other Essays* (London: Chatto and Windus, 1967 and 1973), pp. 33–48.

—— 'Towards Standards of Criticism' in F. R. Leavis *Anna Karenina and Other Essays*, pp. 219–34, p. 221.

—— 'Keynes, Spender and Currency Values' in F. R. Leavis, *A Selection From Scrutiny Volume I* (Cambridge: Cambridge University Press, 1968), pp. 185–96, p. 195.

—— 'Eliot's "Axe to Grind" And The Nature of Great Criticism' in *English Literature In Our Time and The University* (Cambridge: Cambridge University Press, 1979), pp. 85–108, pp. 95–6.

—— '"The Present and the Past: Eliot's Demonstration' in F. R. Leavis, *English Literature In Our Time and the University*, pp. 63–82.

—— 'Why "Four Quartets" Matters In A Technologico-Benthamite Age' in *English Literature in Our Time and The University* pp. 111–32, p. 122.

—— 'Introductory' in F. R. Leavis, *English Literature In Our Time and The University*, pp. 1–35.

—— 'Literature and the University: The Wrong Question' *English Literature In Our Time and The University*, pp. 39–60.

—— 'Luddites? Or Is There One Culture' in F. R. Leavis, *Nor Shall my Sword: Discourses on Pluralism, Compassion and Social Hope* (London: Chatto and Windus, 1972), pp. 77–99, p. 92; pp. 163–98.

—— 'Élites, Oligarchies And An Educated Public' in F. R. Leavis, *Nor Shall My Sword: Discourses on Pluralism, Compassion and Social Hope* , pp. 201–28.

—— 'Pluralism, Compassion and Social Hope in F. R. Leavis *Nor Shall My Sword: Discourses on Pluralism, Compassion and Social Hope*, pp.163–98.

—— 'English, "Unrest" and Continuity' in F. R. Leavis, *Nor Shall My Sword: Discourses on Pluralism, Compassion and Social Hope*, pp. 103–33.

—— 'Two Cultures? The Significance of Lord Snow' in F. R. Leavis, *Nor Shall My Sword: Discourses on Pluralism, Compassion and Social Hope*, pp. 41–74.

—— 'Luddites? or There Is Only One Culture' in F. R. Leavis, *Nor Shall My Sword: Discourses on Pluralism, Compassion and Social Hope*, pp. 77–99.

—— 'Adam Bede' in F. R. Leavis, *Anna Karenina and Other Essays*, pp. 49–58.

—— 'The Organic Community', Letter to *The Spectator*: 10 May, 1963 in F. R. Leavis *Letters in Criticism*, ed. John Tasker (London: Chatto and Windus, 1974), pp. 100–1.

—— 'Four Quartets' in F. R. Leavis, *The Living Principle: 'English as a Discipline of Thought'* (London: Chatto and Windus, 1975), pp. 155–264.

—— Judgement and Analysis' in *The Living Principle: 'English' as a Discipline of Thought* , pp. 71–154.

—— 'Thought, Language and Objectivity' in F. R. Leavis, *The Living Principle*, pp. 19–69.

—— 'Mutually Necessary' in F. R. Leavis *The Critic as Anti-Philosopher* ed. G. Singh (London: Chatto and Windus, 1982), pp. 186–208.

—— 'Joyce and 'The Revolution of the Word"' in F. R. Leavis, *The Critic As Anti-Philosopher*, pp. 121–8.

—— 'Gerard Manley Hopkins: Reflections After Fifty Years' in F. R. Leavis, *The Critic As Anti-Philosopher*, pp. 76–97,.

—— 'Justifying One's Valuation of Blake' in F. R. Leavis, *The Critic As Anti-Philosopher*, pp. 1–23.

—— 'Memories of Wittgenstein' in F. R. Leavis, *The Critic as Anti-Philosopher*, pp. 129–45.

—— 'Standards of Criticism' in F. R. Leavis, *Valuation in Criticism and Other Essays* ed. G. Singh (Cambridge: Cambridge University Press, 1986) pp. 244–52.

—— 'T. S. Eliot and English Literature' in F. R. Leavis, *Valuation In Criticism and Other Essays*, pp. 129–48.

—— 'Valuation in Criticism' in F. R. Leavis, *Valuation In Criticism and Other Essays*, pp. 278–84.

—— 'The literary discipline and liberal education' in F. R. Leavis, *Valuation in Criticism and Other Essays* , pp. 163–83.

—— 'Thought, Meaning and Sensibility: The Problem of Value Judgement' in F. R. Leavis, *Valuation in Criticism and Other Essays*, pp. 285–97.

—— 'Reading Out Poetry' in F. R. Leavis, *Valuation in Criticism and Other Essays'*, pp. 253–75.

—— The Responsible Critic: or the function of criticism at any time' in F. R. Leavis, *Valuation in Criticism and Other Essays*, pp. 194–206.

—— 'Literary Studies: a reply' in F. R. Leavis, *Valuation in Criticism and Other Essays*, pp. 207–17.

## SECONDARY SOURCES

Adorno, Theodor W., *The Culture Industry: Selected Essays on Mass Culture* ed. J. M. Bernstein (London: Routledge, 1991).

—— *Minima Moralia: Reflections from Damaged Life* trans. E. F. N. Jephcott (London: Verso, 1993).

—— *The Jargon of Authenticity* trans. K. Tarnowski and F. Will (London: Routledge and Kegan Paul, 1973).

—— Adorno, *Aesthetic Theory* trans. Christian Lenhardt (London and New York: Routledge, 1984).

—— *Negative Dialectics* trans. E. B. Ashton (London: Routledge, 1973 and 1990).

Adorno, T. W. and Horkheimer, M. *Dialectic of Enlightenment* trans. J. Cumming (London and New York: Verso, 1992).

Adorno, T. W., Benjamin, W. , Black, E., Brecht, B. and LUKÁCS, G., *Aesthetics and Politics*, translation editor R. Taylor (London and New York: Verso, 1990).

Althusser, Louis, *For Marx*, trans. Ben Brewster (London: New Left Books, 1977).

—— *Lenin and Philosophy and Other Essays*, trans. Ben Brewster (London: New Left Books, 1977).

Angell, Norman, *The Press and the Organisation of Society* (Cambridge: Minority Press, 1922).

Annan, Noel, *The Disintegration of an Old Culture* (Oxford: Clarendon Press, 1966).

Appignanesi, Lisa, ed., *Ideas From France: The Legacy of French Theory* (London: Free Association Books, 1989).

Baldick, Chris, *The Social Mission of English Criticism 1848–1932* (Oxford: Clarendon Press, 1983 and 1987).

Barker, Francis *et al. 1936: The Sociology of Literature Volume 2, Practices of Literature and Politics* (Colchester: University of Essex, 1979).

Barthes, Roland, *The Pleasure of the Text*, trans. Richard Millar (Oxford: Blackwell, 1975 and 1990).

—— *Image-Music-Text* trans. Stephen Heath (London: Fontana/Collins, 1977).

Baudrillard, Jean, *Selected Writings*, ed. Mark Poster (Cambridge and Oxford: Polity Press in association with Basil Blackwell, 1988).

—— *Simulations*, trans. Paul Foss et al. (New York: Semiotext(e), 1983).

Bauman, Zygmunt, *Modernity and the Holocaust* (Ithaca: Cornell University Press, 1989).

Bell, Michael, *F. R. Leavis* (London and New York: Routledge, 1988).

Belsey, Catherine, *Critical Practice* (London and New York: Methuen, 1980).

Bender, Gretchen and Druckery, Timothy, eds. *Culture on the Brink: Ideologies of Technology* (Seattle: Bay Press, 1994).

Benjamin, Walter, *One Way Street and Other Writings*, trans. Edmund Jephcott and Kingsley Shorter (London and New York: Verso, 1979 and 1992).

—— *Illuminations*, ed. Hannah Arendt, trans. Harry Zohn (London: Fontana, 1973 and 1992).

Bennett, Tony, *Formalism and Marxism* (London and New York: Methuen, 1979).

Berger, John, *Ways of Seeing* (London: British Broadcasting Corporation in association with Harmondsworth: Penguin, 1972).

Bergonzi, Bernard, *Exploding English: Criticism, Theory and Culture* (Oxford: Clarendon Press, 1990).

Berten, Hans, *The Idea of the Postmodern: A History* (London and New York: Routledge, 1995).

Biaggani, E. G., *The Reading and Writing of English*, preface by F. R. Leavis (London: Hutchinson's Scientific and Technical Publication, 1936).

Bilan, R.P., *The Literary Criticism of F. R. Leavis* (Cambridge: Cambridge University Press, 1979).

Billington, Rachel, Strawbridge, Sheelagh, Greensides, Lenore and Fitzsimons, Annette *Culture and Society* (Basingstoke: Macmillan, 1991).

Bocock, Robert, *Consumption* (London and New York: Routledge, 1993).

Bowie, Andrew, *Aesthetics and Subjectivity: From Kant to Nietzsche* (Manchester University Press, 1990).

Boyers, Robert, *F. R. Leavis: Judgement and the Discipline of Thought* (Columbia: University of Missouri Press, 1978).

Bradford, Richard, ed. *The State of Theory* (London and New York: Routledge, 1993).

Buckley, Vincent, *Poetry and Morality: Studies on the Criticism of Matthew Arnold, T. S. Eliot and F. R. Leavis* (London: Chatto and Windus, 1968).

Bunyan, John, *The Pilgrim's Progress* (Belfast: Ambassador Productions Ltd, 1992).

Burke, Sean, *The Death and Return of the Author: Criticism and Subjectivity in Barthes, Foucault and Derrida* (Edinburgh: Edinburgh University Press, 1992).

Burnham, James, *The Management Revolution* (Harmondsworth: Penguin, 1945).

Burns, Elizabeth and Tom eds, *The Sociology of Literature and Drama: Selected Readings* (Harmondsworth: Penguin, 1973).

Butterfield, H, *The Whig Interpretation of History* (New York: Norton, 1931 and 1965).

Cain, Williams E., *The Crisis in Criticism: Theory, Literature and Reform in English Studies* (Baltimore and London: The Johns Hopkins University Press, 1984).

Calder, Angus and Sheridan, Dorothy, *Speak for Yourself: A Mass Observation Anthology 1937-1949* (London: Jonathan Cape, 1984).

Carey, John, *The Intellectuals and the Masses: Pride and Prejudice among the Literary Intelligensia* (London and Boston: Faber and Faber, 1992).

Casey, John, *The Language of Criticism* (London: Methuen, 1966).

Castles, E. B., *The Coming of Leisure* (London: New Education Foundation, 1935).

Chambers, Iain, *Popular Culture: The Metropolitan Experience* (London and New York: Routledge, 1986).

Charques, R. D., *Contemporary Literature and the Social Revolution* (London: Martin Secker, 1933).

Clark, Jon, Heinemann, Margot, Margolies, David and Snee, Carol eds, *Culture and Crisis in Britain in the Thirties* (London: Lawrence and Wishart, 1979).

Cole, G. D. H. and M. I., *The Condition of Britain* (London: Gollancz, 1937).

Collini, Stefan, *Public Moralists: Political and Intellectual Life in Britain: 1850–1930* (Oxford: Clarendon Press, 1991).

Connerton, Paul, ed. *Critical Sociology: Selected Readings* (Harmondsworth: Penguin, 1976).

Connolly, Cyril, *Enemies of Promise* (London: Routledge and Kegan Paul, 1938 and Andre Deutsche, 1973 and 1988).

Connor, Steven, *Theory and Cultural Value* (Oxford: Basil Blackwell, 1992).

—— *Postmodern Culture: An Introduction to Theories of the Contemporary* (Oxford: Basil Blackwell, 1989).

Cox, C. B. and Dyson, A. E. eds., *The Twentieth Century Mind, History, Ideas and Literature in Britain 2: 1918–1945* (Oxford: Oxford University Press, 1972).

Cross, Gary, *Time and Money: The Making of Consumer Culture* (London and New York: Routledge, 1993).

Crossman, Richard ed., *The God That Failed: Six Studies In Communism* (New York and London: Hamish Hamilton, 1950).

Cunningham, Valentine, *British Writers of the Thirties* (Oxford and New York, 1985).

Day, Gary, ed. *The British Critical Tradition* (Basingstoke: Macmillan, 1993).

Debord, Guy, *The Society of The Spectacle*, trans. Donald Nicholson-Smith (New York: Zone Books, 1967 and 1994).

de Man, Paul, *Blindness and Insight: Essays In The Rhetoric of Comtemporary Criticism* (London and New York: Routledge, 1983 and 1989).

Derrida, Jacques, *Margins of Philosophy* trans. Alan Bass (New York and London: Harvester Wheatsheaf, 1982).

—— *Of Grammatology* trans. Gayatri Chakravorty Spivak (Baltimore and London: The Johns Hopkins University Press, 1976).

—— *Writing and Difference* trans. and with an introduction and notes by Alan Bass (London: Routledge and Kegan Paul, 1978 and 1990).

—— *Positions* trans. and with notes by Alan Bass (London: The Athlone Press by arrangement with the University of Chicago Press, 1987).

de Saussure, Ferdinard, *Course in General Linguistics* trans. W. Baskin (London: Fontana, 1974).

Doyle, Brian Doyle, *English and Englishness* (London and New York: Routledge, 1989).

Drakakis, John ed., *Alternative Shakespeares* (London and New York: Methuen, 1985).

Eagleton, Terry, *Literary Theory* (Oxford: Basil Blackwell, 1985).

—— *Ideology: An Introduction* (London and New York: Verso, 1991).

—— *The Function of Criticism: From 'The Spectator' to Post-structuralism* (London, Verso, 1984).

Easthope, Antony, *British Post-structuralism Since 1968* (London and New York: Routledge, 1988 and 1991).

—— *Literary Into Cultural Studies* (London and New York: Routledge, 1991).

Edwards, Richard, *Contested Terrain: The Transformation of the Work Place in the Twentieth Century* (New York: Basic Books, 1979).

Evans, George Ewart, *The Days That We Have Seen* (London: Faber and Faber, 1975).

Falk, Pasi, *The Consuming Body* (London: Sage Publications, 1994).

Featherstone, Mike, Hepworth, Mike and Turner, Bryan S., *The Body: Social Process and Cultural Theory* (London: Sage Publications, 1991).

Felman, Shoshana, *Literature and Psychoanalysis, The Question of Reading: Otherwise* (Baltimore and London: The Johns Hopkins University Press, 1982 and 1988).

Fish, Stanley, *Doing What Comes Naturally: Change, Rhetoric and the Practice of Theory in Literary and Legal Studies* (Oxford: Clarendon Press, 1989).

Fiske, John, *Understanding Popular Culture* (London: Unwin Hyman, 1989).

Foucault, Michel, *Discipline and Punish: The Birth of the Prison* trans. Alan Sheridan (Harmondsworth: Penguin, 1991).

—— *The History of Sexuality Volume 1: An Introduction* trans. R. Hurley (Harmondsworth: Penguin, 1990).

Fraser, W. Hamish, *The Coming of the Mass Market 1850–1914* (London: Macmillan, 1981).

Freadman, Richard and Rheinhart, Lloyd eds. *On Literary Theory and Philosophy: A Cross Disciplinary Encounter* (Basingstoke and London: Macmillan, 1991).

French, Philip, *Three Honest Men: A Critical Mosaic Edmund Wilson, F. R. Leavis, Lionel Trilling* (Manchester: Carcanet New Press, 1980).

Freud, Sigmund, *Civilization and Its Discontents*, trans. Joan Riviere revised and edited by James Strachey (London: The Hogarth Press, 1930 and 1979).

—— *The Interpretation of Dreams* trans. J. Strachey. Eds. James Strachey and A. Tyson. Revised by Angela Richards (London: Pelican Books, 1976).

—— *On Metapsychology: The Theory of Psychoanalysis* trans. James Strachey. Ed. Angela Richards (Harmondsworth: Penguin, 1991).

Frowe, John, *Cultural Studies and Cultural Value* (Oxford: Clarendon Press, 1995).

—— *Marxism and Literary History* (Oxford: Basil Blackwell, 1986).

Giddens, Anthony, *Capitalism and Modern Social Theory: An Analysis of the Writings of Marx, Durkheim and Max Weber* (Cambridge: Cambridge Univerity Press, 1971 and 1992).

—— *The Consequence of Modernity* (Cambridge: Polity Press, 1990).

Giddens, A. et. al. *The Polity Reader in Cultural Theory* (Cambridge and Oxford: Polity Press in association with Blackwell Publishers, 1994).

Gloversmith, Frank, ed., *The Theory of Reading* (Sussex: Harvester Press, 1984).

Goodheart, Eugene, *The Failure of Criticism* (Cambridge Massachusetts and London: Harvard University Press, 1978).

Grayling, A. C., *Wittgenstein* (Oxford and New York: Oxford University Press, 1988.

Green, Martin, *Children of the Sun: A Narrative of Decadence in England after 1918* (London: Pimlico 1976 and 1992).

Greenwood, Edward, *F. R. Leavis* (Harlow: Longman, 1978).

GROSS, John, *The Rise and Fall of the Man of Letters* (London: Weidenfield and Nicolson, 1969).

Grossberg, Lawrence, Nelson, Gary and Treichler, Paula eds.*Cultural Studies* (London and New York: Routledge, 1992).

Harari, Josué ed. *Textual Strategies: Perspectives in Post-Structuralist Criticism* (London: Methuen, 1980).

Harris, Constance, *The Use of Leisure in Bethnal Green*, preface (London: Lindsey Press, 1927).

Harris, David, *From Class Struggle To The Politics of Pleasure: The Effects of Gramscianism on Cultural Studies* (London and New York: Routledge, 1992).

Harrison, B, *Inconvenient Fictions: Literature and The Limits of Theory* (New Haven and London: Yale University Press, 1992).

Harwood, John, *Eliot to Derrida: The Poverty of Interpretation* (Basingstoke and London: Macmillan, 1995).

Hawkes, Terence, *Meaning by Shakespeare* (London and New York: Routledge, 1993).

Hayman, Ronald, *Leavis* (London: Heinemann, 1976).

Herrnstein Smith, Barbara, *Contingencies of Value: Alternative Perspectives for Critical Theory* (Cambridge Massachusetts and London: Harvard University Press, 1988).

Hilton, John, *Rich Man, Poor Man* (New York: Garland 1938 and 1944).

Hirsch, E. D., *The Aims of Interpretation* (London: University of Chicago Press, 1976).

Hogan, Patrick Colm, *The Politics of Interpretation: Ideology, Professionalism and the Study of Literature* (Oxford and New York: Oxford University Press, 1990).

Hoggart, Richard, *An English Temper: Essays On Education, Culture and Communications* (New York: Oxford University Press, 1982).

Hopkins, Eric, *The Rise and Decline of the English Working Classes 1918–1990: A Social History* (London: Wiedenfeld and Nicolson, 1991).

Hoy, David Couzens, and McCarthy, Thomas, *Critical Theory* (Oxford UK and Cambridge USA: Basil Blackwell, 1994).

Hynes, Samuel, *The Auden Generation: Literature and Politics in England in the 1930s* (London: Pimlico, 1976 and 1992).

Inglis, Fred, *Radical Earnestness: English Social Theory 1880–1980* (Oxford: Martin Robertson, 1982).

Jakobson, Roman, and Halle, Morris *Fundamentals of Language* (New York: Moulton Publishers, 1956).

Jameson, Frederic, 'Postmodernism and Consumer Society' in Hal Foster ed. *Postmodern Culture* (London: Pluto Press, 1985).

Jennings, Humphrey and Madge, Charles eds., *Mass Observation Day-Survey: May 12 1937* (London: Faber and Faber, 1937 and 1987).

Johnson, Lesley, *The Cultural Critics: From Matthew Arnold to Raymond Williams* (London: Routledge and Kegan Paul, 1979).

Jones, Greta, *Social Hygiene in Twentieth Century Britain* (London and Sydney: Croom Helm, 1986).

Joseph, Michael, *Journalism for Profit* (London: Hutchinson, 1924).

Keating, Peter ed., *The Victorian Prophets* (London: Fontana, 1981).

Kermode, Frank, *History and Value* (Oxford: Clarendon Press, 1988).

Kinch, M. B., Baker, William and Kimber, John, *F. R. Leavis and Q. D. Leavis: An Annotated Bibliography* (New York and London: Garland Publishing, 1989).

Knapp, James F., *Literary Modernism and the Transformation of Work* (Evanston: Northwestern University Press, 1988).

Kruger, Barbara, *Remote Control: Power, Cultures and the World of Appearances* (Cambridge Mass. and London: MIT Press, 1993).

Lacan, Jacques, *Speech and Language in Psychoanalysis* translated with notes and commentary by Anthony Wilden (Baltimore and London: Johns Hopkins University Press, 1994).

—— *The Four Fundamental Concepts of Psychoanalysis*, trans. Alan Sheridan (Harmondsworth: Penguin, 1977).

—— *Écrits: A Selection*, trans. Alan Sheridan (London: Tavistock Publications, 1977).

—— *The Seminars of Jacques Lacan: Book 1 Freud's Papers on Technique 1953–1954*, trans. John Forrester (Cambridge and New York: Cambridge University Press, 1988).

—— *The Seminars of Jacques Lacan Book II: The Ego in Freud's Theory and in the Technique of Psychoanalysis* trans. Sylvana Tomaselli with notes by John Forrester (Cambridge: Cambridge University Press, 1988).

Lansbury, George, *My England* (London: Selwyn and Blount, 1934).

Law, Jules David Law, *The Rhetoric of Empiricism: Language and Perception from Locke to I. A. Richards* (Ithaca and London: Cornell University Press, 1993).

Lears, T. J. Jackson, *Some Versions of Fantasy: Towards A Cultural History of American Advertising* (Cambridge and New York: Cambridge University Press, 1984).

Leavis, Q. D., *Fiction and the Reading Public* (London: Chatto and Windus, 1932).

Lefebvre, Henri, *Critique of Everyday Life* trans. John Moore (London and New York: Verso, 1947 and 1991).

le Mahieu, Daniel, *A Culture for Democracy: Mass Communication and the Cultivated Mind in Britain Between the Wars* (Oxford: Clarendon Press, 1988).

Lemaire, Anika, *Jacques Lacan* trans. David Macey (London: Routledge and Kegan Paul, 1977).

Lentricchia, Frank, *Criticism and Social Change* (Chicago and London: The University of Chicago Press, 1983).

Lind, Robert and Helen, *Middletown* (New York: Constable, 1929).

Lindenberger, Herbert, *The History in Literature: On Value, Genre and Institutions* (New York: Columbia University Press, 1990).

Lodge, David, *The Modes of Modern Writing* (London: Edward Arnold, 1977).

Lucáks, Georg Lukács, *Writer and Critic and Other Essays* ed. and trans. Arthur Kahn (London: Merlin Press, 1970).*Essays on Realism*, trans. David Fernbach, ed. Rodney Livingstone (London: Lawrence and Wishart, 1980).

—— *The Theory of the Novel*, trans. Anna Bostock (London: Merlin Press, 1971).

Lyotard, Jean-François , in *The Lyotard Reader*, ed. Andrew Benjamin (Oxford and Cambridge MA: Basil Blackwell, 1989).

—— *The Differend: Phrases In Dispute* trans. Georges Van Den Abeele (Manchester: Manchester University Press, 1988).

Lyotard, Jean-François, and Thébaud, Jean-Loup, *Just Gaming*, trans. Wlad Godzich (Manchester: Manchester University Press, 1985).

MacCannell, Juliet Flower, *Figuring Lacan: Criticism and the Cultural Unconscious* (London and SYdney: Croom Helm, 1986).

Macherey, Pierre, *A Theory of Literary Production* trans. G. Wall (London: Routledge and Kegan Paul, 1978).

Mackillop, Ian, *F. R. Leavis: A Life in Criticism* (Harmondsworth: Allen Lane, The Penguin Press, 1995).

Marcus, Jane, ed. *Virginia Woolf and Bloomsbury: A Centenary Celebration* (London: Macmillan, 1987).

Massumi, Brian, ed. *The Politics of Everyday Fear* (Minneapolis: University of Minnesota Press, 1993).

Mccallum, Pamela, *Literature and Method: Towards A Critique of I. A. Richards, T. S. Eliot and F. R. Leavis* (Dublin: Gill and Macmillan, 1983).

Merquior, J. C., *Foucault* (London: Fontana, 1985).

Modleski, Tania, ed., *Studies in Entertainment: Critical Approaches to Mass Culture* (Bloomington and Indianapolis: Indiana University Press, 1986).

Mowat, C. L., *Britain Between the Wars* (London: Methuen, 1950).

Mulhern, Francis, ed. *The Moment of 'Scrutiny'* (London: Verso, 1979 and 1981).

—— *Contemporary Marxist Literary Criticism* (London and New York: Longman, 1992).

Narasimhaiah, C. D., Betsky, Seymour, Walsh, William and Littlewood, J. C. F., *F. R. Leavis: Some Aspects of His Work* (Mysore: Rao and Raghavan, 1963).

Norris, Christopher, *Truth and the Ethics of Criticism* (Manchester and New York: Manchester University Press, 1994).

—— *The Truth About Postmodernism* (Oxford: Basil Blackwell, 1993).

—— *What's Wrong with Postmodernism: Critical Theory and the Ends of Philosophy* (New York and London: Harvester Wheatsheaf, 1990).

—— *Uncritical Theory: Postmodernism, Intellectuals and the Gulf War* (London: Lawrence and Wishart, 1992).

—— *Derrida* (London: Fontana, 1987).

Ortony, Andrew, ed. *Metaphor and Thought* (Cambridge: Cambridge University Press, 1979).

Orwell, George, *The Road to Wigan Pier* (Harmondsworth: Penguin, 1937 and 1989 ).

—— *Inside The Whale and Other Essays* (Harmondsworth: Penguin, 1957 and 1988).

Overstreet, Henry, *A Guide To Civilized Leisure* (New York: Books for Libraries Press, 1934).

Page, Norman, *The Thirties in Britain* (Basingstoke and London: Macmillan, 1990).

Paget, R., *Babel.* (London: Kegan Paul, 1930).

Perkin, Harold, *The Rise of Professional Society: England Since 1800* (London and New York: Routledge, 1989).

Pitt-Rivers, G. H. L. F., *The Clash of Culture and the Contact of Races* (London: Routledge, 1927).

Pollard, Harold, *Development in Management Thought* (London: Heinneman, 1974).

Priestley, J. B., *English Journey* (London: Heinemann, 1934 and 1968).

Richards, I. A., *Principles of Living Criticism* (London: Routledge and Kegan Paul, 1924 and 1959).

Rickword, Edgell, 'Culture, Progress and English Tradition' in Edgell Rickword, *Literature in Society: Essays and Opinions II 1931–1978*, ed. A. Young (Manchester: Carcanet, 1978).

Robson, W. W., *Modern English Literature*, (London: Oxford University Press, 1970).

Rorty, Richard, *Contingency, Irony and Solidarity* (Cambridge: Cambridge University Press, 1989).

Rowntree, B. Seebohm, *Industrial Unrest: A Way Out* (London: Longman, 1922).

Russell, Gilbert, *Advertisement Writing* (London: Earnest Benn, 1927).

Samson, Anne, *F. R. Leavis* (New York and London: Harvester Wheatsheaf, 1992).

Selden, Raman ed., *The Theory of Criticism: From Plato to the Present* (Harlow and New York: Longman, 1988).

Seltzer, Mark, *Bodies and Machines* (New York and London: Routledge, 1992).

Sheldon, Oliver, *The Philosophy of Management* (London: Pitman, 1923).

Shell, Marc, *The Economy of Literature* (Baltimore: Johns Hopkins University Press, 1978).

Simmel, Georg, *On Individuality and Social Forms*, edited and with the introduction by Donald N. Levine (Chicago and London: The University of Chicago Press, 1971).

—— *The Sociology of Georg Simmel* (New York: The Free Press, 1950).

Smith, Joseph H. and Kerrigan, William eds. *Interpreting Lacan* (New Haven and London: Yale University Press, 1983).

Smith, Malcolm, *British Politics, Society and the State Since the Late Nineteenth Century* (Basingstoke and London: Macmillan, 1990).

Snow, C. P., *The Two Cultures* (Cambridge: Cambridge University Press, 1959 and 1993).

Sontag, Susan, *Illness as Metaphor* (Harmondsworth: Penguin, 1977 and 1987).

Stead, C. K., *The New Poetic: Yeats to Eliot* (London: Hutchinson, 1964 and 1983).

Stevenson, John, *British Society 1914–45* (Harmondsworth: Penguin, 1984).

Sturrock, John ed. *Structuralism and Since: From Levi Strauss to Derrida* (Oxford: Oxford University Press, 1979).

Sturt, George, *Change in the Village* (London: Duckworth, 1912 and 1959).

—— *The Wheelwright's Shop* (Cambridge: Cambridge University Press, 1923 and 1993).

Swingewood, Alan, *Sociological Poetics and Aesthetic Theory* (London: Macmillan, 1986).

Taylor, A. J. P, *English History 1914–1945* (Harmondsworth: Penguin 1970).

Taylor, Frederick Winslow, *The Principles of Scientific Management* (London: Harper Row, 1911 and 1947).

Thompson, Denys, ed., *The Leavises: Recollections and Impressions* (Cambridge: Cambridge University Press, 1984).

Todorov, Tvetan, *On Human Diversity: Nationalism, Racism and Exoticism in French Thought* (Cambridge Massachusetts and London: Harvard University Press, 1993).

Tomlinson, A., *Consumption Identity and Style: Marketing Meanings and the Packaging of Pleasure* (London and New York: Routledge, 1990).

Tredell, Nicholas, *The Critical Decade: Culture In Crisis* (Manchester: Carcanet, 1993).

Tugwell, Rexford, *Industry's Coming of Age* (New York: Harcourt Brace and Co., 1927).

Turner, Graeme, *British Cultural Studies: An Introduction* (Boston and London: Unwin Hyman, 1990).

Veblen, Thorstein, *The Theory of the Leisure Class* (New York: Dover Publications, 1899 and 1994).

Walsh, William, *F. R. Leavis* (London: Chatto and Windus, 1980).

Washington, Peter, *Fraud: Literary Theory and the End of English* (London: Fontana, 1988).

Waters, Chris, *British Socialists and The Politics of Popular Culture 1884–1914* (Manchester: Manchester University Press, 1990).

Watson, Garry, *The Leavises, The 'Social' and the Left* (Swansea: Brynmill, 1977).

Watson, George, *The Literary Critics: A Study of English Descriptive Criticism* (London: Woburn Press, 1973).

Watson, J. B., *The Ways of Behaviourism* (London: Kegan Paul, 1925).

Weiner, Martin, *English Culture and the Decline of the Industrial Spirit, 1850–1980* (Cambridge: Cambridge University Press, 1981).

Widdowson, Peter, ed., *Re-reading English*, (London and New York: Methuen, 1982).

Williams, Raymond, *Culture and Society 1780–1950* (Harmondsworth: Penguin in association with Chatto and Windus, 1975).

—— *Keywords: A Vocabulary of Culture and Society* (London: Fontana, 1983).

—— *Problems in Materialism and Culture* (London: Verso, 1980).

—— *Marxism and Literature* (Oxford: Oxford University Press, 1977).

Wittgenstein, Ludwig, *Philosophical Investigations* trans. G. E. M. Anscombe (Oxford: Basil Blackwell.

Wrighter, William, *The Myth of Theory* (Cambridge: Cambridge University Press, 1994).

Zizek, Slavo, *The Sublime Object of Ideology* (London and New York: Verso, 1988).

## ARTICLES

Adams, H., 'Canons: Literary Criteria / Power Criteria' in *Critical Inquiry* 14:4, 1988, pp. 748–64.

Aithal, S. Krishnamoorthy, 'F. R. Leavis on Criticism and Theory' in *Panjab University Research Bulletin*, 9:1-2, 1978, pp. 17–34.

Anderson, Perry, 'Components of the National Culture' in *New Left Review* 50 July–August 1968, pp. 3–57, p. 53.

Annan, Noël, 'Bloomsbury and the Leavises' in Jane Marcus ed. *Virginia Woolf and Bloomsbury: A Centenary Celebration* (London: Macmillan, 1987), pp. 23–38.

Atkinson, B. J., 'Historiography' in C. B. Cox and A. E. Dyson eds. *The Twentieth Century Mind: History, Ideas and Literature in Britain 2: 1918–1945*,(Oxford: Oxford University Press, 1972), pp. 57–67, p. 62.

Bateson, F. W., 'The Function of Criticism at the Present Time' in *Essays in Criticism* 3:1 1933, pp. 1–27.

—— 'The *Scrutiny* Phenomenon' in *Sewanee Review* 85:1 January–March 1977, pp. 144–52.

Belsey, Catheriney, 'Re-reading the Great Tradition' in *Re-reading English* , pp. 121–35.

Bird, Otto, 'The Two Cultures: The Snow Leavis Controversy' in Otto Bird, *Cultures in Conflict: An Essay in the Philosophy of the Humanities* (Notre Dame and London: University of Notre Dame Press, 1976), pp. 114–32.

Black, Michael, 'The Third Realm: An Expository Essay on "Scrutiny"' in *The Use of English,* 15:4, 1964, pp. 281–8.

—— 'The Third Realm: Part 2' in *The Use of English*, 16:1, 1964, pp. 21–31.

Bradbury, Malcolm, 'The Impact of Literary Theory' in Lisa Appignanesi ed., *Ideas From France: The Legacy of French Theory* (London: Free Association Books, 1989), pp. 7–15, p. 12.

Bredin, Hugh, 'F. R. Leavis's theory of language in *The Living Principle*', in *Critical Quarterly*, 24:2, Summer 1982, pp. 61–8.

Brooker, Peter, and Widdowson, Peter, 'A Literature for England' in Robert Colls and Philip Dodd, *Englishness: Politics and Culture 1880–1920* (London and New York: Croom Helm, 1986), pp. 117–63.

Butterfield, H, 'History and the Marxian Method' in *Scrutiny* 1:4 March 1933, pp. 339–55.

Carey, John, 'Yours Cantankerously', *Observer*, 2 June 1974, p. 32.

Church, Richard, *Christian Science Monitor*, 27 January 1937.

Cordner, Christopher, 'F. R. Leavis and the moral in literature' in Richard Freadman and Lloyd Rheinhart eds. *On Literary Theory and Philosophy: A Cross Disciplinary Encounter* (Basingstoke and London: Macmillan, 1991), pp. 60–81.

Crouch, Colin, 'Research On Corporatism In Britain'. Discussion Paper at the Conference on Organizational Participation and Public Policy, Princeton University, September 1981.

Cullen, Barry, '"I thought I had provided something better"–F. R. Leavis, Literary Criticism and Anti-Philosophy' in Gary Day, *The British Critical Tradition* (Basingstoke and London: Macmillan, 1993), pp. 188–212.

de Man, Paul, 'Semiology and Rhetoric', in Josué Harari ed. *Textual Strategies: Perspectives in Post-Structuralist Criticism* (London: Methuen, 1980), pp. 121–40.

Dodd, Philip, 'Englishness and the National Culture' in Robert Colls and Philip Dodd eds., *Englishness: Politics and Culture 1880–1920* (London and New York: Croom Helm, 1986), pp. 1–28.

Dodsworth, Martin, 'Criticism Now: The Abandonment of Tradition?' in Boris ford ed., *the New Pelican Guide to English Literature Volume 8: The Present* (Harmondsworth: Penguin, 1983), pp. 118–36.

Duncan-Jones, Austin, 'The Organic Community' in *Cambridge Review*, 26 May 1933, pp. 432.

Easthope, Antony, 'The Question of Literary Value' *Textual Practice* 4:3 1990, pp. 376–389.

Edwards, Thomas R., 'High Minds, Low Thoughts: Popular Culture and Intellectual Pastoral' in *Raritan*, 1:1 1981, pp. 88–105.

Featherstone, Mike, 'The Body in Consumer Culture' in Mike Featherstone, Mike Hepworth and Bryan D. Turner eds. *The Body: Social Process and Cultural Theory* (London: Sage Publications, 1991), p. 170–196, p. 175.

Felperin, Howard, 'Leavisism Revisited, Or The Mystifications Of Plain Talk: A Postscript to John Docker' in *Meanjin*, 41:2 1982, pp. 171–9.

Filmer, Paul, 'The Literary Imagination and the explanation of socio-cultural change in modern Britain' in *The European Journal of Sociology* 10:2, 1969, pp. 271–91.

Ford, Dennis, 'F. R. Leavis: The Critic as Moralist' in *Soundings*, 65:2, Summer 1982, pp. 168–80.

Frank, Arthur W., 'For a Sociology Of The Body: An Analytical Review' in Mike Featherstone, Mike Hepworth and Brian S. Turner, eds., *The Body: Social Process and Cultural Theory* (London: Sage Publications, 1991), pp. 36–97.

Freadman, Ralph and Millar, S. R., 'Three Views of Literary Theory' in *Poetics: International Review for the Theory of Literature* 17:1-2, 1988, pp. 9–24.

Freud, Sigmund, *Case Histories I: 'Dora' and 'Little Hans'*,. trans. Alix and James Strachey ed. Angela Richards (Harmondsworth: Penguin, 1977). 'On Negation' in Sigmund Freud, *On Metapsychology: the Theory of Psychoanalysis* trans. James Strachey, ed. Angela Richards (Harmondsworth: Penguin, 1984 and 1991), pp. 437–43, p. 438.

Gervais, David, 'Late Witness: George Sturt and Village England' in *Cambridge Quarterly* 20, 1991, pp. 21-44.

Gregor, Ian, 'English, Leavis and Social Order' in *Twentieth Century Studies* 9 September 1973, pp. 22–31.

Hall, Stuart, 'Cultural Analysis' *The Cambridge Review* January 21 1967, pp. 154–7.

Haskell, Thomas, 'Capitalism and the Origins of Humanitarian Sensibility, Part Two' in *The American Historical Review* 90: 2 June 1985, pp. 534–63.

Hobsbaum, Philip, 'Revaluation: Late Leavis and Earlier' in *Salmagundi*, 52:53 1981, pp. 22–233.

Hoey, Allen, 'The Name on the Coin: Metaphor, Metonymy and Money' *Diacritics* 18:2, Summer, 1988, pp. 26–37.

Honigsbaum, F., 'The Struggle for the Ministry of Health 1914–1919'. *Occasional Papers on Social Administration No. 37* (London: G. Bell and Sons, 1970), pp. 39–56.

Jakobson, Roman, 'Two Types of Language and Two Types of Aphasia disturbance' in Roman Jakobson and Morris Halle, *Fundamentals of Language* (New York: Moulton Publishers, 1956), pp. 69–76.

Jameson, Frederic, 'Postmodernism, or the cultural logic of late capitalism' in *New Left Review* , 1984, pp. 53-92.

Kinch, M. B., '"Saying Everything At Once?" The Prose Style of F. R. Leavis' in *English Studies* 73:6 1992, pp. 517–22.

Knights, L. C., '*Scrutiny* and F. R. L.: a personal memoir' in Denys Thompson ed., *The Leavises: Recollections and Impressions* (Cambridge: Cambridge University Press, 1984), pp. 70–81.

Koestler, Arthur, 'The Initiates', in Richard Crossman, *The God That Failed: Six Studies in Communism* (New York and London: Hamish Hamilton, 1950), pp. 25–32, p. 30.

Lawford, Paul, 'Conservative empricism in literary theory: a scrutiny of the work of F. R. Leavis', Part 1, *Red Letters*, 1:1, pp. 12-15; Part 2, *Red Letters*, 2:2, pp. 9–11.

Lukács, Georg, 'Realism In The Balance', trans. R. Livingstone in Theodor Adorno, Walter Benjamin, Ernest Bloch, Bertolt Brecht, Georg Lukács, *Aesthetics and Politics:* translation editor Ronald Taylor (London and New York: Verso, 1977 and 1990), pp. 28–59, pp. 53–4.

MacCABE, Colin, 'The Cambridge Heritage: Richards, Empson and Leavis' in *Southern Review*, 19:3 November, 1986, pp. 242–9.

MacKILLOP, I. D., 'F. R. Leavis: A Peculiar Relationship' in *Essays in Criticism*, 34:3 July 1984, pp. 185–92.

MacHerey, Pierre and BALIBAR, Etienne, 'On Literature as an Ideological Form' trans. Ian McLeod, John Whitehead and Anne Wordsworth, *Oxford Literary Review* 3 1978, pp. 4-12.

Margolies, David, '*Left Review* and Left Literary Theory', in Jan Clark et. al. *Culture and Crisis in Britain in the Thirties* (London: Lawrence and Wishart, 1979), pp. 67–82.

Marx, Karl, 'The Fetishism of the Commodity' in Connerton ed. *Critical Sociology: Selected Readings*, pp. 73–89, p. 74.

Massumi, Brian, 'Everywhere You Want To Be: Introduction to Fear' in Brian Massumi ed. *The Politics of Everyday Fear* (Minneapolis: University of Minnesota Press, 1993), pp. 3 -38, p. 7.

Miles, P., and Smith, Malcolm, 'Hegemony and the Intellectuals in Interwar Britain' in *Trivium* Volume 20, May 1985, pp. 69–96.

Milner, Andrew, 'Leavis and English Literary Criticism' in *Praxis* 1:2, 1976, pp. 91–106.

Morton, A. L., 'Culture and Leisure' in *Scrutiny* 1:4 March 1933, pp. 324–6, p. 324.

Most, Glenn W., 'Principled Reading: A Review of F. R. Leavis, *The Living Principle: "English" as a Discipline of Thought*' in *Diacritics*, 9 June 1979, pp. 53–64.

Murdock, Graham, 'Dilemmas of Radical Culture: Forms of Expression and Relations of Production' in Francis Barker et. al. *1936: The Sociology of*

*Literature Volume 2, Practices of Literature and Politics* (Colchester: University of Essex, 1979), pp. 21–45, esp. pp. 33–7.

Needham, John, 'Leavis and the Post-Saussureans' in *English* 34: 150 Autumn 1985, pp. 235–50.

Nehring, M., 'What Should the Politics Of Cultural Studies Be?' in *Literature, Interpretation, Theory*, 1:3 March 1990, pp. 229–37.

Neill, Edward, '"Give Up Literary Criticism": F. R. Leavis, The Last Phase' in *English*, 33:1 1984, pp. 23–37.

Norris, Christopher , 'Post-structuralist Shakespeare: text and ideology' in Drakakis, ed., *Alternative Shakespeares* pp. 47–66.

Nuyen, A. T., 'Adorno and the French Post-Structuralist: On the Other of Reason' in *Journal of Speculative Philosophy* 4:4 1990, pp. 310–22

Parker, David, 'The Turn To Ethics In The 1990s' in *The Critical Review* Vol. 33, November 1993, pp. 3–14, p. 13.

Pole, David, 'Leavis and Literary Criticism' in *Philosophy*, 51, 1976, pp. 21–34.

Pound, Ezra, 'How To Read' in *Ezra Pount, Literary Essays of Ezra Pound* edited and with an introduction by T. S. Eliot (London: Faber and Faber, 1954 and 1974), pp. 15–39.

Radway, Janice, 'Mail-Order Culture and Its Critics: The Book-of-the-Month Club, Commodification and Consumption' in Lawrence Grossberg, Gary Nelson and Paula Treichler eds. *Cultural Studies* (London and New York: Routledge, 1992), pp. 512–30.

Rollin, Roger B., 'Against Evaluation: The Role of the Critic of Popular Culture' in Peter Davison, Rolfe Meyersohn and Edward Shils, *Literary Taste, Culture and Mass Communication Volume 14: The Cultural Debate Part Two* (Teaneck New Jersey: Somerset House, 1980), pp. 12–24.

Rose, Gillian, 'Architecture to Philosophy: The Postmodern Complicity' in *Theory, Culture and Society*, 5:2-3, pp. 357–72, esp. p. 368.

Sampson, David, 'Literature versus Society? Recent Trends in Literary Criticism' in *Southern Review* 12:3, 1979, pp. 268–84.

Shuttleworth, Alan, 'A Humane Centre' in Peter Davison et al., *Literary Taste, Culture and Mass Communication Volume 14: The Cultural Debate Part Two*, op. cit. pp. 43–65

Spender, Stephen, in *Criterion*, 16 January 1937, pp. 350-3;

Storey, John, 'Mapping the Popular: The Study of Popular Culture within British Cultural Studies' in *The European English Messenger* 3:2 1994, pp 47–59.

Strickland, Geoffrey, 'F. R. Leavis, and "English"' in Boris Ford ed., *The New Pelican Guide to English Literature Volume 8: The Present*, op. cit. pp. 175–92

Susman, Warren, 'Personality and the Making of Twentieth Century Culture' in J. Higham and P. K. Conkin eds. *New Directions in American Intellectual History* (Baltimore: Johns Hopkins University Press, 1979), pp. 212–26.

Tanner, Michael, 'Literature and Philosophy', *New Universities Quarterly* 30:1 Winter 1975, pp. 54–64 and '"Mutually Necessary": a Rejoinder' *New Universities Quarterly* 30:3 Summer 1976, pp. 313–23.

Thompson, John, 'Social Theory, Mass Communication and Public Life' in Antony Giddens *et al. The Polity Reader in Cultural Theory* (Cambridge and Oxford: Polity Press in association with Blackwell Publishers, 1994), pp. 24–37, p. 29.

Thompson, Laura, 'Mediaspeak', Life Magazine, *The Observer* 8 January 1995, p. 70.

Titlestad, P. J. H., 'F. R. Leavis: Hegemony, Canon, Intelligence, Ideology' in *Theoria*, May 1991, pp 59–71.

Turner, Bryan S., 'Recent Developments in the Theory of the Body' in Mike Featherstone, Mike Hepworth and Bryan S. Turner, eds., *The Body: Social Processes and Cultural Theory* (London: Sage Publications, 1991 and 1992), pp. 1–31.

Willinsky, John, 'Leavis, Literary Theory and Public Education' *Mosaic* 21: 2-3 1988, pp. 165–77, p. 173.

Wright, Iain, 'F. R. Leavis: The Scrutiny Movement and the Crisis' in Jon Clark, Margot Heinemann, David Margolies and Carol Snee eds. *Culture and Crisis in Britain in the Thirties* (London: Lawrence and Wishart, 1979), pp. 37–65, p. 55.

Zangwill, O. L., 'Psychology' in C. B. Cox and A. E. Dyson eds., *The Twentieth Century Mind, History, Ideas and Literature in Britain 2: 1918–1945* (Oxford: Oxford University Press, 1972), pp. 171–95, p. 174.

# Index

All subjects listed here are discussed in relation to Leavis. They are entered alphabetically rather than under his name. Reference is made to the notes only where they continue, in substantial form, issues raised in the main body of the book.

Adorno, T.W. xii, 5, 18, 24–6, 40, 42, 48, 50, 53–4, 62, 66, 68, 74, 83, 90, 93, 115, 125, 164, 176–84, 187, 209, 221–8

Advertising 15, 24–8, 53, 65, 74, 80, 87–91, 94–5, 98–9, 104, 129, 130, 197–201

Aesthetics 141–2, 167–8, 190, 226–7, 232, 259n

Alienation 115–16

Althusser, Louis 110–111

America 34–7, 127

Angell, Norman 13–14

Anderson, Perry 109

Arnold, Matthew 2, 9–10, 23, 40, 44–5
  Culture and Anarchy, 40

Austen, Jane 138, 144

Baldick, Chris ix

Baldwin, Stanley 118

Barthes, Roland ix, 103–4, 205–6, 220

Bateson, F. W. xv, 143–50, 153, 155, 175

Baudrillard, Jean 66, 92, 111, 197–201, 212

Bell, Michael x, 47, 165
  F. R. Leavis, x

Belsey, Catherine x–xi, 218, 240n

Benjamin, Walter 60, 100

Bennett, Arnold 20, 37–8

Bennett, Tony 236n

Bergonzi, Bernard x

Berten, Hans 188

Bilan, R. P. ix

Blake, William 210, 215

Bliss 103–5

Bloomsbury 213

Body, the xii, xiv–v, 51–3, 64, 82, 84–6, 101, 104, 122–8, 134, 152–7, 159, 163, 177, 179, 190–8, 203–6, 221, 229
  and embodiment, 85, 129, 134, 151, 192, 197, 206
  and disembodiment, 128–30, 195–6
  and machinery, 125–6, 190–1

Bocock, Robert 157, 195

Boundaries 13, 17, 29, 32, 40–1, 94, 99, 105, 130, 152, 174, 186–90, 204, 206

Boyer, Robert ix

Bunyan, John 135
  The Pilgrim's Progress, 135, 144–5, 154–5, 201

Burns, Elizabeth & Tom ix

Butterfield, Herbert 109

Bureaucracy 212, 229–30

Capitalism 111, 114, 116, 119, 133, 188–9, 191, 227–8

Carey, John 181

Casey, John ix, 184

Castles, E. B. 49

Charques, R. D. 124

Civilisation 1, 5, 19, 22–31, 41–4, 68, 72–3, 82–3, 85–6, 88, 95, 100, 115, 240n

Class 65–6, 92, 109–10, 124, 134, 137, 194, 263n, 278n

Cole, G. D. H. & M. I. The Condition of Britain, 124

Communism 123

Connor, Steven 181

Consciousness xiv, 10–12, 14, 21, 39–40, 59–61, 64–5, 67, 70, 77, 79, 82–6, 102, 119–20, 122, 128,

136, 148, 155, 175, 205, 211, 243–4n, 255–6n
Consumerism xii–xiv, 47–50, 61, 62, 84, 86, 92–3, 123–8, 130, 133, 157–9, 190–9, 203, 212, 215, 237–8n, 258n
Contract 130–4
Corporatism 52–3, 123–4, 127, 194
Cross, Garry 49, 124–5, 160
  *Time and Money: The Making of Consumer Culture*, 49
Culture 1, 6, 18, 20–31, 41–45, 50, 54, 68, 73, 82–3, 85–6, 88, 93, 100, 111, 121–2, 132, 194, 196, 240n, 246–7n
Culture Industry 177, 180, 187, 199, 208, 216, 223, 225, 227
Culture, Mass 2, 5, 93, 196, 202–3, 222
Cultural Autonomy 120–3
Cultural Studies xv, 117, 225

Debord, Guy 54, 62, 66
Deconstruction 147–8
Defoe, Daniel 135
Depth 5–6, 186–90, 205
Derrida, Jacques x, xii, 42, 82, 147–8, 161, 171–6, 183–4, 206–9, 231, 242n
Desire 27, 38, 72, 75–8, 86, 91, 103–4, 126, 128–30, 134, 153, 156–9, 162–4, 174, 214–16
*Différance* 171–6, 183
Donne, John 156
Doyle, Brian 52

Eagleton, Terry ix, 63, 92, 139
Easthope, Antony ix, 141, 226
Elitism 1, 240n
Eliot, T.S. 126, 181
Empiricism 43, 190, 277n
Empson, William 185
Enactment 134–43
Ethics 142, 167–8, 226–7, 232
Evans, G. E. 51–2
Experience 60, 68, 77–8, 80, 89, 93, 116, 127, 131, 139, 232
Expression 134–43

Falk, Pasi 84, 93, 124–5

Fascism 123
Featherstone, Mike 195, 203
Force 126–7, 129, 134, 162–3, 206–9, 211
Form 221–228
Foucault, Michel x, 2, 82
Franco, General 79
Freud, Sigmund 14, 31, 133, 153, 155–6, 159, 162–3
Frow, John 237n

Gender 100–5, 126–7
Gold Standard, the 7–8, 17, 20, 33, 38, 151
Gosse, Edmund 155
Grierson, John 157

Haddow Report, the 81
Harris, Constance 48
Harwood, John 183
Haskell, Thomas 133
Hayman, Ronald ix
Heidegger, Martin x
Herrnstein-Smith, Barbara 81
Hilton, John *Rich Man, Poor Man*, 124
Hirsch, E. D. 210, 218–19
Hitler 79, 107
Hopkins, Eric 237n
Hopkins, Gerard Manley 189
Human 111, 114, 119–20, 163, 176
Human nature 160

Inglis, F ix
Inwardness 87, 144, 146, 159–62, 178, 203, 205
Isherwood, Christopher *Goodbye to Berlin*, 157
Identity thinking 176–8
Intention 209–11, 219

Jacks, L. P. 48
Jakobson, Roman 21
Jameson, Frederic 188
Johnson, Lesley ix
Johnson, Roy 130
Judgements 4, 80, 114, 162–3, 169, 173, 231

Keats, John 85, 104

Kipling, Rudyard 25

Lacan, Jacques x, xii, 75–80, 82, 84, 86, 91, 129, 130–4, 153, 156, 158, 173, 211–218
Lansbury, George 118
Language 9, 12, 18, 22–4, 28–9, 35, 50, 76, 131, 138–9, 171, 176, 180, 182, 218–19, 224, 231, 243–4n, 269n, 284n
Law, Jules David 190
Lawrence, D. H. 126, 206, 211
*The Rainbow*, 147
Leavis, F. R., works of 'Adam Bede', 194, 197
'Anna Karenina', 153, 221
'Bunyan through Modern Eyes', 135–7, 144
*Culture and Environment*, xv, 45, 47–105, 110, 119, 125, 131, 146, 155, 174, 179, 194, 196, 199, 200, 202, 205, 217, 224
'English, Unrest and Continuity', 142, 166, 220
*For Continuity*, 107
'Henry James and The Function of Criticism', 142, 154
'How to Teach Reading: A Primer for Ezra Pound', xiii
'Johnson and Augustanism', 139
Johnson and Augustan Poetry, 141
'Joyce and the Revolution of the World', 211
Judgement and Analysis, 112, 114, 116, 147, 183, 221
'Justifying One's Valuation of Blake', 165
'Keynes, Spender and Currency Values', 151
'Literary Criticism and Philosophy', 129, 148, 178, 189, 203, 212,
'Literature and Society', 138, 140, 152, 160–1, 190, 194, 198, 207
'Marxism and Cultural Continuity', 107–111, 120, 123, 128, 151, 160

'Mass Civilisation and Minority Culture', xiv, 1–45, 47, 58, 79, 97, 103, 120, 127, 130–2, 151, 186, 202
'Memories of Wittgenstein', 185
'Mr. Eliot, Mr. Wyndham Lewis and Lawrence', 153
'Mutually Necessary', 156, 190, 201, 211, 220–1
*New Bearings in English Poetry*, xiv, 192
'Pilgrim's Progress', 135–8, 144–5, 154–5, 201–26
'Pluralism, Compassion and Social Hope', 191, 210, 215, 220
'Reading out Poetry', 131, 152, 164, 179, 204
'Restatement for Critics', 107–8, 110, 114, 151, 164
*Revaluation*, xiv, 192
'Sociology and Literature', 138, 144–5, 154, 160–1
'Standards of Criticism', 131, 152, 166, 181, 190, 202, 224,
*The Great Tradition*, 221
'The Literary Disciple and Liberal Education', 231
'The Marxian Analysis', 110
'The Responsible Critic: or the function of criticism at any time', 143–5, 148, 151–2, 155, 160, 165, 183, 227
'There Is Only One Culture', 182, 193, 220, 225
'Thought, Language and Objectivity', 141–2, 147, 150–1, 154, 166, 169, 178, 180–1, 184, 186–7, 197, 204, 208–10, 218, 224–5
'Thought, Meaning and Sensibility', 139, 141–2, 150, 156, 164, 167, 178, 187, 193, 197, 204, 208–9, 219–20, 225
*Thought, Words and Creativity: Art and Thought in Lawrence*, 145, 147–8, 207, 220, 225–7
'Towards Standards of Criticism', 113, 198, 204
'Tragedy and the Medium', 139

'T. S. Eliot and English
  Literature', 115, 156, 225
'Two Cultures? The Significance
  of C. P. Snow', 151, 226
'Under Which King, Bezonian?',
  107–8, 111, 115–6, 120–2, 128,
  131, 135, 150
'Valuation in Criticism', 118, 131,
  141–2, 145, 150, 158, 160,
  164–5, 190, 202, 205, 224, 231
'What's Wrong With Criticism',
  xiv, 216
Leavis, Queenie 239n
Lefebvre, Henri 115, 119
  *Critique of Everyday Life*, 116
Leisure 47–55, 73–5, 77, 123
'Life' 126, 129, 134, 149–52, 166–7,
  197, 206, 221, 231–2
Lindsay, Jack *John Bunyan, Maker of
  Myths*, 135
Literary Criticism 2–3, 11, 13, 55–7,
  83–4, 87, 91, 94, 109, 111–14,
  116, 118–19, 120, 126–7, 130–4,
  137, 169
Literature 25–6, 41, 43, 55–8, 73–4,
  78–9, 84, 87–92, 94, 105, 112,
  114, 118, 122, 124, 131, 134–49,
  157–8, 167, 214–5, 217,
  249–52n, 263n
Lukács, Georg 137
Lynd, R. S. & H. M. 33
  *Middletown*, 33, 35–6, 39
Lyotard, Jean-Francois 61–4, 153

Macherey, Pierre 7
Mackillop, Ian ix, 239n, 255n
Margolies, David 109
Marvell, Andrew 143, 146, 151, 153,
  155
  'A *Dialogue Between the Soul and
  the Body*', 143–4, 148, 150, 155
Marx, Karl 91
Marxism xv, 66, 107, 108–12,
  115–17, 119–21, 124, 134–5,
  138, 236n, 262n
Mass Observation 126, 157
Massumi, Brian 125

Meaning 7, 12, 19, 71, 114, 147–8,
  151, 166–7, 172–3, 202, 209–11,
  218–221, 230, 246n
Memory 56, 60, 63, 91
Metaphor 7–10, 15–17, 19–23, 25,
  30–36, 38, 43, 59, 75–6, 79, 82,
  103, 118, 122–3, 128, 133–4,
  149–52, 175, 181, 183, 193, 195,
  206, 242n, 247–8n
Metonymy 21–23, 25, 30–2, 35,
  247–8n
Modernity 59, 128–30, 134, 150, 153,
  155, 169, 186
Morton, A. L. 108
Mosley, Oswald 79
Mulhern, Francis ix, 1, 52, 108, 110
Mussolini, Benito 79

National Government, the 21
*New Verse* 124
Norris, Christopher x, 148, 183
Negative dialectics 176–9, 183

'Obvious', the 31–34, 36–8, 44, 87,
  89, 151–2, 166–7, 189, 207, 228
Oedipus complex 14, 38, 75, 132,
  227, 273n
Organic community 50–8, 60, 64, 66,
  68, 69, 70, 72–3, 76–9, 84–5, 87,
  90–2, 95, 102, 111–15, 117–18,
  121, 128–9, 135, 155, 163, 196,
  207, 249–53n
Orwell, George 50
Overstreet, Henry 49

Paget, Richard 2
Parker, David 232
Perkin, Harold 52, 114
Pitt-Rivers, G. H. L. F. 94
Pleasure xiv, 50–2, 84, 101–2, 104–5,
  203, 205–6, 265n
Poem, the 169–171, 187–8, 198, 208,
  210
Poem, 'thereness' of 165–6, 170,
  173–4, 197–8, 222
Poetry xiv, 43
Pope, Alexander 155
  'The *Dunciad*', 155
Postmodernism 188

Post-structuralism x–xii, 81–82,
    143–9, 167, 176, 218–19,
    229–30, 236n, 246n, 283n
Priestley, J. B. 124
Production 84, 123–8, 145, 190–8,
    203
Professionalism 52, 114, 117–20
Proust, Marcel 60, 63
Public and Private 159–62, 186
Puritanism 144, 154

Race 10

Reading xiii, 26–7, 32, 36, 41–4, 65,
    68–70, 72–3, 80, 83, 85–7, 92,
    96, 98, 100–2, 104–5, 145,
    154–6, 158, 160, 163–8, 170,
    189, 192, 197–201, 204–6
Recognition 11–12, 20, 38, 77–9, 89,
    130, 132, 145, 211–18, 227
Remembrance 53, 60, 63
Repetition 28–32, 36, 43, 44
    *and death instinct*, 162–3
Representation 134–43, 201
Representative 201, 209
Responsibility 80, 219, 225
Richards, I. A. 8–10
Rickword, Edgell 124, 237n
Ridley, M. R. 147
Robson, W. W. 123
Rorty, Richard 22

Samson, Anne 17
Saussure, Ferdinand de x
Science 87–9
Scientific Management xii–xiii, 57,
    74, 76, 101, 112–5, 117–20, 129,
    133, 162–3, 190–1, 193, 198,
    230, 237n, 238n, 255n, 264n
*Scrutiny* 107–8, 110
Seltzer, Mark 125–7, 133, 180, 190–7,
    205–6
Shakespeare, William 87, 135, 204
    *Antony and Cleopatra*, 147
Simmel, Georg 59–60, 125, 202,
    227–8
    'The Metropolis of Mental Life', 59
Significance 166–7, 182, 194, 201,
    218–228, 230

Singh, G xv
Social Darwinism 10
'Something More' xii–xiv, 2, 7, 9, 11,
    12–14, 25, 31, 39–40, 58, 82, 90,
    98–9, 105, 129, 150, 156–7, 174,
    178–9, 182, 189, 194, 249n
Standards 3, 6, 11, 18, 19, 39, 43,
    152, 201, 202
Standard of Living 6–7
Standardization 6, 37, 202
Sterling Crisis, the 21
Stevenson, John 85, 123, 237n
Sturt, George 51, 56–7, 60, 63–74, 78,
    87, 91, 94, 98, 100–2, 112–13,
    135, 255n
    *The Wheelwright's Shop*, 51, 192
Surface 5–6, 186–90, 205
Surveillance 191, 193
Susman, Warren 202

Tanner, Michael ix, 185
Taylor, A. J. P. 124
Taylor, Frederick Winslow 56–7,
    112–14, 126, 191
Techniques xiii, 57
Technologico Benthamite
    Civilisation 193–4, 222
'Third Realm', the 169–223, 273n
Thompson, Denys 45, 239n
Thompson, E. P. 51
Thomson, John 15
Time and Motion Studies 56
Tradition 6, 15–16, 22, 24–5, 28, 41,
    53, 56–63, 78, 118, 122, 132–4,
    149, 159, 179–83, 189, 194,
    197–202, 204–5, 211, 217,
    221–4, 226, 230–1
Tugwell, Rexford 48

Valuation 13, 18, 30, 81, 120, 144–5,
    180, 193, 201, 208, 224, 230–3
Value xi, 3, 11, 13, 19–20, 38, 80–4,
    116–17, 131, 144, 166, 168, 193,
    200, 213, 219–22, 226–8, 233,
    237n, 245–6n

Wall Street Crash, the 17
Walsh, William ix
Washington, Peter 219
Watson, George ix

Watson, John B 2, 83
Weber, Max 212
Wheelwright's craft 55–6, 70, 100–1, 103
Williams, Raymond 47, 117, 249n
   *Culture and Society*, 47

Wittgenstein, Ludwig 183–6
Wordsworth, William 135
Work 50–5, 114, 118, 123
Wright, Ian 108–9, 116–19

Zangwill, O. L. 122